WHAT WAS CONTEMPORARY ART?

WHAT WAS CONTEMPORARY ART?

Richard Meyer

The MIT Press   Cambridge, Massachusetts   London, England

A project of Creative Capital | Warhol Foundation Arts Writers Grant Program

MIT Press books may be purchased at special quantity discounts for business or sales promotional use. For information, please email special_sales@mitpress.mit.edu or write to Special Sales Department, The MIT Press, 55 Hayward Street, Cambridge, MA 02142.

This book was set in Neutra by The MIT Press. Printed and bound in Canada.

Library of Congress Cataloging-in-Publication Data

Meyer, Richard, 1966–
    What was contemporary art? / Richard Meyer.
        p.   cm.
    Includes bibliographical references and index.
    ISBN 978-0-262-13508-5 (hardcover : alk. paper)
1. Art, Modern—20th century. 2. Art—Historiography. I. Title.
N6490.M483   2013
709.04—dc23
2012028404

10 9 8 7 6 5 4 3 2 1

For David Román

Contents

Acknowledgments

I have been at work on this book for nearly a decade. During that time, I have benefited from the input of many individuals and the support of various institutions. It is a pleasure to acknowledge them here.

Three close friends and colleagues—Julia Bryan-Wilson, Christina Kiaer, and Ara Merjian—responded to parts of the manuscript with keen insights and exacting criticisms. I thank them for their generosity of intellect and spirit. Douglas Crimp kindly read the afterword and provided helpful feedback for revision. Connie Wolf shared with me her signature combination of insight, humor, and know-how. Were it not for the critical suggestions, professional example, and abiding friendship of Nancy Troy, I probably would still not be finished with this book.

At the University of Southern California, my professional home throughout most of this project, I was fortunate to work alongside a set of superb colleagues, including Leo Braudy, the late Anne Friedberg, Sarah Gualtieri, Selma Holo, Akira Mizuta Lippit, Maria-Elena Martinez, James McHugh, Tara McPherson, Bruce Smith, and the indefatigable Vanessa Schwartz. While a visiting faculty member at the University of Pennsylvania in 2006–2007, I developed the manuscript in conversation with David Brownlee, Michael Leja, Christine Poggi, Ingrid Schaffner, and Gwendolyn DuBois Shaw. During a stay at the Courtauld Institute of Art in 2010, I was lucky to have Caroline Arscott, Catherine Grant, and Julian Stallabrass as interlocutors. Among the other colleagues who responded to this book at various stages, I thank, in particular, Alex Alberro, Sue-Ellen Case, Huey Copeland, Sharon Corwin, Eda Cufer, Whitney

Davis, Susan Foster, Coco Fusco, Suzanne Hudson, Elisabeth Lebovici, Helen Molesworth, Keith Moxey, Kaja Silverman, Terry Smith, and Michael Taylor.

In 2006, Michael Lobel and I coorganized a colloquium at the Clark Art Institute titled "The Short History of Contemporary Art." The conversations held over that weekend in Williamstown, Massachusetts, shaped my subsequent work on this book. I am grateful to participants Yve-Alain Bois, Julia Bryan-Wilson, Thomas Crow, Darby English, Hal Foster, Ann Gibson, Pamela Lee, and Mignon Nixon, as well as to Michael Ann Holly and Mark Ledbury of the Clark Art Institute.

Three talented Ph.D. students in art history—MacKenzie Stevens and Katie Kerrigan at USC and Claire Grace at Harvard—worked as research assistants on this project. They tracked down images, checked and rechecked archival sources, secured photographic permissions, and offered key suggestions to the author. I am grateful to each of them. Among my other students, both current and former, who contributed to the thinking that went into this book, I am especially grateful to Jason Goldman, Karin Higa, Jason Hill, Rachel Middleman, Leta Ming, Aram Moshayedi, Alexandra Nemerov, and Virginia Solomon. For the translation of Russian-language texts, I thank Nadya Bair. Slide curator Mike Bonnett provided excellent scans of images. Freelance editor Michelle Bonnice became a crucial respondent to the manuscript, making improvements, both large and small, and helping to develop the core argument of the book.

For archival assistance, I thank Michelle Harvey, Michelle Elligott, Miriam Gianni, and Thomas Grischkowsky at the Museum of Modern Art Archives; Wilma Slaight and Ian Graham at the Wellesley College Archives; Janet Moore at the Institute of Contemporary Art, Boston; and Tracey Schuster in Special Collections at the Getty Research Institute. Daphne Cummings kindly provided information about her father, the artist Willard Cummings.

For assistance with permissions and reproduction rights, I thank Kathleen Langjahr at Artists Rights Society, Alison Smith at Vaga, Jill Thomas-Clark at The Corning Museum of Glass, and Jemal Creary at Condé Nast.

Research for this book was generously sponsored by a Creative Capital/Andy Warhol Foundation Arts Writers Grant as well as by funding from the Advancing Research in the Humanities and Social Sciences (ARHSS) program at USC. Additional support was provided by the Office of the Dean and the Department of Art and Art History at Stanford University.

I have been pleased to present parts of this book at many conferences and universities. I thank the organizers who invited me and the audiences who listened and responded at the Melbourne meeting of the International Committee of the History of Art (CIHA), the Paris office of the Terra Foundation for American Art, the Georgia O'Keeffe Museum and Research Center, the University of Pennsylvania, the Hood Museum of Art, the Colby College Museum of Art, Southern Methodist University, New York University, Cooper Union, Swarthmore College, the University of Delaware, the University of Chicago, and the Getty Research Institute.

Roger Conover, my editor at the MIT Press, believed in this project even—and especially—when my own faith wavered. He has been a model editor and a good friend throughout. Matthew Abbate handled the manuscript with precision and sensitivity and designer Erin Hasley made the book beautiful. I thank MIT Press acquisitions assistant Justin Kehoe, art coordinator Mary Reilly, freelance editor Paula Woolley, and indexer Laura Bevir for their excellent work on this project.

Ira Sachs provided moral support and a healthy dose of perspective when I most needed it. Glenn Ligon and the late Anita Steckel furnished artistic inspiration along with the gift of their friendship.

My mother, Sherry Meyer, and her companion, Gladys Eisenstadt, offered intellectual engagement and loving encouragement. I am grateful to these two extraordinary women as well as to my brother and sisters, Bruce, Sharon, Aileen, and Robin Meyer.

My life partner, David Román, not only read the manuscript with great care; his own work on contemporary American theater and performance inspired the thinking that went into this book. I dedicate it to him with love and gratitude.

1 Introduction: The Art-Historical Postmortem

In 1969, a young woman named Rosalind Krauss filed a dissertation in the Department of Fine Arts at Harvard University. Fifteen years later, after she had emerged as one of the leading critical and art-historical thinkers of her generation, Krauss would explain the unorthodox means by which she had devised her dissertation topic:

> I was in fact thinking of a topic in nineteenth-century European art that would have been much more palatable to my professors at Harvard, but it was going to be difficult for me to go to France for a year in the middle of this marriage [she had recently wed Richard Krauss]. I didn't know what to do until one morning I woke up to an announcement on my clock radio that a sculptor had been killed in Vermont. I thought it was Tony Caro, because they said "Bennington, Vermont" where he was teaching. I thought, "Oh, how terrible," because I knew Tony. Then, after a couple of sentences, they repeated the name and I realized it was [David] Smith. I thought, "Um, I now have a thesis topic." I knew they would never allow me to do a dissertation on somebody who was still alive, but he had just died. I went rushing to Harvard to announce this as my topic.[1]

Within the logic of this anecdote, the shift from the imagined death of Anthony Caro to the actual one of David Smith constitutes a passage from personal loss to professional opportunity, from the register of friendship to that of scholarship, from the "terrible" thought that a sculptor Krauss knew firsthand had perished to recognition of the use value of an entirely different sculptor's demise. Death here delivers the artist into history, or at least into the history of art. Sealed off from the possibility of new works, stylistic shifts, imaginative breakthroughs, or creative disappointments, Smith's artistic output could at last be scrutinized, interpreted, and catalogued by the art historian. Krauss could now write a thesis on David Smith—but only, and almost literally, over his dead body.

Even here, however, there was a catch. To make Smith "more palatable," Krauss's advisors approved her topic on the condition that she prepare a catalogue raisonné of Smith's sculpture as part of the thesis. Krauss dutifully researched and photographed some seven hundred sculptures dating from 1932, the year that Smith turned from painting to three-dimensional construction, or what he called "drawing in space," to 1965, the year in which he was killed in an automobile accident (he missed a turn in a road and was crushed inside his pickup truck)—a range represented here by *Construction*, one of Smith's earliest three-dimensional works (no. 4 in Krauss's catalogue raisonné), and *Cubi XXVIII*, the last work he completed before his death.[2]

Given the exhaustive scope of Krauss's catalogue raisonné, the logic that guides the rest of her dissertation is brilliantly paradoxical. In the three-chapter essay that precedes the catalogue, Krauss argues that art-historical chronology and biographical sequence are precisely the wrong tools for understanding Smith's "preeminence" as a modernist sculptor. To explain the absence of biographical narrative from the essay, Krauss writes, "I feel the simple succession of events in Smith's life is as mute and unrevealing about his art as are the simple facts of his sculptural chronology."[3] As though in response to the advisors who required her to locate, photograph, and date some seven hundred sculptures, as well as dig up every public statement, lecture, and radio interview by this famously loquacious artist, Krauss positions her interpretation of Smith's modernism "against the testimony which a brute chronological succession of works provides" and against "any simple idea of symbiosis between David Smith and his historical context."[4] (The first chapter of Krauss's dissertation is titled "Defining Smith's Career: Beyond an Historical Context.")[5]

In describing the parameters of her study, Krauss notes that "while the catalogue of Smith's sculpture which follows this essay contains nearly 700 items, I have dealt explicitly with only about 40. This is because I believe that the quality of Smith's work derives from a particular attitude he had toward sculpture—an attitude which is fully embodied in the masterpieces of his career."[6] Note the self-assurance of Krauss's voice in this passage—the certainty with which she identifies and separates the forty "masterpieces" of Smith's sculptural output from the remainder of his oeuvre.

For Krauss, Smith's best sculptures exemplify how "certain objects or occurrences detach themselves from their historical background and strike [the scholar] with their overwhelming importance."[7] The scholar's task, Krauss continues, "is to understand and to account for their sharpness of focus within his own view."[8] With such statements, we see art history moving away from comprehensive cataloguing toward critical accounts of selected artworks; away from the seven hundred in favor of close readings of the forty. By unraveling the structural logic of the very catalogue raisonné she had compiled, Krauss helped launch the self-critical turn in contemporary art history.[9] In her writing as in that of other leading figures in the field, the present-tense encounter between object and scholar increasingly came to take precedence over the "brute chronological succession" of artworks and the monographic logic of biography.[10]

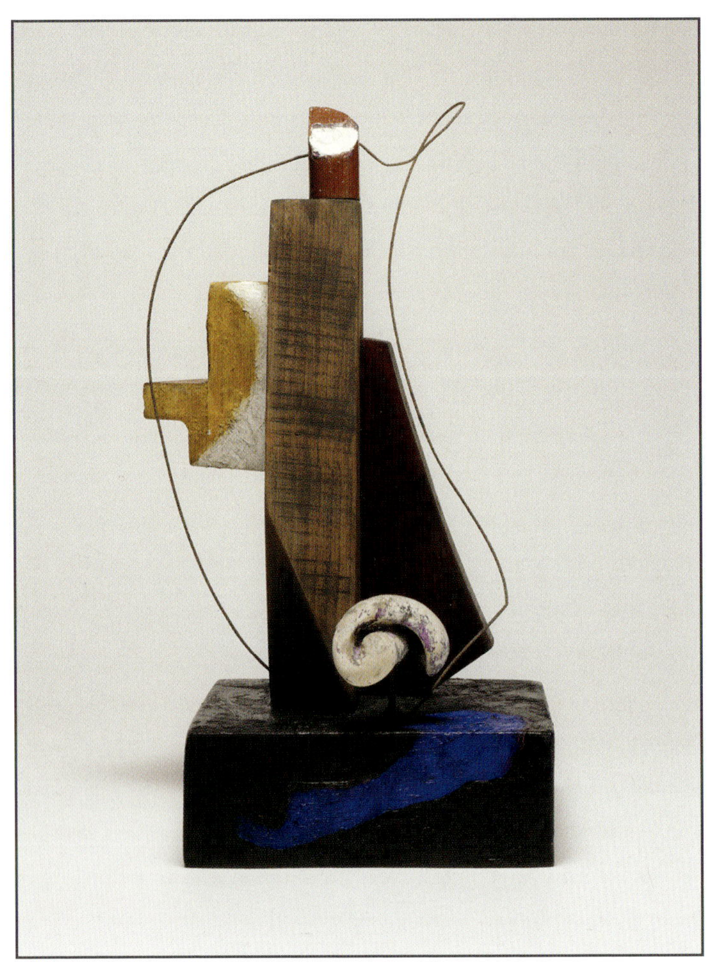

1.1 David Smith, *Construction*, 1932, wood, wire, and plaster, 18½ × 5 × 9½ inches. © Estate of David Smith/Licensed by VAGA, NY.

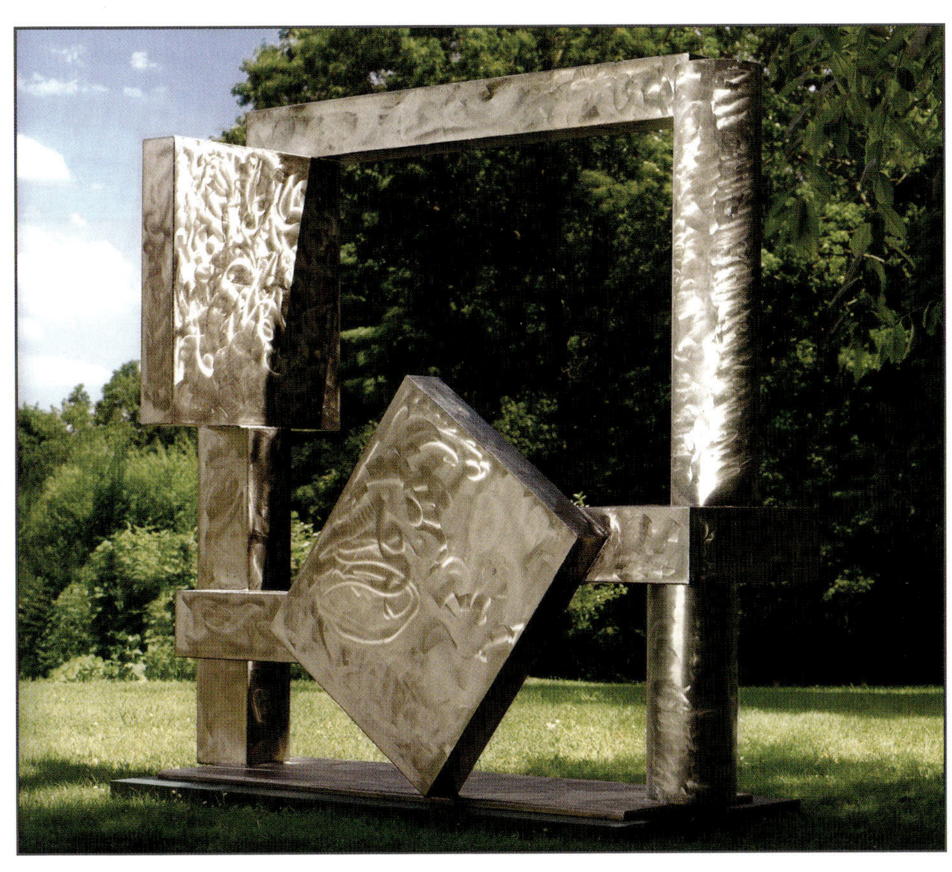

1.2   David Smith, *Cubi XXVIII*, 1965, stainless steel, 108 × 110 × 45 inches. © Estate of David Smith/Licensed by VAGA, NY.

Like her Harvard colleague Michael Fried, Krauss wrote art criticism while pursuing her doctorate in art history in the mid to late 1960s. And like Fried, she was a disciple of the New York critic Clement Greenberg. The preface to Krauss's dissertation notes her debt to modernist criticism above and beyond any academic advisor or art-historical training: "My knowledge of modern painting and sculpture was largely formed and nurtured by the critical essays of, and discussions with, Clement Greenberg and Michael Fried. With their aid, I began, while a graduate student at Harvard University, to write criticism. It was during the kind of contact with modernist works of art involved in that endeavor that my own conviction about American sculpture strengthened, and with it, my desire to write about the work of David Smith."[11] The term "conviction" surfaces repeatedly in Krauss's dissertation.[12] It draws attention to the self-assured judgment of the critic rather than to the purported objectivity and temporal remove of the art historian.[13] As Greenberg would succinctly put the point years later, "The first obligation of an art critic is to deliver value judgments."[14]

Shortly before filing her dissertation at Harvard, Krauss published a two-part article drawn from it in the February and April 1969 issues of *Artforum* magazine.[15] Titled "The Essential David Smith, Parts One and Two," the article blurred the boundary between contemporary art criticism and doctoral research in art history. The intervening *Artforum* issue, March 1969, was given over to the publication of Fried's dissertation in its entirety. *Artforum* readers expecting coverage of contemporary art and film (such as that included in every prior issue of the magazine) were instead offered a book-length treatise titled "Manet's Sources: Aspects of His Art, 1859–1865." Apart from several pages of gallery advertisements and a few letters to the editor, nothing appeared in the issue other than Fried's fourteen-part thesis (complete with 258 endnotes as well as the author's extensive translations of the French sources cited in his text). No explanation for the special issue was offered by the editors.

The anomaly marked by Fried's issue may be suggested visually by comparing the covers of the February 1969 and March 1969 issues. Where the former presents Richard Serra's site-specific, molten-lead sculpture *Splashing* (created earlier that same winter at the Leo Castelli warehouse), the latter reproduces a large detail from Edouard Manet's *The Dead Torero* of 1864. Fried's special issue of *Artforum* bracketed the currentness of contemporary art such that the "clock" of art criticism could be wound back a century.

In another sense, however, "Manet's Sources" was no less contemporary than Serra's *Splashing*. While Fried's subject was over a century old, his project had only just been completed: his dissertation was filed at Harvard two months prior to its publication in the magazine. Like Krauss's two-part article on Smith, the all but instantaneous appearance of Fried's thesis in *Artforum* challenged the divide between art-historical scholarship and contemporary art criticism in 1969.[16] Fried would later comment on his dual practice of art writing at the time: "I kept my activity as an art critic distinct from my work in art history; I never considered writing a dissertation on a living artist or seeking academic credit for my New York reviews. Intellectually, however, it was another story: from the start the distinction between art criticism and art history seemed to me a matter of emphasis rather than of principle, and my understanding of contemporary art had implications for the questions I began to put to the past."[17] At the beginning of this passage, Fried locates criticism and scholarship as separate spheres of production.[18] By the end, however, the two spheres have intersected to such a degree that only a matter of "emphasis" distinguishes them.

Krauss likewise understood the practices of art history and criticism to be "mutually inclusive," but only when realized "in their most supreme

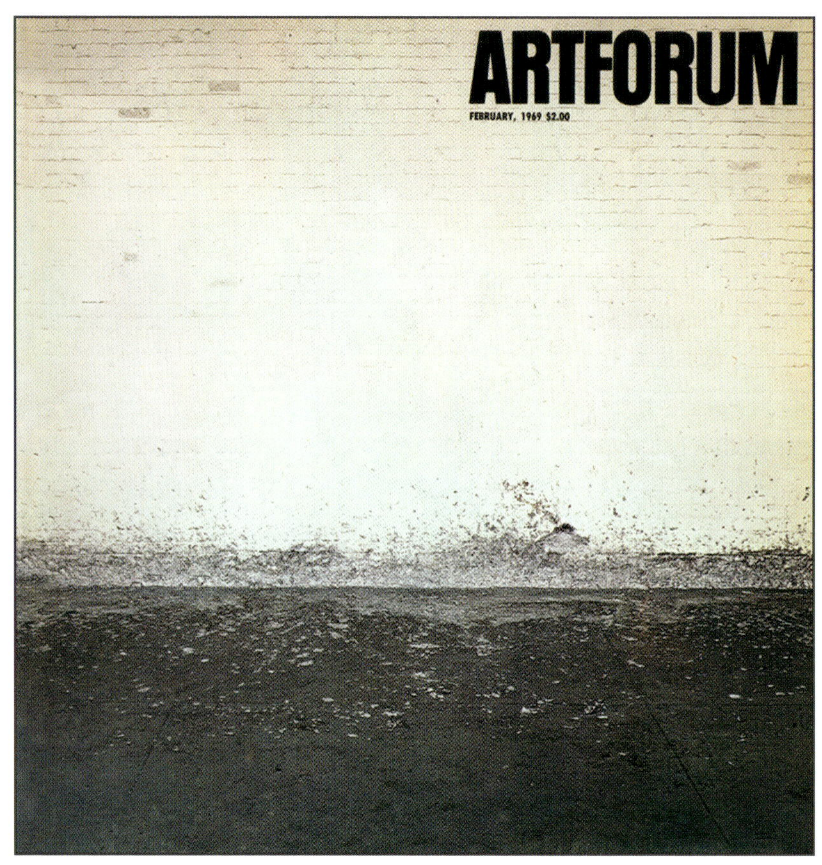

1.3 *Artforum* cover, February 1969. © Artforum.

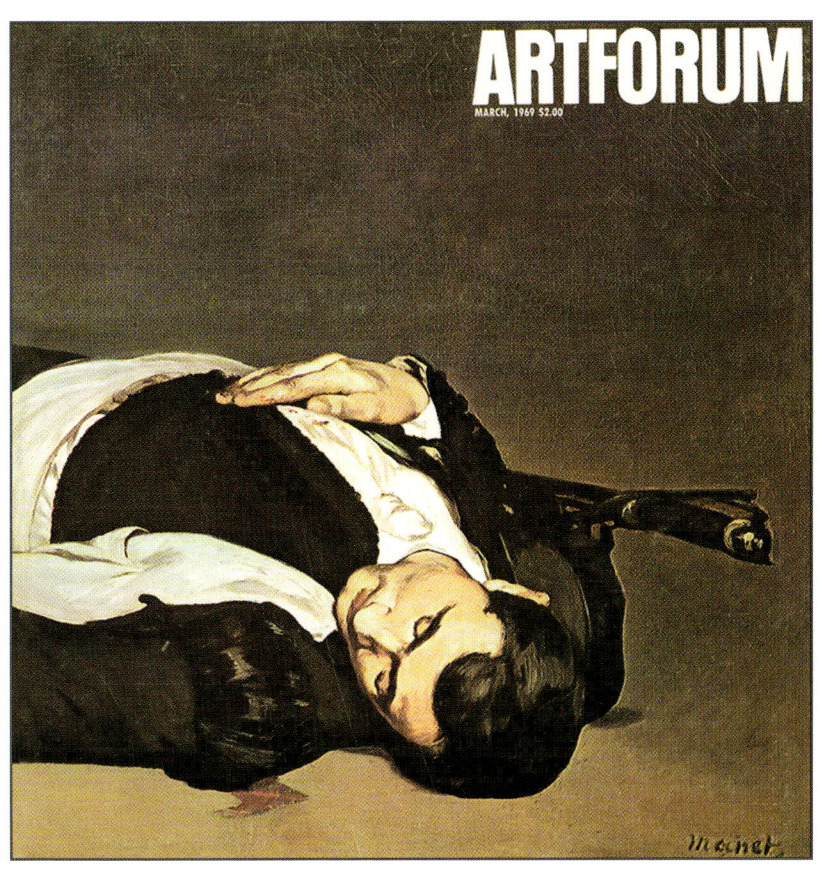

1.4 *Artforum* cover, March 1969. © Artforum.

examples."[19] In lesser cases, she warned, the art historian's dogged insistence on "systematic objectivity" limited his method to bloodless chronology and deadening taxonomy. What remains dazzling about Krauss's dissertation essay is the confidence of her critical voice, the magisterial conviction with which she passes judgment not only on artworks but also on other critics and historians.[20]

Krauss set contemporary critical judgment (or "conviction") against the reductive logic of chronology and biographical determinism. As though rendering this opposition in concrete form, the two halves of her dissertation would ultimately appear as freestanding publications. In 1971, a revised version of the essay was published by the MIT Press as *Terminal Iron Works: The Sculpture of David Smith*. Six years later, Garland Press published the catalogue as *The Sculpture of David Smith: A Catalogue Raisonné*. In the gap that opened between these two accounts of "The Sculpture of David Smith," and in the far greater degree of professional attention that *Terminal Iron Works* received, we see one model of scholarship displacing another. We see art history becoming criticism. And we see art history becoming contemporary.

As the dissertations I now advise attest, artists no longer need to be dead—or even very old—to be the subject of intensive scholarly analysis. Today, dissertations are routinely written on artists who are mid to late career, on recent museum exhibitions and biennials, and on current critical debates in the art world. Tenured and tenure-track jobs are posted for historians of contemporary art, and endowed chairs have been established in the field. In 2009, a new professional society was founded in order to "foster strong scholarship and to promote collegiality within the vital field of contemporary art history."[21] In the United States, at least, contemporary art has emerged not only as a viable area of art-historical study but as, by far, the most popular. In an analysis based on the annual listing of dissertations in progress issued by the College Art Association (CAA), the art historian Michael Lobel observes that "in 1996, American and Canadian dissertations in progress, in all art history fields, numbered 210; by 2005, dissertations in progress, in post-1945 art alone, numbered 214."[22] The number of dissertations on contemporary art history thus exceeded the sum of all dissertations in the discipline a decade before.

In keeping with Lobel's findings, an article by *New York Times* art critic Holland Cotter reported in 2011 that "an overwhelming number" of applicants to art history graduate programs "now declare contemporary art their field of choice: 80 percent was a figure I heard repeatedly—but unofficially—in conversations during the annual College Art Association conference this winter."[23] One source for that figure may well have been Patricia Mainardi, a scholar of nineteenth-century European art, who convened a panel called "The Crisis in Art History" at the 2011 CAA conference. In her opening remarks, Mainardi lamented the preponderance of art history doctoral students ("eight of out every ten") specializing in contemporary art. "Maybe we should drop the word 'history' from 'art history,'" she proposed, a bit caustically, to a hotel ballroom full of art historians.[24]

Consider the following anecdote as further evidence of the rise of what might be called "now-ism" within art history. In 2009, I offered a graduate seminar at the University of Southern California that sought (much as this book does) to historicize the idea of contemporary art. At the first meeting of the course, I was taken aback when a Ph.D. student expressed the hope that we would not have to endure "that long slog through the '90s" before arriving at the current decade of art and criticism. Prior to that semester, I had rarely taught a seminar that reached the 1990s, much less "slogged through" them to arrive at the millennium on the other side.

The students in the class understood the designation "contemporary" differently than I had expected. Rather than referring to art since 1945, art since 1960, or even art since 1970, "contemporary" meant to them the work of artists exhibiting today and in the immediate past. Banksy, Mathew Barney, Sophie Calle, Patty Chang, Sam Durant, Nikki S. Lee, Glenn Ligon, and Catherine Opie were some of the artists on whom students in the seminar had already written or declared their intention of doing so in upcoming projects. In one or two cases, the students were nearly the same age as the artists they wished to study. The history they proposed to chart neatly coincided with the time of their own lives.

In response to this emphasis on the present, I posed to the students a series of questions at once straightforward and admittedly aggressive: "Why are you studying art history if what you really want to do is write about the contemporary moment?" "Where are the archives for your research on contemporary art—in the files of a commercial gallery, in a drawer in the artist's studio, in a theoretical paradigm, in a series of interviews that you intend to conduct with the artist, or in the testimony of the works of art themselves?" "What, if anything, distinguishes your practice as a historian of contemporary art from that of an art critic?" And, finally, "How does the history of art matter to the works you plan to write about and to the scholarly contribution you hope to make?"

One student (not the '90s "slogger") effectively redirected these questions to me. During her admissions interview the previous year, she recalled, faculty had emphasized the close association the doctoral program in art history enjoyed with contemporary art museums, curators, and artists as well as its location in an international center of early twenty-first-century art (namely, Los Angeles). Since "the contemporary" had been used as a device to attract graduate students to the program, she reasoned, perhaps it was the professor (rather than those very students) who should define and defend the relation between contemporary art and art history.

She was right. If graduate students and emerging scholars now take contemporary art for granted as an area of specialization, it is because the discipline of art history invites them to do so. When I started graduate school in 1988, no such invitation was forthcoming. It was understood that "modernists," like everyone else in the program ("medievalists," "classicists," "early modernists," "Americanists," "Asianists"), worked on historical artists, issues, and objects.[25] It might have been conceivable for a modernist to study the early work of a living artist who had reached a certain, golden age. In that case, however, the work at issue would have been old enough for sufficient "historical distance" (say, about forty years) to have been achieved.

None of these ground rules were spoken aloud, nor did they need to be. At the time, there were no professional societies for historians of contemporary art, nor were there tenure-track jobs in the field to which one might aspire. Had someone proposed the practice of something called "contemporary art history," I could only have understood it as an oxymoron. Somewhere along the line, sometime in the (long) 1990s, things changed. The discipline of art history embraced the work of living artists. This book is an attempt to reckon with that shift. But it is also an effort to grapple with the broader dialogue between contemporary art and the historical past. It does so by investing in the power of particular pictures, people, and institutional episodes to illuminate larger patterns of art and culture. By looking in detail at selected art-historical episodes, *What Was Contemporary Art?* ignores others that might have been equally illuminating. Rather than a definitive survey, the book is presented as a modest proposal for putting the "history" back into contemporary art history.

When Is Contemporary Art?

In the last few years, several scholars and critics have situated "the contemporary" as a distinct period in the development of art and culture. According to the art historian Alexander Alberro, for example, "the contemporary" may now be traced to specific sources and a date of origin:

> The years following 1989 have seen the emergence of a new historical period. Not only has there been the collapse of the Soviet Union and its satellite states and the heralding of the era of globalization, but technologically there has been the full integration of electronic or digital culture, and economically, neoliberalism, with its goal to bring all human action into the domain of the market, has become hegemonic. Within the context of the fine arts, the new period has come to be known as "the contemporary."[26]

For Alberro, this "new period" has displaced previous paradigms of twentieth-century art, particularly the concepts of modernism and the avant-garde:

> New forms of art and spectatorship have crystallized in the past two decades. These new forms have come to be discursively constructed as "the contemporary." There is no question that they owe a great deal to their modernist forbearers, and that there is much that carries over into the present. However, since the late 1980s these new modes have outstripped their debt to the past, and the hegemony of the contemporary now must be recognized.[27]

In a formulation that mirrors Alberro's, the editors of the January 2010 issue of *e-flux* journal write that the term "contemporary" "has clearly replaced the use of 'modern' to describe the art of the day. With this shift, out go the grand narratives and ideals of modernism, replaced by a default, soft consensus on the immanence of the present, the empiricism of now, of what we have directly in front of us, and what they have in front of them over there."[28] A few pages later in the same issue, the art critic Cuauhtémoc Medina argues that "above all, 'contemporary' is the term that stands to mark the death of 'modern.'"[29]

In his 2009 book *What Is Contemporary Art?*, the art historian Terry Smith frames the demise of modern art and the concomitant ascent of the contemporary as a global phenomenon of the late 1980s: "We are starting to see that in the years around 1989, shifts from modern to contemporary art occurred in every cultural milieu throughout the world, and did so distinctively in each."[30] And again: "In the visual arts, the big story, now so blindingly obvious, is the shift—nascent during the 1950s, emergent in the 1960s, contested during the 1970s, but unmistakable since the 1980s—from modern to contemporary art."[31] Like Alberro, Smith situates contemporary art within a post-1980s period marked by globalization, digital media, hegemonic capitalism, and spectacular culture.[32]

This book pursues a different tack. Rather than focusing on the past two decades, it takes a longer view of the history of the new. It does not nominate the fall of the Berlin Wall, the rise of the Internet, or the effects of globalization as the origin of "the contemporary." Instead of positioning contemporary art as a stylistic movement or chronological period that comes after the modern, this book returns to earlier moments in the twentieth century when the work of living artists was at issue.[33]

In doing so, it draws on the semantic fact that "contemporary" has not always signified a quality of being up-to-date, current, or extremely recent. Indeed, the first definition of the word given in the *Oxford English Dictionary*—"Belonging to the same time, age, or period; living, existing, or occurring together in time"[34]—conveys coexistence rather than newness. According to the entry, the variant "co-temporary" was in usage during the seventeenth and eighteenth centuries and "became so popular c. 1725 as to almost expel 'contemporary' from use." Although the preference for "co-temporary" faded relatively quickly, this antiquated synonym is a useful reminder that contemporary is, at its core, a relational condition.[35] It takes two, in other words, to be contemporary.

As the art historian Tom McDonough puts it, the original definition of contemporary "might naturally lead us to ask in the case of art: contemporary with what?"[36] By asking "contemporary with what?" we are forced to look beyond the individual artist or masterwork to a broader field of artistic and cultural production. Once we do so, our conception of "contemporary" can no longer be reserved exclusively for those artists whose work is most highly valued by the market, the museum, or the academic discipline of art history. Those artists are "contemporary" to many others who have not been granted—and, in some cases, have not sought—recognition in the pages of art magazines, the halls of biennials or international art fairs, the portfolios of blue-chip galleries, or the PowerPoint presentations of art historians.

This book does not argue that contemporary art is over or that we have arrived at a "post-contemporary" moment of cultural production. But it does retrieve selected episodes in the history of once-current art so as to reclaim the "contemporary" as a condition of being alive to and alongside other moments, artists, and objects. Consider in this context the title of a book published in 1907. Randall Davies's *English Society of the Eighteenth Century in Contemporary Art* focuses on art that portrays British "Society" in the 1700s, not on art contemporary to Davies's own moment of writing or on works that conveyed any particularly modern quality or spirit of innovation. "Society" for Davies meant the elite of the British aristocracy as represented, for example, by a mezzotint after a painted portrait of Mary Somerset, Duchess of

Ormonde, a watercolor drawing of Queen Charlotte and the Princess Royal, or a cut-paper silhouette of a patrician family in their drawing room. For Davies and his contemporaries in 1907, "modern" was a property of work that was original, progressive, and forward-looking, of art that was not so much of its time as ahead of it. "Contemporary," by contrast, described a neutral condition of temporal coexistence between two or more entities. While a portrait of the Duchess of Ormonde attended by an African child-servant was contemporary to eighteenth-century British society, few in 1907 would have called it modern in the sense of being progressive or forward-looking.[37]

Even here, however, the matter of what constitutes contemporary art does not necessarily remain straightforward. The temporal existence of an artwork is not bound by its moment of production or by the life (or death) of its creator. As the Renaissance art historians Alexander Nagel and Christopher Wood write,

> No device more effectively generates the effect of a doubling or bending of time than the work of art, a strange kind of event whose relation to time is plural. The artwork is made or designed by an individual or a group of individuals at some moment, but it also points away from that moment, backward to a remote ancestral origin, perhaps, or to a prior artifact, or to an origin outside of time, in divinity. At the same time it points forward to all its future recipients who will activate and reactivate it as a meaningful event. The work of art is a message whose sender and destination are constantly shifting.[38]

As it persists over time, the artwork may become newly relevant to later works and social-historical contexts. Contrasting the study of art history to that of literature, music, and dance, Thomas Crow has observed that the "unique, physically sensible pattern"[39] of the work of art links the time of its making to that

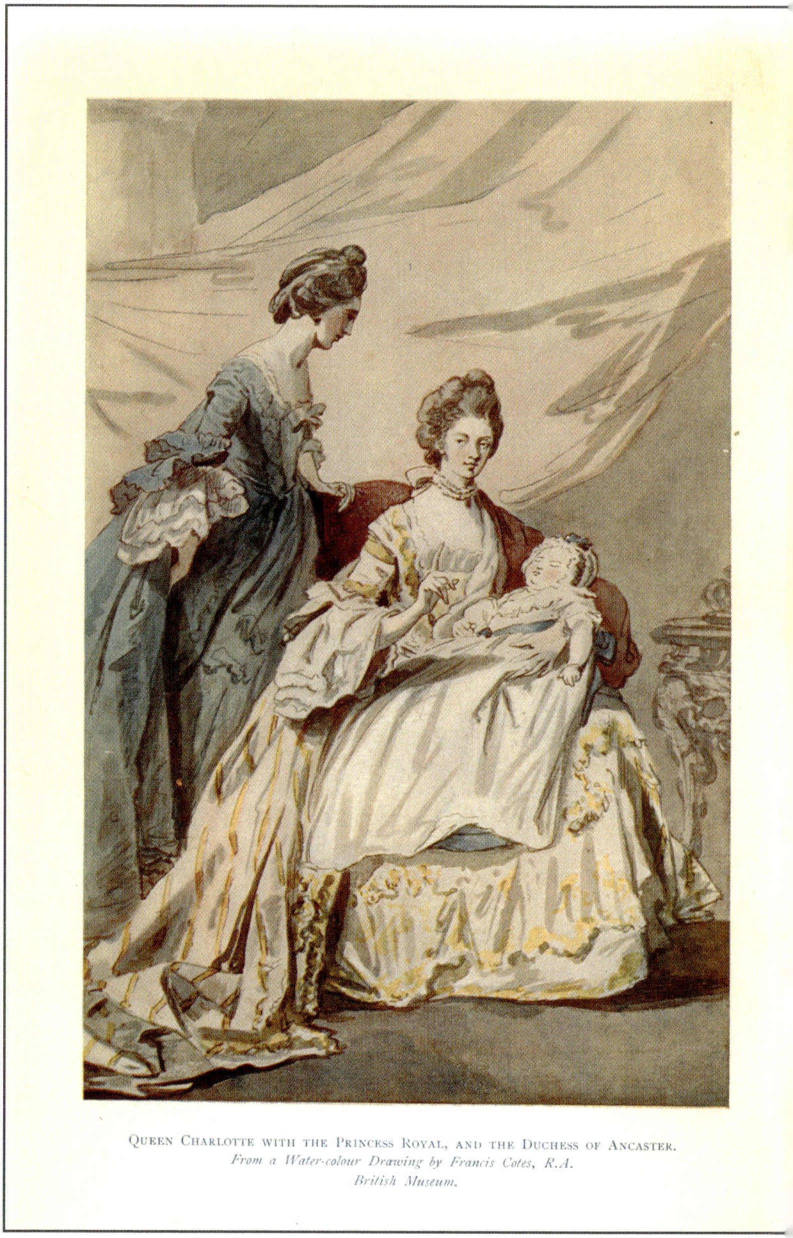

1.5 Title page, Randall Davies, *English Society of the Eighteenth Century in Contemporary Art* (London: Seeley and Co., 1907).

ENGLISH SOCIETY

OF THE EIGHTEENTH CENTURY
IN CONTEMPORARY ART

BY

RANDALL DAVIES, F.S.A.

AUTHOR OF "CHELSEA OLD CHURCH," &c.

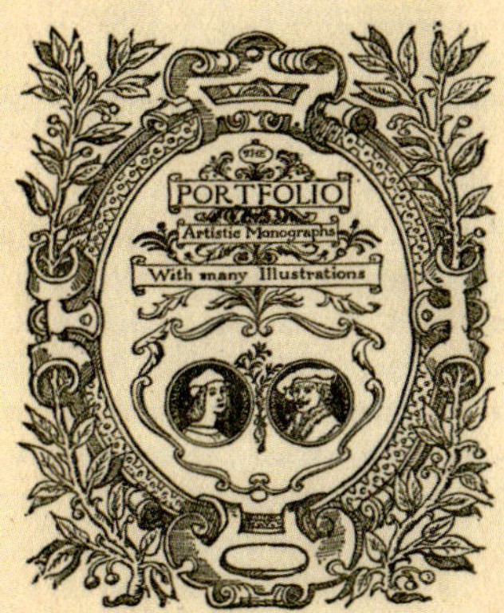

LONDON
SEELEY AND CO. LIMITED, GREAT RUSSELL STREET
NEW YORK: E. P. DUTTON & CO.
1907

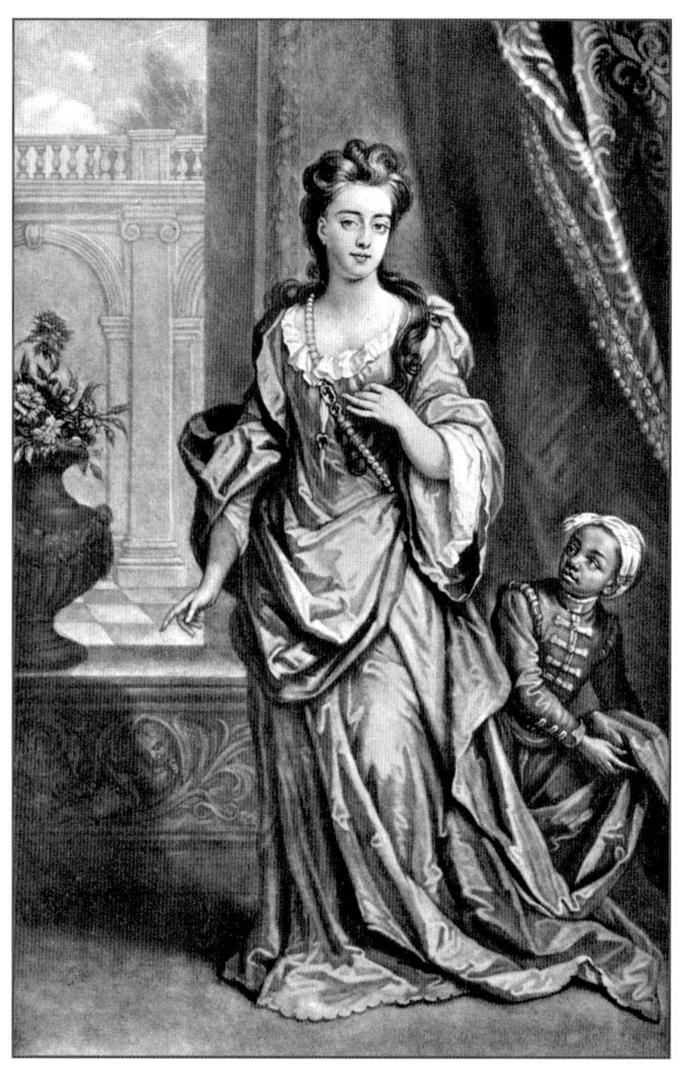

1.6 *The Duchess of Ormonde,* mezzotint after a painting, reprinted in Davies, *English Society of the Eighteenth Century in Contemporary Art.*

of our viewing in a peculiarly vivid manner. For Crow, art is distinguished by its status as an expressive object "from the past that arrives in our midst like a traveler through time."[40] Building on this line of argument, I propose that the category of contemporary art might include not only newly produced works by living artists but also those time travelers that arrive "in our midst" from earlier moments and historical contexts.

Those time travelers sometimes disrupt the distinction between contemporary and historical art by rendering the past newly present. A specific example might be useful here. The eighteenth-century silhouette by Thonard (published by Davies in 1907) cannot help but look contemporary (to the writer of this book in 2012) because of my prior knowledge of the work of the living American artist Kara Walker. In pieces such as *Insurrection! (Our Tools Were Rudimentary, yet We Pressed On)* (2000), Walker draws upon a history of cut-paper silhouettes extending back to the late seventeenth century even as she introduces bodies, gestures, and terrors never before visible in that history.

For all the fierceness of Walker's reckoning with the historical past, her art can do nothing to change the social conditions and inequities that shaped eighteenth-century Society, whether British or American, lowercase or capital s. But Walker can change our retrospective view of those conditions, such that, for example, the "delightful"[41] drawing-room formality of the eighteenth-century scene comes to seem rigid and compulsory, a world of enforced protocols and exacting regulations to which each figure, even the family dog, must submit. Seen "through" Walker's *Insurrection!*, Thonard's rendering of aristocratic privilege begins to unravel. It is as though Walker's insurgent figures may breach the boundaries of Thonard's sedate Society, as though the black-and-blue history of servants and slaves might at any moment overtake the black-and-white patrician family in its drawing room. Walker's art

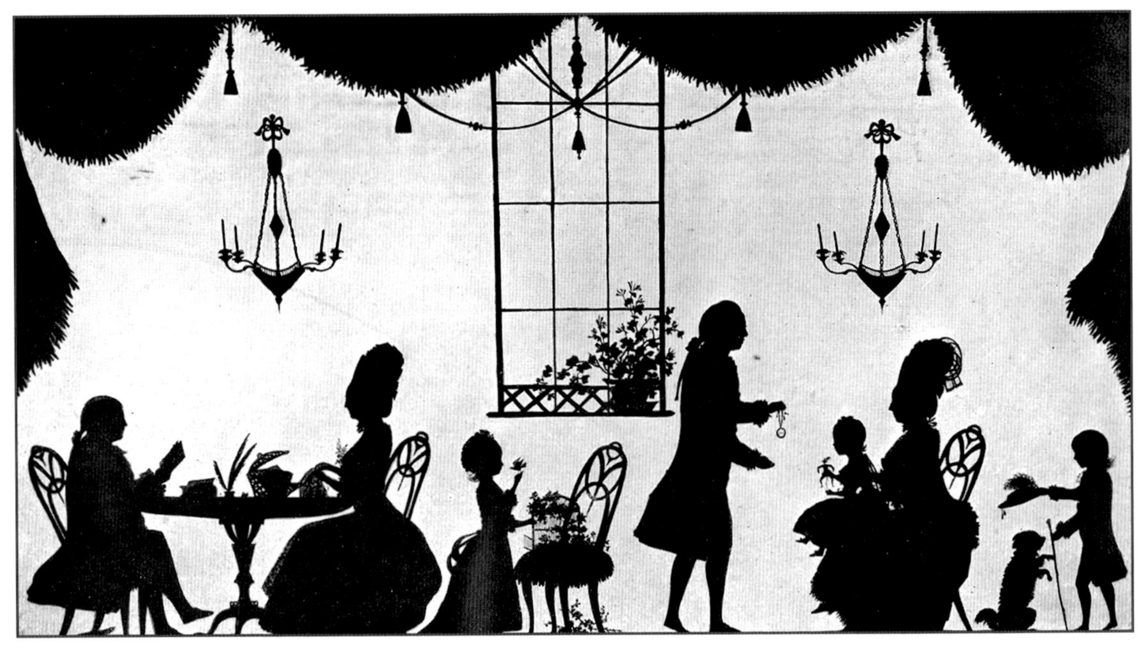

1.7 "A Family Group," from an eighteenth-century silhouette by Thonard. (Collection Sir George Sitwell, 4th Baronet.) Reprinted in Davies, *English Society of the Eighteenth Century in Contemporary Art.*

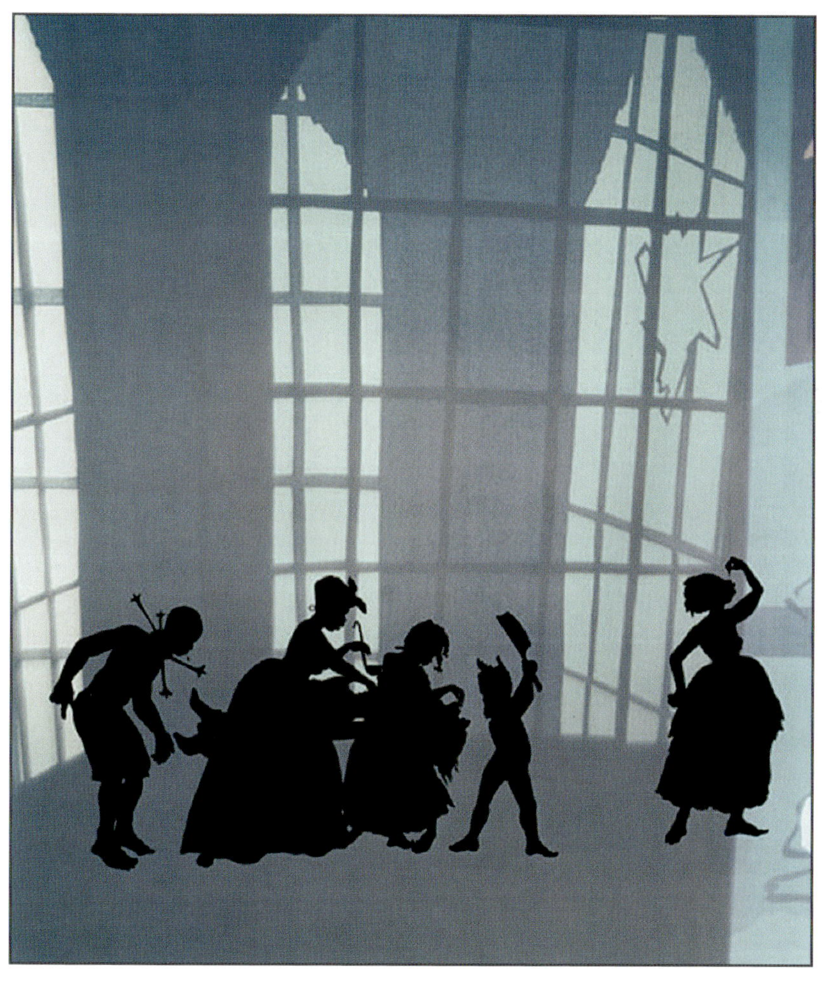

1.8 Kara Walker, *Insurrection! (Our Tools Were Rudimentary, yet We Pressed On)*, 2000, cut-paper silhouettes and light projections. (Courtesy Guggenheim Museum.)

operates according to a dialectical model of history in which the past is no more settled or secure than the present.

The challenges posed by contemporary art are not unique to the current moment or the immediate past. All works of art were once contemporary to the artist and culture that produced them. Part of the task of the art historian, then, is to retrieve a vivid sense of the world into which an artwork was introduced and so to measure the distance between its contemporary moment and the scholar's own. Our return to the past must acknowledge the impossibility of forging a comprehensive account of the artwork "as it really was" while nevertheless attending to the specificity and heft of history. In its persistence over time, the material life of artworks challenges us to think beyond the punctual limits of now and then. "[All art has been contemporary]" reads Maurizio Nannucci's 2010 neon work in the Boston Museum of Fine Arts. To make that glowing text into more than a truism, we need to recognize that all historical art was once current and that all contemporary art will soon be historical. We also need to grapple with how the art of the past informs and reconfigures the contemporary moment.

Making Contemporary Art History

While the emergence of contemporary art history as a field of study may be quite recent, debates over whether such a field should exist are not.[42] In November 1941, the director of the Museum of Modern Art (MoMA), Alfred H. Barr Jr., published an essay in the *College Art Journal* titled "Modern Art Makes History, Too." It pled for more art historians—and especially for more graduate students—to study the art of their own times: "The field of modern art is wide open and crying for scholarly research but how many candidates for Ph.D. or M.F.A. are doing theses in twentieth century art? Or even in late nineteenth century? And if they were would they receive the proudly learned guidance available to them in Medieval or Sumerian archaeology?"[43]

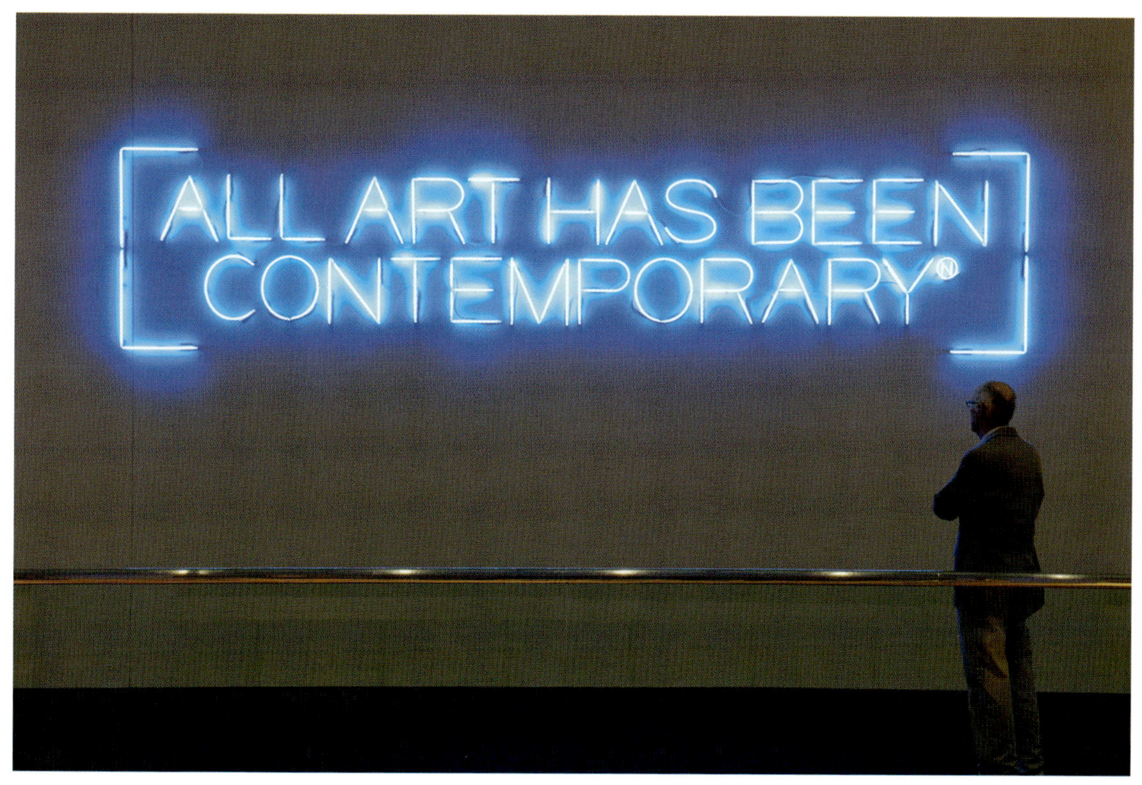

1.9   Maurizio Nannucci, *All Art Has Been Contemporary*, 1999, fabricated in 2011, Neon, transformer, 216⁹⁄₁₆ inches. (Courtesy Museum of Fine Arts, Boston, Museum purchase with funds donated by members of the 2010–2011 Contemporary Art Visiting Committee.)

In arguing for modern art as a field worthy of scholarly attention, Barr will go on to suggest potential research topics on painting and sculpture but also on film, dance, photography, architecture, and industrial design.[44] According to Barr, the study of twentieth-century art offered one special advantage over every other arena of art-historical research: the possibility of direct dialogue between artist and scholar. Barr was both excited by this possibility and distressed that it was so rarely exploited at the time:

> And what opportunities are being lost! Graduate students can't correspond with John [sic] van Eyck, Masolino or Vasari to clear up scholarly problems but they can air-mail Maillol or Siqueiros and write or phone for an appointment with Wright, André Breton, Stieglitz, John Sloan, Balanchine, or D. W. Griffith. (It is already too late to ask art historical questions of Klee or Vuillard, two of the best painters of our time—they died within the year.)[45]

The study of modern art necessarily involved firsthand contact with artists, a category Barr understood capaciously to include painters, sculptors, architects, photographers, choreographers, and filmmakers. Whether most graduate students in 1941 could really have phoned up Frank Lloyd Wright or George Balanchine or D. W. Griffith for an appointment is another matter. Art-historical method demanded that they do so. Or, rather, it would have demanded so had graduate students been permitted to write dissertations on living artists at the time.

The mention of Wright in "Modern Art Makes History, Too" was particularly charged given that Barr had just endured a bitter professional battle with the architect over an exhibition devoted to Wright's work that MoMA opened in 1940.[46] Far from clearing up "scholarly questions" in a straightforward manner, the essays prepared for the MoMA catalogue were seen by Wright as nothing short of a "conspiracy" to distort his achievement and undermine his career. The dispute escalated to the point that, at Wright's insistence, the publication of the catalogue was canceled. In the end, the exhibition was mounted almost entirely by the architect and his students rather than by MoMA's curatorial staff.[47] Both the museum's invitation and a sign posted by the show's entrance specified that the exhibition was "arranged by the architect himself."

A negative review in *Parnassus* magazine described the exhibition as "a bewildering mélange of blue-prints, architectural renderings, scaled models, materials, and photographs" for which "surprisingly enough there is no catalogue."[48] Barr, still furious with Wright about the situation, responded with a letter to the editor that spelled out the museum's conflict with the architect in no uncertain terms:

> I would like to make clear . . . that Mr. Wright . . . was not interested in the plan proposed by our curator—a plan which involved a lucid chronological exposition of Wright's development, particularly as regards his handling of space. For six months, the Department of Architecture had been planning and working upon a catalog which would have comprised a great deal of factual and critical material, including essays by a half-dozen of the foremost architects and architectural historians in this country. Mr. Wright refused to permit the publication of the catalog as planned, although it had been intended as a tribute to him. It was then too late to prepare a new publication. At the beginning of one of our conversations here at the Museum, Mr. Wright announced, "I am a very difficult man." We agree, but we still believe him to be the greatest living architect.[49]

According to Barr, the exhibition planned by the museum would have offered a "lucid chronological exposition of Wright's development." But Wright

F R A N K
L L O Y D
W R I G H T

**THE PRESIDENT AND TRUSTEES OF
THE MUSEUM OF MODERN ART INVITE YOU TO ATTEND
THE PRIVATE OPENING OF A COMPREHENSIVE EXHIBITION
OF THE WORK OF FRANK LLOYD WRIGHT, ARRANGED BY
THE ARCHITECT HIMSELF, ON TUESDAY EVENING, NOVEMBER
TWELFTH, 1940, FROM EIGHT-THIRTY TO ELEVEN O'CLOCK
AT 11 WEST FIFTY-THIRD STREET, NEW YORK CITY.**

THIS INVITATION IS NOT TRANSFERABLE AND WILL ADMIT TWO PERSONS

1.10 Invitation to the exhibition *Frank Lloyd Wright, American Architect*. Exhibition Pamphlet Files, # 114. (Courtesy The Museum of Modern Art Archives, New York.) Digital image © The Museum of Modern Art/Licensed by SCALA/Art Resource, NY.

was not just a leading figure in the history of modern architecture; he was also a living force to be reckoned with. Drawing on his considerable resources at the time, Wright refused to be contained or confined by the museum's "lucid chronological exposition." He would not submit docilely to the terms of his own historicization.

While still on good terms with the museum, Wright drafted a marvelously intricate cover design for the catalogue of the upcoming MoMA exhibition. Dissatisfied with the show's title ("Frank Lloyd Wright: American Architect"), he took the liberty of renaming it "In the Nature of Materials: The Work of Frank Lloyd Wright." Within a few months of submitting the cover design, Wright saw to it that the catalogue was never published. His ill-fated design recalls the discord between the "greatest living architect" and the museum that sought to pay tribute to him. More broadly, the cover illustration suggests the ongoing challenge (and potential hazards) of making contemporary art into history. In "Modern Art Makes History, Too," Barr does not mention the possibility that the artist may prove "a very difficult man" (or woman) or that the professional relationship between artist and scholar may unravel into misunderstanding, mutual resentment, or misrecognition. The unhappy encounter between Wright and the museum suggests the potential for conflict of interest that arises when artists (or, as in more recent instances, dealers, collectors, or museum trustees) intervene in a curatorial process from which they stand to benefit directly.[50]

In "Modern Art Makes History, Too," Barr bemoaned the fact that "the average teacher of art history" has not "really studied the art of the recent past … he loves it little and regards it with suspicion as too ephemeral or too new, too untested by time, or too trivial or eccentric to be worth the serious study of graduate students, let alone undergraduates who he feels should concern themselves with the classics, the values of which seem dependably

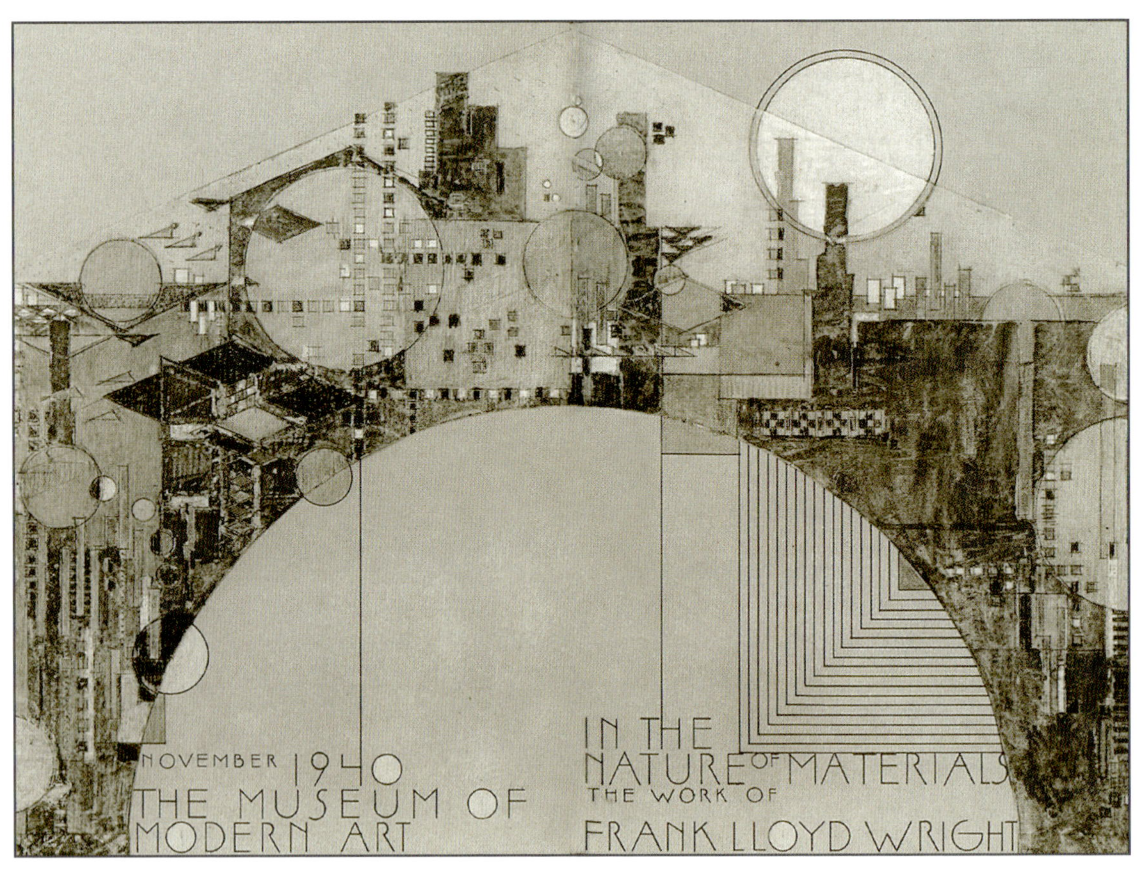

1.11 Frank Lloyd Wright, cover design for the publication planned to accompany the exhibition *Frank Lloyd Wright, American Architect*, The Museum of Modern Art, November 12, 1940–January 5, 1941. © 2012 Frank Lloyd Wright Foundation, Scottsdale, AZ/ Artist Rights Society (ARS), NY.

permanent."[51] But, as Barr goes on to suggest, the values of the past are re-made and reframed by the concerns of the present. The past is not so permanent after all.

In agitating for more students to study the art of their own time, Barr was arguing against the orthodox view that only historical artifacts were worthy of scholarly attention. Today, we face something of the opposite problem from that diagnosed by Barr sixty years ago. Rather than dismissing the art of our own moment as invalid or untested, art historians shower it with ever more scholarly and critical attention through academic conferences, magazine reviews, exhibition essays, blog postings, dissertations, and university press books. We may, in other words, have developed too much love for the new and now, while retaining too little for the old and then. By retrieving fragments of the art-historical past, this book means to temper the demands made by our own contemporary moment, including the demand to be always already "up-to-date."

Scholars of contemporary art frequently seek to interview, correspond with, or otherwise interact with the artists about whom they are writing. The twenty-first-century equivalent of airmailing Maillol might be emailing say, Mathew Barney or, more likely, contacting his gallery in the hopes of setting up an appointment to interview the artist. The protocols and limits of such negotiations have rarely been addressed in the literature on contemporary art. The unpredictability of contemporary art history as a field of study flows in part from the unpredictability of living artists and their responses to the scholars who seek to write about them.[52]

"To grasp reality," the art historian Erwin Panofsky wrote, "we have to detach ourselves from the present."[53] Yet, when scholars are contemporary with the artist on whom we write, we cannot detach ourselves entirely from the present. To share the same moment as the artists we study opens the possibility of a knowledge based on proximity and direct contact rather than posterity and critical distance. But it also courts the risk of rendering the art historian a glorified publicist or ventriloquist for the artist. We need to speak plainly, then, about both the privileges and challenges that follow from being "contemporary with" the artists on whom we focus.

Episodes from the Past

Each of the book's chapters opens with a specific episode in the display, criticism, or study of (then) current art: an undergraduate course at Wellesley College in 1927, an exhibition of newly rendered facsimiles of cave paintings at MoMA in 1937, an institutional dispute over the word "contemporary" in 1948. In each case, I try to reconstruct both the logic and the vividness of these episodes when they were contemporary, when they were "now." The years appended to the chapter titles serve both as punctual markers of the past and as departure points for the open-ended narratives that follow.[54]

What we now call contemporary art history might be said to begin with the introduction of works by living artists into the art-historical curriculum. Chapter 2 focuses on a key moment within that introduction: Barr's undergraduate course on modern art at Wellesley College in 1927. From avant-garde painting in Europe to industrial architecture and automobiles in the United States, from Russian stage designs to German expressionist cinema, the course took the art and culture of its own moment as both subject matter and inspiration. The chapter examines the iconoclastic pedagogy and experimental sense of modernity that shaped Barr's unprecedented class on contemporary art.

Chapter 3 charts a highly selective path through the curatorial program of MoMA under Barr's directorship (1929–1943). It looks in particular detail at the ways in which several exhibitions of premodern art—*Persian Fresco Painting* (1932), *Prehistoric Rock Pictures in Europe and Africa* (1937), and *Italian*

Masters (1940)—were positioned in relation to early twentieth-century art at the time. Far from staying put in the distant past, premodern art kept resurfacing in the exhibition program of the young museum—and it did so not in opposition to contemporary culture but in dialogue with it.

Chapter 4 considers the surprisingly bitter controversy sparked by the decision of the Institute of Modern Art in Boston to change its name to the Institute of Contemporary Art (ICA) in 1948. The change was necessary, according to the institute, because the idea of modern art had collapsed into a narrow version of European modernism. In a public statement announcing its new name, the ICA declared that modern art had become "a cult of bewilderment" that "rested on the hazardous foundations of obscurity and negation, and utilized a private, often secret, language which required the aid of an interpreter."[55] Drawing on the archival files of the ICA and contemporaneous news coverage of the controversy, this chapter reconstructs the symbolic and political stakes of the modern/contemporary divide at midcentury.

The figure of Alfred Barr looms large in what follows, larger, in fact, than I originally anticipated or intended. Before working on this book, I subscribed to the prevailing view of Barr (and the museum he directed) as narrowly formalist and concerned primarily with elite forms of cultural production.[56] The figure I encountered in the pages of Barr's own letters, diaries, and writings—as well as, to varying degrees, in the scholarly accounts of Sybil Kantor, Rona Roob, and Kirk Varnedoe—was a different man altogether.[57] Here was an art history professor who taught his students how to look not only at painting, sculpture, and architecture but also at photography, typography, film, theater, and the design of goods for sale at the local five-and-dime. Here was a museum director who engaged fully with contemporary—or what he often described as "living"—art while insisting on its rootedness in the historical past. In returning to Barr's teaching, writing, and curatorial practice of the

1920s, 1930s, and early 1940s, we may glimpse contemporary art history in the making.

Pictures from the Past

While each chapter returns to a particular time and place, none stays put there. Individual moments of art, criticism, and exhibition open onto other artworks, institutional contexts, and interpretive concerns. Rather than attempting a comprehensive history of works that answer the question, "What was contemporary art?" I have assembled a dossier of selected episodes in that history. As the dossier unfolds, its contents reposition and cross-reference one another.

What Was Contemporary Art? follows from the premise that artworks have the ability to, as Nagel and Wood put it, "generate the effect of a doubling or bending of time."[58] The work of art inhabits different temporalities and contexts, including, but not limited to, its latest moment of reception. As it endures over time, the artwork may act simultaneously as an emissary from the past and an interlocutor in the present, a historical relic and an object of contemporary visual interest.

The works of art discussed in this book are variously European, African, Asian, and North American. My account of their exhibition and critical reception, however, unfolds almost exclusively within the United States. *What Was Contemporary Art?* might therefore be said to propose an alternative definition of "Americanist" art history. Rather than focusing solely on the work of artists born or living in the United States, the book analyzes the idea of contemporary art within American culture during the first decades of the twentieth century.

The images in *What Was Contemporary Art?* are its central objects of investigation and occasionally (via the use of pictorial juxtaposition or surprise) its method of argument. Whenever feasible, images have been reproduced in color and generously sized. To borrow a distinction made by Thomas Crow, this book attempts "to speak to the visual as well as of it."[59] Rather than simply illustrating points already made in the text, the pictures reactivate moments in the history of once contemporary art.

In addition to works of fine art, a range of visual materials makes an appearance in the chapters that follow, including exhibition announcements, installation photographs, illustrated books, posters, magazine covers, and museum brochures. The analysis of such materials often benefits from the practices of close analysis and sustained formal description traditionally reserved for works of fine art. To look with a certain intensity at, say, an ad in *Vanity Fair* magazine featuring a Picasso portrait, a flyer from an artists' protest against MoMA, or a color facsimile of a Matisse painting is not to argue for the aesthetic value of that object or to elevate it to the status of high art. It is, however, to acknowledge that the history of contemporary art extends well beyond the frame of original works.

In each chapter, images are called upon to conjure a sense of the art-historical past and to transport us, however fleetingly, out of the here and now of our current moment. The works reproduced in this book challenge any neat periodization of contemporary art. They were made some time ago but will, in many cases, be so obscure as to qualify as new for many readers. These pictures were contemporary to their own moment. Now, they may be to ours as well.

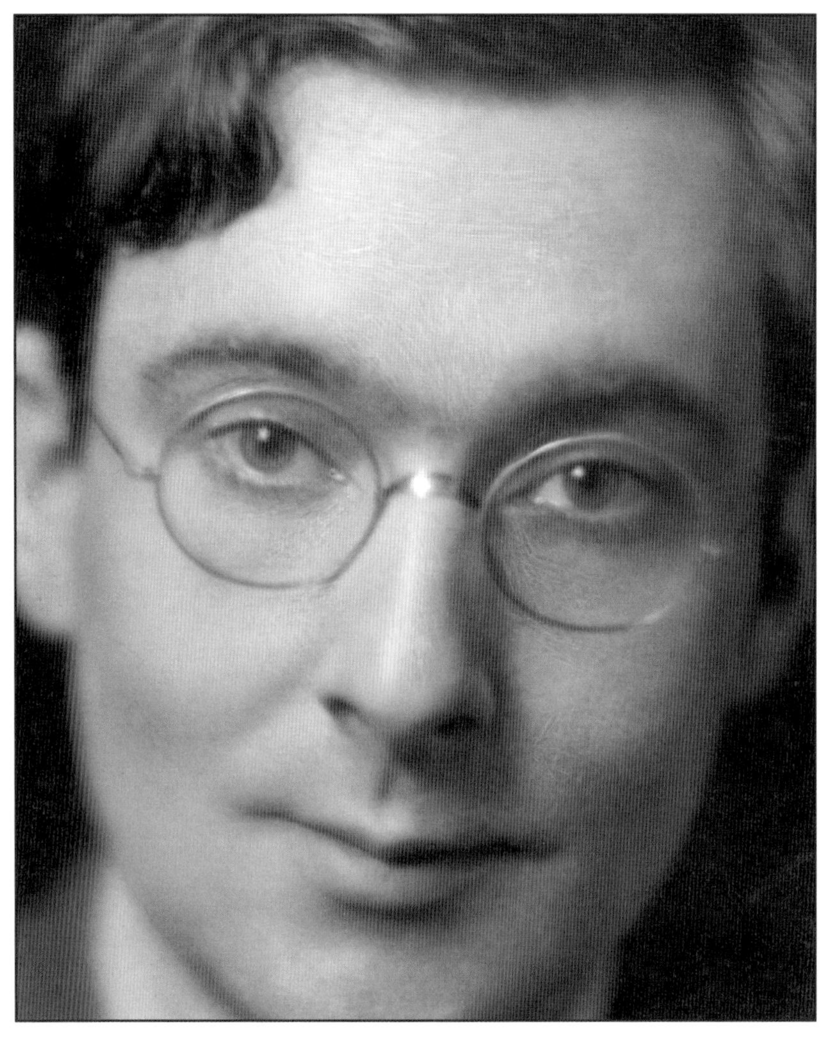

2.1 Alfred H. Barr Jr., c. 1929. Margaret
Scolari Barr Papers, photo albums, box
35. (Courtesy the Museum of Modern Art
Archives, New York.) Digital image © The
Museum of Modern Art/Licensed by SCALA/
Art Resource, NY.

2 Young Professor Barr (1927)

Course Offering

In spring 1927, a professor at Wellesley College offered what is thought to have been the first college course in the United States on contemporary art. The professor was Alfred H. Barr Jr., a twenty-five-year-old *wunderkind* recently appointed to the faculty. His class defied the disciplinary bounds of art history by teaching undergraduates about the art, architecture, design, music, film, and theater of their own moment. Fueled by Barr's experimental pedagogy and expansive, even revolutionary sense of modernity, the course attracted an unusual degree of attention on campus and in the press, even appearing, by the following summer, in the pages of *Vanity Fair* magazine. Little remembered today, the course furnished an important conceptual blueprint for the upstart institution that would ultimately hire Barr away from Wellesley College, the Museum of Modern Art (MoMA) in New York City.[1]

By returning to the methods and materials of the Wellesley course, I hope to retrieve a sense of contemporary art as a newly invented field of study in 1927 and to recall a culture of modernism far more inclusive than that typically associated with Barr. As we shall see, Barr approached teaching the course as part of a broader program of research, criticism, and curating. He conceived of contemporary art as a subject in the making and urged his students to experience it firsthand rather than to study it from a dispassionate remove.

A quick note about terminology may be helpful before proceeding to class. Although Barr alternated between "modern" and "contemporary" in the context of his Wellesley course, the two were not interchangeable in his lexicon. The term "modern," often capitalized to underscore its status as a historical style (following "Renaissance" and "Baroque"), signified for Barr the most innovative art and culture of the nineteenth and early twentieth centuries. "Contemporary," which he rarely capitalized, conveyed a condition of currency or coexistence regardless of artistic form, content, or sensibility. In a letter written in 1929 to Paul Sachs, his Harvard University mentor, Barr would note that "the word 'Modern' is valuable because semantically it suggests the progressive, original, and challenging rather than the safe and academic which would naturally be included in the supine neutrality of the term 'contemporary.'"[2]

Although still a doctoral candidate at Harvard University in winter 1926, Barr was offered teaching positions at Wellesley, Smith, and Oberlin Colleges. They carried comparable salaries and responsibilities, but Wellesley alone agreed to Barr's proposal for a course on modern art.[3] He was hired at the rank of associate professor to teach Renaissance, baroque, and modern art, starting in fall 1926. In his first semester at Wellesley, Barr offered History of the Italian Tradition in Painting. Unlike Italian Renaissance art history classes taught by other Wellesley faculty, Barr's course extended from Leonardo and Raphael all the way "down to Renoir and Cezanne."[4] History of the Italian Tradition in Painting was a prerequisite for Barr's modern art course in spring 1927. In setting this requirement, Barr established a historical basis for the study of twentieth-century art, a field that was, of course, only twenty-seven years old at the time.

Art history courses designated as "Modern" were increasingly common by the mid 1920s.[5] However, as Barr later complained, the art covered in such courses typically "began with Rubens and ended with a few superficial and hostile remarks about Van Gogh and Matisse."[6] In contrast to his teachers at painting (excluding the Far East), and aims to develop observation and æsthetic appreciation as well as to relate important monuments to their contemporary civilization. This course is not open to students who have taken or are taking any other history course in the Art Department.

Open to seniors only. No prerequisites. Three hours a week for a year.
MISS AVERY.

204†. STUDIO PRACTICE. Design.
Open by permission of the department to juniors and seniors who have completed course 103. Three hours a week for the first semester. (Nine hours of studio practice.) MISS LITCHFIELD.

205. SECOND YEAR INTRODUCTORY COURSE IN THE HISTORY OF ART. First Semester—Introduction to Romanesque and Gothic Art, with emphasis on the development in France. Second semester—Introduction to Renaissance Art, with emphasis on the development in Italy. Laboratory work is required.
Open to students who have completed course 101. Three hours a week for a year. MISS AVERY, MISS IGLEHART.

303. HISTORY OF THE ITALIAN TRADITION IN PAINTING. A general review of the problems and schools of the Italian Renaissance; their subsequent development in European painting through El Greco, Velazquez, Rubens, and Poussin down to Renoir and Cezanne. Laboratory work is required.
Open to students who have completed course 205. Three hours a week for a year. MR. BARR.

304. HISTORY OF RENAISSANCE ARCHITECTURE. This course centers in a critical study of the works of representative architects of the Italian Renaissance. It follows the influence of that style on the native architectural expression of France. Laboratory drawing is required.
Open to students who have completed course 205. Three hours a week for a year. MRS. ROGERS.

305. TRADITION AND REVOLT IN MODERN PAINTING. Pictorial organization; expression; representation. Twentieth century painting; its relation to the past, especially the 19th century; to developments in the other arts; to criticism and fashionable aesthetics; to contemporary civilization.
Open to students who have completed course 303. Three hours a week for the second semester. MR. BARR.

†See note on page 42.

2.2 Page from *Wellesley College Bulletin Calendar*, 1926–1927. (Courtesy Wellesley College Archives.)

Princeton and Harvard, Barr created a modern art class focused on the art, architecture, and design of the current moment, which is to say, the 1920s. Although the class extended back to the nineteenth century and carried a prerequisite of coursework on earlier art, it was primarily concerned with contemporary art and culture in the United States and Europe.

The Wellesley course was officially designated Art 305: Tradition and Revolt in Modern Painting, a title whose medium-specificity would prove largely misleading. The class proceeded diachronically across the nineteenth and twentieth centuries as well as synchronically across the visual, performing, and commercial art of the 1920s. The course description in the *Wellesley College Bulletin Calendar* outlined its concerns as "Pictorial organization; expression; representation. Twentieth century painting; its relation to the past, especially the 19th century; to developments in the other arts; to criticism and fashionable aesthetics; to contemporary civilization."[7] As we shall see, the official listing for Art 305 hardly did justice to the remarkably wide range of objects and issues covered by the class.

The relative restraint of the course announcement may have had more to do with the descriptive conventions of college catalogues at the time than with the young professor's vision of the class. In a letter to his parents dated February 1926, Barr shared a first—and rather more detailed—draft of his course announcement:

> Here's the notice for the Wellesley catalogue (in an unedited form) . . . Vision and representation. Pictorial organization. The place of subject matter. The achievement of the past—especially the nineteenth century. The 20th century, its gods and -isms. The painter, critics, dealer, collector; the museum, the academies; the public. Contemporary painting in relation to sculpture, the graphic arts, architecture, the stage, music,

literature, commercial and decorative arts. Fashionable aesthetics: fetish and taboo. Painting and modern life. The Future.[8]

This first description suggests the true sweep of Barr's ambitions for the class. In addition to individual artists and movements (the stock-in-trade of art history classes then as now), the course would address broader questions relating to the collection, display, and criticism of contemporary art and culture as well as the dialogue between modern painting and public life.

The mention of "fetish and taboo" indicates Barr's emergent interest in African and other forms of non-Western art and their influence on European avant-gardes. Among the slides he collected for the Wellesley course were pictures of masks and other ritual objects created by Native Americans, African Bakubas, and Philippine Melanesians.[9] No less intriguing than "fetish and taboo" is the appearance of "The Future" at the end of Barr's draft description. How might the course have addressed "The Future" as well as the past of modern art? One answer may flow from the iconoclastic format of the class within the context of the Wellesley Department of Art.

Alone among Wellesley art history courses, Tradition and Revolt in Modern Painting included no formal midterm or final exam. In addition, Barr designated all the students in the class "faculty" because he wished each to develop her own field of expertise and then instruct the others—as well as him—about it. This gesture, which Barr did not make in his courses on Italian Renaissance or European baroque art, suggests that, as each student in the class was equally contemporary to the art of her own historical moment, each was—or would become—qualified to teach part of the course. As a local newspaper article about the course noted at the time, "The organization into a 'Faculty' makes each individual student responsible for her special division of the subject, with the opportunity of reporting the main outlines of its development to the class at some time during the term."[10]

Nine students (all juniors or seniors) enrolled in Tradition and Revolt in Modern Painting.[11] Early in the semester, two sophomores were permitted to join the class as auditors.[12] All the women in the class were between eighteen and twenty-one years old, while Barr was age twenty-five and the twentieth century had just entered its twenty-seventh year. The course thus narrowed both the usual generation gap between teacher and students and the historical distance between the students and the material they were studying.[13] The participants in Art 305 were themselves contemporary to most of the art at issue in the course.

Every art history class at Wellesley College, save for Barr's Tradition and Revolt in Modern Painting, entailed something called "laboratory work." Introduced into the curriculum in 1897 by department chair Alice Van Vechten Brown, laboratory work required students to sketch, paint, or sculpt copies after photographs or plaster casts of the artworks they were learning about in lecture. The goal was to infuse the historical study of art with a sense of material immediacy through hands-on engagement. The Department of Art likened the method to the laboratory experiments students undertook in science classes. Practical experimentation and a technical knowledge of art were thus emphasized alongside memorization of artists, dates, and monuments. Students might learn, for example, the method of gold-ground panel painting as practiced in the Trecento in Italy, or make comparative sketches after a photograph of a figure from Michelangelo's Sistine Chapel ceiling and a live model attempting the same pose in the classroom. Wildly popular with students, this approach to art history became so closely identified with the college that it was known as the "Wellesley Method."[14]

Tradition and Revolt in Modern Painting dispensed with the Wellesley Method, presumably because the art at issue was not grounded in the logic of mimesis or artisanal craft. Rather than having his students learn the

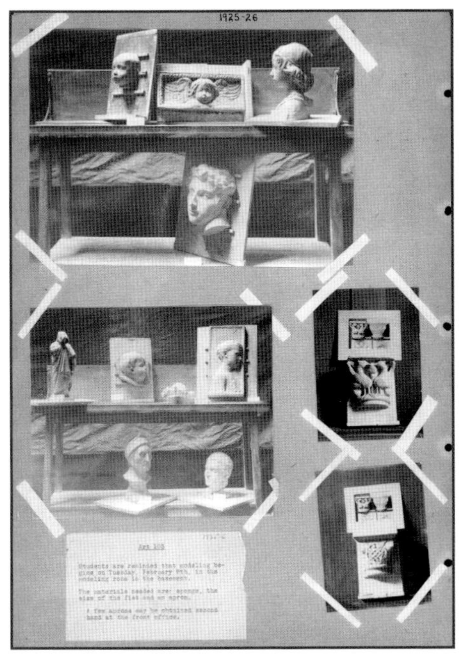

2.3 Photograph from Wellesley College scrapbooks documenting student "laboratory work" for Art 103, 1925–1926. (Courtesy Wellesley College Archives.)

2.4 Photograph from Wellesley College scrapbooks documenting student "laboratory work" for Art 101 and 104, 1931–1932. (Courtesy Wellesley College Archives.)

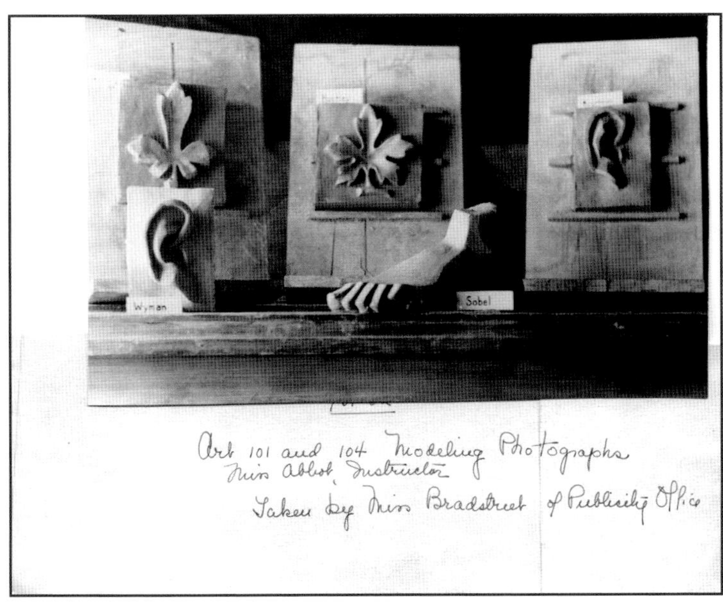

technical procedures of historical art so as to mimic the works of dead artists, Barr asked them to engage with living forms of art, architecture, music, and theater. The course included, for example, an in-class, two-person recital by Barr's roommate at the time, art historian Jere Abbott, along with a "young man in the Music Department" of works by Igor Stravinsky, Arnold Schoenberg, and Les Six (a group of avant-garde composers much inspired by the music of Erik Satie and the poetry of Jean Cocteau). Among the field trips taken by the class were a visit to Cambridge to see the New England Confectionary Company (Necco), which was the largest candy factory in the world at the time, and to Boston to see the Motor-Mart, a new kind of urban structure that combined the functions of parking garage and service station.[15] Barr saw the Necco factory and the Motor-Mart as significant examples of industrial architecture, which he regarded as one of the most advanced forms of contemporary American culture.[16] Completed in 1927, both buildings would have been brand-new or possibly still under construction at the time of the class visit. One way to engage with the future of modernity, then, was to witness it being built or occupied.

"Wellesley and Modernism"

Dazzling in its multidisciplinarity, Barr's modern art course included the study of French, Russian, German, Italian, Dutch, Mexican, and American painting; of architecture and the industrial arts, including the design of automobiles, home and office furniture, and household appliances such as refrigerators; of cartoons, comic strips, magazine illustrations, posters, typography, and popular advertisements; of stage design, dance, music, and film; and of modern criticism and aesthetics. Student "faculty," sometimes working in pairs, were responsible for particular topics, which ranged from industrial architecture to "the study of Jazz and its derivatives," from "theatre arts" to the "history of the movie."

One of the more unusual student projects was senior Mary C. Bostwick's assignment: the publication of an article about Tradition and Revolt in Modern Painting in a local newspaper. Bostwick's class assignment was linked to her membership on the Wellesley Press Board, a group of students who worked as stringers for area newspapers, filing features on campus life for publication. Each member of the Press Board was assigned to a different newspaper and paid a small honorarium for her contribution. Bostwick was employed by the *Boston Evening Transcript*, which on April 27, 1927, published an (unsigned) article titled "Wellesley and Modernism." The piece promoted both Barr's modern art class (by this time three-quarters complete) and the college sponsoring it as vibrantly progressive:

> Wellesley has taken another step in the study of modern artistic achievement, by the semester course in modern art offered by the art department for the first time this year. Almost the first course in any college devoted entirely to painting of the last hundred years, it treats the phases of tradition and revolt in contemporary art, with its development out of the successive trends of the nineteenth century. Since modernist tendencies are not confined to painting, the course makes a study of all the arts, aiming to comprehend the relation of modern expression to twentieth-century civilization.
>
> To keep abreast of the art work of the moment is the ideal of the course, and to acquire familiarity with the names and the accomplishments that are prominent not only in art circles but in all currents of life. … Museums, galleries, and private collections, the theatre and the "movie," are drawn upon for material, and particularly current periodicals, in which are found not only critical material, but new drawings and prints,

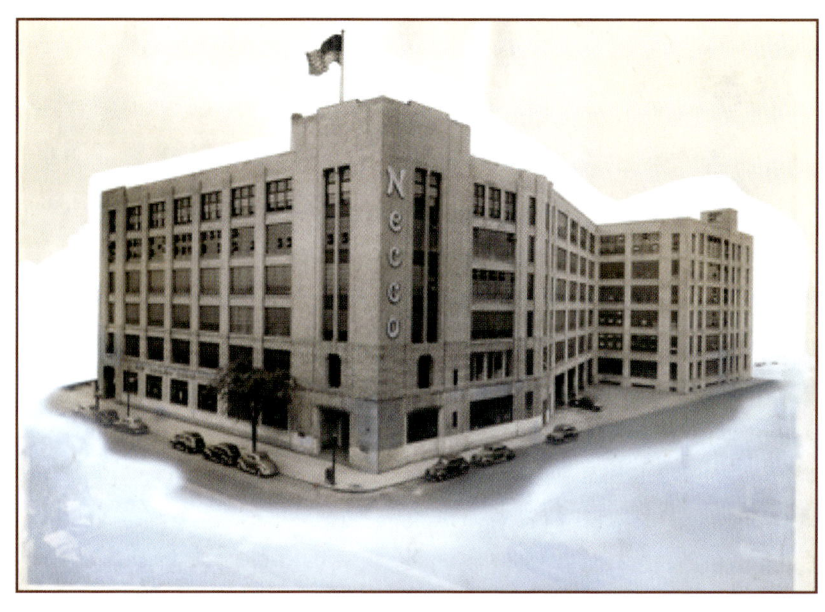

2.5 Necco Building, Cambridge,
Massachusetts, 1927. (Photograph c. 1940.)

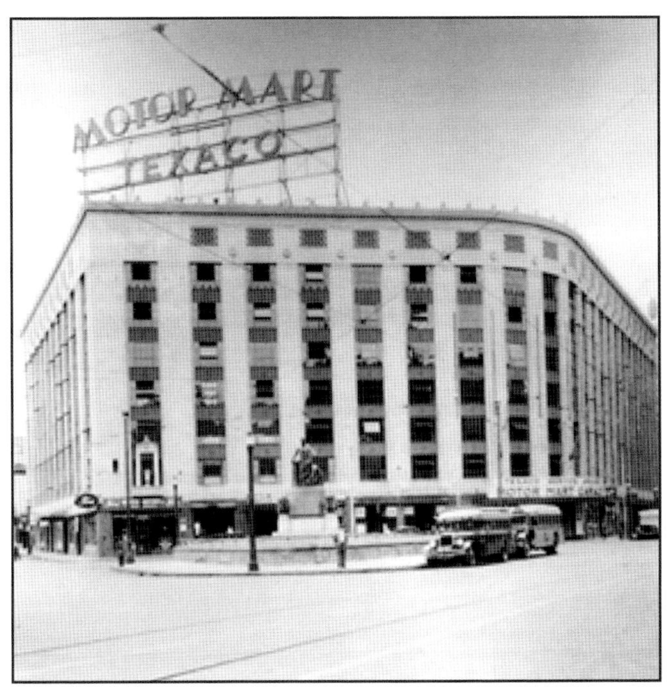

2.6 Motor-Mart, Boston, 1927. (Photograph
c. 1940.)

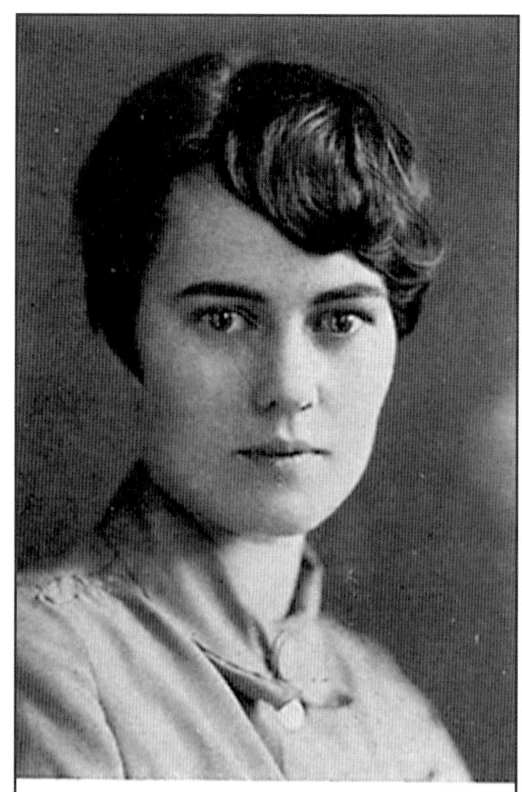

2.7 Photograph of Mary C. Bostwick,
Wellesley Legenda (yearbook), 1927, page 32.
Photograph by Bachrach. (Courtesy Welles-
ley College Archives.)

and the increasingly fine work in advertisements and typography. The class is thus necessarily informal and opens each week with reports on events of timely interest before the more carefully prepared problems are introduced.[17]

According to the article, all members of the student faculty were assigned to work on contemporary examples of art and design. None of the students was asked to report on impressionism, postimpressionism, nineteenth-century art criticism, or the like. None, in fact, was asked to report on paintings of any kind. Presumably, the class as a whole covered nineteenth-century painting and other pre-contemporary materials, while individual students reported on more recent topics and "events of timely interest."

Two trips taken by the "faculty" suggest the range of material taken up by the class. In January 1927, Barr accompanied his students to the National Automobile Show at New York City's Grand Central Palace, where forty manufacturers had three hundred different automobiles on display, including a Reo Flying Cloud that featured Lockheed's latest four-wheel hydraulic brake system and styling by the Italian designer Fabio Segardi; a sporty Dodge roadster "upholstered in gray snakeskin leather"; and a "glorious yellow collapsible coupe" called the Jordan Six.[18]

The class also attended a performance of *The Dybbuk*, a Yiddish play presented in Hebrew by the Moscow-based Habima Players in a production directed by Konstantin Stanislavski's protégé, Evgeny Vakhtangov. Adapted in 1916 from Eastern European folk tales, the play tells the story of a Jewish bride possessed by a dybbuk (demon spirit) on the eve of her wedding. According to Brooks Atkinson's review in the *New York Times*, the Habima Players' expressionist acting, costumes, and set design fueled the visual and physical impact of the performance to such a degree that the play effectively transcended the limits of language: "In spite of an eager audience, to whom

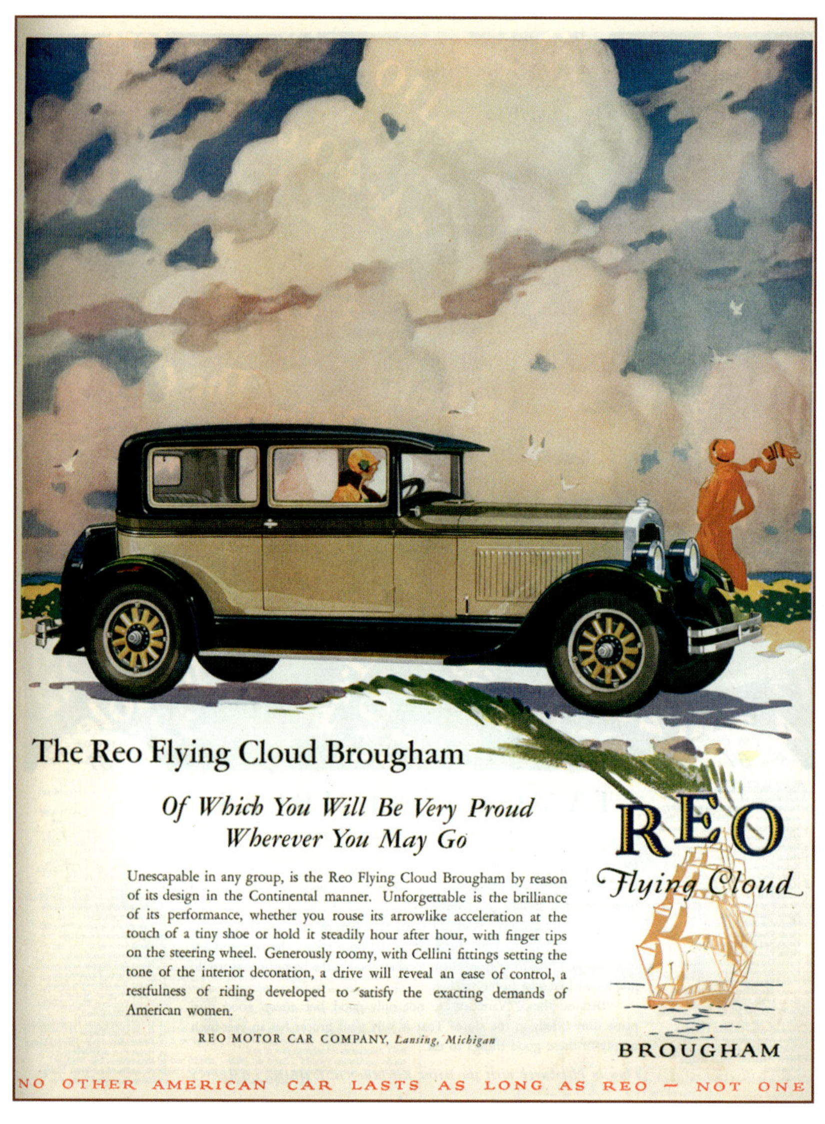

2.8 1927 Reo Flying Cloud Brougham auto advertisement. *Ladies Home Journal*, April 1927.

Hebrew was not an unfamiliar tongue, the spoken words obviously did not matter particularly last night. For the attention was naturally focused upon a highly stylized type of acting developed to a state of plastic perfection."[19] Atkinson proceeded to describe the "extraordinary" makeup that rendered the actors' faces into "grotesque masks" and the angular set design that dramatically skewed the action unfolding on stage. Though Atkinson's review bespeaks the theatrical impact of *The Dybbuk*, no record survives of Barr's response—or that of his students—to the production.[20]

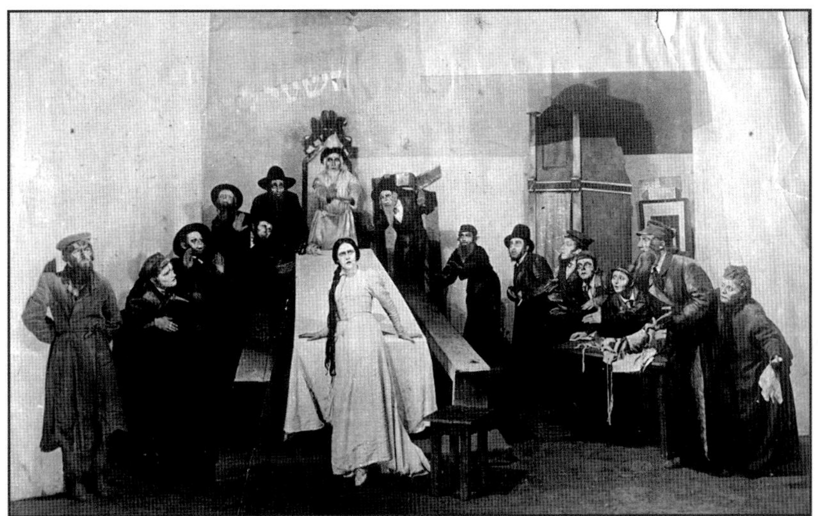

2.9 "The Court of the Tzaddik in *Dybbuk*," 1922, photograph, 5⅞ × 8⅝ inches (15 × 22 cm). (Courtesy The State Central Museum A. A. Bakhrushin from the collection of Federal State Institution of Culture.)

As such class trips suggest, Tradition and Revolt in Modern Painting challenged the strict divides between art and commerce and between elite and mass culture. This is not to say that Barr simply opened the floodgates to all of contemporary culture and let the students pick and choose whatever they liked best. Course activities were structured and selective. The class attended *The Dybbuk*, for example, but not *Gentlemen Prefer Blondes* (also on stage in New York City in January 1927). Students were assigned to see Fritz Lang's *Metropolis* but not the top-grossing film of 1926, *Aloma of the South Seas*. In general, Barr emphasized the European avant-garde (in art, theater, film, and music) alongside those forms of American culture he considered most innovative at the time (industrial architecture, photography, cartoons). The course encompassed "all the arts" because Barr believed that vanguard painting and sculpture could not be understood in isolation from the broader culture of which they were part, a culture of candy factories and Motor-Marts no less than of Henri Matisse and Aristide Maillol.

For one class assignment in particular, students were asked to focus on the material culture of everyday life. As "Wellesley and Modernism" reported, "An amusing experiment connected with the industrial arts is the ten-cent store competition for a 'Still Life' made up of the three best objects to be found which are made of some strictly modern material such as aluminum or papier mache."[21] The goal of the assignment was to find and recombine the "best" modern objects on offer: even at the five-and-dime, distinctions could be drawn.[22]

"A Modern Art Questionnaire"

Barr commenced Tradition and Revolt in Modern Painting with a quiz consisting of fifty terms, mostly proper names, drawn from the world of contemporary arts and letters. These proceeded "from very obvious to somewhat more difficult" and ranged from George Gershwin at the top of list to Das Bauhaus near the bottom, from Alfred Stieglitz (#12) to Arnold Schoenberg (#39), and from Saks Fifth Avenue (#17) to Suprematism (#47). Students were instructed to identify "the significance of each" term "in relation to modern artistic expression."[23] Notably, though set in a course on "Modern Painting," Barr's quiz included only five painters—Matisse (#4), Miguel Covarrubias (#5), John Marin (#7), Wyndham Lewis (#33), and Fernand Léger (#45)—one of whom, Covarrubias, was best known as a caricaturist at the time. What is more, all of the entries referred to figures who were living and, in this literal sense, contemporary in 1927.

No copy of the quiz survives in the holdings of the Wellesley College Archives. A few months after the course ended, however, the quiz was published as "A Modern Art Questionnaire" in *Vanity Fair* magazine. As a result, a substantially larger audience than the eleven young women enrolled in Barr's course would have encountered his quiz in 1927 (the magazine's circulation at the time was 80,000).[24]

In *Vanity Fair*, the quiz was prefaced with commentary by Barr: "This is a primitive among questionnaires having been invented almost a year ago as a preliminary examination to test the student's background for a course in modern art at Wellesley College ... it covers with careful proportion modern expression in architecture, sculpture, painting, graphic arts, music, prose, drama, poetry, the stage, decorative and commercial arts, movies, ballet, and modern criticism, chosen from French, British, Italian, Russian, Germanic and American sources."[25] The publication of Barr's questionnaire in *Vanity Fair* suggests both the novelty of contemporary art as a field of study in 1927 and the liveliness of the dialogue between popular and elite culture. According to "Wellesley and Modernism," "Modern pictorial style has followed into the ordinary environment of life. Publications like the *New Yorker*, *Vanity Fair*,

AUGUST, 1927

A Modern Art Questionnaire

By ALFRED H. BARR, Jr.

THIS is a primitive among questionnaires having been invented almost a year ago as a preliminary examination to test the student's background for a course in modern art at Wellesley College. It lacks the sophistication of the more recent manner. There are no spellbinders such as: Name four important artist-photographers whose names begin with St—, or: What poet wrote in honor of an English naval victory, "We bit them in the bight, the Bight of Heligoland"?, or: What daughter of an American clergyman published in Paris perhaps the most remarkable prose work of the century, written by an Irishman and forbidden in the United States? However, like many primitives it has its own peculiar, if humble, charm. For instance, it covers with careful proportion modern expression in architecture, sculpture, painting, graphic arts, music, prose, drama, poetry, the stage, decorative and commercial arts, movies, ballet, and modern criticism, chosen from French, British, Italian, Russian, Germanic and American sources. Furthermore, the list is carefully graded from very obvious to somewhat more difficult; only the most important accomplishments, **with a** few exceptions, are considered; the usual position of question and answer is reversed; and finally a few actual works of art are represented by photographs or quotations.

WHAT IS THE SIGNIFICANCE OF EACH OF THE FOLLOWING IN RELATION TO MODERN ARTISTIC EXPRESSION?

1. George Gershwin
2. Max Reinhardt
3. Henri Matisse
4. *The Hairy Ape*
5. Miguel Covarrubias
6. James Joyce
7. John Marin
8. UFA
9. Alexandre Archipenko
10. Roger Fry
11. The Zoning Law
12. Alfred Stieglitz
13. *The Cabinet of Dr. Caligari*
14. Aristide Maillol
15. The Imagists
16. Jean Cocteau
17. *Saks-Fifth Avenue*
18. *Petrouchka*
19. Harriet Monroe
20. Paul Claudel
21. Gilbert Seldes
22. Franz Werfel
23. Gordon Craig
24. Forbes Watson
25. Oswald Spengler
26. Luigi Pirandello
27. *Les Six*
28. The Sitwells
29. Edgar Brandt
30. (who wrote this?)
    Thou art come at length
    more beautiful
    than any cool god
    in a chamber under
    Lycia's far coast
    than any high god
    who touches us not
    here in the seeded years;
    ay, than Argestes
    scattering the broken leaves.
31. Polytonic
32. The Barnes Foundation
33. Wyndham Lewis
34. Frans Masereel
35. Frank Lloyd Wright
36. George Antheil
37. John Quinn
38. *Sur-réalisme*
39. Arnold Schönberg
40. *Aria de Capo*
41. John Alden Carpenter
42. Frankl
43. Vsévolöd Meierhold
44. Harold Samuel
45. Fernand Léger
46. (who wrote this?)
    "Silence is not hurt by attending to taking more reflection than a whole sentence. And it is said and the quotation is reasoning. It gives the whole preceding. If there is time enough then appearances are considerable. They are in a circle. They are tendering a circle. They are a tender circle. They are tenderly a circle."
47. Suprematism
48. *Das Bauhaus*
49. Le Corbusier-Saugnier
50. Richard Boleslavsky

Answers on page 96

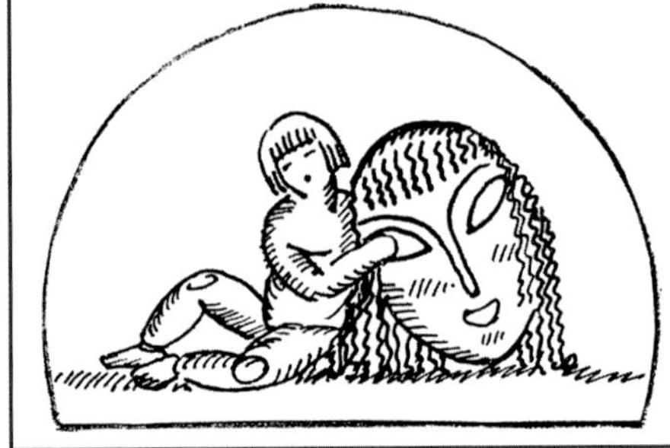

2.10 Alfred Barr, "A Modern Art Questionnaire," *Vanity Fair*, August 1927. (Courtesy Condé Nast.)

and *The New Masses* are particularly rich in their illustrations and advertise-ments."[26] Students in Art 305 were required to read—but, even more, to look at—current issues of these three periodicals throughout the semester. The inclusion of the *New Masses*, a radical left journal committed to Marxist poli-tics, alongside the fashionable *Vanity Fair* and the literary *New Yorker*, might seem discordant. From Barr's perspective, however, in spring 1927 a commu-nist journal and a capitalist magazine might be equally compelling in terms of "modern pictorial style."

At Wellesley, Barr urged his students to approach advertising, illustra-tion, and commercial display as genuine forms of modern expression rather than as debased or fraudulent imitations of the avant-garde.[27] He singled out Saks Fifth Avenue (#27) as especially forward-looking in this regard: "Through its advertisements and show windows, this department store has done more to popularize the modern mannerism in pictorial and decorative arts than any two proselytizing critics."[28]

The "modern mannerism" popularized by Saks Fifth Avenue may be glimpsed in an advertisement published in the September 1927 issue of *Van-ity Fair* (the issue directly following the one with Barr's questionnaire) that presents "we moderns" as a pair of flattened and interlocking male silhou-ettes. The stylized geometry and severely tailored proportions of the men rhyme with the quasi-abstract notations (jagged lines, dipping curves, small semicircles) that float around them. The following year, Frederick Kiesler's sleek design for a Saks show window employed oblique angles, spirals, and a few strategically placed props (a black velvet coat with white fur collar, a black evening purse, and a pair of long white gloves draped over a chair) to elicit a sense of visual mystique.[29] Where Kiesler's window marketed the posh accessories and lightly surrealist allure of fashionable femininity, the Saks haberdashery advertisement in *Vanity Fair* promoted a clubhouse,

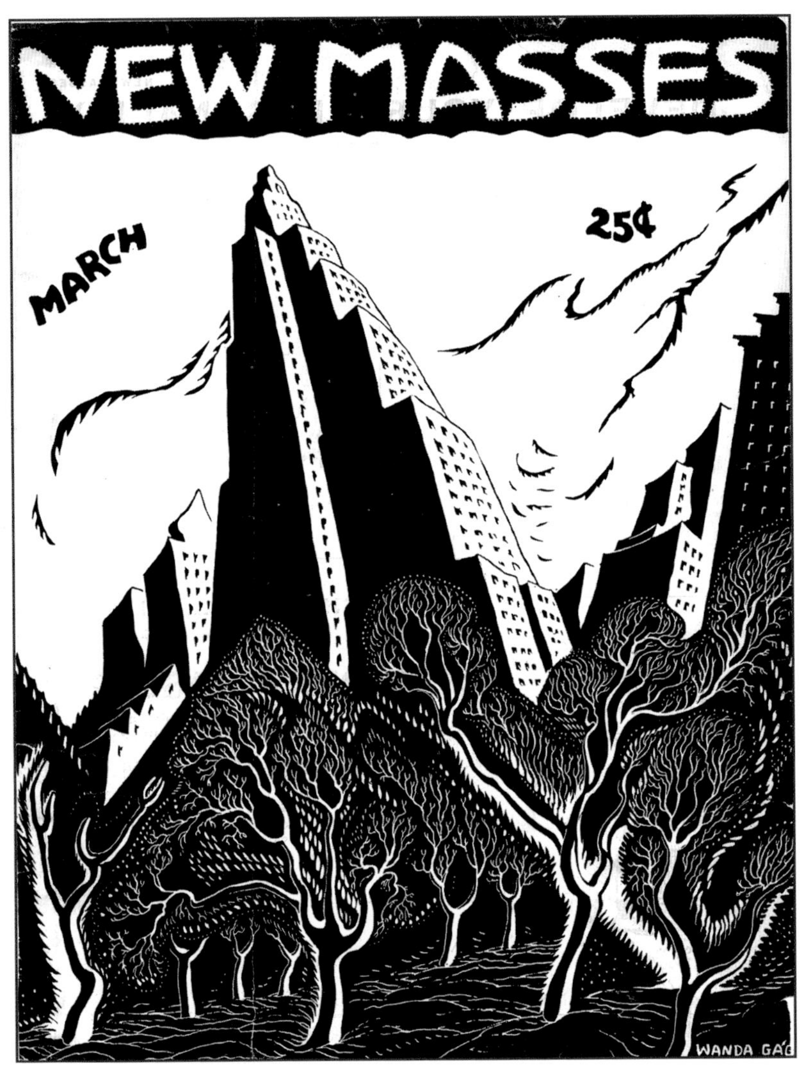

2.11 *New Masses*, March 1927. Cover illustration by Wanda Gág. (Courtesy The Tamiment Library, New York University.)

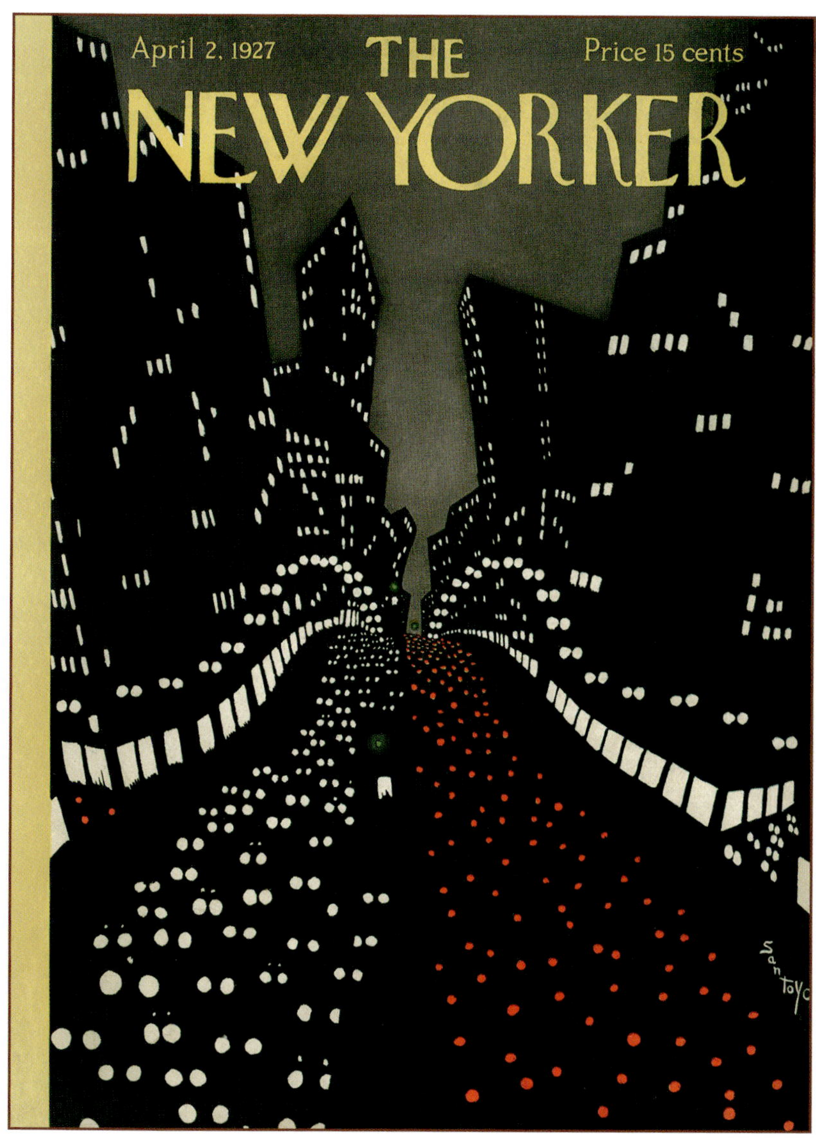

2.12 *The New Yorker*, April 2, 1927. (Courtesy
Condé Nast.)

quasi-cubist version of modernist masculinity.[30] By borrowing from surrealism or cubism to sell clothing, the show window and the menswear ad demonstrated the ways in which "modern pictorial style has followed into the ordinary environment of life."[31]

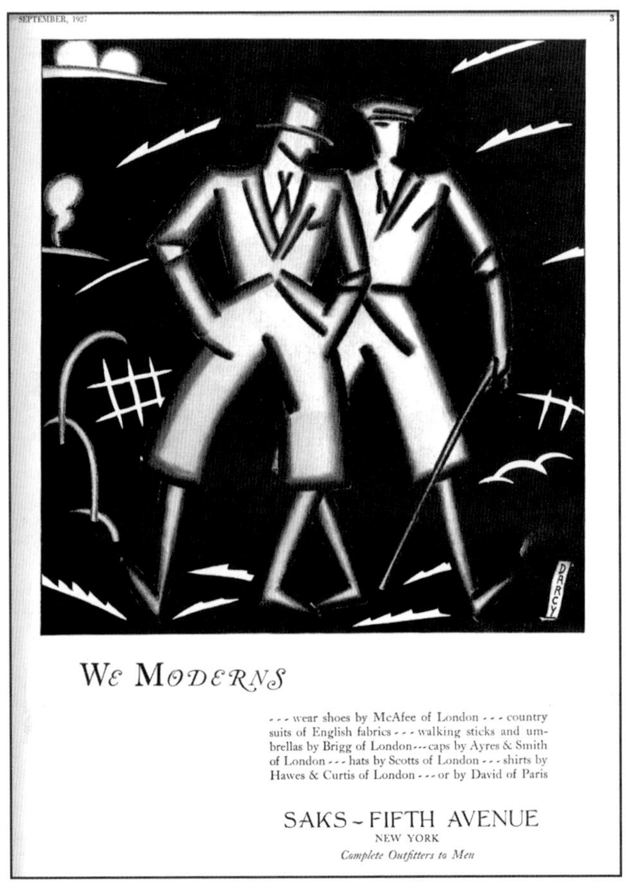

2.13 "We Moderns," menswear ad for Saks Fifth Avenue, *Vanity Fair*, September 1927.

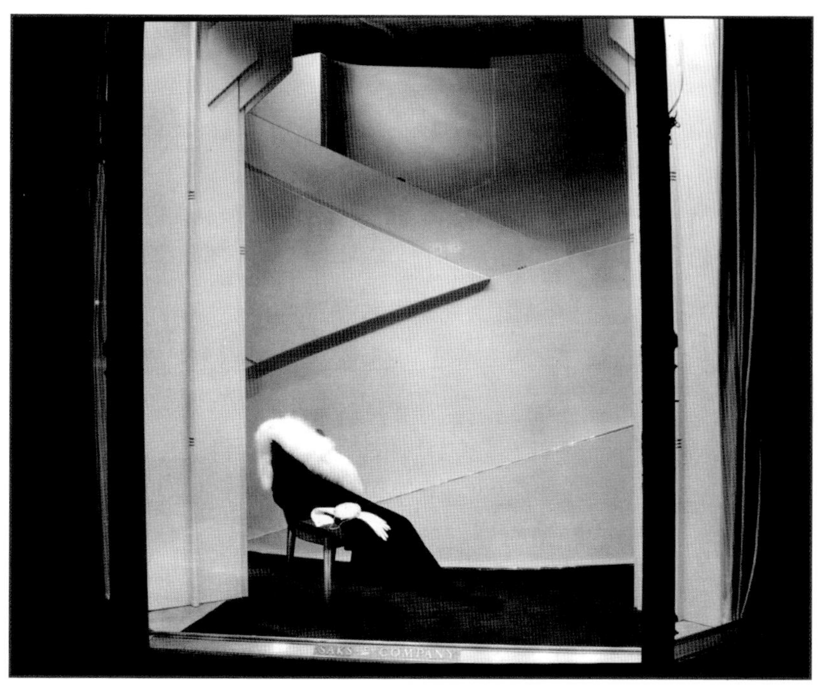

2.14 Frederick Kiesler, Saks Fifth Avenue
show window, 1928–1929. (Courtesy The
Kiesler Archives.)

"The Magazine of Next Season's Modernity"

In the pages of *Vanity Fair*, Barr's questionnaire functioned as a kind of parlor game by which readers might display their knowledge of modern art to themselves and others.[32] Such quizzes were a regular feature of the magazine at the time. "A Theatrical Questionnaire" appeared in the July 1927 issue, following "A Lawn Tennis Questionnaire" in June and "A Questionnaire on Motion Pictures" in April. The questionnaires contributed to *Vanity Fair*'s broader presentation of modernity as both a lifestyle to which readers should aspire and a body of knowledge they needed to acquire. A 1925 subscription advertisement exhorted, "Don't Be a Yesterday, Be a Tomorrow," below an image of two couples in evening dress, one of which ("The Yesterdays") appears smaller and marginally less fashionable than its counterpart ("The Tomorrows"). "Read *Vanity Fair*," the ad exclaims, "The Magazine of next season's modernity."[33] The bottom of the page is divided into nine columns representing the various spheres of culture dealt with in the magazine—"stage," "fashions," "literature," "world ideas," "sports," "dancing," "art," "satire," and "movies."[34]

A 1929 subscription advertisement ramped up the idea of modernity as a test that readers needed to pass. Beside a black-and-white reproduction of a cubist painting, the ad poses a series of questions: "Somebody paid $3,500 for this . . . WHY? Why did Picasso, master draughtsman, choose to paint a portrait like this? Why Braque . . . Matisse . . . Derain . . . Cézanne? What do they mean? What do you say when your pretty dinner partner asks you? Could you even tell if this were wrong side up? You've got to know. Not just gulp soup! One way to find out. Read *Vanity Fair*." In smaller type, the ad promises that readers will "get the habit of knowing all the new and amusing things in all the arts," from music and theater to "talking cinema," from visual art to dance and fashion.

The advertisement contains a number of inside jokes. The painting re-produced—Pablo Picasso's *Portrait of Braque* (1909–1910)—was indeed print-ed upside down. By inverting the portrait, *Vanity Fair* extended and exaggerated Picasso's cubist disturbance of perspectival illusionism and com-positional order. The upending of the painting would have been recognized by readers already familiar with Picasso's *Portrait of Braque* and surmised, perhaps, by others knowledgeable about cubism. What readers might not have known, however, was that the "somebody" who paid $3,500 for the *Por-trait of Braque* was Frank Crowninshield, then editor in chief of *Vanity Fair*.[35] The oblique manner in which the ad alludes to the magazine's editor and his private art collection evoked a sense of social exclusivity (with clues to be decoded by a small group of cognoscenti) and tongue-in-cheek commentary on the abstruseness of modern art ("Could you even tell if this were wrong side up?"). It is worth noting that the portrait had been created some twenty years prior to its appearance in the ad. Though two decades out of date, Pi-casso's *Portrait of Braque* embodied *Vanity Fair*'s modernity far better than, say, the artist's neoclassical paintings of the mid 1920s. The abstraction and ambiguity of the cubist portrait—in conjunction with the ad's playful banter about it—rendered it one of the "new and amusing things in the arts" in 1929. Seven years later, Crowninshield lent the *Portrait of Braque* to Barr's land-mark show, *Cubism and Abstract Art*, at MoMA.[36] In the exhibition catalogue, Barr used the portrait to illustrate an early stage in the development of cubist painting in the years between 1908 and 1912. In this context, the painting was reproduced right-side up.[37]

Like *Vanity Fair*'s subscription campaigns, Barr's quiz might be said to present modernity as an amusing diversion, a test to be passed in order to impress a dinner companion. From this perspective, "A Modern Art Ques-tionnaire" seems well suited to the cover illustration of the issue in which it

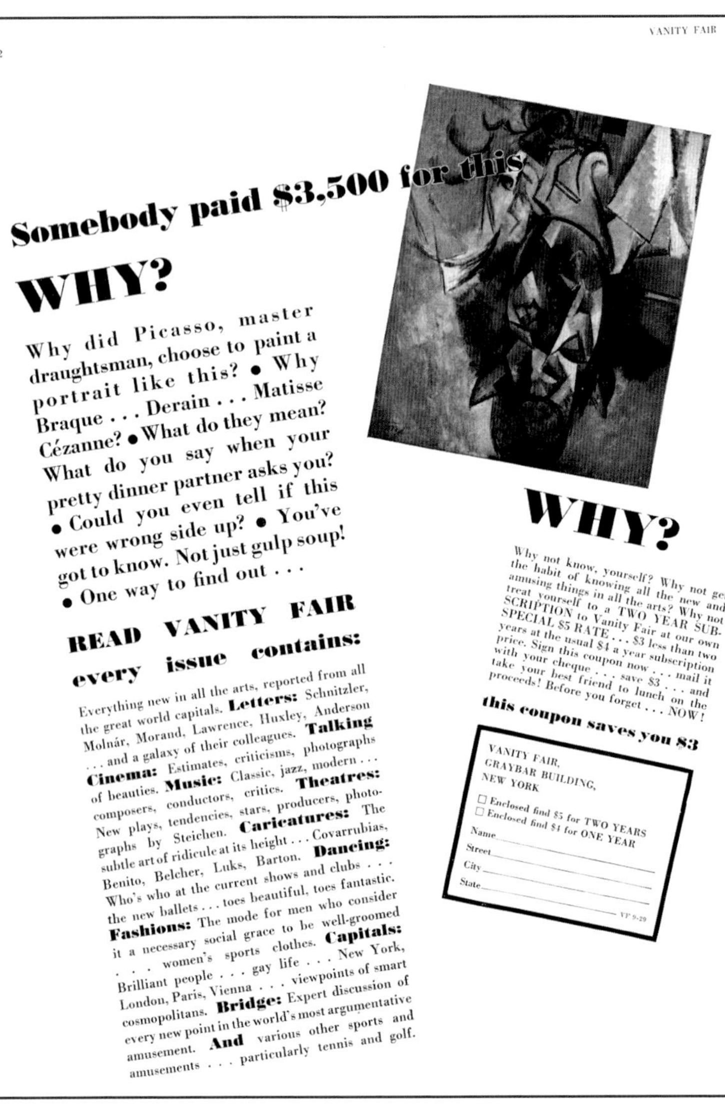

2.15 "Somebody paid . . . ," *Vanity Fair* advertisement, 1929. (Courtesy Condé Nast.)

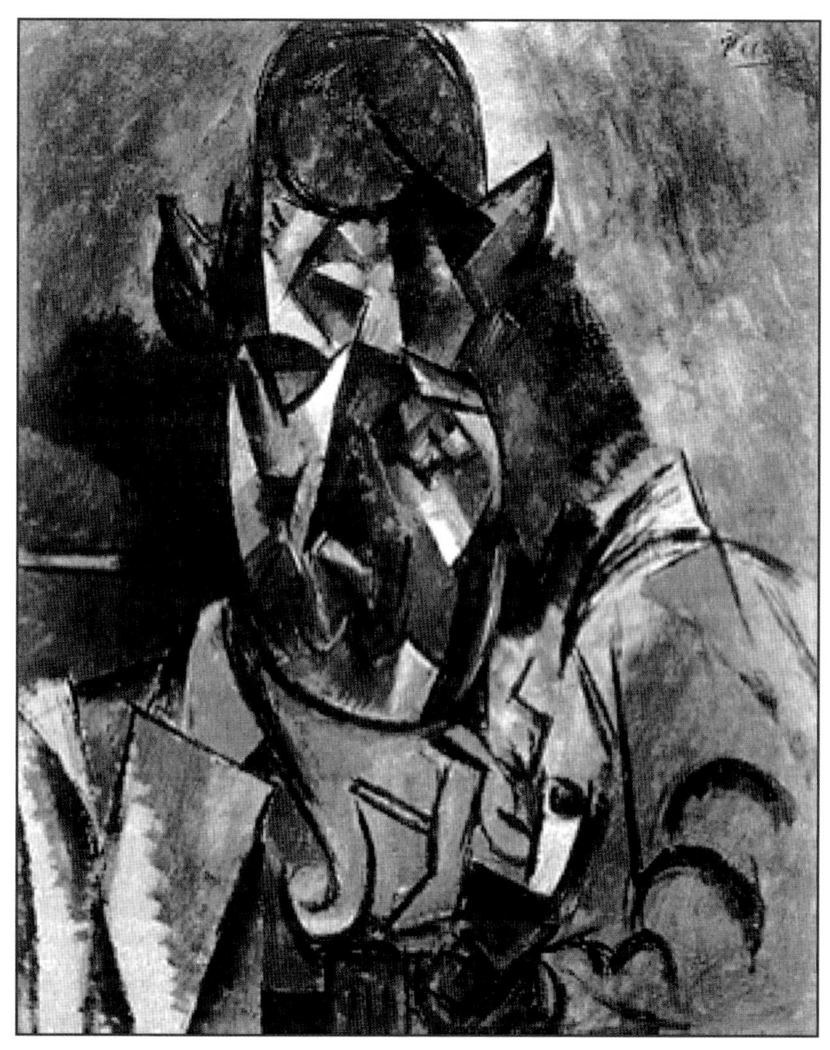

2.16 Pablo Picasso, *Portrait of Braque,* 1909–1910. © 2012 Estate of Pablo Picasso/ Artists Rights Society (ARS), New York.

appeared—a droll cartoon by A. H. Fish of leisure-class comforts and foibles at the beach. Though Barr surely intended his questionnaire to amuse *Vanity Fair* readers, he saw the magazine as more than a trifling pleasure of the elite or, for that matter, a joke at the expense of the masses. Barr subscribed to *Vanity Fair* at least as early as his freshman year at Princeton University, and he discussed its significance for the study of modern art at a public lecture in 1922. In a diary entry from that year, Barr notes that he gave "a talk before the Art Journalists Club on the subject of modern art in recent magazines such as 'Vanity Fair' (!), 'Studio,' etc . . . Bourdelle, Brancusi, etc, . . . [Professor Charles] Morey and the other grey-beards do laugh."[38] The parenthetical exclamation point, like the laughter of Morey (a prominent medievalist with whom Barr studied at Princeton) and "the other grey-beards," suggests the surprise that Barr's serious regard for *Vanity Fair* elicited from established art historians in 1922.[39]

Later in his career, Barr would credit both *Vanity Fair* and the modernist literary magazine *The Dial* with helping to launch his interest in contemporary art. In a memo to a museum colleague in 1941, he noted, "One can look back, and I suppose down, upon these magazines as dilettante, the one [*The Dial*] highbrow, the other [*Vanity Fair*] fashionable, but both succeeded in awakening in me, and many others of my generation, an interest in the work of living artists in various media—from painting and sculpture to movies and photography."[40] In the absence of formal scholarship on living artists, photographers, and filmmakers, magazines such as *The Dial* and *Vanity Fair* helped educate their readers, including Barr, about contemporary art.[41] I discuss below one of *The Dial*'s most significant contributions in this regard—its 1924 portfolio titled *Living Art*. Before doing so, I would like to consider further *Vanity Fair*'s role as an arbiter of contemporary art and culture.

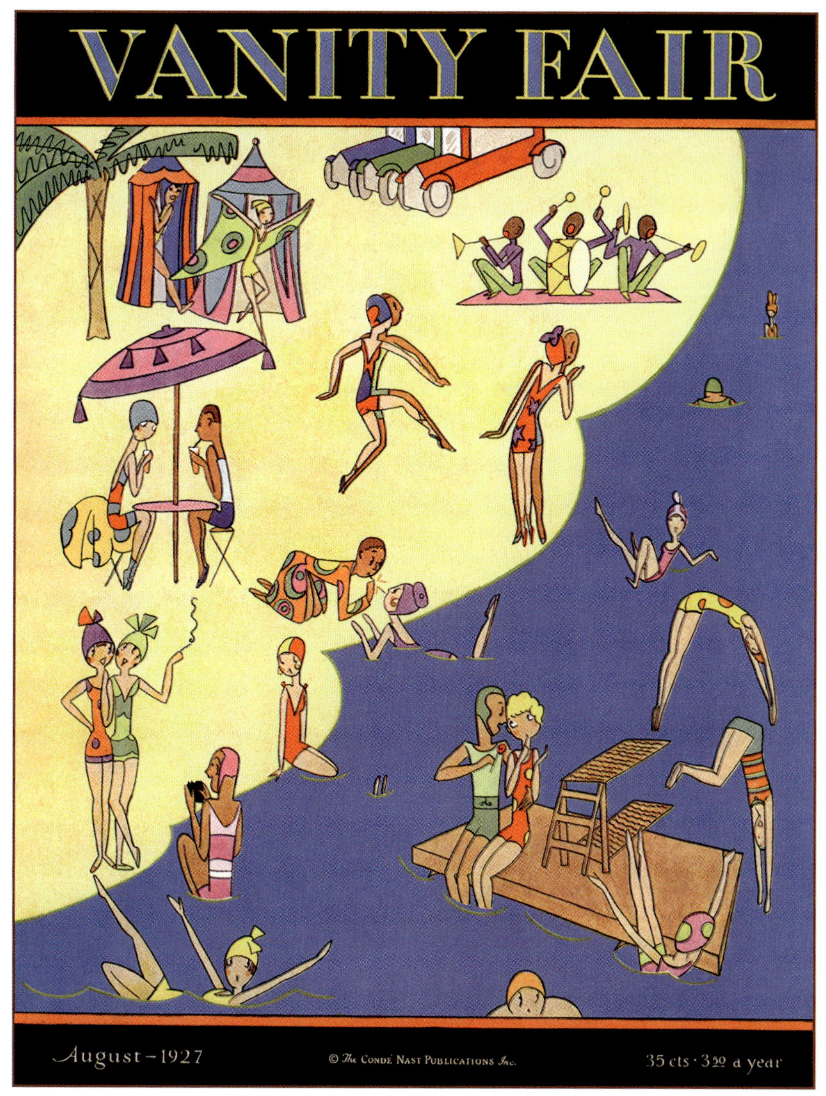

2.17 *Vanity Fair*, August 1927. Cover illustration by A. H. Fish. (Courtesy Condé Nast.)

In addition to serving as the magazine's editor in chief from 1914 to 1935, Crowninshield was the secretary of MoMA's board of trustees and, as such, played a key role in selecting Barr as MoMA's founding director. By way of introducing the new institution to the public, Crowninshield published Barr's article, "An American Museum of Modern Art," in the November 1929 issue of *Vanity Fair*.[42] Long before the two men became professionally acquainted, however, the editor had influenced the art historian. As Helaine Ruth Messer observes in her 1979 dissertation on the history of MoMA, "When Crowninshield became editor of *Vanity Fair*, he wrote a series of profiles on contemporary artists which Alfred Barr remembered reading as a boy growing up in the Middle West. In some cases, as with the piece on Paul Klee, they served as his first introduction."[43]

Vanity Fair's commitment to contemporary art complemented its attention to a broadly visual culture of photography, fashion, advertising, and caricature printed in color and black-and-white.[44] The appearance of Covarrubias (#5) in "A Modern Art Questionnaire" similarly reflected Barr's interest in popular illustration alongside, rather than in opposition to, vanguard painting. It also signaled the contemporaneity of *Vanity Fair*, since Covarrubias was by this time best known for his regular contributions to the magazine. Ultimately, he would create more cover illustrations for *Vanity Fair* than anyone other than Fish, and his name would appear in ads to promote the magazine's cutting-edge status.[45]

A Mexican-born artist and archaeologist, Covarrubias pursued a range of professional projects, from celebrity and political caricatures to ethnographic studies of Balinese culture. Among his best-known contributions to *Vanity Fair* were the "Impossible Interviews," watercolor renderings of imagined confrontations between otherwise unrelated celebrities, such as "Marie of Romania vs. Mae West," "Fritz Kreisler vs. Louis Armstrong," and "Freud vs.

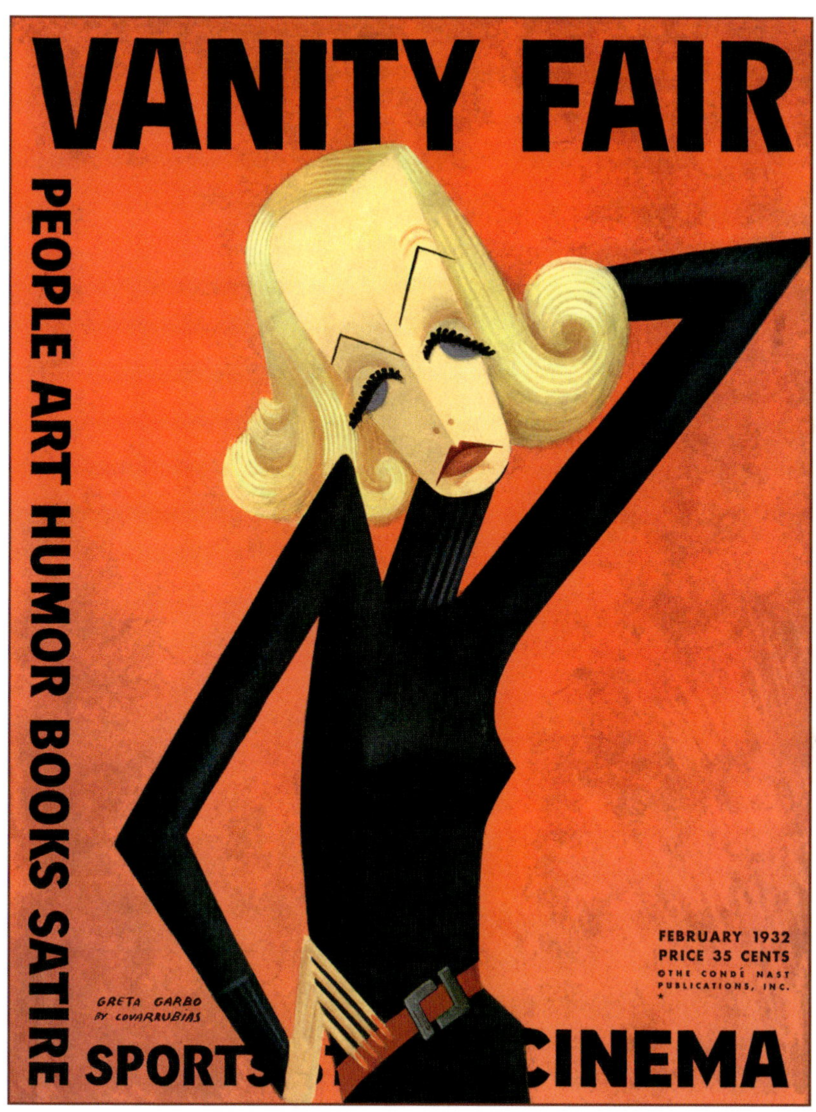

2.18 *Vanity Fair*, February 1932. Cover illustration by Miguel Covarrubias. (Courtesy Condé Nast.)

Jean Harlow." With visual flair and flamboyant color, Covarrubias coupled famous subjects from incongruous social and professional spheres. Rather than choosing sides in these celebrity matchups, he subjected each combatant to comparable forms of pictorial and physiognomic exaggeration. In addition to caricaturing individual celebrities, the "Impossible Interviews" satirized the broader tension between elite and popular culture, between high art and mass entertainment.

Modern Women

Along with proper names such as Covarrubias and Luigi Pirandello (#26), the entries on Barr's "A Modern Art Questionnaire" included two literary quotations, one poetry (#3) and the other prose (#46), both prefaced by the question, "Who wrote this?" The poem began:

Thou art come at length
More beautiful
Than any cool god
in a chamber under
Lycia's far coast.

The prose passage concluded with the lines, "They are in a circle. They are tendering a circle. They are a tender circle. They are tenderly a circle." Both entries cited the work of female modernists—H. D. (Hilda Doolittle) and Gertrude Stein, respectively.[46] Two other female literary figures, the poets Edna St. Vincent Millay and Harriet Monroe (whom Barr identified as the "matriarch of the Chicago school"), featured in the questionnaire as well.[47] The appearance of female modernists on Barr's quiz raised the issue of gender and creative achievement, which was especially pertinent in the context of the Wellesley course where all the participants, save for the professor himself, were women.[48]

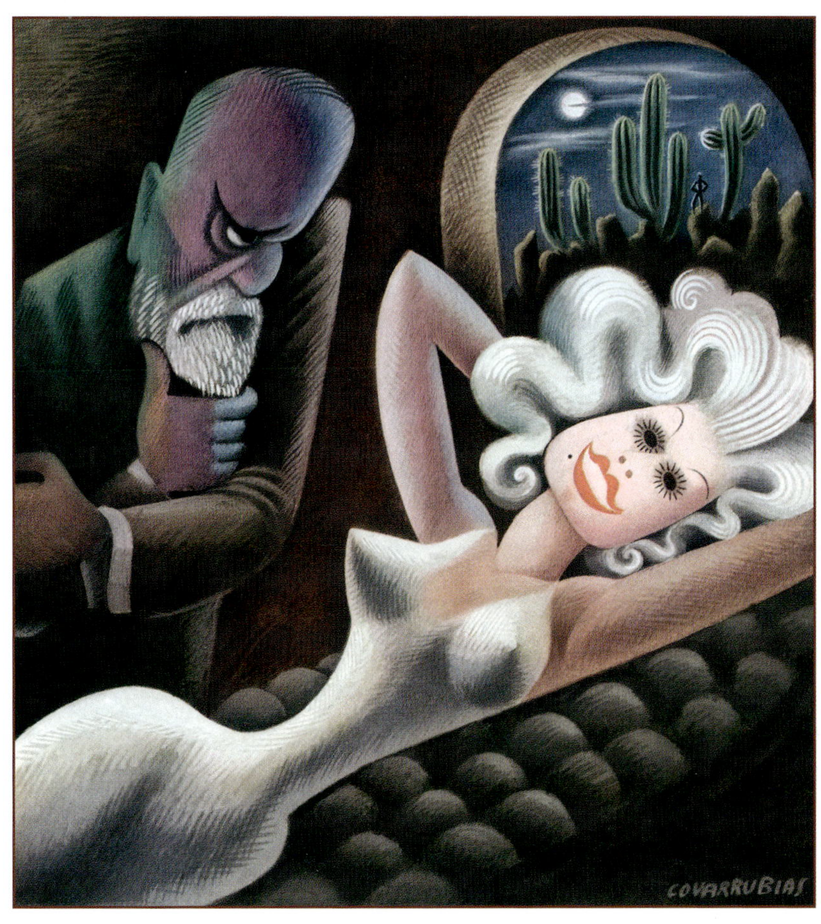

2.19 "Impossible Interviews," *Vanity Fair* (illustration of Greta Garbo and Sigmund Freud by Miguel Covarrubias). (Courtesy Condé Nast.)

The institutional foundation for Barr's class was prepared by the female professors who preceded, worked alongside, and, in the case of Alice Van Vechten Brown, hired him at the college. Founded in 1875, Wellesley was among the first American colleges to establish a freestanding art department and, by 1900, was "the sole college in the country in which it was possible to major in the history of art."[49] A course in museum training, the first of its kind in the nation, was established in 1911 as part of a small graduate program.[50] In her 1915 history of Wellesley College, Florence Converse noted that "In addition to work with undergraduates, the [art] department offers courses to graduate students who wish to prepare themselves for curatorships, or lectureships in art museums, and Wellesley women occupy positions of trust in the Metropolitan Museum in New York, in the Boston Art Museum, in museums in Chicago, Worcester, and elsewhere."[51] By 1928, the announcement for the graduate program could mention "museum directors" (alongside librarians, curators, assistants, and instructors) as positions to which "women graduates" might aspire.[52]

When it was first founded, Wellesley sought to educate young women to become cultivated amateurs, accomplished wives and mothers, community-minded volunteers, and, for those who remained unmarried, teachers.[53] The college's motto, *Non ministrari, sed ministrare* (Not to be ministered unto, but to minister), suggests the combination of female fortitude and civic-minded service it sought to instill. By the late 1920s, Wellesley graduates were increasingly entering a professional labor force not only as teachers but also as social workers, journalists, librarians, businesswomen, and, in a few cases, museum professionals.

Barr's designation of the young women in his contemporary art course as "faculty" and his collaborative approach to teaching drew upon a campus environment that likewise fostered a strong sense of female authority and student achievement. Several of the students in Barr's class would go on to notable careers in modern art, including two who worked at MoMA during his directorship. Ernestine Fantl was hired in 1932 as a curatorial assistant at the museum and was promoted, in 1935, to curator of architecture and industrial art.[54] Reportedly the only student to pass the preliminary quiz in January 1927, Fantl moved to London in 1937 and became a fashion editor for the *Sunday Times*. Nearly fifty years after graduating from Wellesley College, Fantl would publish a memoir, *With Tongue in Chic*, in which she recalled Barr's class as marking the beginning of "the most exciting part of my life":

> Alfred (he was too young to be called Professor for long) possessed the greatest attribute of a teacher. He was an eye-opener. He opened our eyes to architecture as well as to modern painting and sculpture. . . . Alfred made us aware of all aspects of art and design. He sent us to the five and ten cents store to select a dollar's worth of useful objects which we thought well designed, and let us mount an exhibition of them. Besides taking us to Boston's museums and galleries and concerts, he took us to the movies, for he was an early Garbo fan.[55]

At the Museum of Modern Art, Fantl would organize exhibitions such as *Modern Exposition Architecture* and *Posters by A. Mouron Cassandre* and work closely with Barr on the research and installation of the landmark show *Cubism and Abstract Art*. In several cases, the visual objects and architectural designs curated by Fantl were first introduced to her in the context of the Wellesley course.

Helen Franc, one of two sophomores who audited Barr's class, later worked as an editorial assistant at MoMA and ultimately rose to the position of senior editor in the Department of Publications.[56] Her guide to the museum's collections, *An Invitation to See*, remains in print. A third student in the

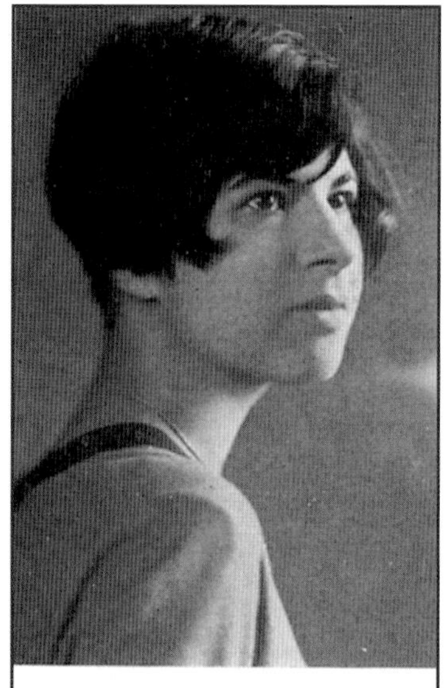

course, Katharine Sterne, became an art reviewer for the *New York Times* in the early 1930s and served on the editorial staff of *Parnassus*, a journal of art criticism and history published by the College Art Association.[57] Barr's Tradition and Revolt in Modern Painting thus helped to prepare its student faculty for sustained—and in several cases—lifelong engagements with contemporary art and culture.

2.20 Ernestine Fantl, *Wellesley Legenda* (yearbook), 1927. (Courtesy Wellesley College Archives.)

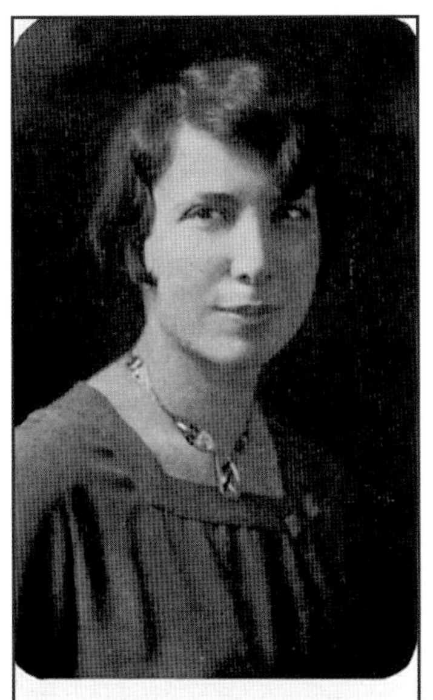

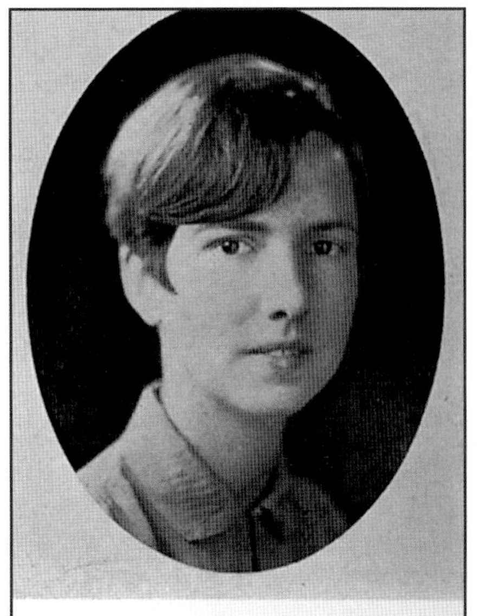

2.21 Helen M. Franc, *Wellesley Legenda* (yearbook), 1929. (Courtesy Wellesley College Archives.)

2.22 Katharine G. Sterne, *Wellesley Legenda* (yearbook), 1928. (Courtesy Wellesley College Archives.)

Reproductions and Originals

One of Barr's firmest convictions as a teacher was that his students should, whenever possible, experience art firsthand rather than through the mediation of black-and-white lantern slides projected within the confines of a darkened classroom. In addition to taking the students to see theater, films, and architecture, Barr organized exhibitions of modern paintings, drawings, posters, and book designs on campus. When original works of art were not available, he sought out exhibition-quality prints and color facsimiles. According to "Wellesley and Modernism," "As an important variation from the usual methods of study, fine colored reproductions are used whenever procurable in place of photographs, since modern art cannot be fully understood without color."[58]

During the first month of class, Barr organized *Reproductions of Famous Works of Modern Artists* at the Farnsworth Art Museum on the Wellesley campus. Among the painters represented in facsimile were Pierre-August Renoir and Paul Cézanne (both of whom would have been familiar to students who had enrolled in Barr's History of the Italian Tradition in Painting course the previous semester) as well as Matisse, Picasso, Pierre Bonnard, Marie Laurencin, Charles Demuth, and John Marin. According to a notice in the *Christian Science Monitor*, "The artists are men [sic] whose works are not well represented in the public galleries of Boston and the reproductions are not mere colored prints but reproductions which are so technically perfect as to recreate the originals adequately."[59] The reproductions both compensated for the absence of original works of modern art in the Boston area and in a sense were called forth by that absence. Their technical perfection, according to the *Christian Science Monitor*, rendered them sufficient representations of modern art—the next best thing, we might say, to seeing the paintings firsthand.

Barr's 1927 exhibition *Reproductions of Famous Works of Modern Artists* anticipates Walter Benjamin's 1936 essay "The Work of Art in the Age of Mechanical Reproduction" (which would itself become one of the most widely reproduced critical texts of the twentieth century). According to Benjamin,

> Even the most perfect reproduction of a work of art is lacking in one element: its presence in time and space, its unique existence at the place where it happens to be. This unique existence of the work of art determined the history to which it was subject throughout the time of its existence. This includes the changes which it may have suffered in physical condition over the years as well as the various changes in its ownership. The traces of the first can be revealed only by chemical or physical analyses which it is impossible to perform on a reproduction; changes of ownership are subject to a tradition which must be traced from the situation of the original.[60]

Barr would have agreed with Benjamin about the irreducibility of works of art to their printed reproduction, no matter how technically "perfect." As a teacher, he was keenly aware of the importance of seeing modern art in person and complained repeatedly about the difficulty of doing so in Boston. Shortly after arriving at Wellesley, Barr voiced this complaint in an open letter to the *Harvard Crimson*. Published on the paper's front page under the headline "'Boston Is Modern Art Pauper'—Barr," his letter kicked off with the observation: "It is surprising, even shocking, to the stranger to find so little interest in Modern pictures in Boston and Cambridge, places which have a deserved reputation as centers of alert cultivation of the Seven Arts. One may search in vain for the works of the foremost living painters in the Boston Museum, in Fenway Court [the private museum of Isabella Stewart Gardner], or in the Fogg."[61] Barr proceeded to list some of most influential modern artists whose work was missing from local museums and contrasted this deficiency with the holdings on offer in other cities and countries: "It is actually impossible for an amateur to study . . . a single painting by Cezanne, Van Gogh, Seurat, Gauguin, masters who are honored the world over—in London, Paris, Berlin, in Italy, Russia, Scandinavia, in the Low Countries, in Chicago and New York and Cleveland—but not in Boston." By way of underscoring the provincialism of Boston, Barr dryly observed that "one must actually travel to Worcester to see paintings by Gauguin and Redon."[62]

Barr's letter to the *Harvard Crimson* set off something of a scandal, in part because of how it was covered by other newspapers and magazines. A notice in *Art News*, for example, attributed to Barr a view of Boston as "a barren waste" and an "art desert," thereby extending his critique of the city's modern art holdings to its entire cultural scene. In a letter to the magazine's editor, Barr called the notice "an unfortunate misrepresentation" and a "journalistic distortion" of his prior statements. "It would be folly to make such an assertion regarding a city which has the greatest Oriental and Classical collections in America and where interest in art thrives even though it be a decade behind Cleveland, Chicago, or Worcester, Mass."[63] Even as he sought to set the record straight, Barr could not resist the opportunity to mention Boston's inferiority with regard to recent art. When he lamented that Boston is "a decade behind Cleveland, Chicago, or Worcester, Mass.," Barr articulated modernity as an uneven condition wherein certain cities and regions lagged "behind" the pace of vanguard culture. Boston, in his view, had fallen out of contemporaneity by at least a decade.

Somewhat surprisingly, Barr's affiliation with Harvard was not mentioned by the *Harvard Crimson*. Though still a doctoral candidate living in Cambridge, he was identified as "Professor Alfred H. Barr, Jr. of the Wellesley Fine Arts department" and, more simply, as a "Wellesley Critic." Had it been disclosed, Barr's Harvard affiliation would no doubt have inflected the second half of his letter, which partially exempted the university's own museum from the backwardness otherwise endemic to Boston: "The Fogg Museum with hitherto very limited space and funds has not been party to this spirit [of conservatism]. Its splendid collection of drawings is carried through to Picasso and in the new Museum there is to be ample room for contemporary expression."[64] Barr then applauded one of the Fogg's current shows: "In the Print Room at present is an exhibition of recently acquired facsimiles and photographs published by *The Dial* in 1923. There are paintings in oil, watercolour, and tempera, drawings in crayon and pencil reproduced so miraculously that under glass it is impossible to detect them from originals. Picasso is there, Bonnard and Matisse, Vlaminck and Signac, and the Americans, John Marin and Charles Demuth, three of whose watercolors the Fogg acquired several years ago."[65] If this checklist sounds familiar, it is because the same *Dial* portfolio would be shown by Barr a few months later in *Reproductions of Famous Works of Modern Artists* at Wellesley College.

Titled *Living Art*, the *Dial* portfolio featured twenty color facsimiles of paintings, prints, and watercolor sketches and ten black-and-white photographs of sculpture. The technical excellence of the portfolio was widely remarked upon at the time of its publication. In the *New Republic*, Lewis Mumford exclaimed, "The process that created these facsimiles is faithful beyond the dreams of ordinary color photography or engraving; so that these pictures resemble the originals, not as the things of this world favor their platonic archetypes, but as the seal corresponds to the signet. In short, Mr. [Scofield] Thayer, [editor of *The Dial* and publisher of the portfolio,] has not merely reproduced 'Living Art': he has enriched it."[66]

In his letter to the *Harvard Crimson*, Barr likewise emphasized the "miraculous" technical perfection of *Living Art* and the near impossibility of

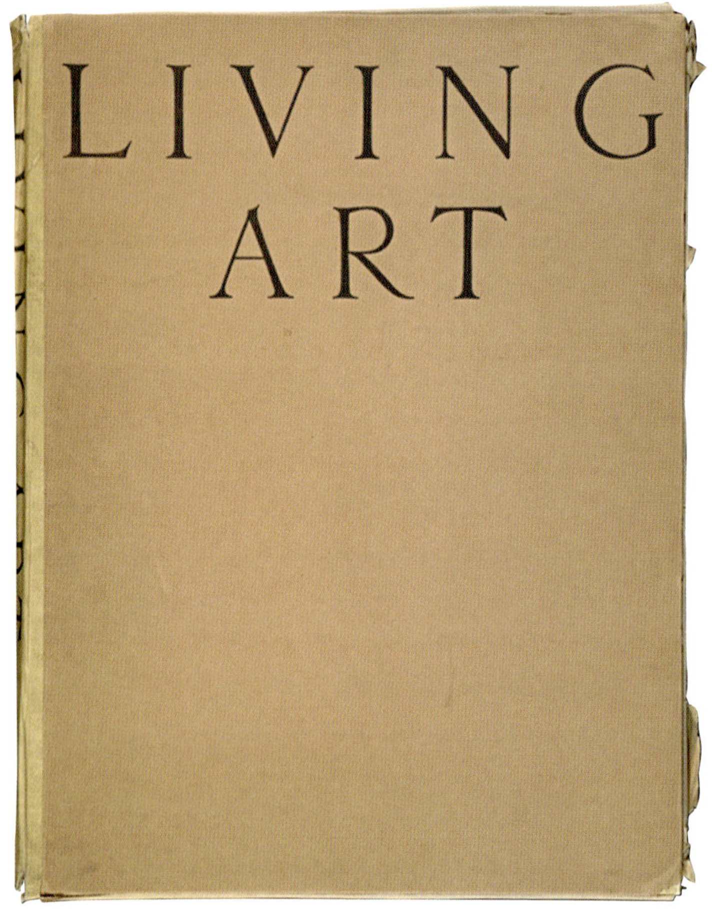

2.23 *Living Art: Twenty Facsimile Reproductions after Paintings, Drawings and Engravings and Ten Photographs after Sculpture by Contemporary Artists*, cover, published by The Dial in 1923; preface by Scofield Thayer. (Photography by the Getty Research Institute, Los Angeles.)

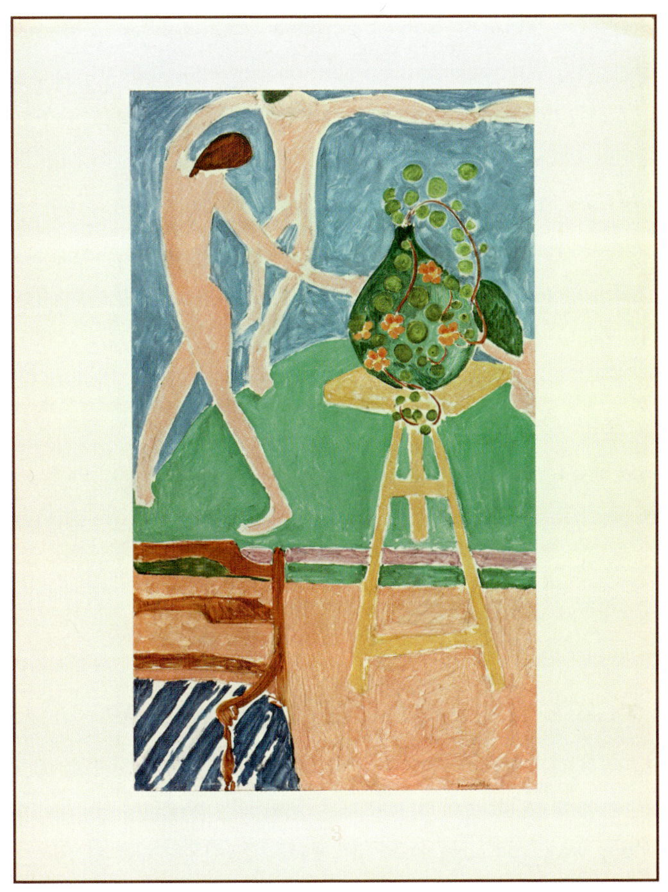

2.24 Facsimile of Henri Matisse, *Nasturtiums with the Painting Dance*, 1923, in *Living Art: Twenty Facsimile Reproductions after Paintings, Drawings and Engravings and Ten Photographs after Sculpture by Contemporary Artists*. (Photography by the Getty Research Institute, Los Angeles.) © 2012 Succession H. Matisse/Artists Rights Society (ARS), New York.

distinguishing the facsimile from the original work of art, at least when both were under glass. He neglected to mention, however, that the *Dial* portfolio had been newly donated to the Fogg and that the donors, as announced in the press the week before, were "Alfred H. Barr and Jere Abbott, graduate students at Harvard."[67] Without Barr and Abbott's gift, there would have been no exhibition in the Fogg Print Room in November 1926 to praise. Barr embraced the progressive spirit of the Fogg's exhibition of the portfolio while effacing his own role in bringing it about.

At the time he wrote "Boston Is Modern Art Pauper," Barr was seeking additional color reproductions for use in his upcoming modern art class at Wellesley while trying to stretch his modest budget for course materials as far as possible. To do so, he enlisted the help of the New York-based dealer J. B. Neumann, a key figure in the introduction of early twentieth-century German painting to the New York art world. In a letter dated October 12, 1926, Barr gently prodded the dealer:

> You will remember, I trust, how very generously you offered to help me with material for my course in *Contemporary Art*. I have an absurdly small amount—a little over $200.00, but with your aid I hope to make it go a long way. You suggested (if I remember rightly) that you could import books and prints for me at dealers prices. ... Boston is very dead so far as contemporary art is concerned. Sargent and Dodge McKnight are still the last word, but there are many who would be interested if they could see good originals or perfect reproductions.[68]

Barr evinces obvious distaste for the artists who mark "the last word" in local taste—John Singer Sargent, the society portraitist and painter of the grandiose *Triumph of Religion* allegories at the Boston Public Library, and Dodge McKnight, a New England watercolorist favored by local elites such as

Isabella Stewart Gardner but largely ignored outside the region. Sargent was no longer a contemporary artist (in the literal sense that he had died the previous year) or, in Barr's estimation, a genuinely modern one. McKnight, though alive, was equally outdated from the perspective of the Wellesley professor.

Though lamenting the moribund state of Boston's contemporary art scene, Barr nevertheless held out hope that the display of "good originals or perfect reproductions" might inspire public interest in modern art. While on the Wellesley faculty, Barr not only encouraged his students to become "aware of all aspects of art and design" but also published in the pages of the *Harvard Crimson*, the *Wellesley College News*, and *Vanity Fair*. In so doing, he sought to persuade multiple audiences to open their eyes to a wide spectrum of living art and artists.

"Queer and Incomprehensible"

Two months after *Reproductions of Famous Works of Modern Artists*, Barr organized a quite different kind of exhibition on campus. For *Progressive Modern Painting from Daumier and Corot to Post-Cubism*, he borrowed thirty-five paintings and drawings from collections in New York, Boston, and Cambridge. No prints or facsimiles were included. Among the works on display were a Georges Seurat study for *A Sunday on La Grande Jatte*, an Edgar Degas portrait, a Georgia O'Keeffe painting of flowers, and a Man Ray still-life painting.

Barr used his connections in New York, Cambridge, and Boston to bring "progressive modern painting" to campus. His loan exhibition was just as innovative as the course it accompanied. The critic from the *Christian Science Monitor* wrote approvingly that "the use of originals in art education in America is going to enliven the subject, to say the least. It is hoped that this free lending of canvases will be encouraged at colleges, for it will help in developing taste."[69] The reviewer went on to note that the current exhibition offered "a fine opportunity indeed for the young women of Wellesley to see what cubism and the impressionisms are all about."[70] While the eleven students in Barr's seminar constituted its most immediate audience, *Progressive Modern Painting* was open to all of the "young women of Wellesley" as well as to the college's faculty, staff, and visitors.

In a curatorial conceit that anticipated his later career at MoMA, Barr wrote descriptive wall texts for the majority of works on view in the Wellesley exhibition. Such object labels were not a convention of museum display at the time. Indeed, the *Christian Science Monitor* complained that the exhibition relied too heavily on Barr's captioning: "Mr. Barr has put some elucidating remarks beneath most of the pictures as a means of bridging the gap for the newcomer. Appreciating the importance of such a system for classroom purposes, one feels in the very necessity of the 'footnotes' a criticism of these pictures. Modern pictures, many of them, grow out of too self-conscious theory. The painters are lost in the means. If they are insistent upon abstraction (or a disinterest in subject matter) they must get their ideas across like pure music, without explanation."[71] Notwithstanding their pedagogical function, the abstract pictures on display should, according to this critic, speak for themselves.

The critic for the *Christian Science Monitor* was not alone in expressing reservations about Barr's exhibition. *Progressive Modern Painting* was met with a decidedly mixed response from the Wellesley student body, judging from a report published in the college newspaper. In "Seniors Find Modern Artist Queer and Incomprehensible," the *Wellesley College News* relayed a prevailing sense of frustration among students who had seen and responded to the exhibition: "The *News* has had the privilege of seeing a series of brief criticisms on the exhibition of modern art written by members of the senior art classes. These opinions seem singularly unanimous in expressing feelings of dislike, disgust, or of bewilderment. Many girls frankly stated their complete lack of understanding and consequent displeasure. Only a few expressed pleasure in the exhibition but most were interested."[72] The article focused on the question of female pleasure—and displeasure—in the face of modern art. It aligned the displeasure of the "girls" with "feelings of dislike, disgust," and incomprehension.[73] Yet the *News* also reported that most of the students "were interested" in the art on display. Taking an interest in modern art was not, then, the same thing as taking pleasure in it. The distinction between visual pleasure and aesthetic interest would remain crucial to Barr's effort to expand the audience for twentieth-century art and culture.

One week prior to the appearance of "Seniors Find Modern Artist Queer and Incomprehensible," Barr published a remarkable defense of the exhibition in the *Wellesley College News*. He opened the article by citing the overheard remarks of two female visitors "of the older generation." The first visitor denounces the show as politically subversive: "Bolshevist Art! That's the trouble with Modern Education! Showing students this sort of thing!"[74] The second embraces the show as an opportunity for learning: "Well! This is refreshing. Now we can find out what's going on in the world." The one speaker worries about the deleterious effect the show might have on younger viewers ("Showing students this sort of thing!"), while the other focuses on discovery ("Now we can find out what's going on in the world"). For Barr, these two responses "express quite succinctly the closed and open mind" of audiences for modern art. The attitude of most Wellesley viewers, he reasoned, would fall somewhere between the panicked dismissal of the former and the free-thinking embrace of the latter.

In the remainder of the article, Barr argued that the abstraction and apparent incomprehensibility of modern painting were, in fact, historically

SENIORS FIND MODERN ARTIST
QUEER AND INCOMPREHENSIBLE

W.C. News 4/28/27

The NEWS has had the privilege of seeing a series of brief criticisms on the exhibition of modern art written by members of the senior art classes. These opinions seem singularly unanimous in expressing feelings of dislike, disgust, or of bewilderment. Many girls frankly stated their complete lack of understanding and consequent displeasure. Only a few expressed pleasure in the exhibition, but almost all were interested. Quotations from some of the comments follow.

2.25 "Seniors Find Modern Artist Queer and Incomprehensible," *Wellesley College News*, April 28, 1927. (Courtesy Wellesley College Archives.)

specific effects of its "emancipation" from the labors of verisimilitude and storytelling:

> Painting has been for centuries subordinate to the church, to illustration, to portraiture, to interior decoration. Painting has preached sermons, preserved the appearances of persons and events, or documented scientific research. Today increasing literacy, the radio, camera, and the moving picture render the utilitarian services of painting superfluous, so that painting is rapidly becoming as useless as sonnets or string quartets. Now this is vital to the understanding of why modern painting is misunderstood: the public has not kept pace with this revolutionary emancipation. It sill looks to the artist for stories, for the imitation of natural objects, or for pleasing decorative color.[75]

The rise of radio, film, photography, and popular literature has superseded the long-standing need for painting to tell stories, preserve likenesses, or prettify interiors. Yet the public, whose desires lag behind the pace of modernity, still wants painting to perform its old services. The "revolutionary emancipation" of modern painting requires viewers who are equally liberated from traditional conceptions of art.

To this broadly historical argument, Barr added a final flourish of pure visuality. "In so short a space it is impossible to develop further an apologia for this exhibition of modern painting. Apologies end where they begin—in words. These pictures demand to be looked at—again—and again—and then again. Only by this means may they be understandingly enjoyed."[76] Plainly Barr wanted viewers to grapple with the "queer and incomprehensible" force of modern painting rather than to search in vain for familiar stories or reassuring moral lessons.

It is worth noting that Barr's defense of modern painting took the form of an article in the student newspaper rather than, as might be expected from a member of the faculty, a letter to the editor. Barr treated the *Wellesley College News* seriously as a forum for public debate and contemporary art criticism. He offered himself as a participant—rather than the ultimate authority—in such debate. Rather than telling students what to think about modern painting, he urged them to look (and look and look again) for themselves. In effect, Barr was advocating a pedagogy of firsthand viewing. Leave behind the realm of words, he advised the readers of the *Wellesley College News*, leave behind this very article and go see the paintings in the Farnsworth Art Museum for yourself. The point of bringing original works of contemporary art to campus was not to convince students of a particular argument or moral about modern life but to get them to look at the world in a fresh way.

Writing the Contemporary

In May 1928, Barr published his first piece of architectural criticism. Rather than treating the work of Frank Lloyd Wright, the Bauhaus, or Le Corbusier (#35, #48, and #49, respectively, on "A Modern Art Questionnaire"), he focused on a building designed by one F. C. Lutze, a little-known engineer based in Boston. The building was the Necco factory, and Barr's account of it drew on the class trip he took with his Wellesley students the previous year.[77]

In the article, Barr extolled the factory's functionalist design and geometric appeal. He wrote approvingly of the varying size, proportion, and glazing of the windows, including the random play of open and closed casements across the facade.[78] He praised the factory's giant smokestack as enhancing the building to which it belonged "somewhat as an Italian basilica and its campanile are mutually complimentary."[79] He commended Lutze's decision to leave visible the exterior ventilators, process pipes, and dust collectors at the

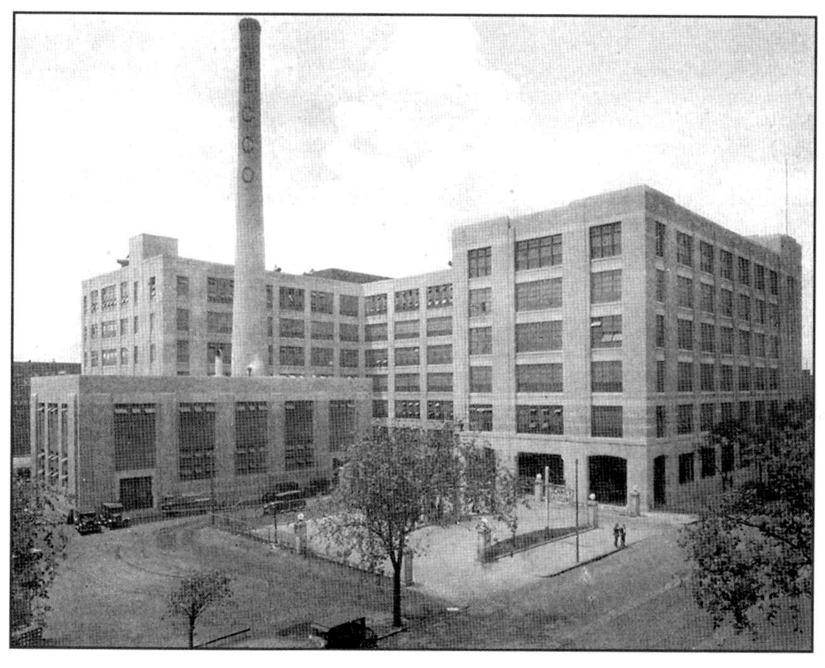

2.26 The Necco factory, *The Arts*, May 1928.

rear of the factory rather than "concealing them behind a false attic or parapet as our architects by means of Baroque cupolas conceal the rotund water tanks of skyscrapers."[80] Barr's admiration for industrial machinery infused his description of the "interior filled with an amazing complex of dynamos, boilers, automatic sprinklers, miles of process pipes, filters, refrigerators, pulverizers, dehumidifiers, and pumps."[81]

At Barr's request, his friend and Harvard roommate Jere Abbott shot photographs to accompany the article.[82] Several of these pictures, including a worm's-eye view of the smokestack and process pipes, bespeak Abbott's familiarity with contemporaneous photography in the Bauhaus and Russian constructivism. Like László Moholy-Nagy and Aleksandr Rodchenko, Abbott exploited oblique angles, thrusting architectural forms, tipped perspectives, and extreme foreshortening to suggest the dynamism of industrialized modernity and the new vantage points it commanded. Where Rodchenko famously reoriented the facade and fire escape of his apartment building on Miasnitskaya Street in Moscow, Abbott cropped, tilted, and quasi-abstracted the Necco factory's chimney and process pipes into a sleekly geometric composition.

It was not simply the architectural design of the Necco factory—or, for that matter, of Rodchenko's apartment house—but also its pictorial reorientation by the photographer that conveyed modernity. The photographs imply the active stance of the photographer who shifts position, crouches, lies down on the ground, or climbs up to the roof to achieve a radically unexpected viewpoint. The art historian Leah Dickerman has aptly described this effect as "camera vision": "Vertigo and disorientation become productive forces, thrusting the viewer out of a firmly grounded visual world, and forcing a conscious repositioning. Granted mobility, the dispersal and multiplication of the camera's points of view replace the fixed panoramic viewpoint of classical perspective."[83] Rodchenko's dynamic "camera vision" thus provided a metaphor for the transformation of everyday life by revolutionary politics and perspectives.

Though he did not share Rodchenko's radical politics, Abbott mobilized his own "camera vision" in the series of severely cropped and tilted views of the Necco factory reproduced in *The Arts*. Barr's accompanying essay likewise meant to challenge traditional perspectives on architecture. For Barr, the limestone and brick factory qualified as one of the "most living and beautiful buildings in New England" in part because of its refusal to hide functionalism behind unnecessary ornament. Notice that the word Barr opts for here is neither "modern" or "contemporary" but "living," a term of high praise in this context.

Built by an engineer rather than a classically trained architect, the immense factory deserved, according to Barr, to be called "architecture even though it be as far removed from the Beaux-Arts tradition as a Frigidaire refrigerator is from a Louis Quinze Victrola."[84] The Necco factory (which opened in 1927), like the Frigidaire refrigerator (which debuted in 1919), suggest just how far Barr's conception of modernity extended beyond painting, sculpture, and Beaux-Arts architecture.

Barr's Wellesley course served as a springboard for publications such as "The Necco Factory." Rather than treating teaching and research as distinct fields of endeavor, Barr linked his pedagogical practice directly to his research, curating, and writing about art. While at Wellesley, Barr developed both a popular and a scholarly voice, a voice that variously addressed the readers of the *Wellesley College News*, the *Harvard Crimson*, *The Arts*, and *Vanity Fair*. Rather than imagining that his role as a professor was to convey established knowledge to his students, Barr conceived of the class as a laboratory for the study of a culture very much in the making.

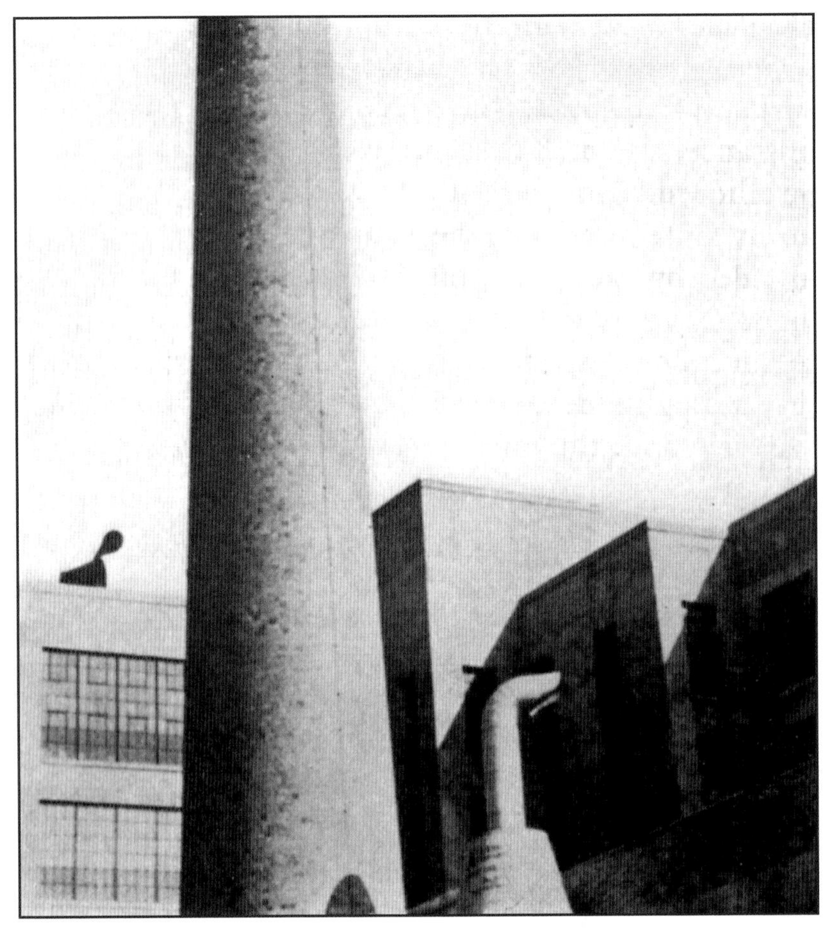

2.27 Jere Abbott, photograph of Necco
factory, 1927. (Figure 4, Alfred Barr, "The
Necco Factory," *The Arts*, May 1928.)

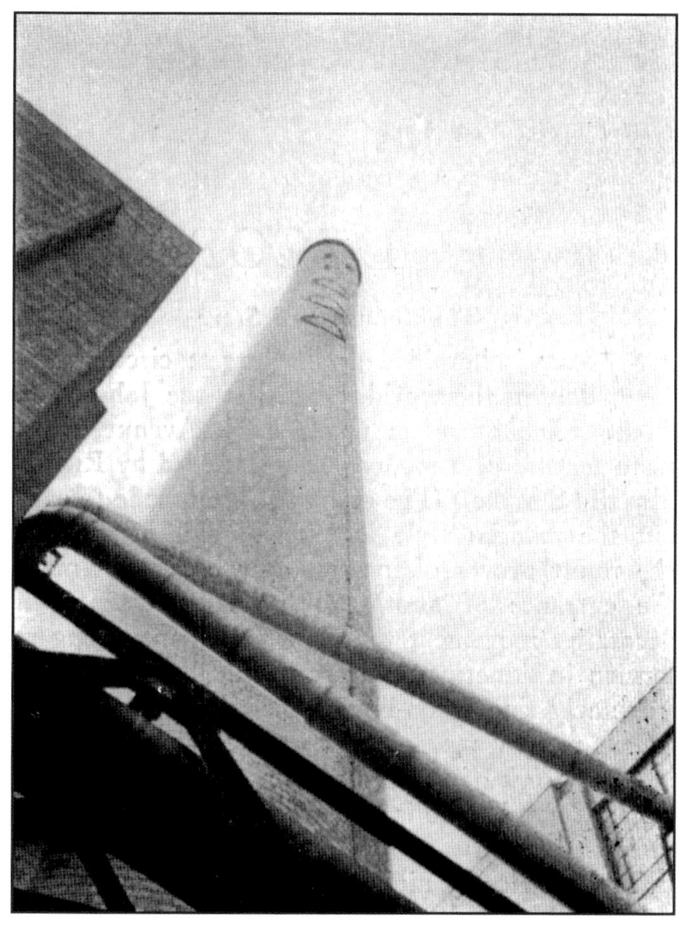

2.28 Jere Abbott, photograph of Necco factory, 1927. (Figure 5, Alfred Barr, "The Necco Factory," *The Arts*, May 1928.)

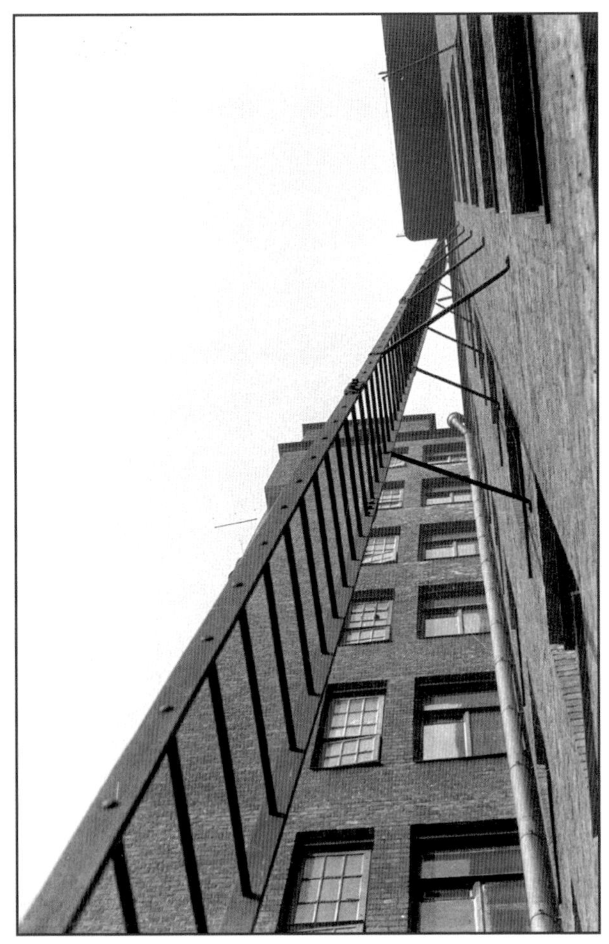

2.29 Aleksandr Rodchenko, *The Fire Escape*, from the series *House on Miasnitskaya Street* (*Dom na Miasnitskoi*), 1925. (Courtesy A. Rodchenko and V. Stepanova Archive.) © Estate of Alexander Rodchenko/RAO, Moscow/VAGA, New York.

In this context, it is worth remembering Barr's dual status as both teacher and student. As Sybil Kantor has pointed out, Barr periodically "attended [Paul] Sachs's museum course with Abbott"[85] during the 1926–1927 academic year. Sachs's Harvard course, officially known as Museum Work and Museum Problems, helped mold a generation of curators and museum directors in the interwar United States.[86] Even as Barr organized exhibitions in conjunction with his Wellesley course, he was learning how to be a museum man at Harvard. When he designated each of the students in Art 305 a member of the faculty, Barr might well have been thinking of his own, concurrent roles as professor and graduate student.

Taking Leave

While teaching his modern art course at Wellesley, Barr applied to the Carnegie Corporation for funding to go abroad the following year. He sought, as his letter of application put it,

> a grant to enable me to study for a year in Europe. . . . I wish to study contemporary European culture. . . . My choosing the modern field for my special study needs, perhaps, further explanation since such a choice is infrequent even among students of my age. First of all, I believe that the older periods are comparatively well supplied with teachers and scholars, while the modern field has scarcely been touched by American scholars. Also, I must confess, perhaps naively, that I find the art of the world in which I live far more absorbing and vitally interesting than the art of, say, the XVIIIth dynasty in Egypt—or even that of the trecento in Italy. And finally, I feel increasingly a sincere and urgent demand on the part of undergraduates and the general public to be assisted in the comprehension of the art of the past thirty years, which is often so strange

and puzzling but which is, after all, very living and important both in itself and as an expression of our amazing though none too lucid civilization.[87]

Barr framed his proposal to study abroad as a response to a "sincere and urgent demand" on the part of college students and members of the general public to understand the art of their own day. He characterized this art as "absorbing and vitally interesting" but also "strange and puzzling." For Barr, the urgency of contemporary art outdistanced the appeal of every other period of artistic production, from ancient Egypt to the early Italian Renaissance.

Although his application was rejected by the Carnegie Corporation, Barr took the trip anyway, with the help of funds secured by Sachs, his Harvard mentor.[88] In July 1927, he sailed for London, where he met up with Abbott. Traveling together, the pair visited Rotterdam, Amsterdam, and Berlin, followed by four days at the Bauhaus in Dessau. Barr recorded his visit in a hastily scribbled diary of appointments. He sat in on Josef Albers's design course, discussed photography with Moholy-Nagy, dined with Herbert Bayer and his wife, visited the studio of the painter Lyonel Feininger, looked at drawings with (and by) Paul Klee, and met with Bauhaus founder and architect Walter Gropius. Even before Barr's arrival in Dessau, however, the school had shaped his pedagogy: "Gropius' ideal of bringing together the various visual arts influenced my course in modern art at Wellesley in 1926–27. It included architecture, industrial design, graphic arts, painting, sculpture, films, photography. A few years later the Bauhaus also influenced my plan for the Museum of Modern Art."[89]

Barr's visit to Dessau seems only to have heightened his esteem for the Bauhaus. He was almost certainly recalling his trip with Abbott when he wrote, in 1937, "Ten years ago, Americans visited the Bauhaus at Dessau as a place of pilgrimage where the philosophy and practice of modern design were in the process of clarification."[90] In his preface to MoMA's exhibition on the Bauhaus in 1938, Barr enumerated the school's principles, including its ambition to "bring together various arts of painting, architecture, theatre, photography, weaving, typography, etc. into a modern synthesis which disregards conventional distinctions between fine and applied arts."[91]

Barr contrasted the adventurous, multidisciplinary spirit of the German design school with the stodgy traditionalism of architectural training in the United States. Looking back upon the late 1920s (again from the vantage point of 1938), he wrote:

> Some of the younger of us had just left college where ... the last word in imitation Gothic dormitories had windows with one carefully cracked pane to each picturesque casement. Others of us, in architectural schools, were beginning our courses with gigantic renderings of Doric capitals, or ending them with elaborate projects for Colonial gymnasiums and Romanesque skyscrapers. It is no wonder then that young Americans began to turn their eyes toward the Bauhaus as the one school in the world where modern problems of design were approached realistically in a modern atmosphere.[92]

Barr's admiration for the Bauhaus would remain much in evidence throughout his long career at MoMA, from *Bauhaus: 1919–1928*, a comprehensive exhibition organized by Gropius and Bayer for the museum in 1938, through the frequent appearance of Bauhaus artists in the museum's shows and its staunch promotion of modernist design in keeping with Bauhaus principles. That the Bauhaus movement, with its sprawling oeuvre expressed across an astonishing diversity of media, has had such a profound impact on American perceptions of modernity is due in some measure to Barr's "eye-opening" encounter in Dessau in 1927.

"Such Abundance"

Following their visit to the Bauhaus, Barr and Abbott returned to Berlin to secure visas to travel to Russia. The pair left Berlin on Christmas Eve and traveled by train through Poland to Moscow. Intending to stay three or four weeks, they remained in Russia for nearly three months, two of which were spent in Moscow, followed by several weeks in Leningrad. Both men kept diaries during their stay, and Barr's in particular conveys their excitement upon arrival in Russia: "We feel as if this were the most important place in the world for us to be. Such abundance, so much to see: people, theaters, film, churches, pictures, music and only a month to do it in, for we must attempt Leningrad and perhaps Kiev. It is impossible to describe the feeling of exhilaration."[93] In an entry dated two days later, Barr reiterated, "We'd rather be here than any place on earth."[94]

Barr's diary bespeaks his desire to see as much as possible—"people, theaters, film, churches, pictures, music"—while in the Soviet Union. With the help of May O'Callahan, a wealthy Irish expatriate living at the Hotel Luxe in Moscow, Barr and Abbott met the constructivist theorist Sergei Tret'yakov and, through him, the artists Aleksandr Rodchenko and Varvara Stepanova, the filmmaker Sergei Eisenstein, the theater director Vsevolod Meyerhold, and the architect Moisei Ginzburg. Early in their visit, Barr and Abbott were also introduced to Diego Rivera, who was visiting Moscow as part of an official delegation sent by the Mexican Communist Party in honor of the tenth anniversary of the Russian Revolution.[95]

Barr and Abbott pursued an extremely active itinerary during their two months in Moscow—attending the theater, films, concerts, dance programs, and museums while frequently meeting with artists, architects, magazine editors, and writers. With the help of their Russian translator, the two men also spent a good deal of time seeking out art books, photographs, magazines, posters, and other printed matter about contemporary Soviet culture. In addition, Barr and Abbott researched and purchased materials on the history of Russian icons dating back to the eleventh century. Their exploration of revolutionary art and culture in the Soviet Union thus unfolded alongside an inquiry into religious art of the Middle Ages. As at Wellesley, Barr's enthusiasm for contemporary Soviet art and living Russian artists did not dampen his pursuit of other, more traditional art-historical concerns.

Barr's visit to the Soviet Union occasioned encounters with a wide, indeed global, range of art and culture. While in Russia, he read Tret'yakov's manuscript of a "bio-interview" with a Chinese boy living in Moscow, saw Rivera's "complete series of photographs of his Mexico City murals," and admired the fruits of Eisenstein's "great hobby" of collecting prints and books by and about the nineteenth-century French satirist Honoré Daumier. Which is to say, Barr encountered French, Chinese, and Mexican culture while in Moscow as well as revolutionary Russian art, theater, and film. Poised between the Leninist New Economic Policy of the mid 1920s and Joseph Stalin's first five-year plan (1928–1932), Moscow at that moment was a site of dynamic artistic production but also, as Barr's diary suggests, of state censorship and increasingly centralized control over the arts. In his entry for January 6, 1928, for example, Barr notes that he and Abbott "wrote our journals all morning since [the] exhibition to which Diego Rivera was to take us was closed suddenly. Two reasons were given by the Mexican—first, there were portraits of some of the opposition [to Stalin], second, because in a group representing Lenin's funeral some figures were nude."[96]

Barr and Abbott's trip to Russia was also an encounter with the Soviet critique of American capitalism. The two men attended a screening of *The Extraordinary Adventures of Mr. West in the Land of the Bolsheviks* (1924), a comic film by Lev Kuleshov that uses American cinematic methods to satirize

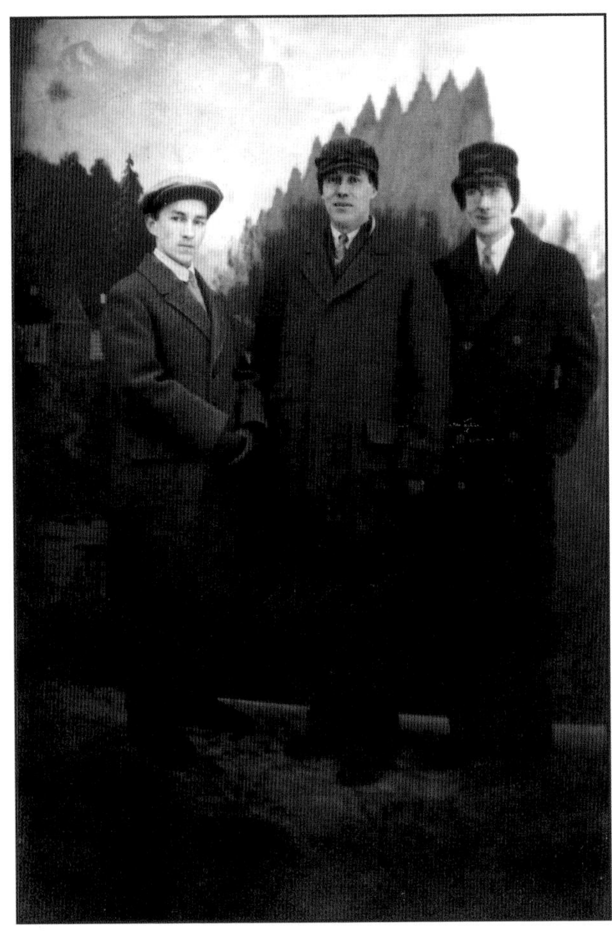

2.30 Jere Abbott (center) and Alfred H. Barr Jr. (right) in Moscow with their translator Petr Likhatchew (left), February 13, 1928. Photographer unknown. Alfred H. Barr, Jr. Papers, 9.F.71. (Courtesy The Museum of Modern Art Archives, New York.) Digital image © The Museum of Modern Art/Licensed by SCALA/ Art Resource, NY.

an American visitor ("Mr. West") and his cowboy companion ("Jeddy") as they encountered those "mad, savage Russians" in the Soviet Union. Barr—another American abroad in the Soviet Union but by no means a naively anti-Soviet, pro-American idealist in the mold of "Mr. West"—described Kuleshov's film as "a good subject but handled very badly."[97]

How might we see Barr's trip abroad (what he called his "special study") in relation to the Wellesley course he taught the previous spring and would offer again the following year? As Elizabeth Jones has pointed out, while in Russia, "Barr collected books, pamphlets, programs, photographs with singular patience and persistence."[98] Drawing on this research, he published five articles in relatively rapid succession on topics that included Eisenstein's films, the Lef (Left Front for the Arts) group of revolutionary artists, medieval Russian icons, and constructivist architecture. The first of the five articles—and the only one published in Russian—appeared in the journal *Sovetskoe kino* (Soviet film) just as Barr was leaving the country. Titled "Za grantsei: Ruki" (Abroad: Hands), Barr's article focused on an experimental film by Stella F. Simon, an American photographer studying film in Berlin. Barr had seen the film, which consisted entirely of hand gestures, and met Simon during his visit to Berlin several weeks before arriving in Moscow. As was his habit, Barr procured still photographs from the director at that time. He not only provided three of these film stills to *Sovetskoe kino* but also agreed to contribute an article to accompany them.

The circumstances under which Barr came to write for *Sovetskoe kino* suggest both his interest in—and distance from—the radical art and politics of the Lef group. In his entry for January 3, 1928, Barr writes that he went

> to see Rodchenko and his talented wife [Varvara Stepanova]. Neither spoke anything but Russian but both are brilliant, versatile artists. R. showed us an appalling variety of things—suprematist paintings

(preceded by the earliest geometrical things I've ever seen, 1915, done with compass)—woodcuts, linoleum cuts, posters, book designs, photographs, kino set, etc., etc. He has done no painting since 1922, devoting himself to the photographic arts of which he is a master . . . R.'s wife is managing editor of [*Sovetskoe*] *Kino*. When I showed her Mrs. Simon's film she was much interested and asked for four stills to reproduce with an article. It will be fun to be paid in rubles (if any). I arranged to get photographs of Rodchenko's work for an article. We left after 11:30—an excellent evening—but I must find some painters if possible.[99]

Even as Barr seems to savor the prospect of this cross-cultural exchange ("It will be fun to be paid in rubles (if any)"), his view of modern art is tested by the constructivist dismissal of painting as bourgeois and counterrevolutionary. Just after he characterizes Stepanova and Rodchenko as "brilliant, versatile artists," Barr describes the latter's work as "appalling" in its variety, then insists that he "must find some painters if possible." Stepanova, for one, was irritated with Barr's insistence on painting during this first encounter. Her account of their meeting (as recorded in the artist's diary) provides an instructive contrast to Barr's:

> Those Americans came to call: one of them dull, dry, and bespectacled—Professor Alfred Barr; the other cheerful and young—Jere Abbott. Surmised that Barr was traveling at Abbott's expense. Rodchenko speculated that Abbott was the child of wealthy parents.
>
> Barr is interested only in art—painting, drawing. He turned our whole apartment upside down. They made us show them all kinds of old junk. Toward the end Barr got all hot and bothered. Abbott is the more interested in new art.[100]

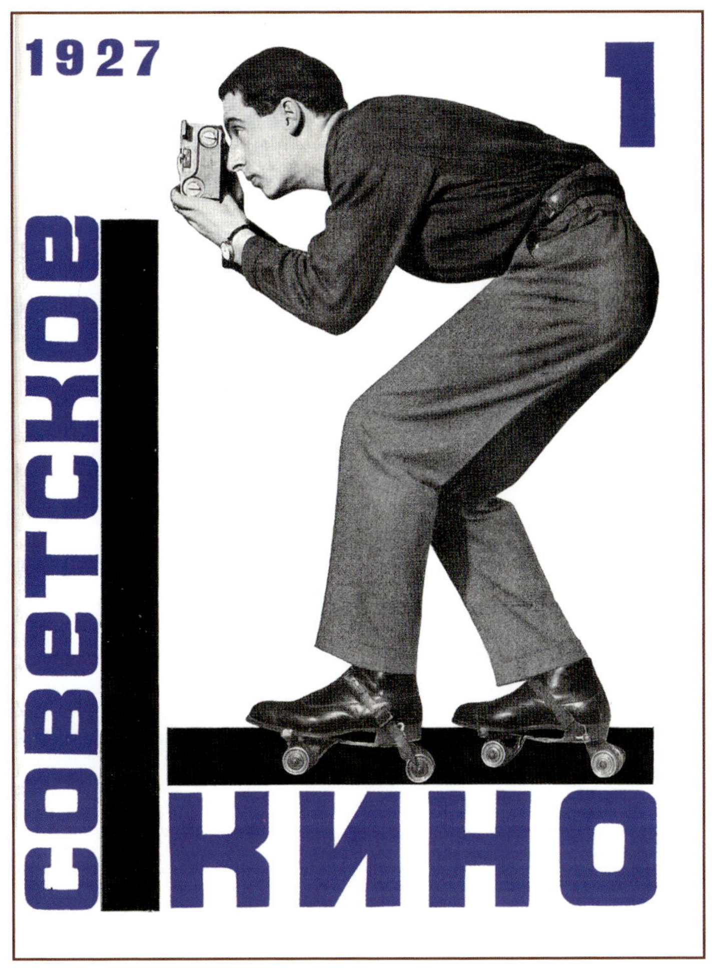

2.31 *Sovetskoe kino* 1 (1927), cover.

Barr struck Stepanova as conventional and dryly academic by comparison to his "cheerful and young" (and, as the Russian couple correctly surmises, affluent) companion.[101] At the same time, although Stepanova judged Abbott to be "the more interested in new art," it was Barr who would contribute to *Sovetskoe kino*.

Barr's article on Simon's *Hands* (1926) appeared in the March 1928 issue of the magazine, the cover of which featured a smokestack, telephone wires, and electrical cables photographed at an oblique angle. The article's main title, "Abroad," referred most directly to the fact that Simon's film had been produced in Germany. But "abroad" also named Barr's position as a foreign visitor to Moscow and a guest essayist in *Sovetskoe kino* as well as the novelty of an American professor contributing an article about an experimental film made in Berlin by an American woman to a state-sponsored magazine published by constructivist artists in Soviet Russia. "Za grantsei" embodied Barr's interest in cross-cultural exchange and the global circulation of art. It also marked an important departure for the author, who had never published on film before, much less in Russian translation. "Movies require a new critical apparatus," he confided to his diary several weeks into drafting the essay for *Sovetskoe kino*. Barr seemed to adapt quickly to this "new apparatus," publishing an essay on Eisenstein (in English) shortly after his return to the United States.[102] Barr never had occasion to contribute to Stepanova's magazine again: by late 1928, *Sovetskoe kino* had been "liquidated" as part of Stalin's policy of "cultural revolution."[103]

Most often designed by Stepanova, the covers of *Sovetskoe kino* combined typography, geometry, and photomontage to create a dynamic sense of Soviet film on the move.[104] Barr's diary captures a hint of this dynamism. Into his journal, the American pasted four Soviet postage stamps, a small sketch in colored pencil, the program from an Alexander Scriabin concert that

ЗА ГРАНИЦЕЙ

РУКИ

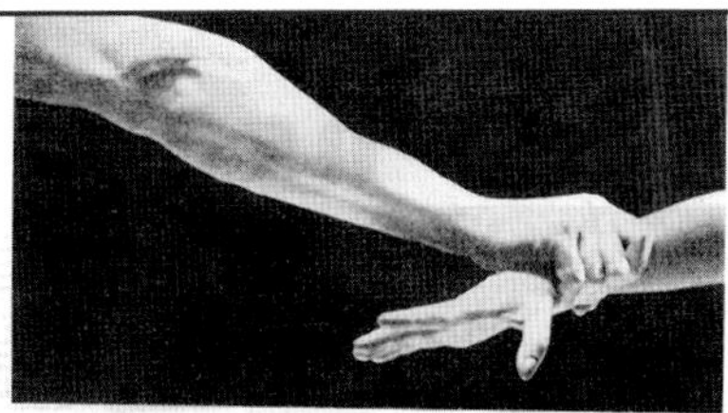

МЕЛОЧИ

„НЕ ИГРА"

НА ОЛИМПЕ

ЦЕНЗУРА ВЕЗДЕ

ФИЛЬМА ДЛЯ ВСЕХ

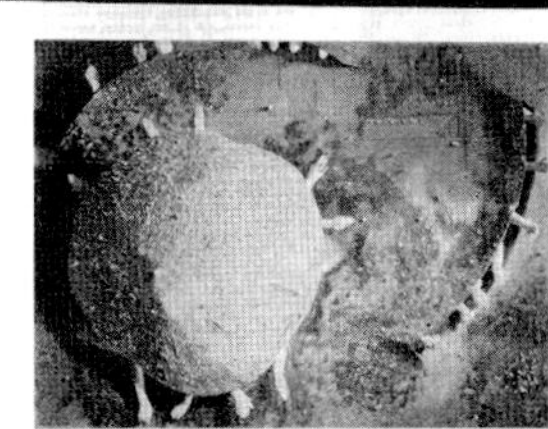

КАК РОДИЛАСЬ „ПАРИЖАНКА"

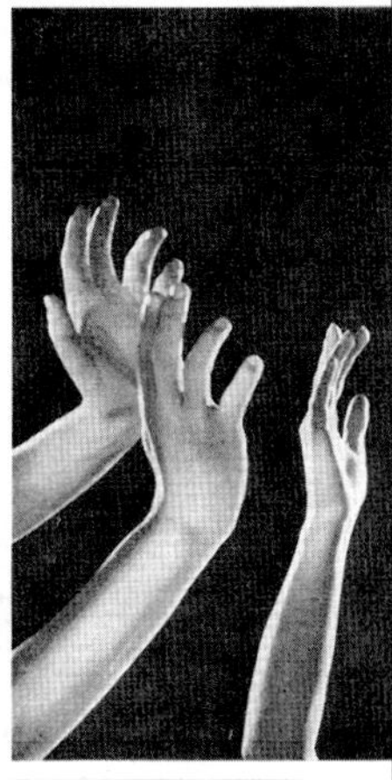

2.32   Spread from article by Alfred Barr,
"Za Grantsei: Ruki (Abroad: Hands)," *Sovetskoe kino* 1 (1928): 26–27.

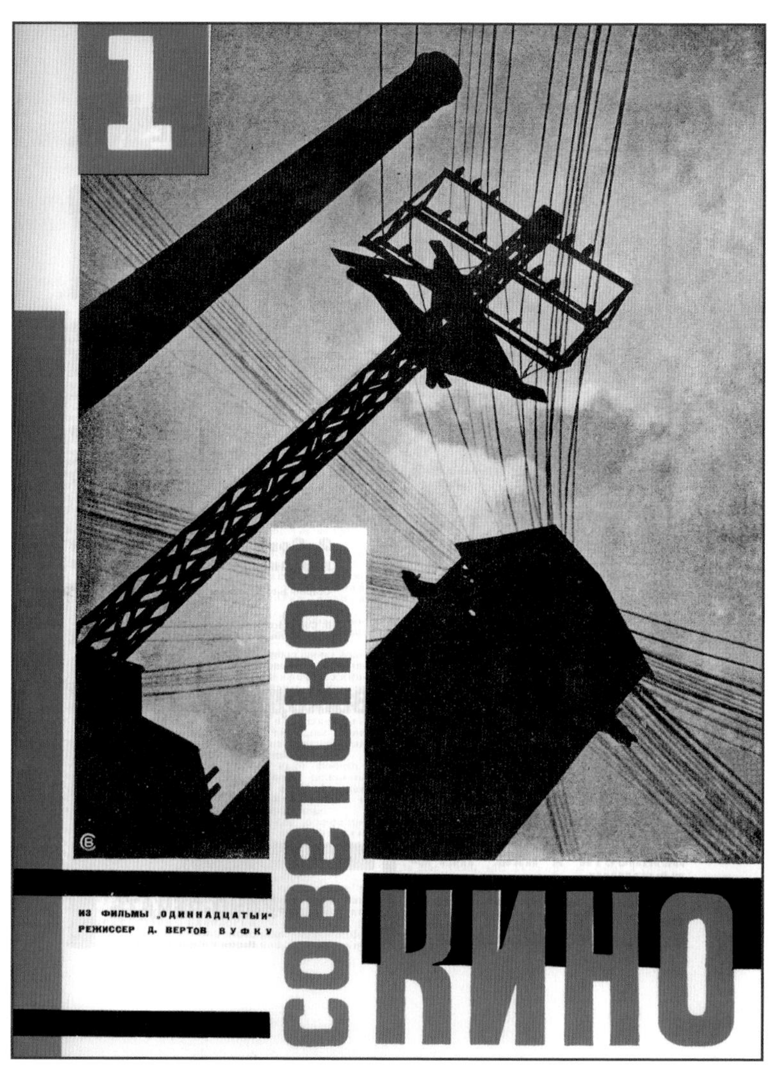

2.33 *Sovetskoe kino* 1 (1928). Cover
design by Varvara Stepanova.

he attended shortly after arriving in Moscow, and two foldout *kino* (movie) brochures: one for Vsevolod Pudovkin's 1926 film *The Mother* (based on the Maxim Gorky novel); the other for Eisenstein's *The Battleship Potemkin* (1925). I mention these details to suggest the physicality that is the small object informally known as Barr's "Russian Diary" (today housed in the Houghton Library at Harvard University).[105] The diary is not merely a transcript of ideas but a visual and material embodiment of Barr's encounter with Soviet culture. It is as though Barr's admiration for Eisenstein's montages and Stepanova's typography were made manifest in his diary's combination of cursive writing and printed information, text and image, English and Cyrillic. Throughout his visit to Moscow, Barr engaged as directly as possible in the culture of contemporary art, film, theater, music, and dance, just as he had instructed his Wellesley students to do back in Massachusetts.

"Fine Artistic Talent"

During the 1928–1929 school year, Barr taught Tradition and Revolt in Modern Painting for the second and, as it turned out, last time. To accompany this version of the class, Barr organized an exhibition of contemporary European, Russian, and American posters and book covers, some of which he had acquired during his extended trip abroad the previous winter. In its emphasis on the commercial and political uses of modernism, the exhibition recalled Barr's recent encounters with both the Bauhaus in Dessau and Lef artists in Moscow.

In its article on the exhibition, the *Wellesley College News* addressed the thorny relation of art and commerce head-on:

> After one has seen the exhibition of Modern European Posters and Commercial Typography in the Art Museum collected by Professor Barr, the old question concerning commercial art arises. Can it be classified

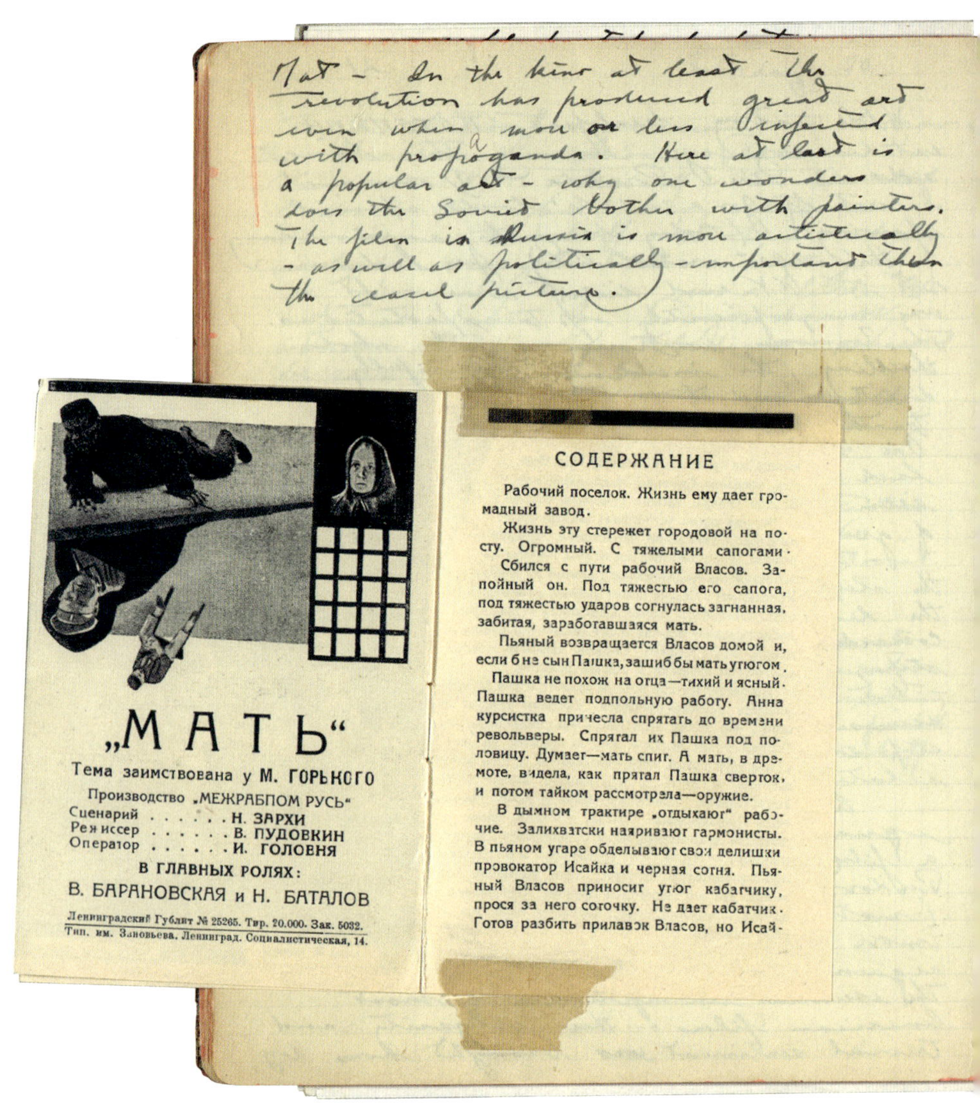

2.34 Alfred Barr, "Russian Diary," 1927–1928.
(Courtesy Houghton Library, Harvard University.)

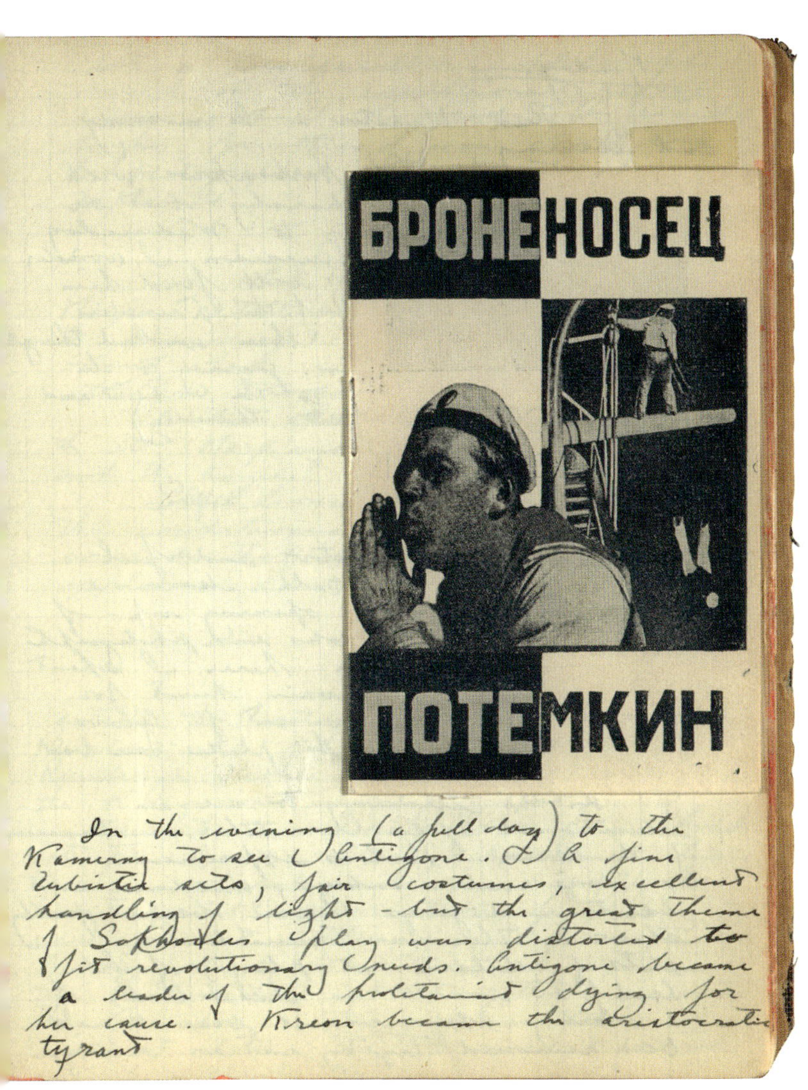

In the evening (a full day) to the
Kamerny to see Antigone. A fine
cubistic sets, fair costumes, excellent
handling of light - but the great theme
of Sophocles' play was distorted to
fit revolutionary needs. Antigone became
a leader of the proletariat dying for
her cause. Kreon became the aristocratic
tyrant

among the fine arts? Fine artistic talent has lent itself to these advertisements which bear a practical relationship to the economic and social life of the different countries represented. Whether or no the result is fine art, it shows that modern art is not entirely separated from the utilitarian ends of modern life.[106]

At the end of the unsigned article, the author muses about the "comparatively sluggish development" of American posters in comparison to their European counterparts: Does the problem with American poster design reside in the fact that "we do not demand and hence necessitate the merging of the fine arts with the economic and social ends of our age? Are we too materialistic—or too unadventurous?"[107] Overall, the article is remarkable for the complexity and sophistication with which it approaches the question of poster design within the context of contemporary culture.

In its acknowledgment of the "fine artistic talent" evidenced in the posters, the *News* seems more impressed by this exhibit than with Barr's prior show, *Progressive Modern Painting*, which it had characterized as "queer and incomprehensible." One irony of the *News*'s shift in reception is that the poster show included several objects that might justifiably have been characterized as "Bolshevist Art"—one of the charges leveled, according to Barr, by a member of the "older generation" against the earlier exhibition.[108] A productivist poster by A. Vedeneev, for example, offered what Barr described in a wall text as "high powered industry at full speed (but controlled by the worker)."[109] The poster's proletarian subject makes a telling contrast with the French and English transit posters on display elsewhere in the same exhibition. Where E. McKnight Kauffer's "From Winters Gloom to Summers Joy," a poster created for the London underground in 1927, traces time in terms of seasonal change (from bulky winter overcoat to tennis whites) and corresponding color contrasts (heavy black and gray contours give way to sunny shards of yellow and green), Vedeneev's poster, the text of which reads "Industrialism is the road to socialism," measures time in terms of political and economic advancement as gauged by the shift toward a worker-controlled society. The arrow on the machine's dial points to the number 10, which is magnified to mark the tenth anniversary of the October Revolution. According to the *Wellesley College News* article, "The Russian posters are more virile [than the English or French], perhaps because their aim is nationalistic rather than hedonistic."[110]

Written in the present tense, the article does not merely describe the contents of the exhibition; it engages them critically. The article's central question—Can posters "be classified among the fine arts"?—is never answered directly. Instead, the problem of artistic hierarchy gives way to the observation that "modern art is not entirely separated from the utilitarian ends of modern life."[111] By the time he left Wellesley to take up his new position at MoMA in the summer of 1929, Barr had helped create a vibrant culture of contemporary art at the college, one that extended from course offerings and campus exhibitions to highly informed art criticism in the college newspaper.

Barr's multidisciplinary conception of MoMA was shaped not only by the Bauhaus but also by the pedagogy he fashioned for teaching contemporary art to the young women at Wellesley. In the late 1920s, Barr exposed college students to a culture of modernity that extended from the paintings of Matisse to the windows of Saks Fifth Avenue, from the posters of the London Underground to those of post-revolutionary Russia. His conception of a new museum likewise encompassed not only modernist painting and sculpture but also architecture, industrial design, commercial illustration and typography, film, photography, and furniture. Indeed, Barr later characterized his 1929 proposal for the new Museum of Modern Art as "simply the subject headings of the Wellesley course."[112]

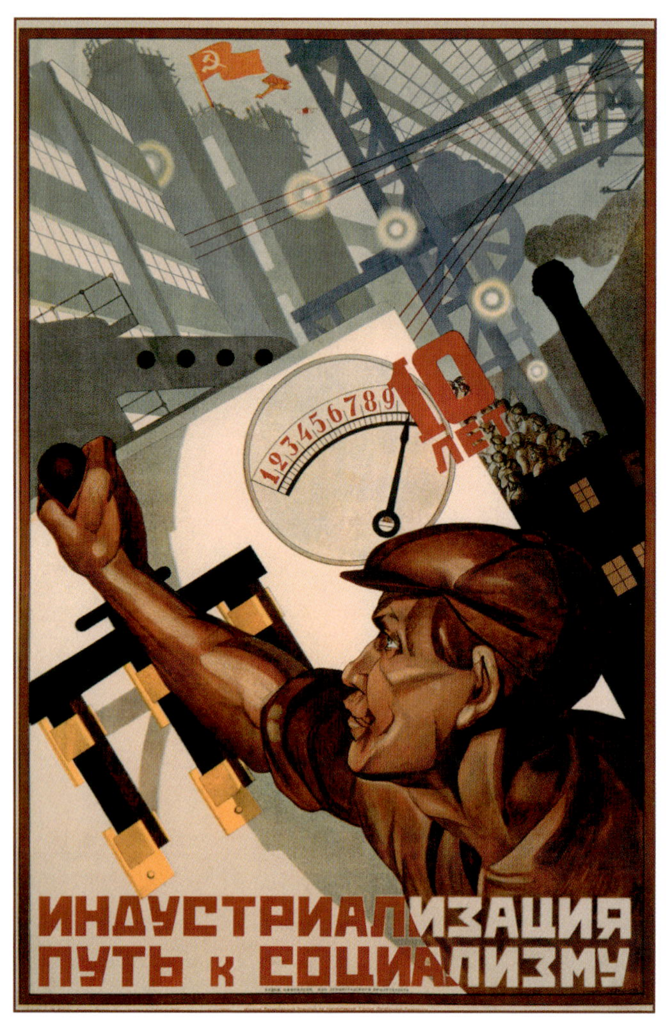

2.35 A. Vedeneev, *10th Anniversary of October Revolution*, poster, 1927.

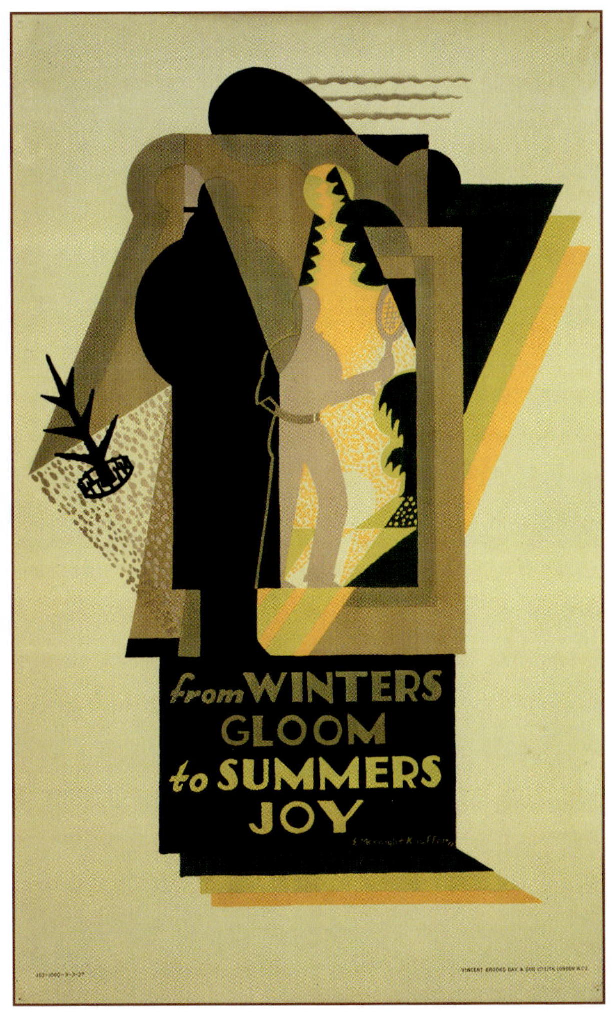

2.36 Edward McKnight Kauffer, *From Winters Gloom to Summers Joy*, 1927. Lithograph, 40⅛ × 25 inches. (Collection The Museum of Modern Art.) Digital image © The Museum of Modern Art/Licensed by SCALA/Art Resource, NY.

Postscript: Candy to Chromosomes (2004)

I have revisited Barr's modern art course at Wellesley in such detail because I wish to retrieve something of its adventurous pedagogy and genuinely multidisciplinary understanding of contemporary art. What might Barr's Tradition and Revolt in Modern Painting class look like if it were offered today—what art and industrial architecture, what posters, magazines, theater, and film could we call upon to, as "Wellesley and Modernism" put it, "stimulate an interest among the students in the vital and revolutionary creative work which is an integral part of civilization"?[113]

By way of suggesting the difficulty of adapting Barr's course to our contemporary moment, I offer a brief update on the Necco factory. The New England Confectionary Company is no longer based in Cambridge, having relocated to Revere, Massachusetts, in 2002. In 2004, the Necco factory building reopened as the global research headquarters of Novartis, a Swiss-held biomedical and pharmaceutical corporation. Barr's beloved chimney (which he likened to the campanile of an Italian church) has been demolished, and the power plant at the heart of the old factory building is now the company cafeteria. The signature space of the redesigned building is a six-story, amoeba-shaped, skylighted atrium with capsule-like elevators and exposed steel shafts that distantly recall the machinery of the former candy factory.[114]

The lead architect for the "adaptive redesign" of the factory told a reporter from the *Boston Globe* that "In its day, the Necco building was a demonstration of manufacturing. In our day it will be a demonstration of research."[115] Given the broader shift in American culture toward ever more specialized forms of research and development, how are we to make our own research as art historians relevant to the social and material conditions of contemporary life? How, in other words, are we to instill in our students (and in ourselves) a sense of art history as something more than a conversation that happens among nicely dressed people sealed in an artificially lit glass bubble?

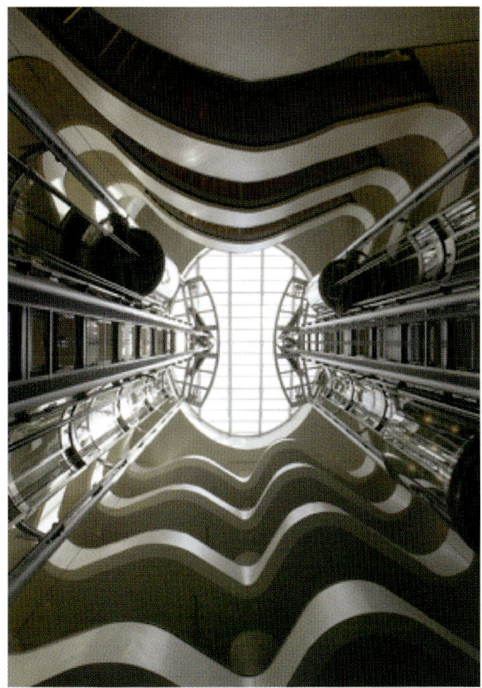

2.37 Novartis global research headquarters (in the site of the former Necco factory), atrium, elevators, and skylight, 2004.

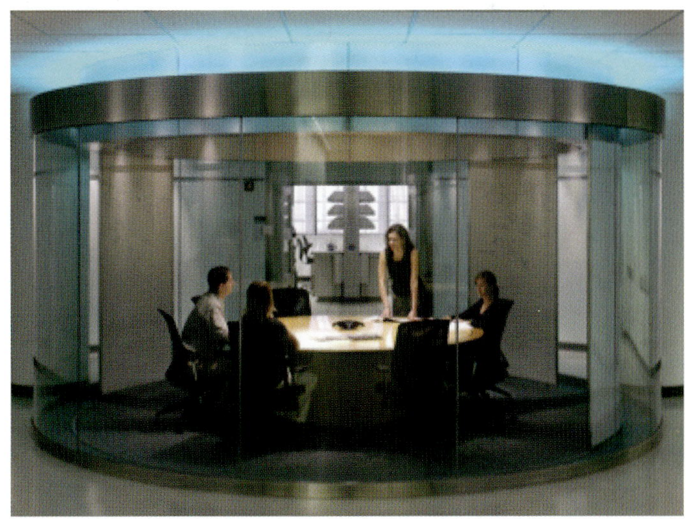

2.38 Novartis global research headquarters, conference room, 2004.

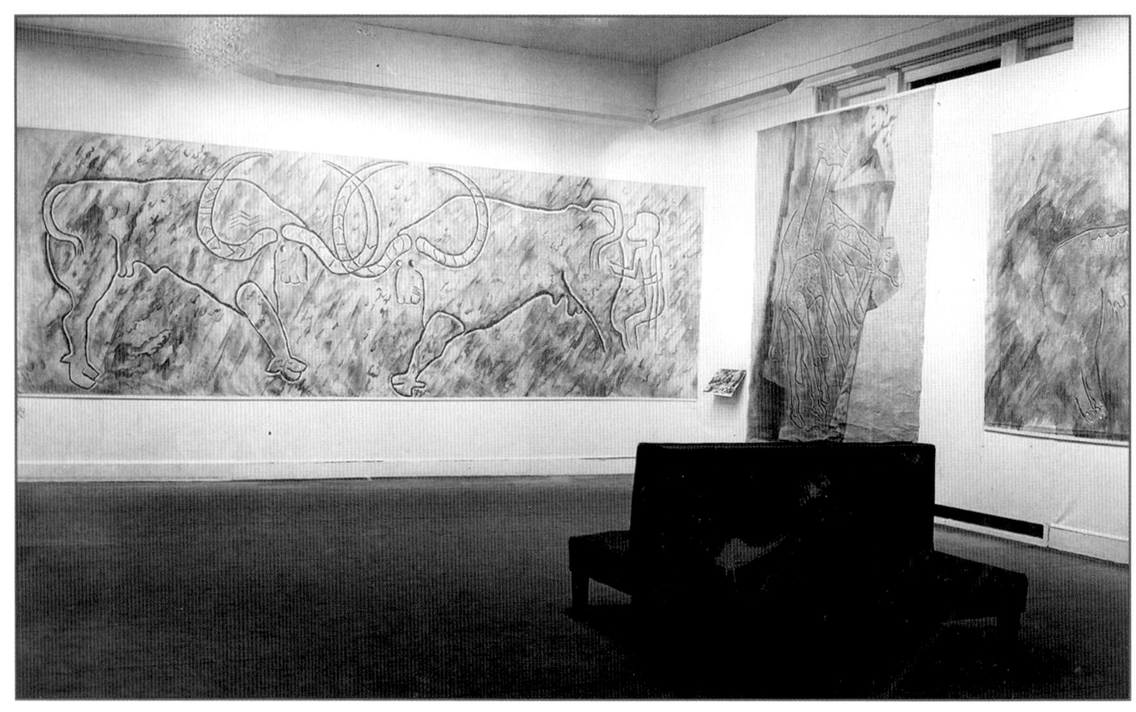

3.1 Installation view of the exhibition *Prehistoric Rock Pictures in Europe and Africa*, April 28–May 30, 1937. The Museum of Modern Art, New York. Photographic Archive. (Courtesy The Museum of Modern Art Archives, New York.) Photographer: Soichi Sunami. Digital image © The Museum of Modern Art/ Licensed by SCALA/Art Resource, NY.

3 Prehistoric Modern (1937)

You can be a museum or you can
be modern, but you can't be both.

Gertrude Stein

In April 1937 an unusual exhibition opened at the Museum of Modern Art (MoMA). Titled *Prehistoric Rock Pictures in Europe and Africa*, it consisted of copies of Paleolithic and Mesolithic cave paintings, many of which were rendered at the monumental scale of the originals. Why were works such as these on view in a museum dedicated primarily to late nineteenth- and early twentieth-century art? What version of "modern art" licensed an exhibition of pictures whose origins were as remote from the contemporary moment as humanly imaginable?

This chapter returns to a period, the 1930s and early 1940s, when the story of modern art was still up for grabs, when multiple versions were unfolding, jockeying alongside and sometimes contradicting one another. Rather than integrate those versions into a coherent narrative—or claim that MoMA succeeded in doing so—I want to retrieve some of the lesser-known strands of the story. These strands unravel the idea of modern art as a coherent period style that neatly precedes the "contemporary." And they loosen the ties binding MoMA to a prescriptive narrative of formalist modernism.

Under the directorship of Alfred H. Barr Jr. (from 1929 to 1943), the museum mounted several exhibitions that extended far beyond and, chronologically speaking, centuries (or, in the case of *Prehistoric Rock Pictures*, millennia) before modernist painting and sculpture. Rather than bolstering the narrative of nineteenth- and twentieth-century art as a unidirectional drive toward abstraction, these exhibitions challenged the very idea of chronological sequence and art-historical influence. Far from staying put in the distant past, premodern art kept resurfacing in MoMA's exhibition program, and it did so not in opposition to contemporary culture but in dialogue with it. This chapter attempts to listen in on that dialogue.

What Is Modern Art?

Barr repeatedly sought to expand the curatorial reach of the museum beyond the strictures of European art of the late nineteenth and early twentieth centuries, and to explain why it was necessary to do so. A case in point is provided by his response to a questionnaire circulated by the *New York Times* critic Edward Alden Jewell in 1931 to a select group of museum directors, art historians, and artists.[1] Among the questions posed by Jewell:

What is modern art?
How do we know it when we see it?
Is it still on the crest of the wave or is it on the decline?[2]

In Barr's response to the questionnaire (which was distributed by MoMA as a press release and excerpted in the *New York Times*), he refused to privilege any particular pictorial style, national school, or chronological period: "Modern art may be defined in many ways but for the Museum of Modern Art specific definition is unwise especially if a definition be taken as an indication of policy. The first principle of the Museum's program is flexibility and capacity for change. The moment the Museum's attitude crystallizes, it betrays its purpose."[3]

By insisting on the ever-shifting program of the museum under his direction, Barr neatly eluded the question of whether modern art was "on the crest of the wave" or "on the decline." Lest this response be seen as evasive, he added that "at the present time, the Museum is concerned primarily with the work of those early 20th Century artists who seem progressive and alive, together with the work of the past especially the 19th Century which is related to the present either by direct ancestry or analogy." By prefacing this remark with "at the present time," Barr acknowledged that art which seems "progressive and alive" today may not seem so tomorrow. The museum's engagement with "the work of the past . . . which is related to the present"[4] would therefore shift as new forms of contemporary art—and with them, new relations to the history of art—emerged in the future.

As though to underscore his refusal to limit modern art to the nineteenth and twentieth centuries, Barr concluded his response to the questionnaire by noting that "In the future the Museum plans an exhibition which may include Dutch primitives such as Jerome [sic] Bosch, Baroque mannerists such as El Greco, Paleolithic cave drawings, Boeotian bronzes, T'ang figurines, Russian ikons, Persian miniatures, and 20th Century sculpture and painting. The general public will frequently be unable to tell the new from the old but it will learn to tolerate the strange even though it is contemporary."[5]

Whether viewers could distinguish "the new from the old" was less important to Barr than their willingness to engage with radically unfamiliar forms of artistic expression. The goal of the exhibition Barr described was not to identify a premodern object (a Tang figurine, say, or an El Greco painting) as the lone source for a specific artist or movement in the late nineteenth or early twentieth century; rather, it was to create a dialogue between modern and historical art—and, no less importantly, between European and Asian cultural achievement—in which neither would be subservient to the other.

The "future exhibition" Barr described to the *New York Times* never came to pass.[6] With materials ranging from Paleolithic drawings to Boeotian bronzes, the show may well have been beyond the logistical and financial capacities of the museum at the time. Nevertheless, several of the objects mentioned by Barr in this context—Russian icons, Persian paintings (though in wall-sized rather than miniature format), and Paleolithic drawings (in facsimile)—surfaced in his publications or in MoMA's curatorial projects of the 1930s.[7] Rather than setting up a developmental narrative in which these artworks gave rise to the modern, Barr sought to understand the place of the past within the present moment. In what follows, I look at four case studies in which historically remote objects became newly relevant to the contemporary moment.

Russian Icons

"Revolutions have as a rule not been kind to religious art." With this memorably understated line, Barr opens his essay on Russian icons in the February 1931 issue of *The Arts*. To make the claim concrete, Barr points to the destruction of Catholic relics under Henry VIII and Oliver Cromwell, the Calvinist burning of "Dutch and Flemish primitives" in the sixteenth century, and the smashing of church sculptures during the French Revolution. To these examples, Barr counterposes the Bolsheviks:

> The Russian revolution has pursued a far more enlightened program, though not without certain curious contradictions. Lenin himself was not interested in art—in fact he confessed a distaste for cubism—but both he and Trotzky recognized the importance of preserving works of art, however ruthless they may have been in the destruction of human lives.

The fact that the Winter Palace was not sacked after its capture in 1917 is strong evidence of the discipline—and historical consciousness—of the men who directed the October Revolution at its very inception.[8]

Barr praises Vladimir Lenin and Leon Trotsky for preserving works of art rather than, in the manner of previous revolutionaries, defiling them. Though he mentions the "ruthless ... destruction of human lives," Barr does not dwell on the disparity between the preservation of religious icons by the Soviet state and its persecution of religious clergy, including the imprisonment, torture, and execution of over a thousand priests in the years following the Russian Revolution.[9]

While Barr lauds the revolutionaries for their "discipline and historical consciousness," he repeatedly criticizes the Russian Orthodox Church for its "general indifference ... toward the artistic and archaeological value of its icons and frescoes,"[10] an indifference made manifest in the "oily soot" that has blackened the paintings over centuries of exposure to candlelight and oil lamps in poorly ventilated churches. Throughout the article, Barr positions the icons as aesthetic objects in need of both study and modern preservation while framing their religious function as antimodern and uncivilized. In his account, the church's neglect of the art formerly in its care stands in for wider practices of barbarism:

> Whatever one's religious beliefs, it can scarcely be denied that the Russian church from a social point of view often worked for evil. It encouraged superstition of the most primitive order. Icons were worshipped almost as fetishes and employed for all manner of magical as well as devotional purposes. Rasputin's power would have been impossible in a more enlightened religious tradition. Politically the church as a body

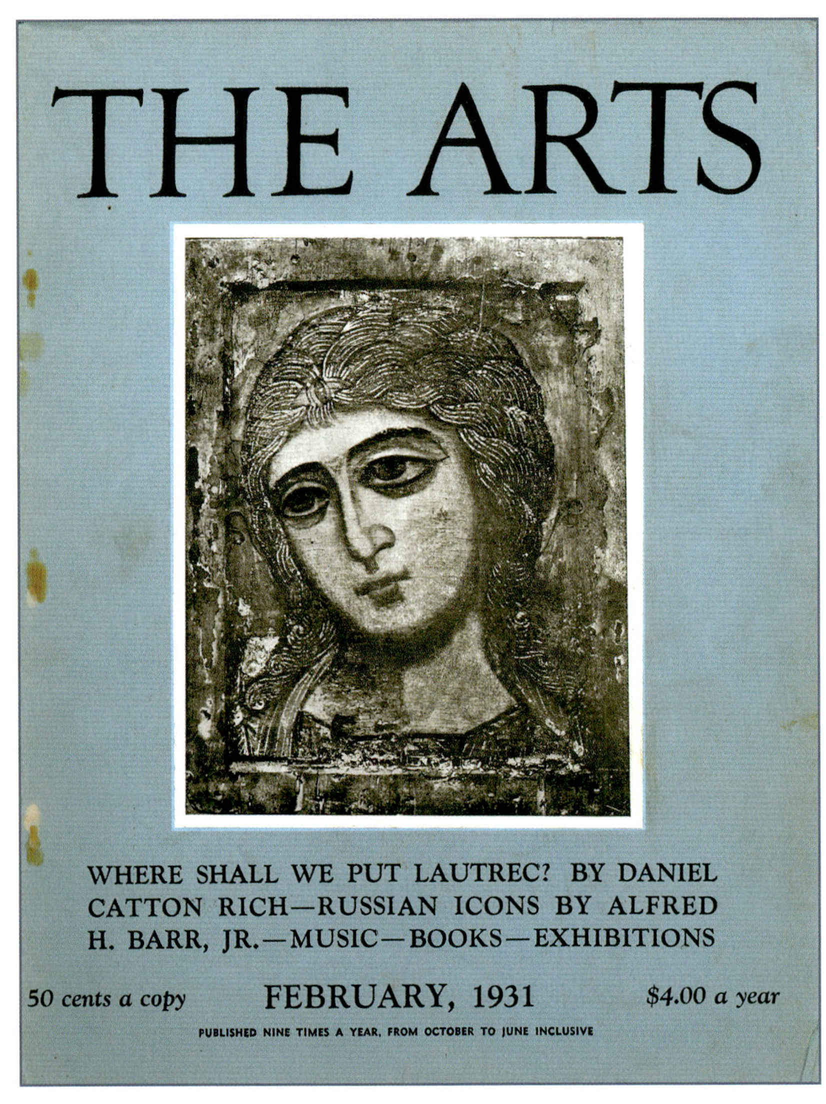

3.2 *The Arts*, February 1931.

was often aligned with the forces of oppression. As late as 1912 the entire clergy of the country was mobilized by the government in an attempt to suppress liberal tendencies in the Duma elections. These facts are not irrelevant when one learns of certain objections raised against the exhibition of icons now on view at the Metropolitan Museum.[11]

The Soviet government had organized the show of Russian icons at the request of the Boston Museum of Fine Arts, where the exhibition was mounted prior to its presentation at the Metropolitan. Legal challenges from the American government nearly precluded the exhibition from being seen in either museum since, as Barr noted, "so far as our State Department is concerned, the Russian Government is officially non-existent."[12] In both Boston and New York, the exhibition provoked protests among Russian-born American émigrés (many of whom had fled after the October Revolution), who argued that the icons had been confiscated illegally by a godless regime. In its coverage of the protests, the *New York Times* cited a letter sent by the National League of Americans of Russian Origin to the president and trustees of the Metropolitan Museum of Art. The letter posed the following questions to the museum's board: "Do you realize with whom you are trafficking when borrowing the Russian icons from what some people choose to call the Soviet Government? Can you fully grasp the measure of indignation which policies of this sort arouse in the minds of right-thinking Russians?"[13]

The Metropolitan's official letter of response avoided the ethical issues raised by the Soviet appropriation of the icons by defining the works as secular rather than sacred: "These icons are old paintings. They come from various museums and galleries in Russian cities. Some of them have long been museum pieces illustrating the history of Russian art."[14] From reading the Metropolitan's letter, one would hardly know that these objects ever had a religious function at all. Barr, for his part, bluntly criticized the double standard whereby those who objected to the exhibition of Russian icons "have continued to tolerate the presence in our museums of Flemish, Spanish, and Italian primitives, many of which were removed from their original chapels by none too pious means."[15] Barr further denounced the protestors as "for the most part counter-revolutionary Russians from whom sympathetic interest can scarcely be expected."[16]

Given that Barr has often been characterized as apolitical (or, more precisely, as depoliticizing) in his approach to modern art, his defense of Soviet cultural policy in 1931 comes as something of a surprise. The urgency of Barr's voice in "Russian Icons" may be attributed in part to the recentness of his encounter with Soviet culture. Barr's three-month visit to Moscow and Leningrad, from December 1927 to March 1928, discussed in chapter 2, involved a dynamic engagement with contemporary art, film, theater, and artists as well as with medieval religious icons. As scholar Sybil Kantor has noted, "Barr's diary has as many entries on viewing icons as on viewing modern art."[17] During the trip, Barr visited several collections of Russian icons and sought out reproductions of them for research and teaching purposes. His diary entry from January 24, 1928, for example, reports that he was "eager to see and talk icons; a great new field is opening up, if only material (books and photographs) were available here. I spent the afternoon in a vain hunt for books. Found a set of Grabar [Igor Grabar's multivolume *History of Russian Art*] for 40 rubles but the plates are bad."[18]

Barr found better reproductions when he visited the Soviet Central State Restoration Workshops, the official headquarters for the study and restoration of prerevolutionary art.[19] He was especially impressed by "the recovery of ikons which goes on from year to year since the founding of the state laboratory by Igor Grabar. The cleaning methods resemble [the] Fogg's enlightened policy."[20] This was high praise indeed, as Harvard University's

Fogg Museum possessed one of the most advanced conservation labs in the world at the time. Barr noted a salient difference between the two laboratories, however, when he observed that the conservation of the icons in Moscow had been "made possible through the anti-religious policy of the Soviet [state]."[21] Rather than destroying the icons as counterrevolutionary, Grabar and his workshop repurposed them as part of the cultural heritage of a newly secularized, nonreligious nation. The icons were meant both to celebrate the visual brilliance of Russian culture and to stand, by way of contrast, as a sign of the premodern past that the contemporary Soviets had transcended.

In addition to repairing and, in some cases, attributing the icons to an individual painter for the first time, the Restoration Workshops produced copies of particularly important or fragile works. According to Barr, "six of the oldest and most valuable icons are represented in the exhibition by copies which are technically miraculous. They were made within the last four years by the same expert craftsmen who cleaned the originals."[22] It is no longer the icons themselves but rather the technical perfection of their modern copies that qualifies, from Barr's perspective, as "miraculous." In the exhibition catalogue, Grabar (who organized the show on behalf of the Soviet government) expanded upon the wondrous effect of the facsimiles:

> [T]hese copies have not been made in the usual way. They constitute a new type of archaeological facsimile; for they reproduce exactly not only the general character of the originals and the impression conveyed by them, but their whole make-up, their structure, their technical peculiarities, even their defects, and this at the exact stage of exposure to which the originals have been brought. A copy of this kind may almost be said to replace the original; when the two have been compared, it has often been impossible for experts and students of ancient Russian to distinguish the copy from the original.[23]

The almost perfect copy might also be said to be an almost perfect displacement of the work's original function. The "expert craftsmen" who made painted facsimiles of the icons after the 1917 Revolution were doing so in the name of contemporary socialist policy, not religious devotion. In effect, the communist state sought to uncouple the icons from their sacred function and present them, newly restored and museum-ready, as the rightful patrimony of the Soviet people.[24]

After devoting the first third of his essay to the fate of Russian icons since the revolution, Barr offers a stylistic history of their development from the eleventh through the seventeenth centuries. In tracing this history, he does not argue for the icons as sources for modernist painting—whether by Kazimir Malevich, Matisse, or any number of other artists for whom such a connection might be adduced. "Russian Icons" proposes no genealogy of modernism. For Barr, the twentieth-century relevance of the icons resides not in their stylistic influence on contemporary art but in their material and symbolic reclamation by the Soviet state. The socialist repurposing of prerevolutionary painting provides the contemporary context for Barr's art-historical analysis.

Barr concludes the essay with a work from his own collection that bridges the gap between premodern past and postrevolutionary present—an enamel box with its top painted in the style of the seventeenth-century Stroganov School of icon painting. "The subject," Barr writes, "is the Soviet Trinity—Soldier, Worker, and Peasant—surrounded by factory chimneys and Fordson tractors (but they are really St. Theodore the Stratelate, St. Demetrius of Thessalonika, and St. Nichols of Myra, unwillingly masquerading in honor of St. Marx)."[25] Though refashioned into a properly proletarian subject, the painted box top brings with it the imprint of religious iconography that cannot be entirely stamped out. Purchased on the street for a few rubles by an American visitor to Moscow in 1928, the box top bespeaks the persistence

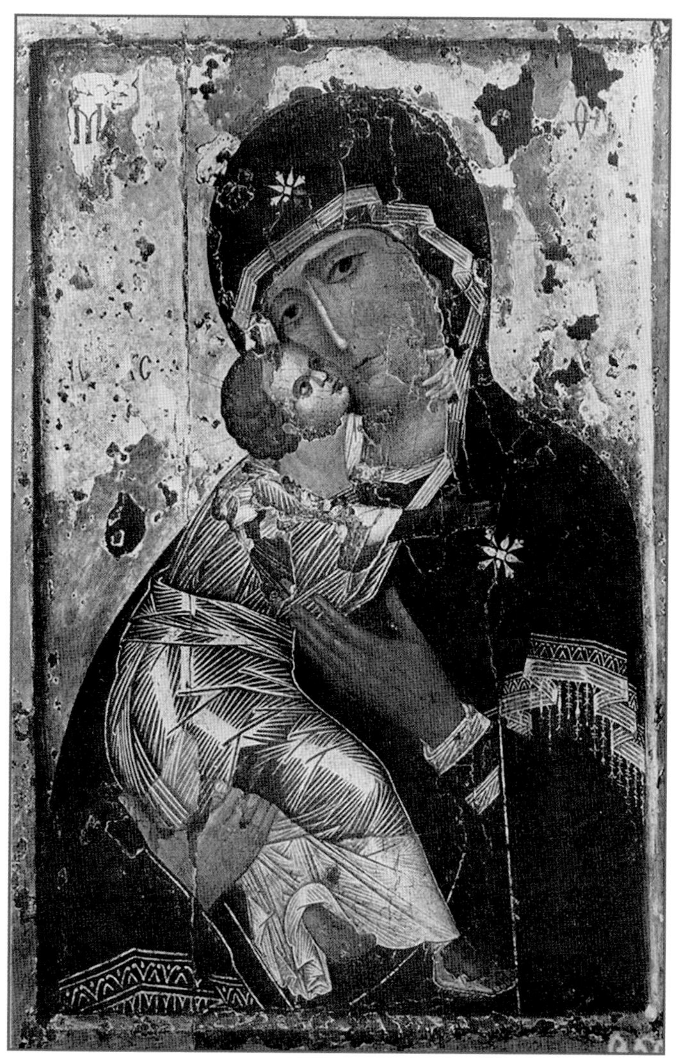

3.3 The Vladimir *Mother of God*, twentieth-century copy by Bryagin of an eleventh-century icon; figure 1 in Barr, "Russian Icons," *The Arts* 17, no. 5 (February 1931).

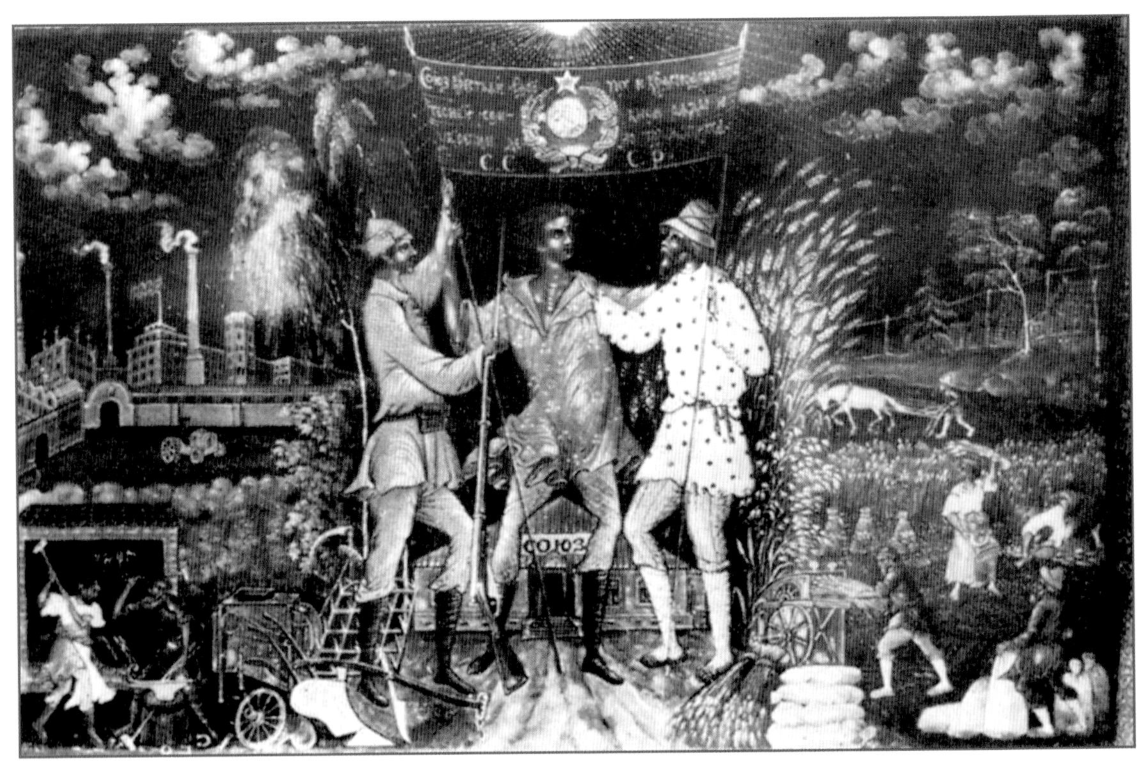

3.4 "The Soviet Trinity—Soldier, Worker, and Peasant," enamel box top painted in the Stroganov style of a seventeenth-century Russian icon; figure 19 in Barr, "Russian Icons," *The Arts* 17, no. 5 (February 1931).

of the prerevolutionary past. The saints "unwillingly masquerading in honor of St. Marx" embody Soviet political ideology even as they point back to the history of the Russian Orthodox Church and its devotional practices. Barr's nomination of "St. Marx" pokes fun at the anti-religious tenets of communism by irreverently elevating Marx to the status of Christian holiness.

Finally, it is worth remembering that these icons were reproduced in the pages of an American art magazine and that Barr's English-language commentary was occasioned by a concurrent exhibition at the Metropolitan Museum of Art. The works on display in the exhibition could not be extricated from the political and interpretive conflicts they provoked in 1931. The tradition of icon painting was not merely an artifact of a distant past but a living force within contemporary Soviet culture. And when the restored icons and recently minted facsimiles were displayed in Boston and New York, they sparked disputes over the legacies of religious art and revolutionary politics in the present moment. The history of Russian icons from the eleventh through seventeenth centuries was still being written—and rewritten—in the twentieth.

Persian Fresco Painting

An exhibition titled *Persian Fresco Painting* opened at MoMA in October 1932.[26] It featured not one fresco. The show consisted instead of over one hundred gouaches on colored paper made by Sarkis Katchadourian, "a living Persian artist" in the words of the museum's press release.[27] Born to Armenian parents in Iran and trained as a painter in Paris, Munich, and Rome, Katchadourian had recently spent two years copying sixteenth- and early seventeenth-century palace frescoes in Isfahan, Iran.

Jointly sponsored by MoMA and the American Institute for Persian Art and Archaeology, *Persian Fresco Painting* was promoted as both an important display of Near Eastern art and a "surprisingly modern" precedent to twentieth-century School of Paris painting.[28] A version of the exhibition had been presented in Paris the previous year at the Musée Guimet, the French national museum of Asian art. The catalogue to MoMA's show could thus report, somewhat immodestly, on the success of its immediate predecessor: "The public flocked in thousands to see this exhibition which offered an insight into the opulent civilization of Safavid Isfahan. . . . Coming in from the gray atmosphere of a Paris winter, the observers were enchanted by the graceful, linear designs of these water colours, and by their delicate harmonies of rose, carmine, vermilion, golden yellow, dull gold, and powdery blue."[29] Yet it was not only the visual pleasure and delicate color harmonies of the paintings that drew the Parisian crowd:

> While the great appeal of these paintings lay in their exotic, almost decadent beauty, the throngs which continued to come to the Guimet found in them . . . something more significant. . . . The history of modern art was being written in the showing of these designs from seventeenth century Isfahan. Gui Monnereau writing in *Echo de Paris*, saw Marie Laurencin in some of the portraits of women, a Modigliani in the painting of a woman bathing, and even Picasso, at the Ali Kapu [Palace]. The correspondent of *Figaro* reported that it was the opinion of many visitors to the exhibition that in the seventeenth century the Persians were already imitating M. Henri Matisse, but without any insipid quality and with far finer draftsmanship. Observers agreed generally that these frescoes, in their freedom from direct representation and in their combination of daring draftsmanship and charming conventionalization, were distinctly in the post-war manner.[30]

This passage shifts freely between seventeenth-century frescoes and twentieth-century European paintings while largely ignoring the mediating hand of Katchadourian, the (twentieth-century) copyist. In this account, the frescoes do not simply anticipate the School of Paris by three hundred years, they collapse historical distance altogether so as to inhabit the same pictorial moment as Matisse, Amedeo Modigliani, and Picasso. To say in 1932 that the murals are "distinctly in the post-war manner" is to date them to the early twentieth century rather than to the early seventeenth. And, conversely, to comment that the Persians were "already imitating M. Henri Matisse" is to backdate the French painter by some three centuries. The logical impossibility of such statements hardly invalidated the affinity they proposed between Safavid frescoes and School of Paris easel paintings. To the contrary, the counterhistorical practice of "finding" modern art in "Persian fresco paintings" seems to have fueled the positive response of the critics. The *New York Times*, for example, observed that it was "[n]o wonder a French critic at once thought of Marie Laurencin. Calligraphically the work also brings before us Matisse, who has often been credited with having gone to Persian sources. You will encounter, indeed, ever so many of our best and some of our most fashionable moderns here."[31] The idea that visitors would encounter "some of our most fashionable moderns" at the exhibition neatly elides that fact that Katchadourian (rather than Matisse or Marie Laurencin) is the modern artist who painted the works on view.

To the extent that the labor of the copyist is downplayed, the Persian frescoes emerge as marvelously, almost miraculously, up to date. This effect is particularly evident in the museum's press release when it cites a French critic exclaiming of the reconstructed murals, "How modern they are! . . . Modern art dating from the sixteenth and seventeenth centuries, modern art from Asia, that is what these paintings seem to be."[32] The astonishment expressed by the critic in the face of "modern art from Asia" bespeaks the prevailing view of European (and especially French) art of the nineteenth and early twentieth centuries as definitively modern.

This not to say that the historical specificity of the original frescoes was elided altogether by the exhibition. The catalogue discusses the flowering of Persian art and architecture under Shah Abbas the Great (reigned 1588–1629) and describes in some detail the two structures housing the frescoes copied by Katchadourian—Ali Qapu (Sublime Gate) and Chihil Sutun (Forty Columns)—at the Safavid palace complex in Isfahan. Although it includes forty-two full-page illustrations of twentieth-century facsimiles, the exhibition catalogue features only two small images of original frescoes. While acknowledging the difference between historical fresco and modern facsimile, the catalogue largely absents the former from view.

But not entirely. Comparison of the photograph captioned "Decoration in the Ali Kapu" in the catalogue with the illustration of the facsimile titled "The Feathered Cap" begins to suggest the disparity between seventeenth-century original and twentieth-century copy. The facsimile repairs the damages wrought on the original over the prior three centuries, crisply delineating the otherwise faded and time-worn composition. Whereas the palace fresco extends across the surface of a recessed niche with a pointed arch, Katchadourian's copy conforms to the rectangular dimensions of its paper ground. What is more, the niche at Ali Qapu is part of a larger decorative program that includes the intricate (if badly weathered) ornamental patterns on the surrounding walls and a second niche into which a wooden frame has been set. Finally, the fresco at Ali Qapu does not hang on the palace wall, as would an easel painting, but has been applied directly to it. Short of severing the plaster ground of the fresco from the larger structure of which it is part, the original painting is immovable. Katchadourian's copies, by contrast, could be rolled up and shipped with relative ease from Isfahan to Paris or New York. They were made to be portable. Following their display at MoMA, for example, the facsimiles were shown at the Arts Club of Chicago and the Leicester Galleries in London.[33]

The copies were also—and not incidentally—for sale. A "Price List of Is-fahan Frescoes Reconstructed by S. Katchadourian" is preserved in MoMA's archival files for the 1932 exhibition. Though the works had just been shipped from Paris, all the prices are listed in U.S. dollars. They range from $204 for the smaller pictures to $816 for the grandest. That the purpose of the list was to enable sales (rather than, for example, to establish insurance values) is made clear in an accompanying note: "The prices are retail prices, and include the 15% sales commission allowed museums." Whether any sales were made during the run of the exhibition is not known.

Along with a designated price, each facsimile came with its own title. "The Feathered Cap," "Preparing for the Feast," "Portrait of a Lady," and "Pilgrims of Love" are typical, although several titles consist of a line or two from the *Rubáiyát of Omar Khayyam*, such as "While you live Drink!—for once dead you never shall return" (quatrain 35). Assigned by Katchadourian, the titles conjure a series of discrete vignettes or narrative scenes. In their original context, the palace frescoes carried neither titles nor verses. Striking a tone of slight condescension, the exhibition catalogue states that "the designations which have been furnished by the artist seem to offer no advantage other than to that public which demands titles."[34] The public that "demands" titles is a modern (and likely a Western) one accustomed to freestanding works of art in galleries and museums. Like the facsimiles themselves, the titles insist on the boundedness of the figures and suppress the densely patterned, multidimensional surround for which they were conceived. They encourage viewers (including potential buyers) to regard each composition as an autonomous picture rather than as part of a unified decorative program.

A photograph taken at Ali Qapu in 2010 shows how the mural on which Katchadourian based "The Feathered Cap" looks today, following extensive restoration of the palace. In this view, we can see that the niche in which the

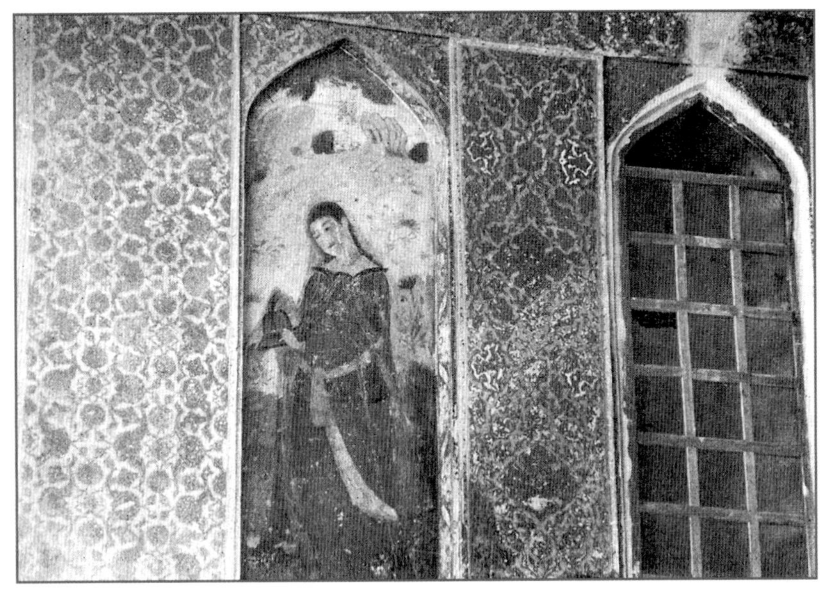

3.5 "Decoration in the Ali Kapu," seventeenth-century original, in *Persian Fresco Paintings, Reconstructed by Mr. Sarkis Katchadourian from the Seventeenth Century Originals in Isfahan* (New York: American Institute for Persian Art and Archaeology, [1932]).

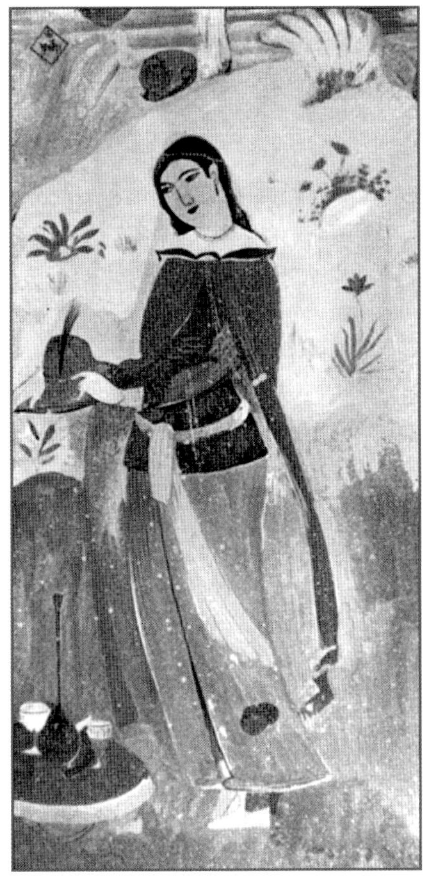

3.6 Sarkis Katchadourian, "The Feathered Cap," twentieth-century copy, in *Persian Fresco Paintings, Reconstructed by Mr. Sarkis Katchadourian from the Seventeenth Century Originals in Isfahan* (New York: American Institute for Persian Art and Archaeology, [1932]), n. 32. (Courtesy The Museum of Modern Art, New York.) Digital image © The Museum of Modern Art/Licensed by SCALA/ Art Resource, NY.

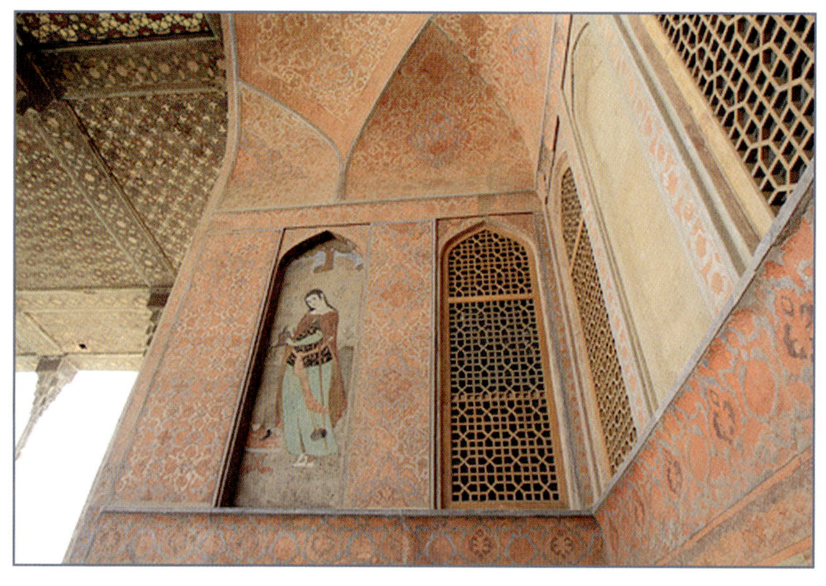

3.7 Corrine Bonnell, photograph of Ali Qapu
taken in 2010. (Courtesy Corrine Bonnell.)

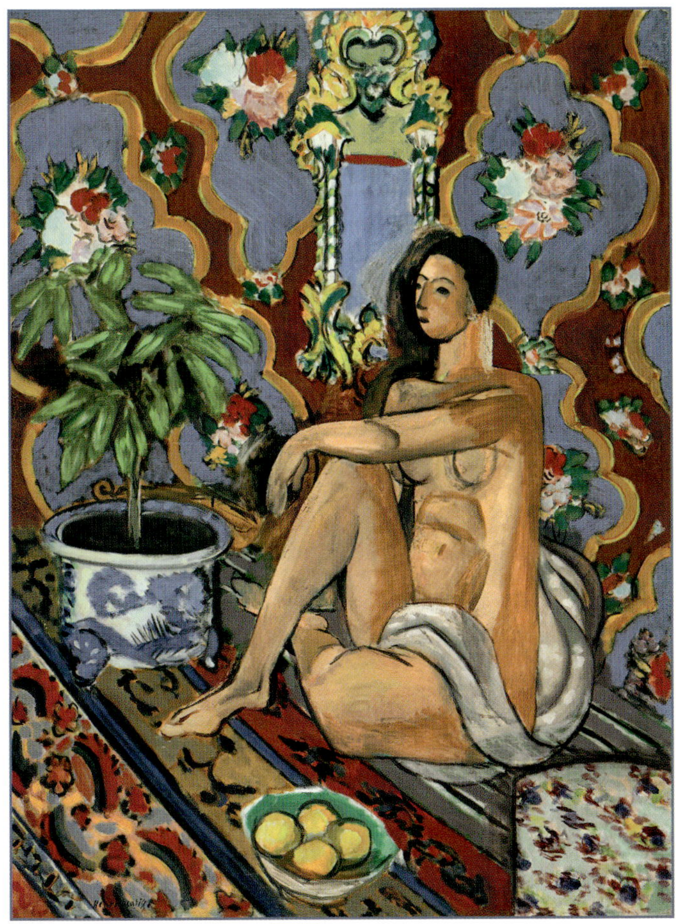

3.8 Henri Matisse, *Decorative Figure* on an *Ornamental Background*, 1925–1926, oil on canvas, 130 × 98 cm. Photographer: Philippe Migeat. © 2012 Succession H. Matisse, Paris/ Artists Rights Society (ARS), NY. (Collection Musée National d'Art Moderne, Centre Georges Pompidou, Paris, France.) Photo credit: CNAC/MNAM/Dist. Rénuion des Musées Nationaux/Art Resource, NY.

female figure appears is but one element in a spectacular, multitiered environment that includes decorative painting—variously floral, geometric, and figurative—on virtually every surface of the palace.[35] The appeal of Islamic art, architecture, and design for modernist painters of the early twentieth century lay in the play of color and pattern freed from the labors of strict verisimilitude as well as in the dynamic dialogue between figuration and abstraction.[36] In Matisse's *Decorative Figure on an Ornamental Background* (1925-1926), for example, neither the female nude nor the surrounding blue arabesques and brilliantly patterned surfaces takes visual precedence; indeed, at certain moments (the black contour lines at the left of the face and shoulder, for example), it is difficult to determine just where the "decorative figure" ends and the "ornamental background" begins.

In a review titled "Modernism from Persia," the *New York Journal American* projected this dizzying visual effect into the chronological realm by claiming that the facsimiles of the Ali Qapu frescoes were both a precedent for and an advance upon modern art:

> If French modernists are thought to need "ancestors" these Persian pictures can certainly be counted among them, being soundly artistic albeit hitherto unrecognized forerunners of the modern. . . . What is centrally similar . . . is the attempt at pure painting, expression of line, and color and design rather than representation of nature. As the Persians have managed the matter better than the modernists, achieving more clarity and more poetry, all the public interested in modern art can profit from studying the exhibition. It makes so plain how art can be abstract and at the same time natural, at once a mental and a sensual delight.[37]

Once again, recent French and centuries-old Persian paintings are aligned on formal terms, with the older art paradoxically outdistancing the new in terms of "pure painting" and modernist "clarity" of design.

Although *Persian Fresco Painting* was extremely well-received in New York (as it had been in Paris), there was at least one dissenting voice among the Americans. The critic for the *New York Sun* compared Katchadourian's copies at MoMA to the original Persian miniatures from the fourteenth to the sixteenth centuries in the permanent collection of the Metropolitan Museum. The comparison was not to MoMA's advantage:

> These copies of the old murals in the Palace of Ali Kapu do not warm the American blood to the extent that the precious miniatures in the Metropolitan Museum Collection do. How could they? After all, they are copies and the copyist can never secure all the spirit of the original. They seem cloyingly sweet and rather restricted in range. There is some frank love-making in them, a great deal of wine-bibbing and some loosely indicated ideals of pulchritude but nothing that seems first-hand. It is not the least likely that they will supersede the miniatures in the affections of our students. There is, as was said before, a quite interfering something that stands between the modern student and these old murals, and that something is probably Sarkis Katchadourian, the artist who made these copies.[38]

For this critic, Katchadourian's copies provide neither an adequate window onto Persian fresco painting nor a successful artistic project in their own right. The "quite interfering something" that stands between the "old murals" and the "modern student" is the figure of the copyist. The flaws ascribed to Katchadourian's paintings by the critic from the *New York Sun* ("cloyingly sweet," narrow in range, inauthentic in spirit) render visible what the other reviewers and the exhibition catalogue largely elide—the labor and limits of the artist's translation of faded palace murals into freshly painted pictures for display (and sale) to contemporary audiences.[39] The distance between seventeenth-century palace fresco and twentieth-century facsimile could not, it seems, be painted entirely out of the picture.

Prehistoric Rock Pictures

Like *Persian Fresco Painting*, MoMA's 1937 exhibition *Prehistoric Rock Pictures in Europe and Africa* consisted entirely of copies. In this case, the copies were watercolor paintings and photographic prints, although only the watercolors approximated the monumental scale of the prehistoric originals. According to an article in the *Bulletin of the Museum of Modern Art*, "The facsimiles reproduce the exact colors and, with a few exceptions, the exact dimensions of the original pictures as they now appear, with chips, cracks and weathering faithfully copied in order to present a complete and accurate cultural document."[40] The facsimiles did not show how the rock pictures would have looked in the Paleolithic or Mesolithic moment of their creation. Rather, the copies conveyed how the pictures appeared at the time of their early twentieth-century rediscovery, whether "in the rock shelters of the African bush, on the rock shores of Scandinavian fiords, and on the limestone walls of the subterranean caves of France and Spain."[41] Prehistory and modernity speak to each other across the widest expanses of time and geography through the mediation of pictorial facsimile and museum exhibition.

All the watercolors and photographs on display in *Prehistoric Rock Pictures* were borrowed from the Forschungsinstitut für Kulturmorphologie (Research Institute for the Morphology of Civilization), a German scientific organization based in Frankfurt am Main directed by the ethnologist Leo Frobenius. Between 1904 and 1932, Frobenius led twelve major research expeditions to study rock art in Egypt, the Sudan, South Africa, Scandinavia, eastern Spain, and southern France, among other sites. During these expeditions, several thousand prehistoric pictures were documented for the first time.

The Forschungsinstitut employed watercolorists to copy rock art pictures in situ and to do so, whenever possible, at scale. While the expedition staff included photographers, Frobenius felt that the watercolorists better captured the essence of cave paintings. In the catalogue to the MoMA exhibition, he explains why:

> Neither the study nor the reproduction of prehistoric rock pictures is easy. If the rock surface were smooth and all on one plane, if the lighting were regular and of the necessary strength and texture, if the colors and incisions were clear cut and not criss-crossed and pocked by erosion, then "perhaps" one would need only to avail oneself of a camera. But only "perhaps." For a lens cannot differentiate between that which is essential and that which is not. The result is that it is extremely difficult if not impossible to obtain an accurate conception of a rock picture from a photograph.
>
> So there is nothing left but to have the pictures copied by hand, something which is not easy and which can be done satisfactorily only by those who have, so to speak, immersed themselves in the material and are sensitive to the spirit and mentality of an age which has passed. This will be hard for some people to understand. But the fact remains that every picture, whether carved into the rock by prehistoric man, drawn by a child or painted by a Raphael, is alive with a certain definite spirit, a spirit with which the facsimile must be infused.[42]

Frobenius introduces the need for painted copies as a response to the technical difficulties presented by prehistoric art (craggy, irregular surfaces,

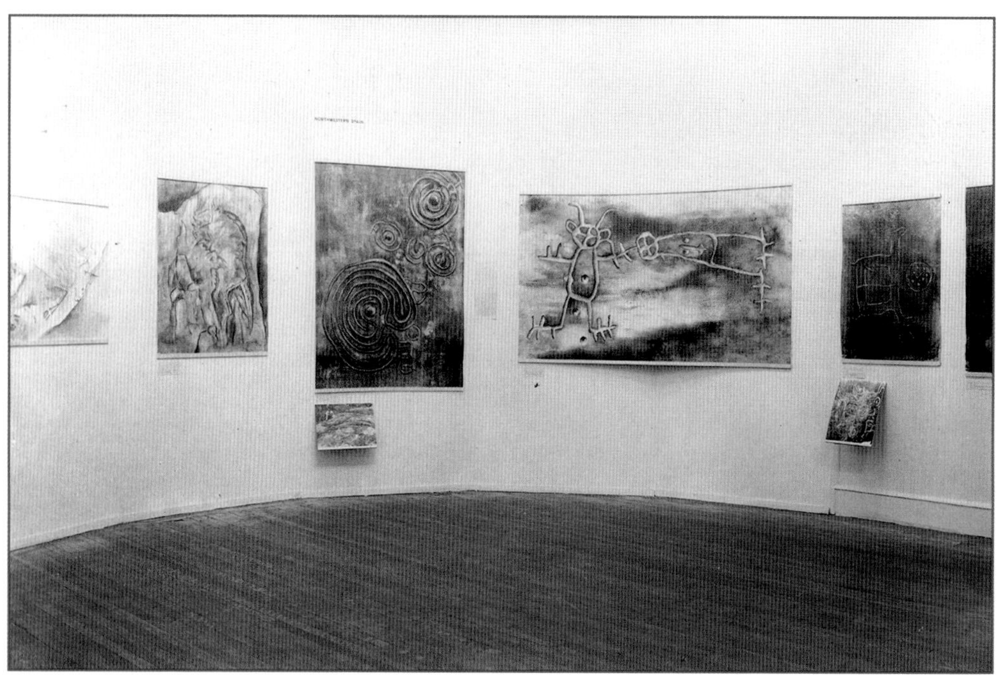

3.9 Installation view of the exhibition *Prehistoric Rock Pictures in Europe and Africa*, April 28–May 30, 1937. Section titled "Northwestern Spain." The Museum of Modern Art, New York. Photographic Archive. (Courtesy The Museum of Modern Art Archives, New York.) Photographer: Soichi Sunami. Digital image © The Museum of Modern Art/Licensed by SCALA/Art Resource, NY.

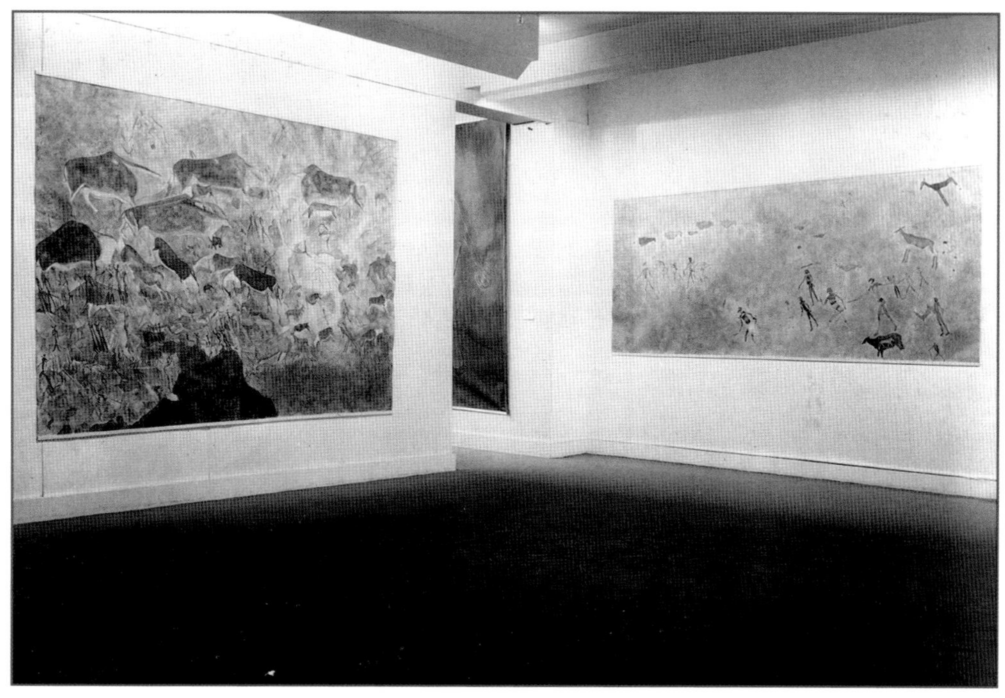

3.10 Installation view of the exhibition
*Prehistoric Rock Pictures in Europe and
Africa*, April 28–May 30, 1937. The Museum
of Modern Art, New York. Photographic
Archive. (Courtesy The Museum of Modern
Art Archives, New York.) Photographer:
Soichi Sunami. Digital image © The Museum
of Modern Art/Licensed by SCALA/Art
Resource, NY.

uneven lighting, and physical deterioration). By the end of the passage, how-ever, technical challenges have transformed into spiritual ones. Far from a mere copyist, the facsimile painter must become "sensitive to the spirit" of a cave painting so as to "infuse" that spirit into the picture's reproduction on canvas. On this account, the painter must intuitively tap into or channel the prehistoric past, or at least that part of the past that remains "alive" in the contemporary moment. In so doing, the copyist revives primeval pictures for the modern world.

Barr struck a similarly mystical note in his preface to the exhibition cata-logue: "We can, as modern men, no longer believe in the magic efficacy of these rock paintings; but there is about them a deeper and more general mag-ic quite beyond their beauty as works of art or their value as anthropological documents. Even in facsimile, they evoke an atmosphere of antediluvian first things, a strenuous Eden where Adam drew the animals before he named them."[43] In his paean to the beauty and "general magic" of the rock paintings, Barr pauses briefly to acknowledge that we are looking at modern copies rather than prehistoric originals, but then he is off on another track. "Even in facsimile," he claims, the pictures return us to "antediluvian first things." Barr conjures a primeval moment of mark-making as far removed from the present day as possible. Yet the status of the rock pictures as twentieth-century cop-ies—and of their viewers as "modern men"—nevertheless lingers on the scene.

The dialogue between modernity and prehistory informs a photograph in the *Bulletin of the Museum of Modern Art* showing an artist at his easel in the Mtoko cave in Southern Rhodesia (now Zimbabwe) during the ninth expedition of the Forschungsinstitut. The artist stands on a ladder so as to reach the upper section of the canvas on which he works. The photograph reveals a second ladder in the background (perhaps for the use of another copyist) as well as an array of supplies, camping equipment, and a pup tent in the foreground. Though the easel at which the painter stands is sizable, both artist and easel are dwarfed by the scale of the cave in which they temporarily reside.

The renderings visible on the cave wall appear to be part of a wider pictorial field that stretches beyond the photographic frame. From the camera's vantage point, the renderings do not cohere into a unified composition (a rock art "picture" or "mural") that could be easily copied by the watercolorist. But even if the cave renderings were more resolved, the facsimile artist would still need to translate them from an irregular, partially eroded, and sloped terrain onto a flat, smooth, geometrically bounded canvas. He would still be making a portable painting from pictorial forms embedded in rock and earth. In an article on "Rock Paintings of Southern Africa," the British archaeologist H. C. Woodhouse observed that prehistoric artists "were not subjected to the tyranny of a frame but only limited by the extent of the rock-face."[44] Modern copyists, however, were necessarily bound by the limits of their canvas.[45]

In its review of *Prehistoric Rock Pictures*, the *New York Times* acknowledged the hard-won achievements of the expedition artists:

> A great deal of credit should go to the artist who, often under the most difficult circumstances, made these splendid facsimile drawings in color. Some of them are enormous. One rock painting of elephants, quagga [a kind of zebra], antelopes, "formlings" and figures found in Southern Rhodesia covers, as reproduced, an entire wall of the museum. But all of the work exhibited, whether the examples be large or of slight dimension, reveals careful and sympathetic artistry.[46]

Notwithstanding such critical praise, the facsimile painters were not acknowledged by name in either reviews or the exhibition catalogue for *Prehistoric Rock Pictures*. The anonymity of the modern copyists paralleled that of

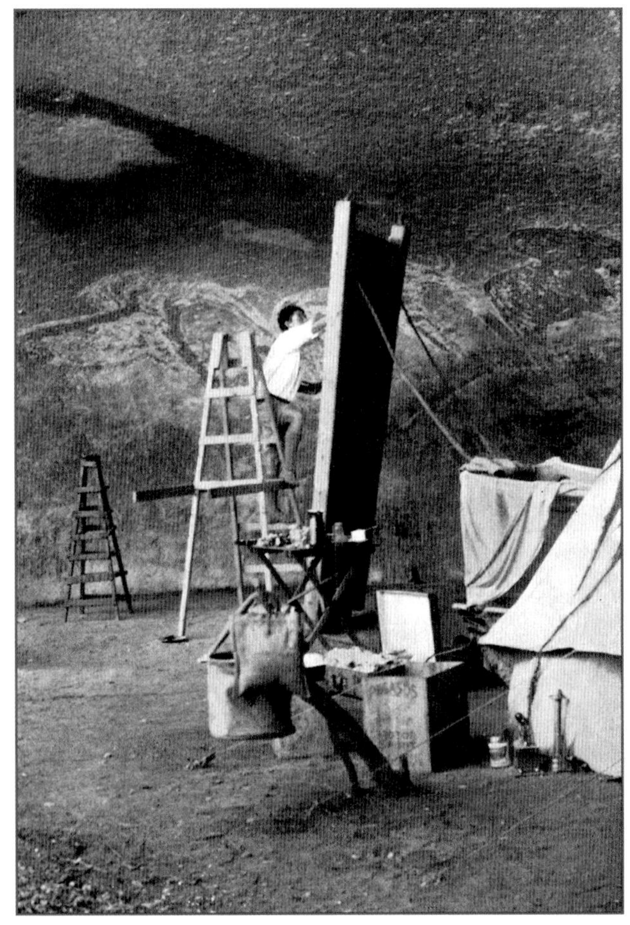

3.11 Douglas Fox, "Prehistoric Rock Pictures in Europe and Africa," *Bulletin of the Museum of Modern Art* 4, no. 5 (April 1937): 7. (Courtesy The Museum of Modern Art Archives, New York.) Digital image © The Museum of Modern Art/Licensed by SCALA/Art Resource, NY.

the prehistoric picture makers they emulated, with the difference being, of course, that the copyists were known and very much alive.

Within the logic of the exhibition, the copyist remained an ambiguous, slightly shadowy figure—perhaps even more elided than Katchadourian was from *Persian Fresco Painting*. Were MoMA visitors meant to understand the facsimile painter as an artist in his or her own right? Were viewers supposed to better appreciate prehistoric rock art by looking at the copy or by looking through it to the imagined original? What, in other words, was the intended effect of presenting a modern copy of a prehistoric Mtoko cave painting in a midtown Manhattan art museum in 1937?

Because many of the facsimiles retained the scale of the original cave paintings, *Prehistoric Rock Pictures* featured spectacular, gallery wall–sized renderings of animals, human figures, and abstract forms. Barr applied his hallmark style of exhibition display: white or beige walls; ample floor space; and spare use of furniture, which included, in this case, a double-sided bench in the middle of the room and a guard's folding chair against a wall (see figure 3.15). Even the wall text, which at MoMA could be quite extensive, was here kept minimal and unobtrusive. In the context Barr fashioned for them, the copies functioned not only as documentations of prehistoric art but as aesthetic forms in their own right, not only as transcriptions of a Paleolithic and Mesolithic past but also as quasi-abstract pictures in a contemporary art museum.

By translating the cave pictures into discrete compositions on rectangular sheets of canvas, the facsimiles nudged prehistoric rock art closer to modern easel painting. So too did the catalogue's description of the copies held at the Forschungsinstitut as an "actual gallery on canvas of more than three thousand facsimiles of prehistoric art, the only collection of its kind in the world."[47] Note that it is the modern replicas—rather than the prehistoric cave paintings on which they are based—that constitute this remarkable gallery. Claims of authenticity and uniqueness ("an actual gallery on canvas," "the only collection of its kind in the world") are thus made on behalf of a multitude of painted copies.

According to MoMA's official chronicle of its early years, it was Barr's idea to bring *Prehistoric Rock Pictures* to the museum. Having seen an exhibition of the facsimiles in Frankfurt in 1936, Barr "made a selection of about one-fourth of the material and arranged for copies to be made. The reproductions were in color, made by artists who accompanied the expeditions under the direction of Professor Leo Frobenius to centers of prehistoric art in Africa and Europe."[48] By this account, the facsimiles displayed at MoMA were copies of copies, each reproduced at Barr's behest for the purpose of exhibition in the United States. The copies would have been nearly contemporaneous with their exhibition in New York, in the sense that they were produced between summer 1936 (when Barr visited Frankfurt) and spring 1937 (when *Prehistoric Rock Pictures* opened at MoMA).

In his review of the exhibition for the *Magazine of Art*, Robert Goldwater argued that the discovery and critical reception of cave paintings in the nineteenth and twentieth centuries revealed more about modern taste than about prehistoric society:

> The opinions concerning this art, from its early neglect [in the late nineteenth century] by those investigators who could not fit it into their picture of what a "primitive" art should be, through those who wished to consider it a manifestation of the purely decorative instinct of mankind, down to the present view (surely more in accord with all the evidence) of its combined social efficacy and aesthetic use, have been a rather accurate if somewhat belated reflection of the changes of taste in the contemporary period. Even today the exotic appeal of this art, as with

that of any other "primitives," may influence the close affinity to modern art which is often found in it; yet we must recognize this exoticism as an important factor in the constitution of the modern eye.[49]

The "modern eye" creates the "exotic appeal" of prehistoric rock pictures, in part by aligning those pictures with the underlying exoticism of twentieth-century artworks that draw on archaic, non-Western, or otherwise "primitive" sources. Goldwater's review of *Prehistoric Rock Pictures* anticipates the publication of his landmark book *Primitivism in Modern Painting*, in which he observes that it was modern European artists—rather than African, Oceanic, aboriginal, or prehistoric peoples—who engaged in a "ferocious primitivizing" of visual form.[50] In his review of *Prehistoric Rock Pictures*, as in his book the following year, Goldwater insisted on the difference between the modern taste for primitivism and the complex histories and traditions of "so-called primitive" art.

In the catalogue to *Prehistoric Rock Pictures*, Barr argued for the twentieth-century relevance of the exhibition on somewhat different grounds. He contrasted the cave paintings to contemporary (which is to say, 1930s) government-sponsored murals in the United States:

> Until recently our own mural art was usually an architect's after-thought, a mere decorative postscript. Now, under the government art projects, it has seemed at times an artificial adjustment to the artist's economic needs rather than the result of any very urgent communal necessity (beyond the preservation of society's self-respect which might suffer if the artist starved). The mural art of the Spanish caves and African cliffs was, on the contrary, an integral and essential function of life, for these painted animals were almost certainly magic symbols used to insure the successful hunting of the real animals. Today walls are painted so that

the artist may eat, but in prehistorical times walls were painted so that the community might eat.[51]

While attributing both magical powers and communal benefit to the cave paintings, Barr all but dismisses the publicly funded murals of his own day. Where prehistoric rock pictures served a fundamental purpose within the society of their makers, contemporary American murals of the 1930s were merely, in Barr's view, an "artificial adjustment" to the material needs of individual artists.[52] The contrast not only brings the cave paintings up to date—it renders them superior to their twentieth-century counterparts.

U.S. government-sponsored murals were not the only contemporary pictures to which Barr compared prehistoric cave paintings. As a companion to *Prehistoric Rock Pictures*, he mounted *Twelve Modern Paintings*, an exhibition of early twentieth-century European works at MoMA. Modernist techniques of willful regression—crude, sticklike figures; seemingly random marks, doodles, and scribbles; distortions of scale; scratched and scored surfaces—were placed in conversation with the "magic" (as Barr put it) of the facsimile cave paintings. According to *Time* magazine, "a small show of advanced abstractionists like Klee, Miro, Arp and Masson was added to the exhibit by Director Barr to show that some living painters are not very distant in spirit from the Mtoko masters."[53] (Note the elevation of the prehistoric makers to "Mtoko masters," a kind of Paleolithic precursor to both the European old masters and the "advanced abstractionists" of the twentieth century.) No installation shots of *Twelve Modern Paintings* survive, so it is difficult to judge the effect of the show as a companion to *Prehistoric Rock Pictures*. We do know that the facsimiles and photographs of rock pictures were displayed on the first three floors of the museum, while the modern exhibition was on the fourth. Thus, while modern and prehistoric art could be seen on the same visit to the museum, they could not be viewed side by side.

Some sense of the dialogue between modern and prehistoric pictures may be gleaned by comparing a view of one of the smaller galleries of *Prehistoric Rock Pictures* with a section of the previous year's landmark exhibition *Cubism and Abstract Art*. The photograph of *Cubism and Abstract Art* shows a two-part carved wooden biomorph by Henry Moore on a plinth and six works by Paul Klee on the wall. A painting such as Klee's *Abstract Trio* (1923) fairly represents the kind of "advanced abstraction" Barr would select for *Twelve Modern Paintings* the following year. Rather than claiming that Klee (or any other twentieth-century painter) was inspired by a specific rock art mural, Barr presented the discovery and reproduction of prehistoric art as a condition of modern life that shaped the use of simplified, distorted, and biomorphic forms in contemporary art. On his account, prehistoric art helped inspire modernist abstraction without fully explaining or exhausting it.

In his essay for the exhibition catalogue for *Cubism and Abstract Art*, Barr positioned abstraction as both a phenomenon unique to the twentieth century and as a pictorial project centuries in the making. By the early 1900s, he argued,

> the pictorial conquest of the external visual word had been completed and refined many times and in many different ways during the previous half millennium. The more adventurous and original artists had grown bored with painting facts. By a common and powerful impulse they were driven to abandon the imitation of natural appearance. "Abstract" is the term most frequently used to describe the more extreme effects of this impulse away from "nature."[54]

Barr's narrative of abstraction as a rejection of verisimilitude stretches back five hundred years, more or less to the Italian Renaissance. Had it reached back another millennium or so, that narrative might have addressed

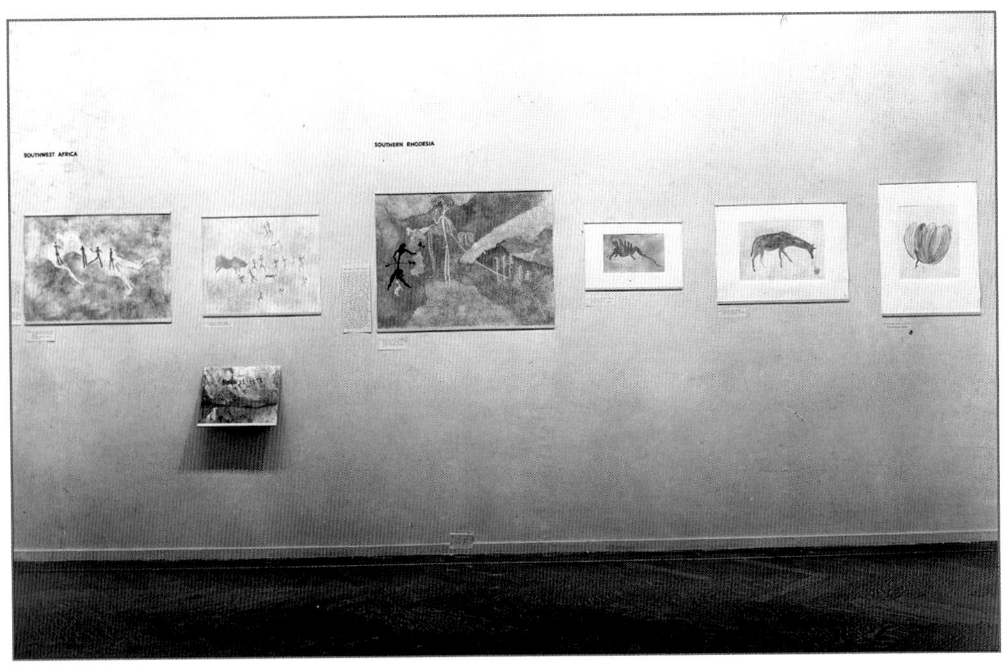

3.12 Installation view of the exhibition
*Prehistoric Rock Pictures in Europe and
Africa*, April 28–May 30, 1937. The Museum of
Modern Art, New York. Photographic
Archive. (Courtesy The Museum of Modern
Art Archives, New York.) Photographer:
Soichi Sunami. Digital image © The Museum
of Modern Art/Licensed by SCALA/Art
Resource, NY.

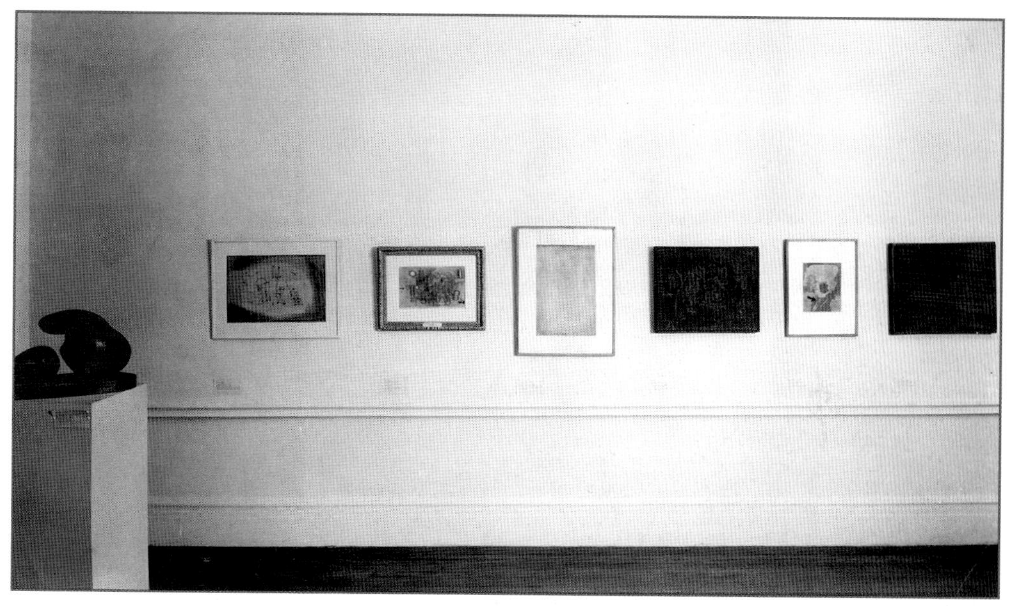

3.13 Installation view of the exhibition *Cubism and Abstract Art*, March 2–April 19, 1936. The Museum of Modern Art, New York. Photographic Archive. (Courtesy The Museum of Modern Art Archives, New York.) Photographer: Beaumont Newhall. Digital image © The Museum of Modern Art/ Licensed by SCALA/Art Resource, NY.

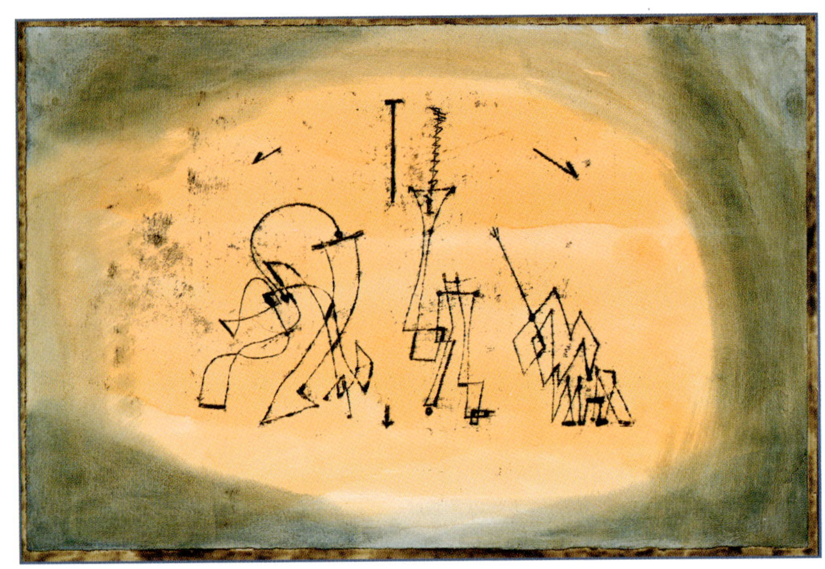

3.14 Paul Klee, *Abstract Trio*, 1923, watercolor and transferred printing ink on paper, bordered with gouache and ink, 12½ × 19¾ inches. © 2012 Artists Rights Society (ARS), New York. (The Berggruen Klee Collection, The Metropolitan Museum of Art, New York.) Image © The Metropolitan Museum of Art. Image source: Art Resource, NY.

the question of whether certain cave paintings qualified as abstract art. Several of the facsimiles in *Prehistoric Rock Pictures* include geometric forms for which no material referent or symbolic meaning has been deciphered. Here is how Douglas C. Fox, Frobenius's research assistant, described these forms in the MoMA catalogue: "There are other equally typical pictures for which we have no explanation. They show sausage or cigar-like forms standing neatly in rows. We call them *formlings*. Perhaps it may be that they portray the peculiar formations of the granite landscape or that the ones in which human figures occur reflect the belief, more current in the Near East, that man was born out of the rock or, in alluvial territories, was shaped in and of the earth."[55] Though Fox begins by asserting that "we have no explanation" for the formlings, he then proceeds to offer two—that they represent rock formations or that they illustrate an origin story about the birth of mankind out of rock and earth. To this day, the question of what the formlings represent is debated within archaeological circles. The formlings have variously been said to represent mud huts, cornfields, quivers, mats, xylophones, grain bins, beehives, clouds, pools of water, the human abdomen, and, most recently, termites and their nests.[56] Researchers remain convinced that the formlings must represent something—not an abstract idea or imaginary presence, but a tangible, nameable *thing*. Because no agreement has been reached as to the identity of that thing, "uneasiness and pessimism concerning the interpretation of these images has ... lingered into the present."[57] If the formlings continue to frustrate archaeological efforts to interpret them, perhaps it is because those efforts do not allow for the possibility of a genuinely abstract prehistoric picture—a picture of shapes and forms that cannot be deciphered or translated into anything else.

The perceptual challenge posed by the formlings is unwittingly made manifest in the *Prehistoric Rock Pictures* catalogue. Alone among the rock pictures illustrated, a Makumba cave mural consisting entirely of formlings has been divided, without comment, into two sections printed one above the other on a single catalogue page. A reader otherwise unfamiliar with the mural would likely assume that the original consisted of two stacked rectangles, rather than one continuous, horizontal field. In a further departure from the visual logic of the mural, each half of the illustration has been printed upside down and backward. Thus, the one entirely abstract picture in the catalogue is also the only work to have been subdivided, reversed, and upended in reproduction.[58] It is as though the difficulty posed by abstraction to twentieth-century viewers has disoriented the illustration and printing of the Makumba cave picture.[59]

In his essay "Cubism and Abstract Art," Barr wrote that "Abstract art today needs no defense. It has become one of the many ways to paint or carve or model. But it is not yet the kind of art which people like without some study and some sacrifice of prejudice."[60] Beyond the intrinsic ("exotic") appeal of cave paintings, the exhibition of *Prehistoric Rock Pictures* provided museum-goers with an alternative access route to twentieth-century abstraction. An access route is not, however, equivalent to a Rosetta stone. The museum did not offer the facsimiles of prehistoric art as decryption keys to unlock the hidden meaning of twentieth-century abstraction, nor did it present the modern paintings and sculptures as a means by which to decode rock art. Rather, the museum offered visitors the opportunity to engage in what Barr called a "comparison of various artistic experiences."[61]

In staging that comparison, MoMA refrained from side-by-side juxtaposition of prehistoric and modern art, of Paleolithic "then" and contemporary "now." And for good reason: there were no Paleolithic artifacts on display at the museum in 1937. The watercolor facsimiles and photographs of prehistoric art on the first three floors of the museum, like the paintings by André

Masson and Matisse on the fourth, were all products of the twentieth centu-ry. Indeed, given that the MoMA exhibition consisted of newly painted copies of the copies Barr had seen the previous summer in Frankfurt, the water-color facsimiles in *Prehistoric Rock Pictures* were almost certainly the most recent—and in this sense, the most contemporary—pictures on display at the time. Moreover, from our vantage point today, it is difficult to look at photo-graphs of museum galleries full of giant facsimiles without conjuring up later abstract paintings of similar scale by Jackson Pollock, Robert Motherwell, Adolph Gottlieb, and other members of the New York School. This is not to argue for a causal relationship between *Prehistoric Rock Pictures* in 1937 and abstract expressionist painting of the 1950s (though we do know that Gott-lieb, for one, attended the show). It is to point out, however, that the MoMA exhibition asked visitors to engage with abstract and quasi-abstract painting on a monumental scale. A string of similar invitations would be issued in the decades to follow.

While *Prehistoric Rock Pictures* and its companion show were on view in April and May 1937, MoMA offered an additional pair of exhibitions: *Paintings by Paul Cézanne from the Museum* showcased pictures from the permanent collection by the postimpressionist painter, while *Color Reproductions of Paintings by Cézanne* extended those holdings through the use of full-scale facsimiles. In this pair of exhibitions, reproductions were called upon only when an original painting was not available, and the copies (and copyists) had no independent standing at all. In *Prehistoric Rock Pictures*, the facsimiles functioned quite differently. The copies of cave paintings on display were not simply surrogates for unavailable original works. They were handmade pic-tures produced by living (if unnamed) artists, and they stood in not only for the Paleolithic and Mesolithic cave paintings on which they were based but also for the modern art they were said to resemble and inspire. In this sense,

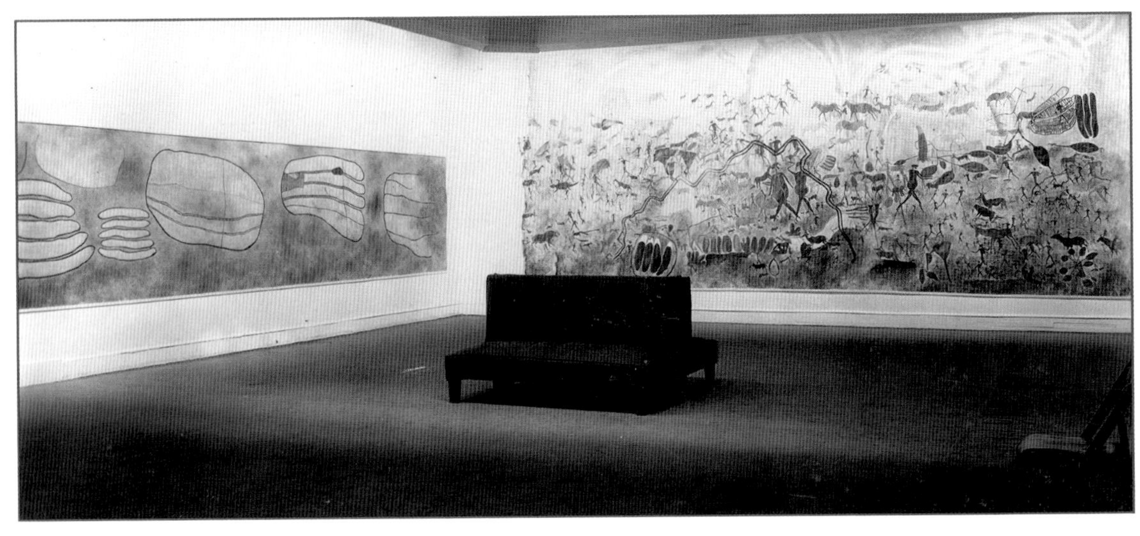

3.15 Installation view of the exhibition *Prehistoric Rock Pictures in Europe and Africa*, April 28–May 30, 1937. The Museum of Modern Art, New York. Photographic Archive. (Courtesy The Museum of Modern Art Archives, New York.) Photographer: Soichi Sunami. Digital image © The Museum of Modern Art/Licensed by SCALA/Art Resource, NY.

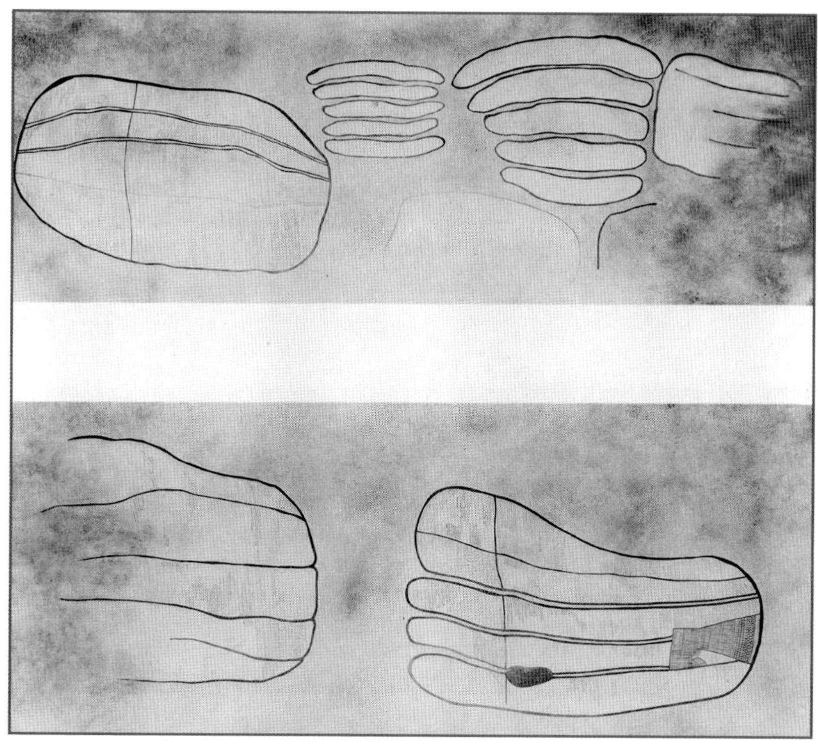

3.16 Detail from the exhibition catalogue for *Prehistoric Rock Pictures in Europe and Africa* (New York: Museum of Modern Art, 1937). (Courtesy The Museum of Modern Art Archives, New York.) Digital image © The Museum of Modern Art/Licensed by SCALA/ Art Resource, NY.

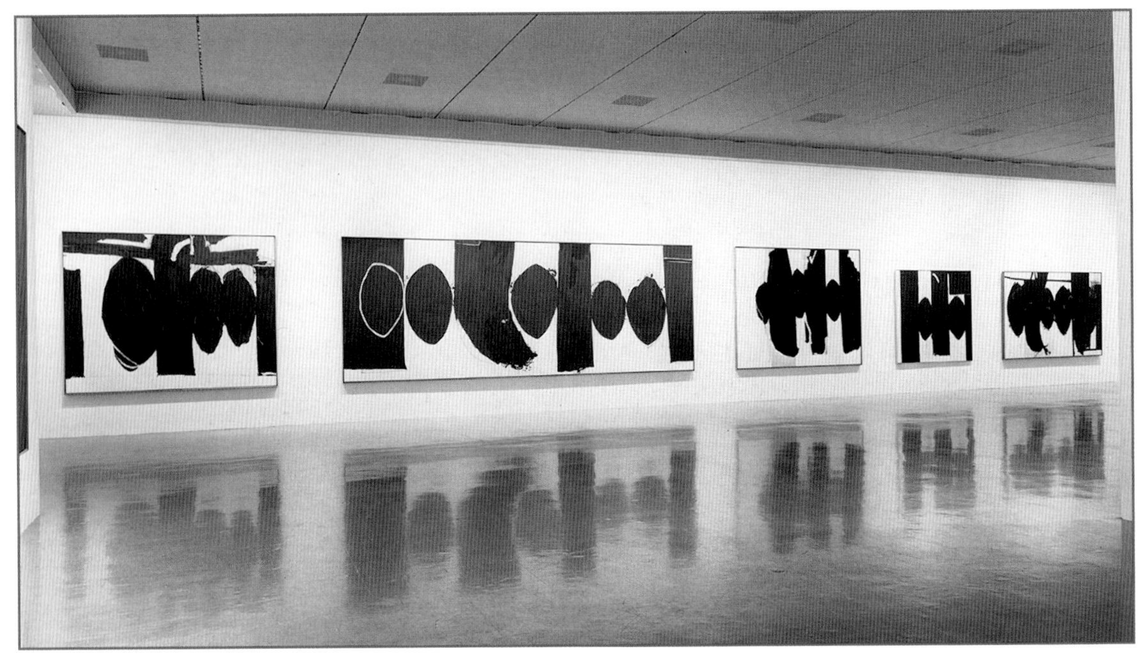

3.17 Installation view of the exhibition *Robert Motherwell*, October 1–November 18, 1965. The Museum of Modern Art, New York. Photographic Archive. (Courtesy The Museum of Modern Art Archives, New York.) Photographer: Rolf Petersen. Digital image © The Museum of Modern Art/Licensed by SCALA/Art Resource, NY.

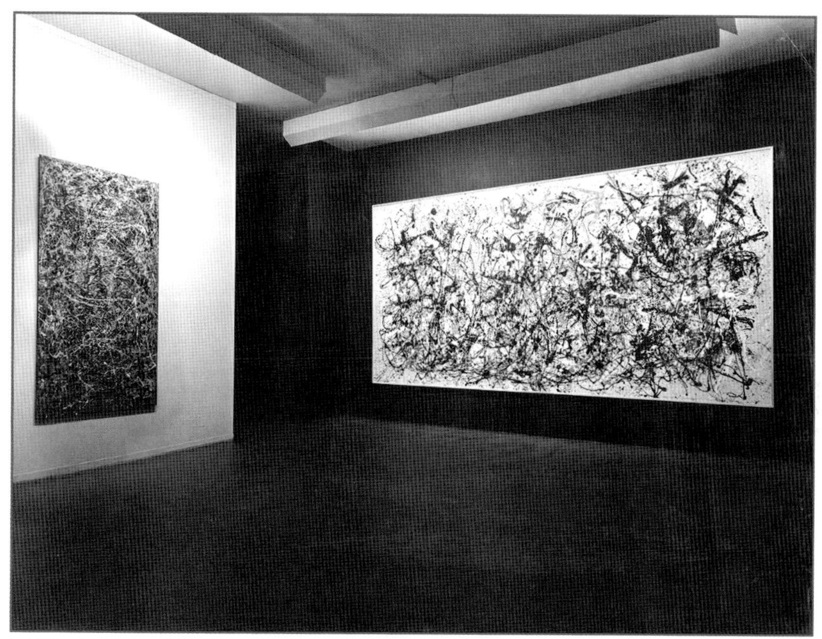

3.18 Installation view of the exhibition *15 Americans*, April 9–July 27, 1952. The Museum of Modern Art, New York. Photographic Archive. (Courtesy The Museum of Modern Art Archives, New York.) Photographer: Soichi Sunami. Digital image © The Museum of Modern Art/Licensed by SCALA/Art Resource, NY.

modernist abstraction and surrealist figuration could be seen at MoMA not only in the dozen twentieth-century paintings in the companion show on the fourth floor but also on the other three floors, in the floating biomorphs and enigmatic formlings of prehistoric cave paintings refashioned into works on canvas and exhibited within the institutional space of modern art. The 1937 exhibition offered a dialectic of prehistoric past and modern present in which the two could unexpectedly trade places—the most archaic forms of picture making becoming a sign for the most avant-garde art at the time. Crucially, there was a third term mediating between the contemporary and the prehistoric, namely the hand-painted facsimile.

From the Paleolithic to the Present

In an article published in the summer 1929 edition of the *Wellesley Alumnae Magazine*, Barr wrote,

> So far as art is concerned, the age in which we live is unique in at least one respect. We know, or at least can know if we take the trouble, far more about the art of the past than could any previous age. This is especially true of the modern artist who very frequently surrounds himself with a bewildering variety of photographs and books on the art of any period from the Paleolithic to the present and of any nationality from Aztec to Cambodian to East African negro. To understand the modern artist it is necessary in many cases to understand what he admires, whether it be a Tang figurine, a French primitive, or Raphael. Now understanding doesn't necessarily imply archeological knowledge, but it does require visual experience, and more valuable still, *comparison* of various artistic experiences. For this purpose, museums are valuable, but they're not always available. Fortunately, like the artist, we can own books, and look

at reproductions and enrich ourselves and prepare ourselves for a real understanding of that extraordinarily interesting and exciting period of art, the early twentieth century.[62]

Rather than searching "archaeologically" for a singular source (whether Paleolithic or French primitive, Aztec or East African) to unlock the meaning of a modern artwork, Barr directs our attention to the wider field of images that the twentieth-century artist inhabits and admires, to the broadly visual culture that shapes the making of contemporary art. On this account, the relation between modern art and the historical past cannot be traced along a linear path of stylistic influence or chronological sequence. Nor, for that matter, can the relation between Western and non-Western cultures. To understand twentieth-century art, we must engage in a *comparison* (the italics are Barr's) not only of individual artworks but also of the visual experiences they provoke. The artwork stands, then, not only as an envoy from the past but also as a living force—a visual experience—in the present. Though a direct visual encounter with the artwork is preferable, it is not always possible. For this reason, prints and illustrated books, as well as photographs and facsimiles, are necessary. Recall in this context Barr's gift (with Jere Abbott) of the *Dial* portfolio *Living Art* to the Fogg Art Museum at Harvard in 1926 and his exhibition of *Reproductions of Famous Works of Modern Artists* at Wellesley College in 1927.

Throughout the 1930s, MoMA sponsored exhibitions of both premodern and non-Western art, including shows of Aztec, Mayan, and Incan art (1933) as well as exhibitions such as *African Negro Art* (1935) and *Prehistoric Rock Pictures*. In other words, Barr's references to Paleolithic, Aztec, and East African art in his Wellesley essay anticipated the content of specific shows that would be mounted by MoMA during his tenure as director.

Rather than searching for iconographical sources, Barr sought to position modern art in broader dialogue with the historical and, on occasion, the prehistorical past. This dialogue was mediated by new scientific findings (such as the discovery of Paleolithic and Mesolithic rock art in the late nineteenth and early twentieth centuries), enhanced practices of visual reproduction (such as improved technologies of printing and lithography), and shifting social and political conditions. For Barr, art was more than a series of relics lodged in the distant past. On the one hand, the history of art was continually being reshaped by the conditions of the present. On the other, no genuine understanding of contemporary art could emerge in the absence of historical consciousness. In 1932, he wrote: "Modern painting may seem confusing but it must be remembered that the whole history of art as well as much scientific and psychological knowledge is available to the contemporary painter. He picks and chooses what he wishes."[63] By acquainting ourselves with the histories and knowledge that matter most to the living artist, viewers may come to understand an otherwise inscrutable work of contemporary art. And in doing so, we may, according to Barr, "give the picture, itself, a chance to live!"[64] His pursuit of "the whole history of art" had brought Paleolithic pictures to MoMA in 1937; three years later, Barr ventured into what many regarded as an even more surprising territory for a museum devoted to modern art.

"Old (and New) Masters"

In January 1940, MoMA mounted *Italian Masters*, an exhibition of Renaissance and baroque art on special loan from the Italian government. In contrast to *Persian Fresco Painting* and *Prehistoric Rock Pictures*, *Italian Masters* was predicated on the authenticity and unique aesthetic value of the artworks in it. The show featured world-famous paintings such as Sandro Botticelli's *Birth of Venus*, Raphael's *Madonna of the Chair*, and Titian's *Portrait of Pope Paul*

III, as well as a Michelangelo bas-relief of the Madonna and Child in marble, none of which had ever before been displayed in New York City. In installing *Italian Masters*, Barr placed the works "in almost perfect chronological sequence" across thirteen galleries on the museum's second floor. No natural light was permitted in the galleries, and only one or two of the available walls in each room were utilized for displaying art. Large areas of the galleries were left in relative darkness so as to showcase, by way of contrast, the dramatically lit paintings and sculptures. The four works Barr considered genuine masterpieces—those by Andrea del Verrocchio, Botticelli, Michelangelo, and Titian—were given galleries to themselves.[65]

MoMA successfully promoted the show as a once-in-a-lifetime opportunity for New York's museum-goers: *Italian Masters* became the most popular exhibition in the museum's history, attracting nearly 300,000 visitors during its three-month run. To accommodate public demand, the museum remained open until 10 p.m. (rather than its usual closing time of 6 p.m.) during the exhibition, which was also extended by two weeks.[66] According to Barr's own account of the show, "The rather severe interior of the Museum galleries was not very noticeable since only the walls on which pictures hung were lit and the great crowds prevent any sense of barrenness."[67] The spareness of the exhibition space was offset by the throngs of spectators streaming through. In this way, the presentation of Renaissance artworks was animated by the living presence of contemporary audiences.

The austerity of Barr's curatorial approach is thrown into greater relief when compared to the presentation of the same exhibition at the Art Institute of Chicago, its immediately previous venue.[68] The Art Institute covered its gallery walls in richly patterned wallpapers and borrowed wrought iron candlesticks from St. Thomas the Apostle Church to impart a sense of old world grandeur.[69] An encyclopedic (rather than predominantly modern)

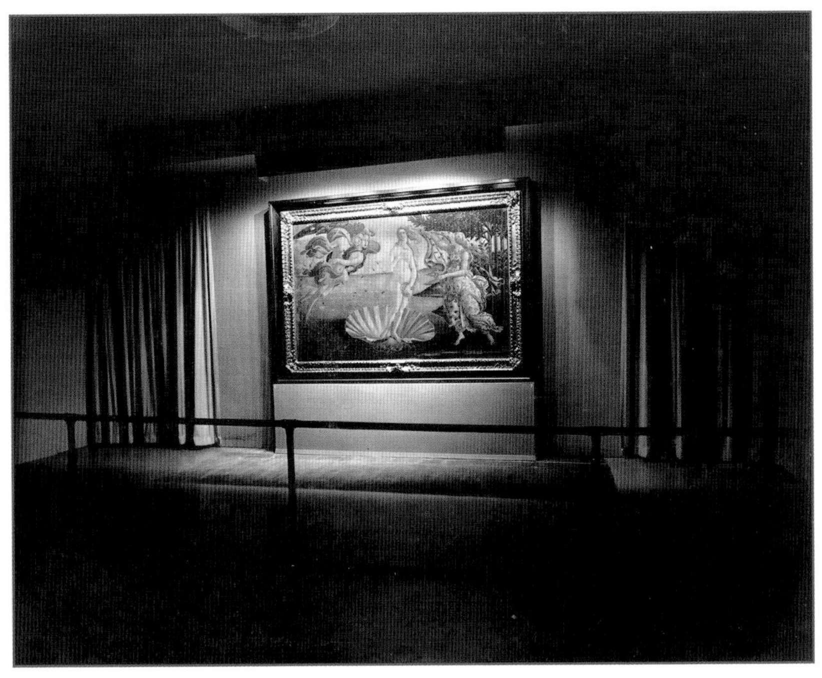

3.19 Installation view of the exhibition *Italian Masters*, January 26–April 7, 1940. View of Botticelli's *Birth of Venus*. The Museum of Modern Art, New York. Photographic Archive. (Courtesy The Museum of Modern Art Archives, New York.) Photographer: Soichi Sunami. Digital image © The Museum of Modern Art/Licensed by SCALA/Art Resource, NY.

museum, the Art Institute of Chicago sought to suggest the richness of Renaissance décor while stopping short of full period-room reconstruction. "The exhibition has been gloriously installed," wrote the critic for the *Chicago Tribune*, who further noted that the galleries "have been redecorated in a manner that resembles sixteenth century damask, or brocade, as the case may be and hung with the Italian works."[70] Edward Alden Jewell of the *New York Times* was similarly captivated by the manner in which the rooms in Chicago "simulated those of rich, sedate Italian palaces" and helped to create an "atmosphere that was firmly yet unobtrusively and always tastefully Renaissance. Viewing them one could imagine these works as they might have appeared in the halls of the Medicis and Borgias, related to a period, to the life of a period."[71]

Jewell admired the decorous, appropriately Italianate effect of the show as installed in Chicago. Yet he was even more exuberant about the countervailing strategy taken up in the New York installation:

At the Museum of Modern Art the whole effect is once more radically changed. Now there might never have been a sixteenth-century palace. There might never have been, at least in any comprehensive sense, a Renaissance. Aside from the famous objects themselves, the sole protagonists in this striking museum drama are space and light, both of which would be *de trop* in the cluttered gloom of, for instance, the Uffizi. What happens is astonishing. In rigorous detachment, divorced from all the past and reinstated as in a kind of timeless voice, these works of art begin to live a life of their own. This each perforce must do, or cease to be. It seems a kind of supreme last test—the most dramatic moment they have known in centuries.[72]

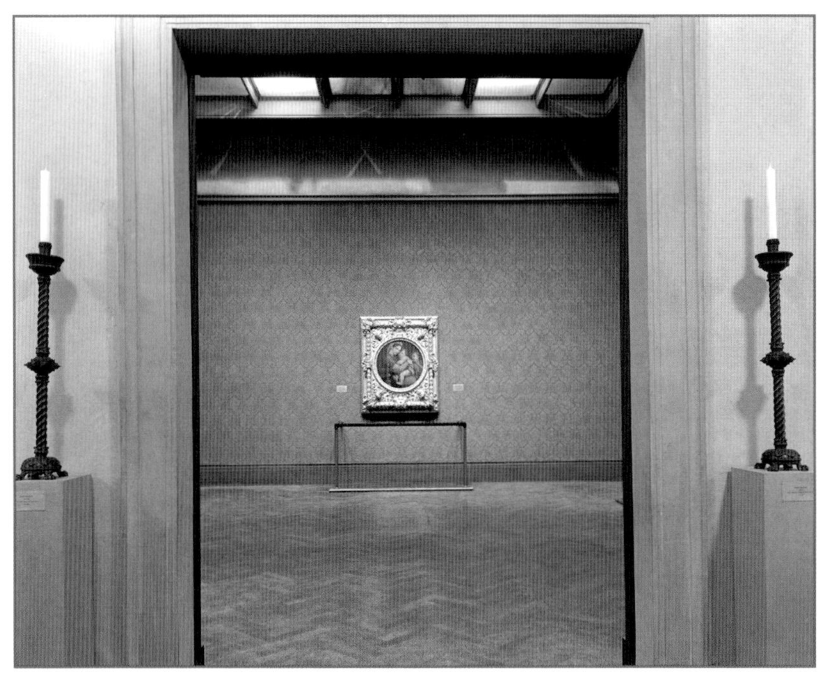

3.20 Installation view of the exhibition
Masterpieces of Italian Art, 1939. Art
Institute of Chicago. (Courtesy Art Institute
of Chicago Archives.)

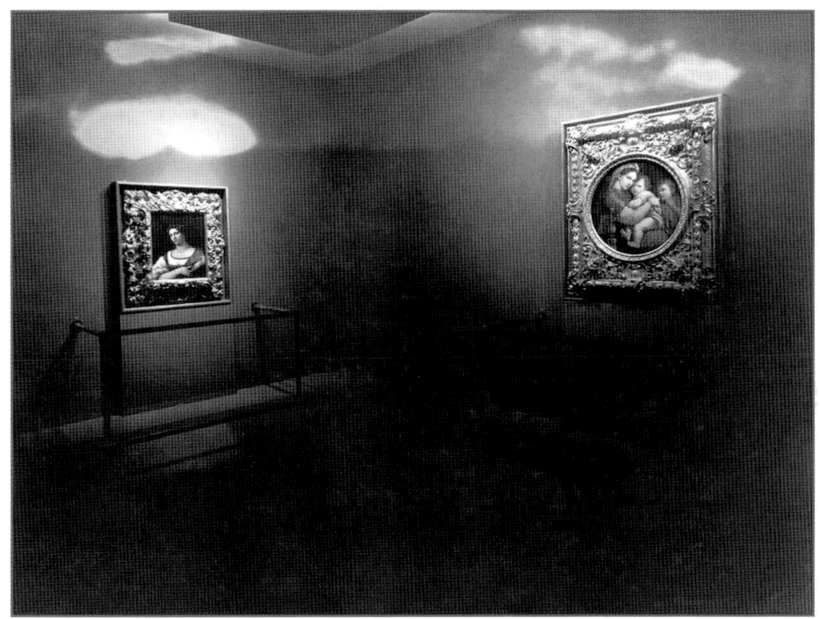

3.21 Installation view of the exhibition
Italian Masters, January 26–April 7, 1940. The
Museum of Modern Art, New York. Photo-
graphic Archive. (Courtesy The Museum of
Modern Art Archives, New York.) Photog-
rapher: Soichi Sunami. Digital image © The
Museum of Modern Art/Licensed by SCALA/
Art Resource, NY.

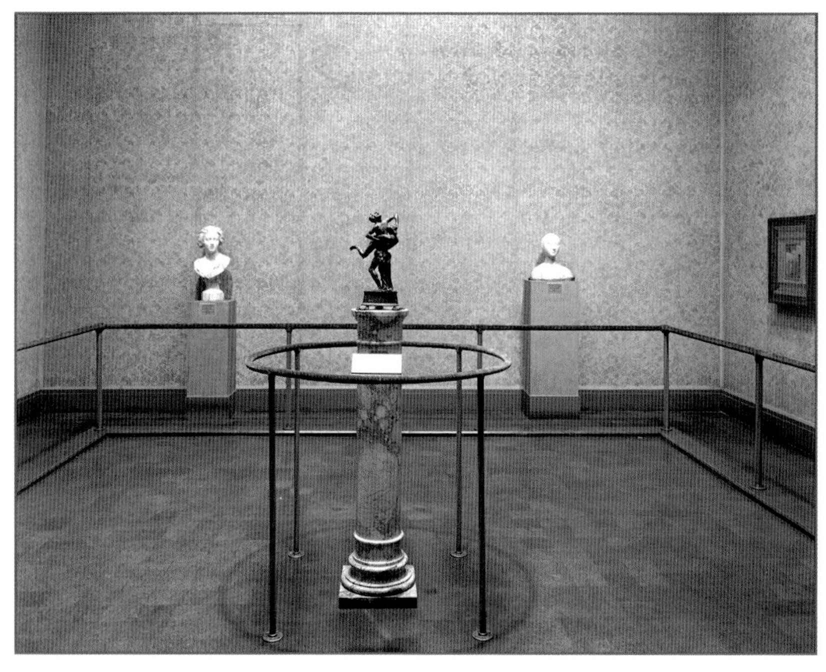

3.22 Installation view of the exhibition
Masterpieces of Italian Art, 1939. Art Institute
of Chicago. (Courtesy Art Institute of
Chicago Archives.)

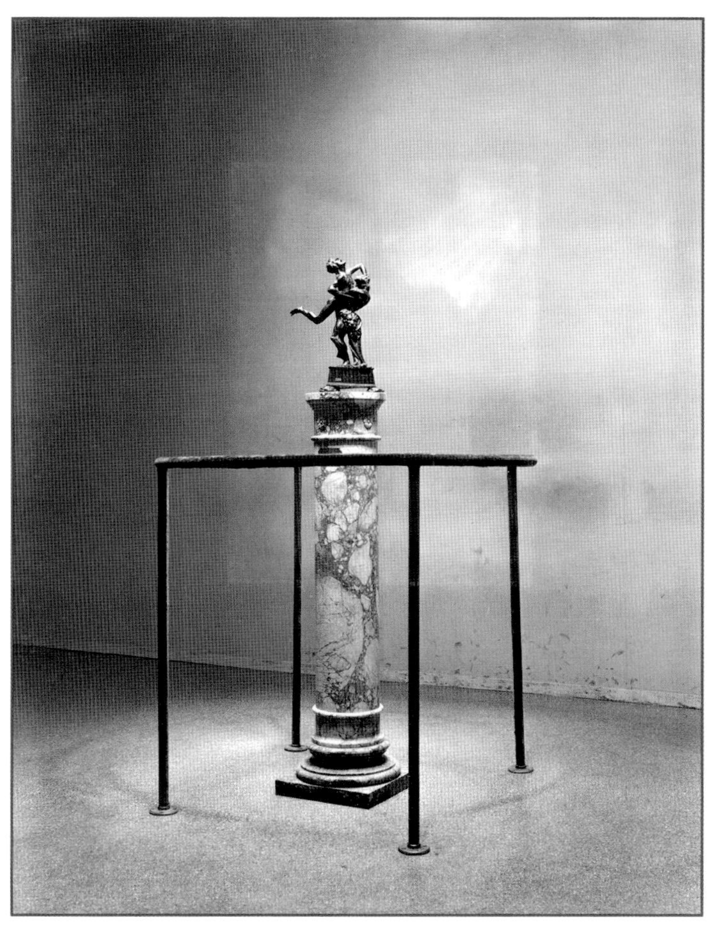

3.23 Installation view of the exhibition *Italian Masters*, January 26–April 7, 1940. The Museum of Modern Art, New York. Photographic Archive. (Courtesy The Museum of Modern Art Archives, New York.) Photographer: Soichi Sunami. Digital image © The Museum of Modern Art/ Licensed by SCALA/Art Resource, NY.

For Jewell, the minimalist "drama" of light and space revives the works in *Italian Masters* to such an extent that they "begin to live a life of their own." The Renaissance paintings and sculptures are all but reborn in the starkly modern environment they inhabit at MoMA, in which each work is presented as a freestanding aesthetic object. According to Barr's notes on the installation, "No effort of any kind was made to suggest a period atmosphere, either by wall coverings or accessories. In other words, the works of art were considered as objects valuable in themselves and isolated from their original period."[73]

Within the space of MoMA's galleries, Barr stripped the Renaissance works of any historical or decorative context that might intrude upon the visual experience of the objects "in themselves." Though he could do little to offset the ornate frames in which several of the paintings were lodged or the marble base on which the Pollaiuolo bronze of *Hercules and Antaeus* rested, Barr otherwise sought to surround the works with as much cool emptiness as possible.

In MoMA's press release for the exhibition, board president Stephen Clark addressed the apparent contradiction of presenting fifteenth- to eighteenth-century art at a museum dedicated to the modern:

> Our acceptance of this exhibition of Italian masterpieces does not indicate a change in the established policy of the Museum or any shifting of its emphasis on the contemporary arts. Our primary interest is, and will continue to be, in the field of modern art. Great masterpieces of art are not, however, bound by any period and the influence of the Italian Renaissance and Baroque traditions upon the modern artist is fundamental and continuous. We are, therefore, glad to be given the opportunity to show these priceless masterpieces to the public of New York City.[74]

Unbound from any one historical period, the Italian masterpieces are said to embody a "continuous and fundamental" tradition on which the modern artist draws. By way of tracing that tradition, Barr produced the diagram "Italian Painting and Sculpture, 1300–1800" for the inside front cover of the catalogue. Comprising broken and solid lines pointing in multiple directions, the diagram recalls, albeit in slightly less complicated form, Barr's famous developmental flow-chart of abstraction from his 1936 *Cubism and Abstract Art* exhibition. As though anticipating a comparison of Renaissance to modern art, Barr included a second diagram on the inside back cover of the *Italian Masters* catalogue, tracing how modern art derived from "three great traditions of European painting" rooted in Italy.

By way of bringing the second diagram to life, Barr and his curatorial staff paired *Italian Masters* with *Modern Masters from European and American Collections*, which featured canvases by Gauguin, Georges Seurat, and Edgar Degas, as well as two paintings each by Pierre-Auguste Renoir, Cézanne, and van Gogh. Save for Gauguin, all of these artists appear as descendants of Giotto on Barr's genealogical chart. In mounting the *Modern Masters* show as a companion to *Italian Masters*, MoMA revived the comparative strategy used for *Prehistoric Rock Pictures* three years earlier. In this case, however, abstract painting and sculpture were largely avoided in favor of figurative works that could relate more persuasively to the representational form and humanist focus of Renaissance art.

Writing in the *New York Times*, Jewell described *Modern Masters* as "a small group of nineteenth and twentieth century paintings and sculpture displayed on the first floor. The experience proves mildly suggestive in a general way and makes possible a few striking individual juxtapositions."[75] While Jewell found the Renaissance and baroque works "astonishing" in their newly modern surrounds, *Modern Masters* he deems only "mildly suggestive." It

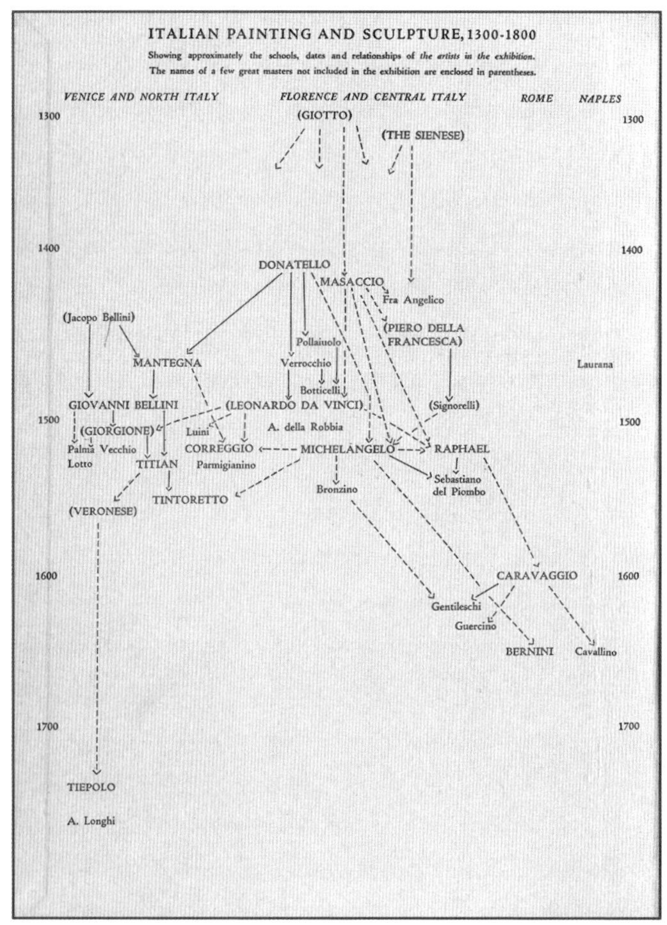

3.24 Alfred H. Barr Jr., chart of "Italian Painting and Sculpture, 1300–1800," exhibition catalogue for *Italian Masters* (New York: Museum of Modern Art, 1940), inside front cover. (Courtesy The Museum of Modern Art Archives, New York.) Digital image © The Museum of Modern Art/Licensed by SCALA/ Art Resource, NY.

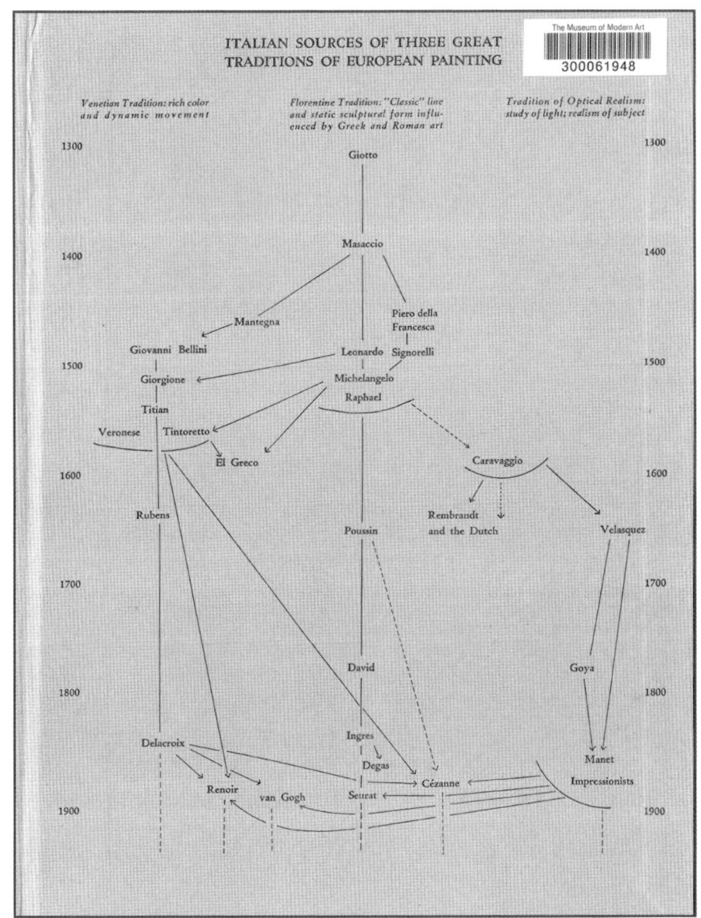

3.25 Alfred H. Barr Jr., chart of "Italian Sources of Three Great Traditions of European Painting," exhibition catalogue for *Italian Masters* (New York: Museum of Modern Art, 1940), inside back cover. (Courtesy The Museum of Modern Art Archives, New York.) Digital image © The Museum of Modern Art/Licensed by SCALA/Art Resource, NY.

is as though the Italian works have been so reanimated by their display at MoMA that there is no need for a literal comparison to modern painting and sculpture. Though Jewell refers to "individual juxtapositions" of recent and Renaissance artworks, the two exhibitions were on different floors of the museum. Visitors could not engage in a direct comparison of, say, Michelangelo's marble *Madonna and Child* and Jacob Epstein's bronze of the same subject from roughly four hundred years later.

In other ways, however, the museum was far from subtle in setting up the shows as pendants. The two exhibition catalogues shared the same dimensions and each featured a color reproduction of a single painting (Fra Angelico's *The Naming of John the Baptist* and Henri Rousseau's *Sleeping Gypsy*, respectively) against a somberly hued monochrome ground. In the foreword to *Modern Masters*, curator Dorothy C. Miller characterized the relation between the two exhibitions as a kind of competition:

> Imaginary contests between the heroes of antiquity and their modern counterparts have always had a certain fascination. Here, within the Museum of Modern Art, some such trial of strength may actually take place, for the Museum, believing in the power and quality of the modern artist, has not hesitated to accept the challenge made possible by its act of hospitality toward the Italian masters. Whichever side, the old or the new, seems to triumph, one fact is sure: the great indebtedness of the modern masters to the work of their ancestors of the Italian Renaissance and Baroque—a debt that is continually being paid not only by the explicit homage which modern artists so often offer to the past but by the ever-changing illumination which the art of the living throws upon the art of the dead.[76]

By way of further dramatizing the "imaginary contest" between the two exhibitions, MoMA asked visitors to vote for their favorite artworks in each.

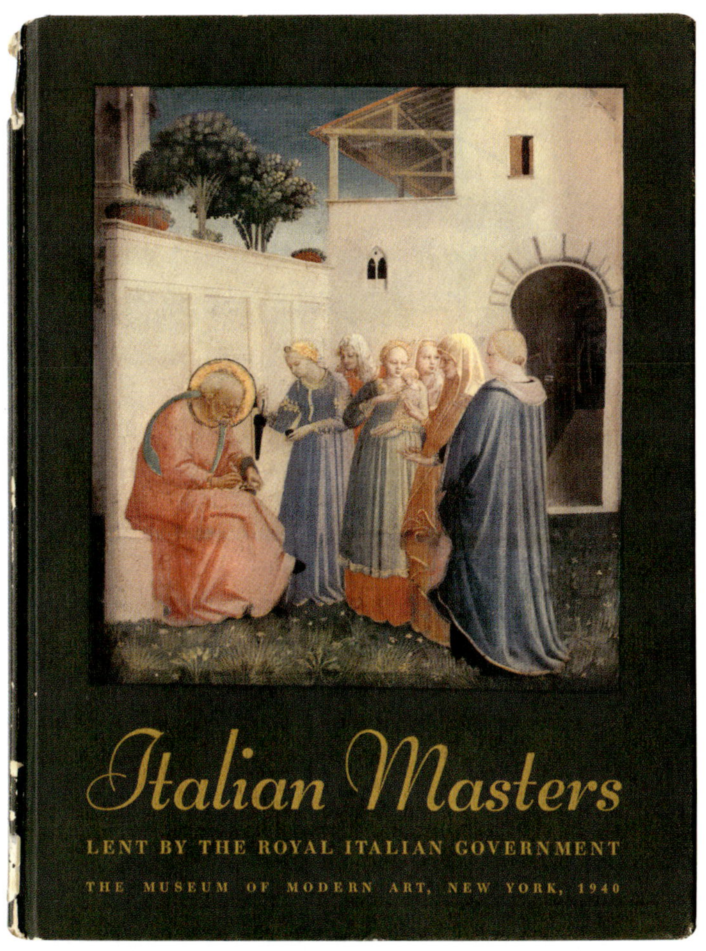

3.26 Exhibition catalogue for *Italian Masters*
(New York: Museum of Modern Art, 1940),
cover. (Courtesy The Museum of Modern
Art Archives, New York.) Digital image © The
Museum of Modern Art/Licensed by SCALA/
Art Resource, NY.

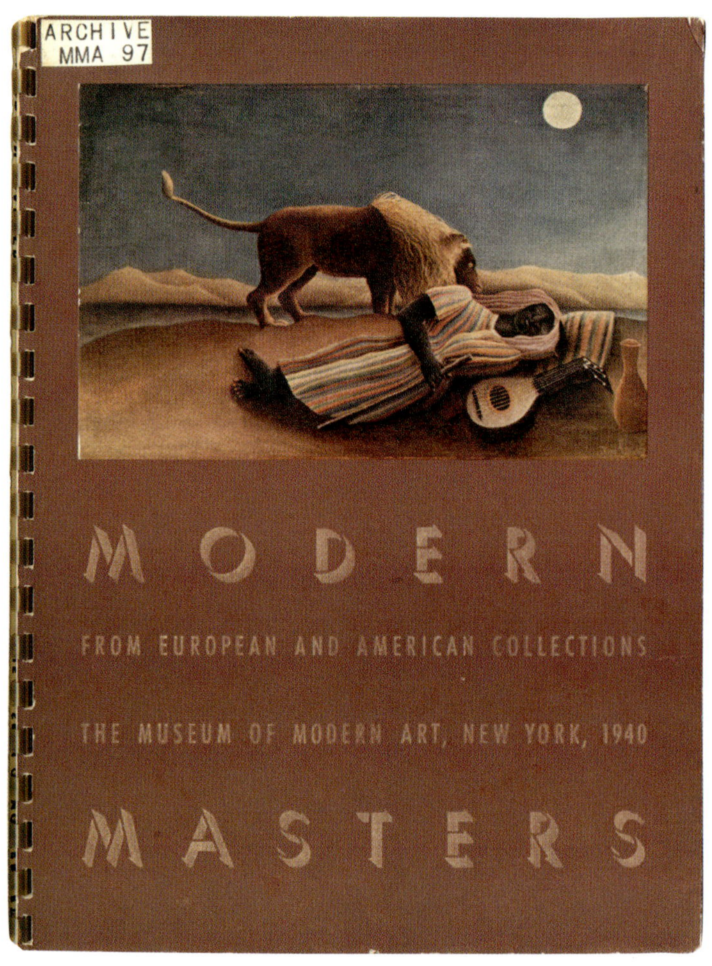

3.27 Exhibition catalogue for *Modern Masters from European and American Collections* (New York: Museum of Modern Art, 1940), cover. (Courtesy The Museum of Modern Art Archives, New York.) Digital image © The Museum of Modern Art/ Licensed by SCALA/Art Resource, NY.

Upon entering the shows, viewers received a checklist of the works on display and were encouraged to rank them in order of preference.[77] Barr was especially pleased that Titian's *Portrait of Pope Paul III* was voted the public's favorite in *Italian Masters* rather than, as had been widely anticipated, Botticelli's *Birth of Venus* (which came in third behind Raphael's *Madonna of the Chair*). The top three vote-getters among the modern works were, in order of popularity, Renoir's *Little Margot Berard* (1879), James McNeill Whistler's *Symphony in White, No. 1: The White Girl* (1862), and Thomas Eakins's *Leticia Wilson Jordan Bacon* (1888).[78] None of the twentieth-century works on display—not the Picasso, Matisse, Joan Miró, or Edouard Vuillard paintings nor the Constantin Brancusi bronze—ranked among the public's favorites. Perhaps the concurrent *Italian Masters* exhibition had skewed the preferences of visitors toward the older art on display in *Modern Masters*. Or perhaps the School of Paris was still too abstract or abstruse on formal grounds to elicit popular appeal.

It did not, in any case, escape the notice of Italian officials that none of its nation's artists were included in *Modern Masters*.[79] Shortly after the show opened, the Italian government proposed an exhibition of exclusively Italian twentieth-century art that it would organize for MoMA. Barr wrote a carefully worded response declining the offer. In doing so, he cited concerns "about the unavoidable uncertainties caused by the war, which indeed may considerably involve both Italy and the Unites States before the exhibition could be arranged."[80] As Barr's letter suggests, the *Italian Masters* and *Modern Masters* exhibitions coincided with an extremely fraught moment in political relations between the United States and Italy. The "Royal Italian Government" that lent the Renaissance and baroque works to MoMA was ruled only nominally by King Victor Emmanuel III. Military and political power was vested in the Italian prime minister and Fascist Party leader Benito Mussolini. In the wake of Adolf Hitler's invasion of Poland in September 1939, and the consequent declaration of war on Germany by France and England, both Italy and the United States were being drawn more deeply into the European conflict. On January 8, 1940, the *New York Times* published an article titled "Italy Is Preparing for Spread of War" which warned that "The frequent consultations that Signor Mussolini is having with military leaders leave no doubt that Italy is engaged in an extensive reorganization of the fighting forces. Moreover, these meetings support the view . . . that the European conflict will spread to other European sectors and that negotiations for peace are farther away than ever."[81]

Given the escalating crisis in Europe, the opening of *Italian Masters* on January 26 could hardly avoid political overtones. Consider, for example, the radio address made on the occasion by Italy's ambassador to the United States, Prince Ascanio Colonna. Delivered in his native tongue, the ambassador's remarks were not broadcast to American audiences but were heard throughout Italy on EIAR, the official radio station of the Fascist Party:

> [I]t is not without meaning that the masterpieces which originate from our ancient churches, from our great museums, from our palaces with all their glorious memories should be gathered, at the behest of the leader of Fascist Italy, in this city which is rightly considered as the most impressive accomplishment of the labor, the daring, and the art of modern times.
>
> This tie that is being thus established between the ancient and the modern, between the human genius of the glorious past and the dynamism of our hard times, cannot but give to men a stronger perception of their duties and a deeper sense of pride and responsibility in the defense of Western Civilization of which these masterpieces are amongst the highest expressions. . . . The long voyage that these pictures and

statues had to make in order to come to the United States is probably their last one, and, therefore, in the future it will only be possible to admire them under those skies that have nourished the dream of their creators.[82]

The ambassador aligns the Renaissance masterworks on display at MoMA with a defense of Western Civilization and a discourse of nationalist patrimony ("our ancient churches, our great museums, our palaces"). Mussolini likewise argued that the triumph of Fascism would entail the rebirth of Italy as a cultural and imperial power, a modern-day revival of the ancient Roman empire. The *Italian Masters* exhibition might thus be seen as an example of what the art historian Emily Braun has called "the Fascist appropriation of the Renaissance—the most prestigious period in the history of the fine arts to which Italy could lay exclusive claim."[83]

When Ambassador Colonna mentioned that "the long voyage that these pictures and statues had to make … is probably their last one," he was referring to a law passed in June 1939 that restricted the loan or export of any Italian artwork whose absence would "represent a substantial loss to the national patrimony."[84] Known as the Bottai Law, this policy was part of a broader set of restrictions, which included prohibitions on intermarriage and the exclusion of Jews from public schools, imposed by the Fascist government as a "defense of the race."[85] The effort to legislate racial purity within the Italian body politic went hand-in-hand with an insistence on a national art cleansed of foreign influence and intermixing.[86]

The political implications of the *Italian Masters* exhibition were left largely unacknowledged by the American press in 1940.[87] Newspaper stories were far more focused on the awesome monetary value of the art on display than on any symbolic message conveyed from Mussolini.

The most serious criticism of *Italian Masters* came not from the press or the public but from the Museum's own Advisory Committee. The committee deemed *Italian Masters* a betrayal of MoMA's mission insofar as "an exhibition of old masters could do nothing to develop an interest in modern art" and therefore "could not be justified in the eyes of the public and would result in more damage to the Museum's reputation than gain." In a highly unusual gesture, the committee voted to censure the exhibition.[88] In response, Barr wrote a letter to the committee's chair in which he sought to explain the decision to proceed with the show:

> I realize that the Advisory Committee feels that the exhibition has little do with modern art or the Museum's program. I must confess that I do not see the exhibition in this light. We have in the past shown African negro art of the last four or five centuries, Pre-Columbian art of five to ten centuries ago and prehistoric rock paintings, some of which dated from 20,000 or so B.C. Each of these exhibitions was of great interest in itself and was justified because it seemed to throw some light upon twentieth century taste and, in some cases, had a direct influence on the "art of our time" (or at least the painting of twenty years ago).[89]

Barr defended the display of premodern art and artifacts at MoMA on two counts. First, the works shown were of "great interest" in their own right; second, they illuminated some aspect of contemporary taste. Even here, Barr was careful to distinguish between the "painting of twenty years ago" and "art of our time" (that is, 1940), perhaps because the twentieth-century works he had in mind were cubist, Dada, and surrealist works of approximately two decades prior.

One particularly prominent member of the Advisory Committee, cultural impresario Lincoln Kirstein, so disapproved of the plan to mount *Italian*

Masters that he sent a letter of objection under separate cover from the committee's official censure: "I cannot but think that the publicity given the Italian pictures would not also give rise to the greatest protest on the part of people who are already carping against the Museum. This would be a terrific handle for all those who insist that the Museum has not got the courage of its convictions, that it is not good to American artists, and in this instance is directly against its own policy of being a museum for contemporary work."[90] Kirstein was reacting against MoMA's practice throughout the 1930s and early 1940s of situating modern art within a wide field of cultural production and world history. Barr argued that shows such as *Prehistoric Rock Pictures* and *Italian Masters* contributed to "a real understanding of that extraordinarily interesting and exciting period of art, the early twentieth century."[91] Detractors like Kirstein believed, however, that MoMA was delving all too liberally into nonmodern, non-Western, and non-art exhibitions. And the complaint they most frequently leveled against the museum was that it was, as Kirstein put it, "not good to American artists." Both *Italian Masters* and *Modern Masters* would be adduced as cases in point.

How Modern?

Ten days after the *Italian Masters* show closed in April 1940, approximately thirty members of an organization called American Abstract Artists (AAA) picketed MoMA to protest their perceived exclusion from its program of exhibitions.[92] Their central grievance was that MoMA had ignored the vanguard efforts of living American artists in favor of foreign, out-of-date, or crassly populist exhibitions. AAA staged its picket to coincide with the opening of *PM Competition: The Artist as Reporter*, a competition organized by MoMA and the tabloid newspaper *PM* in an effort to discover "fresh new talent" in the field of journalistic illustration.[93] That the museum would sponsor a show of visual reportage was particularly galling to the members of AAA who believed that realist modes of illustration were antithetical to the spirit of any genuinely modern art. According to AAA member George L. K. Morris, the group "felt that if the Museum of Modern Art had space for newspaper sketches it certainly wasn't true that they had no space for abstract American art."[94] And if *The Artist as Reporter* was a slap in the face to contemporary abstract artists, so too was *Italian Masters*, which Morris described as "the most astonishing reversal of the museum's entire history."[95]

A flyer designed by AAA member Ad Reinhardt and titled "How Modern Is the Museum of Modern Art?" was distributed during the picket. It sarcastically suggested that, as the museum was now in the business of exhibiting old master paintings ("Caravaggio, Raphael, Bronzino!"), why not open its doors to the entire history of civilization ("How easy to justify a Praxiteles show! How revolutionary the Egyptians! And an Eighteenth Century JAPANESE!")? This last reference alluded to an exhibition of woodblock prints by the Edo-period theater artist Sharaku that had opened at the museum two weeks prior to the protest.[96] At a moment of mounting political tensions between Japan and the United States, printing the word "Japanese" in capital letters underscored the status of the Sharaku exhibition—if not of the museum that was sponsoring it—as un-American. Also running throughout the flyer was the suggestion that MoMA was more concerned with "show business" and the generation of revenue than with serious curatorial display. Among the questions printed on the flyer: "Is the Museum a Business?" and, in smaller type, "How about Billy (Acquacade) Rose as the newest trustee?" By nominating a nightclub promoter and vaudeville producer to the MoMA board, the flyer lampooned the purported stature of both the museum and its trustees.

Reinhardt used eight different typefaces for the handbill, including one reminiscent of medieval manuscript illumination, as well as various font sizes

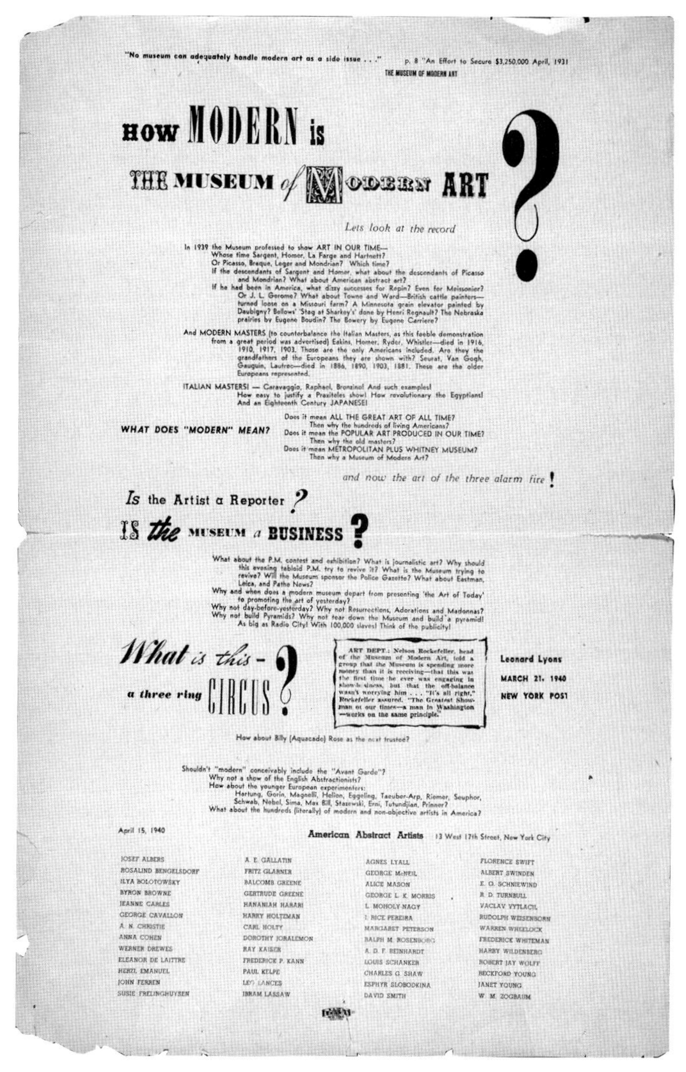

3.28 *How Modern Is the Museum of Modern Art?* Flyer created by the American Abstract Artists group, April 15, 1940. Charles Green Shaw papers. (Courtesy Archives of American Art, Smithsonian Institution.)

and indentations of text. These typographic shifts wittily underscored the message that MoMA was both inconsistent in its policies and outmoded in its exhibitions and collection. Under the headline "Artists Denounce Modern Museum," the *New York Times* described the flyer's critique of MoMA: "Even the curlicue type in which the challenge was set expressed the contempt of the rebels, for it conjured up the velvet antiquity and the theatrical bill posters of the Gay Nineties."[97]

For the members of AAA, the problem was not that MoMA ignored American art altogether; it was that the American art exhibited at the museum was either too old, too conventional, or too popular to qualify as authentically modern.[98] The flyer was especially scathing about the geriatric roster of American painters in the *Modern Masters* exhibition ("Eakins, Homer, Ryder, Whistler—died in 1916, 1910, 1917, 1903. Those are the only Americans included. Are they the grandfathers of the Europeans they are shown with?"). AAA sought to challenge both the association of American art with nineteenth-century academic realism and the alignment of twentieth-century abstraction with the European avant-garde. AAA framed MoMA as disloyal to the American "Avant Garde" in its own backyard. And underwriting this critique was the claim that American abstract painting and sculpture genuinely qualified as "the Art of Today" while the work of the foreign, dead, or otherwise outdated artists shown at MoMA did not.

Postscript: Modern Art, Five Thousand Years Ago (1946)

Six years after AAA posed the question, "How Modern Is the Museum of Modern Art?" the museum proposed an unlikely answer. In 1946, MoMA launched a multimillion-dollar fundraising campaign for a proposed addition to its building on Fifty-third Street.[99] The brochure announcing the campaign featured three multicolored images captioned "Modern art 5,000 years ago . . . ,"

"Modern art yesterday . . . ," "and Modern art TODAY." At the left, reproduced on a black ground, was a detail from a watercolor facsimile after an African cave painting featured in *Prehistoric Rock Pictures*. Much like the exhibition itself, the notion that cave paintings were "Modern art 5,000 years ago" simultaneously updated the prehistoric and backdated the modern. At the center, "Modern art yesterday" was illustrated, against a light pegboard ground, by a worm's-eye view of the terra-cotta figure of the angel Gabriel from an *Annunciation* group by the Florentine sculptor Andrea della Robbia. The sculpture dates from approximately 1465, which would hardly seem to be anyone's idea of "yesterday" in 1946. At the right, "Modern art today" was represented by three images: the International Style facade of the museum's building (completed in 1939 by Philip Goodwin and Edward Durrell Stone) photographed from an oblique angle; Picasso's neoclassical drawing of four dancers from 1925; and a Bauhaus-like overlay of three transparent geometric forms (square, circle, slender rectangle) in primary colors. "Modern art today" was thus presented as a dynamic relationship among different media (drawing, photography, painting, design) and stylistic forms (neoclassicism, geometric abstraction, International Style architecture).

The brochure cleverly telegraphed Barr's abiding conviction that modern art was not a period style or chronological designation but rather an attitude of nonconformity and abiding innovation.[100] As Barr would put it two years later, "The word modern, or its equivalent, has been used probably since the beginning of civilization to denote what innovators created and what conservatives and reactionaries disliked."[101] By these lights, the concept of "modern" stretched all the way back to the "beginning of civilization" even as it continued to shift so as to defy established orders and academic formulae. The modern was, paradoxically, both everlasting and ever-changing.

There is another way to understand the temporal scrambling of the objects reproduced in the fundraising brochure. All the works had been

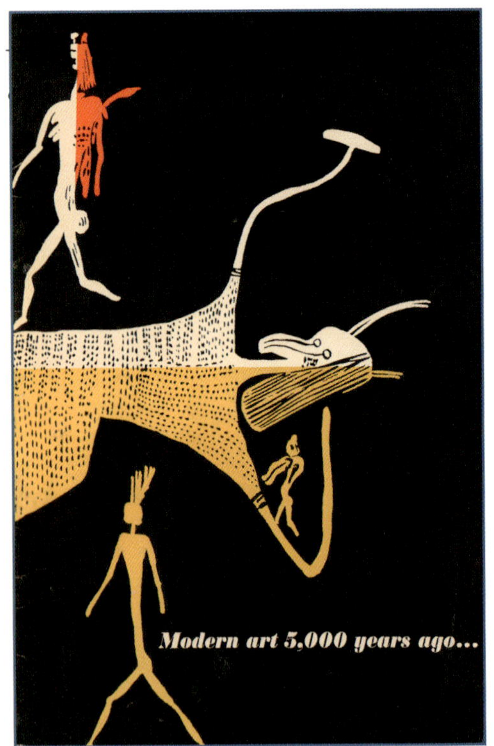

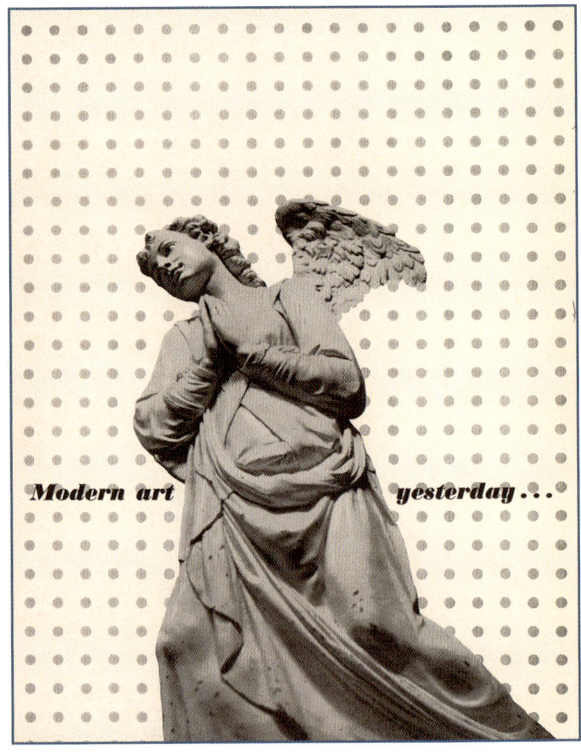

3.29–3.31 Brochure, "Modern Art 5,000 years ago . . . ," "Modern art yesterday . . . ," "and Modern art TODAY," 1946. Reports and Pamphlets, 1940s. The Museum of Modern Art Archives, New York. (Courtesy The Museum of Modern Art Archives.) Digital image © The Museum of Modern Art/Licensed by SCALA/Art Resource, NY.

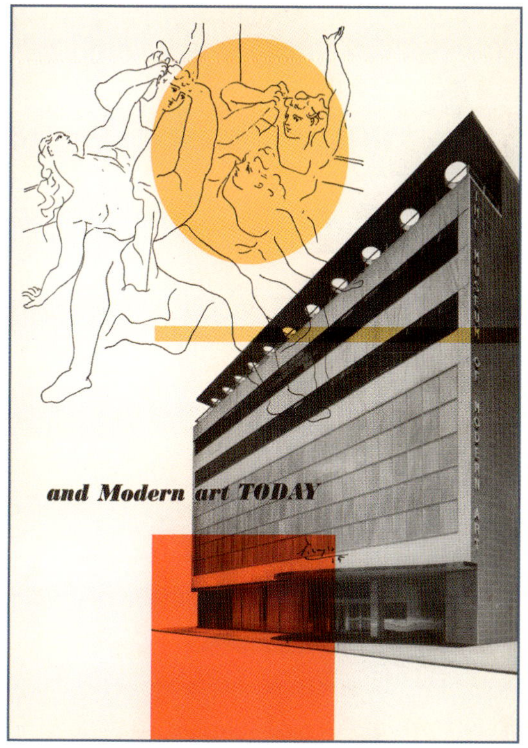

displayed by MoMA in the previous decade—the Picasso drawing, acquired through the bequest of Lizzie Bliss in 1935, was included in the Picasso retrospective of 1939–1940; the facsimile of the African cave painting was part of *Prehistoric Rock Pictures* in 1937; the museum's Fifty-third Street building opened in 1939; and the Andrea della Robbia angel (along with the rest of the figures in the group) was exhibited in *Italian Masters* in 1940. MoMA's proposal positioned modern art not only as a temporal designation but most importantly as a critical lens through which to look at a wide expanse of cultural objects and aesthetic innovations. Perhaps, in the end, too wide.

The experimental nature of MoMA in the 1930s and early 1940s, including its commitment to premodern exhibitions, has been lost or largely ignored by scholars who have characterized the museum and its founding director as narrowly modernist. According to Terry Smith, for example, "Barr's reduced, decontextualized, and exclusionary view of Modern art's history was immediately institutionalized in the exhibitions program and the slowly growing permanent collection" of the museum in the 1930s.[102] Historians William Scott and Peter Rutkoff likewise argue that "by the eve of World War II, under Barr's supervision, MoMA had reduced the rich and diffuse range of modern work to a narrow, almost sectarian, aesthetic."[103]

Such characterizations belie the breadth of the museum's exhibition programs and curatorial vision in the 1930s and 1940s. That vision located modern art not only in late nineteenth- and early twentieth-century Paris but also in seventeenth-century Persia, in fifteenth-century Florence, and in the caves and rock shelters of prehistory. According to a 1933 staff memo outlining the future direction of MoMA, "the Museum should frankly state its right to appraise, by exhibition, any art of any age from a modern point of view."[104] Safavid palace frescoes, Paleolithic rock pictures, and Italian Renaissance paintings and sculpture arrived "like travelers through time" at MoMA during Barr's directorship. Through the mediation of contemporary copies and curatorial practice, premodern and prehistoric art became spectacular exhibitions in the present moment.

Barr's dialectical vision of modern art remains instructive for early twenty-first-century students of contemporary art history. Barr understood the time frame of modern art to include both the present and the distant past, especially as the latter was rediscovered and reimagined in the current moment. In 2009, the art historian Miwon Kwon offered a similarly expansive view of contemporary art as that which is "presumed to embody the newness of the present" but can also "engage prehistoric artifacts, revive ancient techniques or materials, and invest in outmoded images, ideas, and methods. That is to say, contemporary art may be of the present but can newly mobilize the past."[105] Barr's mobilization of historical and prehistoric art in the early years of MoMA now constitutes a past that may itself be newly engaged in our contemporary moment. That has been the aim of this chapter.

'MODERN' OR 'CONTEMPORARY'—WORDS OR MEANINGS?

Feb. 17th '48

As they say in the obituary notices, "Museum of Modern Art, please copy."

Modern distemper

Boston Museum Hits 'Cult of Bewilderment'

Asks Artists To Affirm The 'Truth'

Art Institute Changes Name

Boston Institute Wants No Part Of 'Modern Art;' Alters Name

Institute of Modern Art Has Changed Its Name

TO ASSUME NEW NAME

And from the glass-blocked citadel that is the Museum of Modern Art in New York came this classic answer: "No statement," it said. "And no comment."

MODERN ART LOSES ITS FACE IN BOSTON

Trustees Alter Name of Institute in a Move Against Cultural 'Double Talk, Chicanery'

Art Institute Changes Name

By Dorothy Adlow

The Institute of Contemporary Art is the new name of the art organization which has been known to us as the Institute of Modern Art. Midseason, its officers convened, called in the press, and announced this radical and revealing change of title. This nonprofit educational institution can now continue its varied activities in our community with a greater sense of freedom.

It was not lightly that the change of one word in a title was made. Officials think long and carefully about such matters. The adjective "modern" has assumed a connotation which obscures the broad purpose of the Institute's function. We know that "modern art" conveys a meaning to the layman associated with distortion, distaste, violence, ugliness, unconventionality, bewilderment, ciate and foster. But it is the function of this Institute to encourage the artist in his primary role of spiritual leadership. "The artist should not take refuge in private cynicism . . . . he must come forward with a strong, clear affirmation of truth for humanity."

The Institute maintains an interest in the artist's creative impulse whether he works in a mood of experiment or with a preference for tradition. It will put on exhibitions, publish pamphlets and books, promote the integration of art with industry. It desires above all to free itself of the damaging association with the cultism, the exoticism, the deliberately cryptic nature of so much modern art. It wishes to promote art in the community as something wholesome, enhancing and healthy.

Contempotary Takes Place of Modern for Institute

IN changing its name to the Institute of Contemporary Art, on the ground that "so-called 'modern art'" has given rise to a "cult of bewilderment and double-talk," the Institute of Modern Art of Boston has clearly taken a poke at its sister city's Museum of Modern Art, not to mention the Modern Art Dyers & Cleaners Corp., of 1218 Third Avenue; the Modern Art Greeting Card Company, of 39 East Twentieth Street; and the Modern Art

4.1 Clippings on ICA controversy from James S. Plaut Papers. (Courtesy Archives of American Art, Smithsonian Institution.)

4 Midcentury Contemporary (1948)

Manifesto

On February 17, 1948, the Institute of Modern Art, formerly known as the Boston Museum of Modern Art, announced that it was once again—and for the last time—changing its name. In a public statement released that day, the institute declared that modern art had become "a cult of bewilderment" that "rested on the hazardous foundations of obscurity and negation, and utilized a private, often secret, language which required the aid of an interpreter."[1] The statement concluded by proclaiming: "In order to dissociate the policy and program of this institution from the widespread and injurious misunderstandings which surround the term 'modern art,' the Corporation has today changed its name from The Institute of Modern Art to THE INSTITUTE OF CONTEMPORARY ART."[2]

At once deliberately worded and wildly provocative, the statement (soon to be known as the Boston manifesto) charged that modern art had been betrayed by the very critics and curators who sought to explain it: "Paradoxically, interpretation itself became a barrier to the natural function of art—free, unimpeded contact with the observer. Valid artistic expression was often exploited for purposes of propaganda or sensationalism; and once the gap between artist and public was widened sufficiently, it became an attractive playground for double-talk, opportunism, and chicanery at the public expense."[3] According to the manifesto, the act of interpretation had imposed itself, unnaturally, between artist and audience, and the abstruse claims made on behalf of modern art had precluded the public's ability to understand and enjoy it: "In the last analysis an innocent phrase, modern art, denoting simply the art of our times, has come to signify for millions something unintelligible, even meaningless."[4] On this account, the problem confronting the institute issued from the mystification of the idea of "modern art" as much as from the artworks themselves. The newly christened Institute of Contemporary Art promised, in response, to strive for exhibitions and explanations of art that were "conscientious and forthright."[5]

Officially titled "Modern Art and the American Public," the statement was professionally printed as a bifold brochure and distributed by the institute to 10,000 individuals in the arts, journalism, and higher education.[6] Another 30,000 copies were distributed to the mailing list of the Steuben Glass Company, a purveyor of hand-cut glass and engraved crystal whose president, Arthur A. Houghton Jr., served on the institute's board of trustees.[7] If the manifesto's aim was to capture public attention, it could hardly have been more successful. From *Newsweek* to the *New Yorker*, from the *Chicago Tribune* to the *Hartford Courant*, newspapers and magazines covered the story under headlines befitting a scandal: "Modern Art a Sham to Boston Institute"; "Modern Art Loses Its Face in Boston"; "Boston Museum Hits 'Cult of Bewilderment'"; "Boston Institute Wants No Part of 'Modern Art,' Alters Name."[8]

In an article titled "The Boston Tea Party," the journal *American Artist* compared the "splash" made by the announcement of the Institute of Contemporary Art (ICA) to the hurling of tea into Boston Harbor by Massachusetts colonists more than a century and a half before. Where the colonists protested the British policy of "taxation without representation," the ICA was defying the "hypnotic spell" of "so-called modern art," which, in the words of *American Artist*, "has for too long been bamboozling the public."[9]

As the Boston Tea Party helped spark a revolutionary war, so the ICA would now fight for American independence from foreign influence on aesthetic grounds. While largely tongue-in-cheek, the linking of the Boston manifesto to the Boston Tea Party positioned modern art as an oppressive force that needed to be overthrown. The Boston institute would vanquish European modernism in the name of a contemporary, authentically American art.

The Museum of Modern Art (MoMA) initially refrained from publicly responding to the Boston manifesto. As *Newsweek* dryly noted, "from the glass-blocked citadel that is the Museum of Modern Art in New York came this classic answer: 'No statement,' it said. 'And no comment.'"[10] With the ICA in the role of rebellious upstart, MoMA was cast as the imperious sovereign coolly refusing to discuss the insubordination of provincial subjects.

According to James S. Plaut, director of the ICA and principle author of its manifesto, the renaming of the institute was necessary because the once "innocent idea of modern art" had become narrowly associated with the European avant-garde and, more especially, with the School of Paris. As Plaut would later recall, "We thought the word 'contemporary' was a more wholesome and more permissive word, with broader implications, and we decided to change our name for these two reasons: that it would give us our independence symbolically, without relationship to anyone else, and that it would imply a broad range of activity."[11] How had modern art come to seem so shady and disreputable, at least to Plaut and the institute he directed, in 1948? And why should "contemporary," by contrast, have suggested something "wholesome and permissive"?

In 1929, Alfred H. Barr Jr. had argued that the term "'Modern' is valuable because semantically it suggests the progressive, original, and challenging rather than the safe and academic which would naturally be included in the supine neutrality of the term 'contemporary.'"[12] Two decades later, the ICA would insist that modern art had come to "describe a style which is taken for granted; it has had time to run its course and, in the pattern of all historic styles, has become both dated and academic."[13] The ICA sought to define modern art as a stale period style whose time had past.[14] Barr argued, by contrast, that modern art was not a style that could be superseded but an experiment still very much in the making.[15]

Far from a solely semantic distinction, the midcentury split between "modern" and "contemporary" opened onto broader questions (and accusations) of Continental elitism and leftist dogma on the one side and of reactionary politics and American isolationism on the other.[16] In an essay titled "The Frightening Freedom of the Brush," the art historian Serge Guilbaut has carefully reconstructed the political stakes of the rift between MoMA and its unruly Boston affiliate in 1948. According to Guilbaut, the Boston manifesto "signaled (perhaps unintentionally) that the ICA no longer believed in the implications of internationalism, experimentation, and progressivism that the term modern once carried."[17]

The ICA's description of modern art as a visual language of secrecy and deception reinforced cold war cultural politics at the time, including the suspicion that abstract and otherwise nonnaturalistic art was un-American and tacitly, if not manifestly, Communist.[18] Even as the Boston manifesto insisted that "[w]e are unalterably opposed to extremism of the diehard conservative kind," its rhetoric echoed anti-Communist attacks on modernist art by conservative politicians and self-appointed watchdog groups such as the Society for Sanity in Art.

In this context, Guilbaut discusses the 1947 episode in which the U.S. Congress recalled an exhibition of contemporary American paintings that had been purchased by the U.S. State Department for display abroad. Titled

Advancing American Art, the exhibition was attacked by conservative politicians and the anti-Communist press as subversive of national ideals.[19] An article in the February 1947 issue of *Look* magazine featured images of seven paintings from the exhibition by artists including Ben Shahn and Yasuo Kuniyoshi under the headline "Your Money Bought These Paintings." According to *Look*, the painters employed "symbolism, trick perspectives, and bold color to express themselves" while departing from the reassuring realism "which is popular in the U.S. today."[20] The *Republican News* made the political implications of this departure clear when it accused several of the artists in the exhibition of belonging to the Communist Party.[21] Given the controversy over *Advancing American Art*, it is not surprising that the Boston manifesto became similarly freighted with anti-Communist politics. Though Red baiting may not have been Plaut's intention, the vivid wording of the ICA's statement (with its charges of "a cult of bewilderment"; "a private, often secret, language"; "double-talk, opportunism, and chicanery"; "world chaos and social unrest") dovetailed with far more conservative, even reactionary, voices at the time.[22]

In renouncing modern art, the ICA was renouncing MoMA as well. According to Plaut, "'Modern Art' in the Forties had come to mean, to many people, only the avant-garde of art and the most extreme forms of contemporary expression. Indeed, as the program of the Museum of Modern Art revealed at the time, they had little interest in anything other than 'abstract art.' All other forms of contemporary art were ignored and what had happened, in our view, was that a kind of academy of the left, with all its prejudices and unrealities, had emerged."[23] It is demonstrably untrue that MoMA showed "little interest in anything other than abstract art" in the 1940s. In just the first year of that decade, the museum mounted exhibitions of newspaper sketch illustrations, late eighteenth-century Japanese woodblock prints, Renaissance

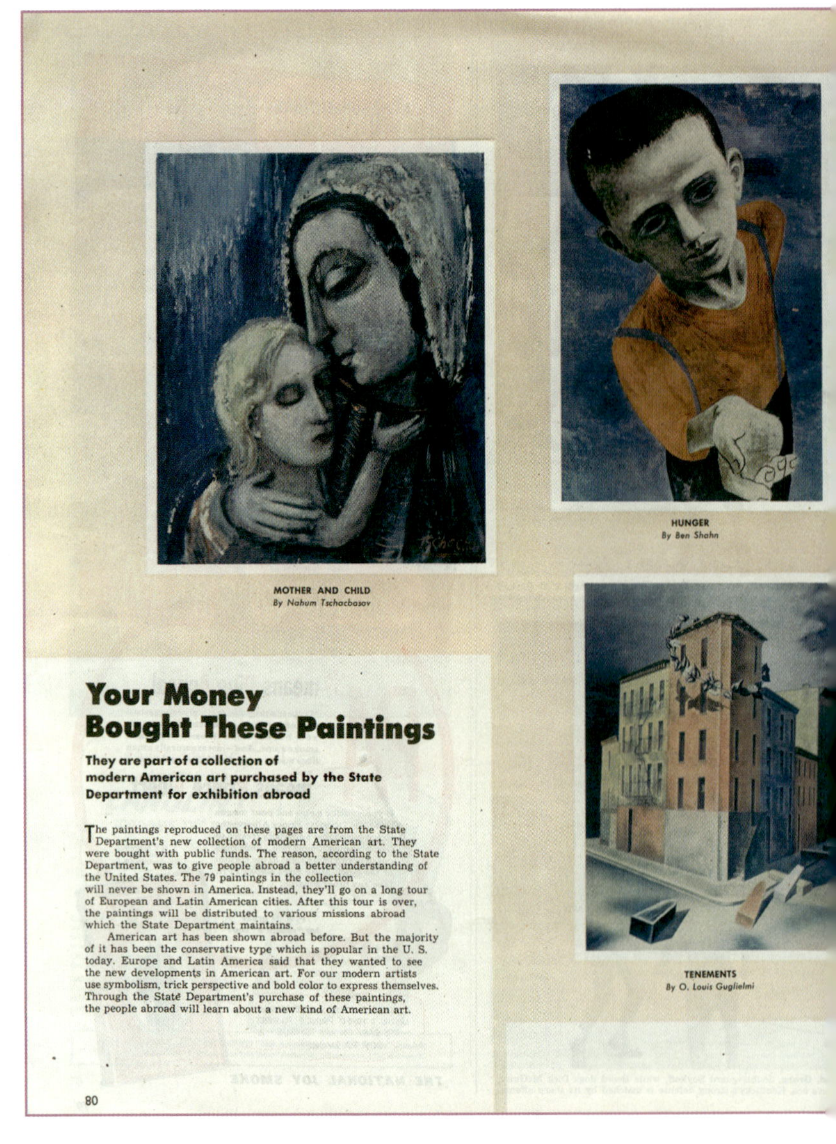

Your Money Bought These Paintings

They are part of a collection of modern American art purchased by the State Department for exhibition abroad

The paintings reproduced on these pages are from the State Department's new collection of modern American art. They were bought with public funds. The reason, according to the State Department, was to give people abroad a better understanding of the United States. The 79 paintings in the collection will never be shown in America. Instead, they'll go on a long tour of European and Latin American cities. After this tour is over, the paintings will be distributed to various missions abroad which the State Department maintains.

American art has been shown abroad before. But the majority of it has been the conservative type which is popular in the U. S. today. Europe and Latin America said that they wanted to see the new developments in American art. For our modern artists use symbolism, trick perspective and bold color to express themselves. Through the State Department's purchase of these paintings, the people abroad will learn about a new kind of American art.

80

4.2 "Your Money Bought These Paintings,"
Look, February 1947.

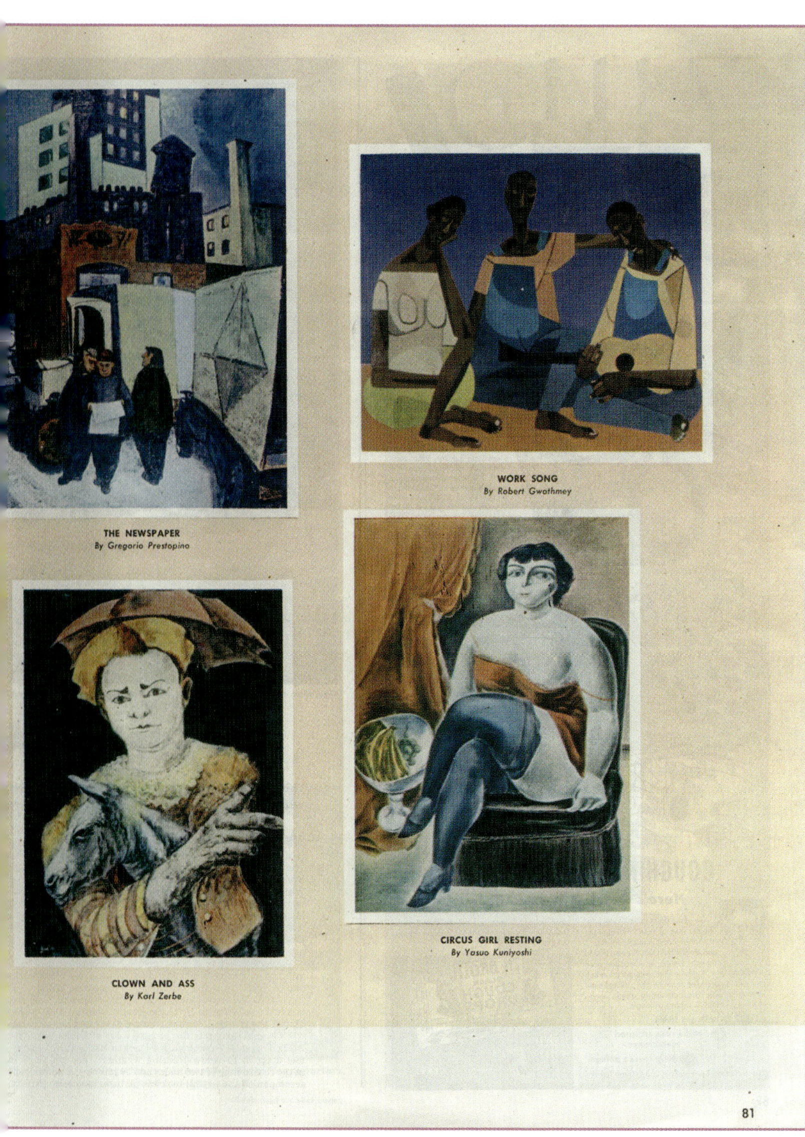

THE NEWSPAPER
By Gregorio Prestopino

WORK SONG
By Robert Gwathmey

CLOWN AND ASS
By Karl Zerbe

CIRCUS GIRL RESTING
By Yasuo Kuniyoshi

and baroque art, and Mexican art from the pre-Columbian period to the (then) present moment. It was, of course, just these sorts of exhibitions that provoked Ad Reinhardt and the members of the American Abstract Artists to ask, "How Modern is the Museum of Modern Art?" But where the American Abstract Artists criticized MoMA as insufficiently modern, the Boston manifesto suggested that modern art had itself become both passé and narrowly partisan.

Among the first critics to challenge the ICA in print was Clement Greenberg, the leading proponent of modernist painting at the time and, arguably, the most influential art critic of his generation. Writing in the pages of *The Nation*, Greenberg pointed out that the Boston manifesto, while replete with negative judgments about modern art, was devoid of specific examples as to what might qualify as contemporary: "The Institute's statement claims, among other things, that 'modern art' describes a style which is taken for granted . . . [but] what, exactly, has come along to supplant it and render it dated? For nothing could be either dated or academic unless something else has appeared to supersede it and make it seem so by contrast. Where, in other words, is the new contemporary art that has made the Institute of Contemporary Art change its name?"[24]

For Greenberg, the manifesto's failure to define "the new contemporary art" suggested that the Boston institute's real goal was not to promote innovation but rather to attack modernist painting. Greenberg characterized the Boston manifesto as a backlash against the rise of abstraction in the United States: "The spreading recognition in this country of the fact that its most significant art is tending to become more and more exclusively abstract . . . has begun to provoke a determined counter-reaction."[25] The Boston institute's change of name was, for Greenberg, a symptom of such "determined counter-reaction." At the moment when the new ICA released its manifesto, Greenberg was arguing for abstract painting—and specifically for the painting of Jackson Pollock (who showed his first drip paintings in January 1948)—as the most advanced form of contemporary art in America and as the rightful heir to the modernist legacy of Gustave Courbet, Edouard Manet, and the European avant-gardes of the early twentieth century.

To the institute's claim that it spoke on behalf of the public, Greenberg responded with withering disdain: "As for the public—which public? The millions who, as the Institute says, find 'modern art' something unintelligible and even meaningless? The same millions also prefer Norman Rockwell to Courbet, and neither the Institute of Contemporary Art nor any other institute will in our day and age ever persuade them to comprehend the standards that make Courbet the one to be preferred."[26] In his earlier writings, Greenberg had dismissed Rockwell's paintings of small-town American life as "kitsch" (which he defined as "the debased and academicized simulacra of genuine culture") while nominating Courbet as "the first real avant-garde painter" for his attempt "to reduce his art to immediate sense data" and "to demolish official bourgeois art by turning it inside out."[27] As Greenberg saw it, the rift between the ICA and MoMA turned not only on the question of abstraction but also on the gap between conventional taste and its modernist demolition, between Rockwell on the one hand and Courbet on the other. According to his 1939 essay "Avant-Garde and Kitsch," "Where there is an avant-garde, generally we also find a rear-guard."[28] In 1948, Greenberg found a "rear-guard" at the ICA in Boston.

There was, however, a salient problem with Greenberg's argument. The ICA never presented Rockwell or the *Saturday Evening Post* as exemplary of contemporary art, nor did it exhibit "chromeotypes, magazine covers, illustrations, ads, slick and pulp fiction, comics, Tin Pan Alley music, tap dancing, [or] Hollywood movies" to name some of the other forms of mass culture Greenberg characterized as egregiously low. The ICA should not, therefore, be reduced to a repository of midcentury American kitsch. Nor, as we saw in the last chapter, should MoMA be seen as the exclusive preserve of the modernist avant-garde in the 1930s and 1940s.

While the Boston manifesto suggested a pronounced split between MoMA and the ICA in 1948, the two institutions remained closely intertwined at the time. Hanging in the institute's galleries at the moment the ICA announced its controversial name change was a retrospective of the leftist American artist Ben Shahn—an exhibition organized jointly by MoMA and the institute and presented in New York just prior to its appearance in Boston. Among the works on display at the retrospective was a poster from 1944 featuring a skeletal, blank-eyed boy holding out his hand alongside text instructing viewers to register and vote. Commissioned by a federation of trade unions, the Congress of Industrial Organizations (CIO), Shahn's poster reproduced his antiwar painting *Hunger* that was included in *Advancing American Art*.[29] Openly critical of American imperialism, war, and class inequity, Shahn was among the artists most often attacked as Communist during the previous year's controversy over the State Department's exhibition. His art combined social realist content with formally skewed perspectives, distortions of scale, and deformations of the figure.

The Shahn retrospective belies the contention that MoMA showed only abstraction or was dedicated exclusively to the European avant-garde in the 1940s. At the same time, the exhibition's display at the Boston institute challenges Greenberg's view of that institution as reactionary in its aesthetic and ideological affiliations. The work of Ben Shahn could not, in short, be confined to either side of the modern/contemporary divide as delineated by the Boston manifesto. In its blending of modernist form and Americanist content, of avant-garde technique and realist subject matter, Shahn's art subverted the starkly oppositional logic at the heart of the institute's public statement. But if the very art on the walls of the institute did not match the message of its manifesto in February 1948, what works would?

In what follows, I respond in some detail to the question posed by Greenberg: What was "the new contemporary art that ... made the [Boston] Institute change its name"?[30] What forms of visual art and culture provoked the shift from modern to contemporary in the 1940s? What did the category of contemporary allow that the modern foreclosed or denied? By way of answering these questions, I will examine the history of the Boston institute before it branded itself "contemporary," which is to say, before 1948.

"The Secession of Boston"

Founded in fall 1936 as a regional satellite of MoMA, the Boston Museum of Modern Art initially operated with "no permanent staff or permanent home" and so relied on local museums and galleries for exhibition space.[31] Through the initiation of membership fees and an annual ball, the museum raised sufficient funds within two years to rent a dedicated space, hire Plaut (a twenty-six-year-old assistant curator at the Museum of Fine Arts in Boston) as director, and engage a small secretarial staff. By late 1938, the Boston Museum of Modern Art could define itself as "an autonomous institution with its own gallery"[32] rather than as a regional outpost of MoMA's main branch in Manhattan.

In early 1939, Plaut announced his first major policy decision as director: the museum would henceforth be known as the "Institute of Modern Art."[33] While far less controversial than the institute's later renaming as

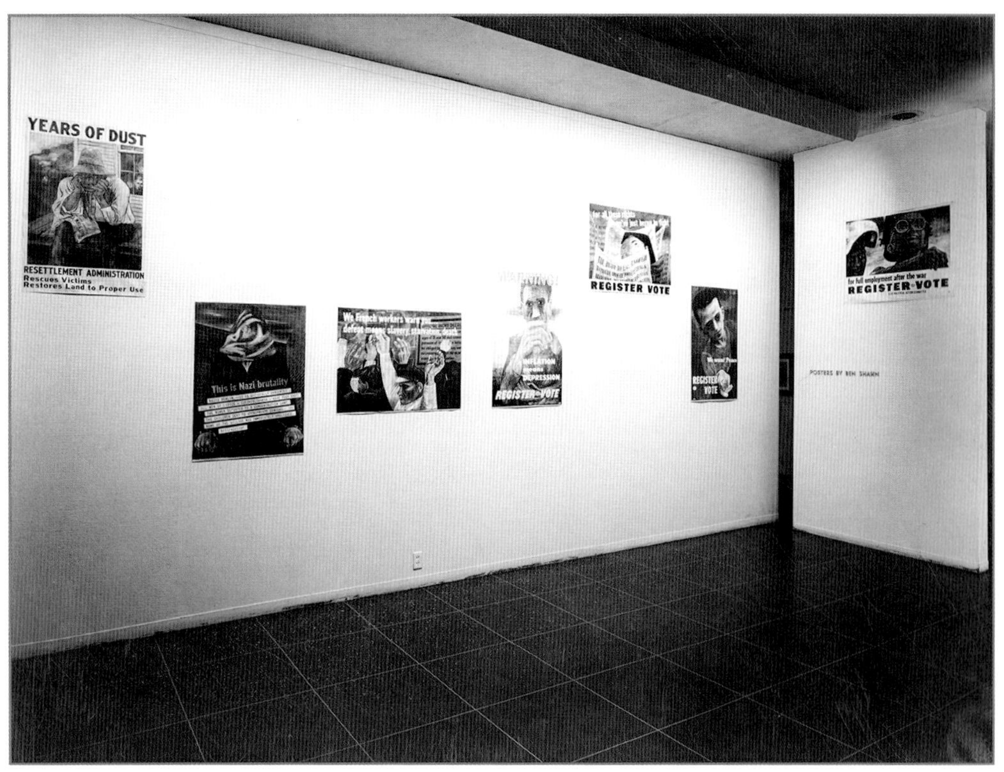

4.3 Installation view of the exhibition *Ben Shahn*, September 30, 1947–January 4, 1948. The Museum of Modern Art, New York. Photographic Archive. (Courtesy The Museum of Modern Art Archives, New York.) Photographer: Soichi Sunami. Digital image © The Museum of Modern Art/Licensed by SCALA/ Art Resource, NY.

4.4 Ben Shahn, *We Want Peace, Register, Vote*, 1946. © VAGA, NY. Lithograph of original tempera painting, 41¼ × 27 inches. (Collection The Museum of Modern Art, New York. Gift of S. S. Spivack.) Digital image © The Museum of Modern Art/Licensed by SCALA/ Art Resource, NY.

"contemporary," this initial change signaled a shift away from both MoMA and its director, Alfred Barr.[34] In distancing itself from New York, the Boston institute also broke with the traditional conception of the museum as a site for the collecting and preservation of works of art. MoMA staff member Monroe Wheeler referred to the episode, only partly in jest, as "the secession of Boston."[35] An "Institute of Modern Art" suggested a place of research and experimentation, a laboratory within which to test hypotheses. In renaming itself, the Boston Institute would likely have had its neighbor, the Massachusetts Institute of Technology (MIT), in mind. Upon its founding in 1861, MIT's emphasis on laboratory training, practical exercises, and class excursions represented a marked contrast to traditional forms of university-based scholarship.[36]

As we saw in the last chapter, MoMA also sought to operate as an "exhibition laboratory" in the 1930s and early 1940s. Unlike MoMA, however, the Boston institute did not acquire art. According to the March 1939 issue of the *Institute of Modern Art Bulletin*, "we are not a museum in the strictest sense, since we have no permanent collection of works of art. The word 'institute' more accurately defines our aim, which is to encourage general interest in the development of modern art in all its aspects, by means of loan exhibitions, lectures, research facilities, and sponsorship of related activities."[37] The Institute of Modern Art was to function as a testing ground for ideas and exhibitions rather than as a repository of artworks. By studying and displaying modern art without acquiring it, the institute would remain unburdened by the symbolic weight (and actual cost) of a permanent collection. As Nathan Saltonstall, the president of the institute, pointed out, even the most forward-looking collection of modern art consisted of "objects never long contemporary."[38] The only way to remain truly up to date, then, was to reject the premise of a permanent collection altogether.[39] In doing so, the Institute of Modern Art was already on the path to becoming "contemporary" (in the sense of being continually alive to the current moment), though it had not yet fixed on that term to describe its overall mission.[40]

Notwithstanding its newly named Institute of Modern Art, Boston remained a backwater so far as twentieth-century art was concerned—or so *Time* magazine (published in New York City) would claim in 1939:

> With the instinct of a patrician grandmother, Boston has taken to its bosom all that is dated and fine and foreign in the way of art. The Fogg Museum at Harvard is the liveliest school of art history in the U.S.; the Fine Arts Museum is eminent for its scholarly array of Oriental and other treasures; the Isabella Stewart Gardner Museum is probably the choicest large-scale clutter among U.S. private-made-public collections. From these institutions, however, few people would get the idea that there are artists alive and sweating now.[41]

The passage contrasts the physical immediacy of contemporary artists ("alive and sweating now") with the historical remoteness ("dated and fine and foreign") of the contents of Boston's art museums. *Time*'s characterization of Boston's hidebound attitude toward the work of living artists recalls Barr's critique of the city in the pages of the *Harvard Crimson* more than a decade earlier: "It is surprising, even shocking, to the stranger to find so little interest in Modern Pictures in Boston and Cambridge, places which have a deserved reputation as centers of alert cultivation of the Seven Arts. One may search in vain for the works of the foremost living painters in the Boston Museum, in Fenway Court, or in the Fogg."[42]

While both Barr (in the late 1920s) and Plaut (in the late 1930s and 1940s) sought to develop an audience for contemporary art in the Boston area, they did so with radically different understandings of what such a project would entail. Barr aimed to open local audiences to what he saw as the most challenging forms of art and design at the time.[43] Plaut, by contrast, increasingly sought to distance the Institute of Modern Art from work that was too abstract, abstruse, or otherwise (in his view) too foreign to American sensibilities.

In 1939, Plaut drafted a brochure titled "Emotionalism in Modern Painting" in which he wrote that "true art must never lose sight of nature—must always remain within the limits of naturalistic representation."[44] Abstract art could only engender a "synthetic and artificial" experience among viewers."[45] Plaut was equally uncomfortable with surrealism, which he viewed as "deliberately perverse" and the "manifestation of deranged minds."[46] Plaut's antipathy to both abstraction and surrealism shaped his growing discomfort with the term "modern art." Speaking on a 1940 radio show in Boston, he proclaimed that "When you say 'modern art' to the average man, he thinks only in extremes and jumps to the conclusion that you are referring to the unintelligible performances of the most wild-eyed, unbalanced, and violently leftist painters."[47] "Unintelligible performances" was code for abstraction, and "wild-eyed, unbalanced, violently leftist painters" likely referred to surrealist artists.

Plaut's message to radio listeners in 1940 might be paraphrased as follows: if the "average man" is alienated by modern art, the problem lies not with the man but with the art. The job of the Boston institute, then, would be to present an alternative vision of what the art of the mid twentieth century might be, a vision the institute would ultimately name "contemporary." When Plaut insisted that "we are not carrying the torch of extreme modernism,"[48] he meant to distance the institute from the most radical forms of abstraction and surrealism and from the New York museum (MoMA) most closely associated with them. MoMA's exhibitions of *Cubism and Abstract Art* (1936) and *Fantastic Art, Dada, and Surrealism* (1936) would have been known to Plaut, not least because the latter traveled to the Boston Museum of Modern Art in 1937.[49]

"Oncoming" Americans

The institute's commitment to "non-extreme" forms of modern art was closely linked to its promotion of figurative painting and especially, though not exclusively, of New England artists. In 1941, Plaut co-curated *Fifty Oncoming American Painters* at the Institute of Modern Art to showcase what he argued was the newfound vitality and autonomy of American art. To promote the exhibition, Plaut wrote a feature article in *ARTnews* in which he underscored the youth of the participating artists (most were under thirty-five years of age) and predicted that their names, while for the most part little known at the time, were ones "with which we will probably have to reckon before long."[50]

Titled "50 Rising American Painters 50," the article suggested that the artists featured in the exhibition were breaking free of foreign (and particularly French) influence and that this was, indeed, why they were rising: "These fifty leave you with the dominant impression that American painting is freeing itself from the bonds of imitation and mannerism."[51] Though Plaut mentions in passing that the show included a few abstractionists, all the individual artworks described in "50 Rising American Painters 50" were figurative, as were all those reproduced in the press at the time.[52] Willard Warren Cummings's *Portrait of Mr. and Mrs. Cutler*, for example, accompanied Plaut's article in *ARTnews*, while Yvonne Twining's *River View* appeared in both the *Christian Science Monitor* and the *Boston Herald*. The latter declared it "All-American Art" while noting that "the independent artist is always out in front in any fight for freedom."[53] How Twining's crisply realist view of the

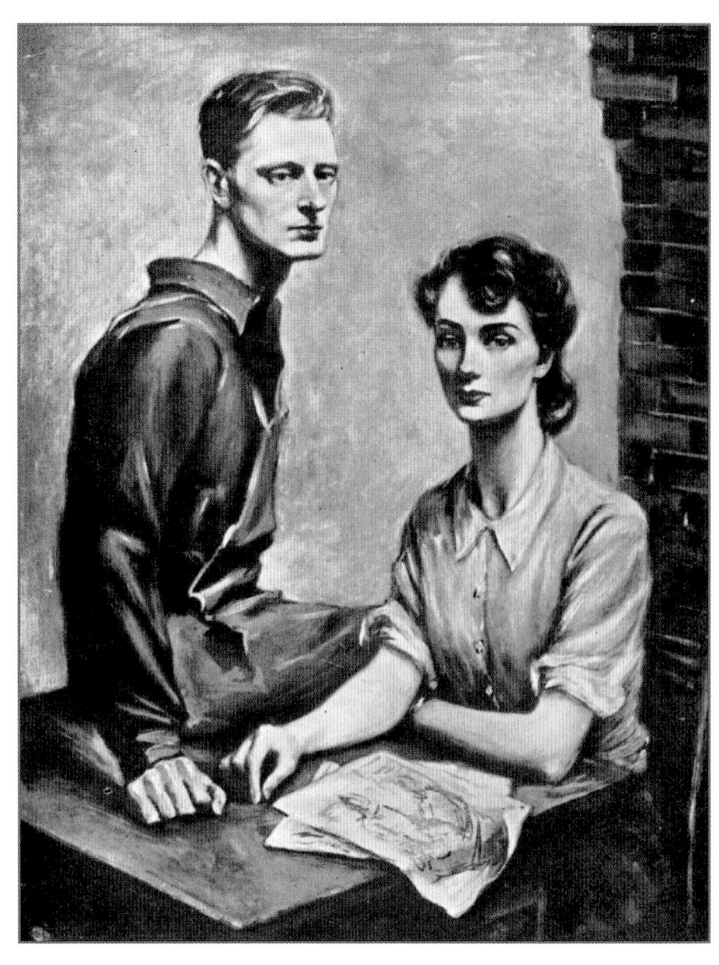

4.5 Willard Cummings, *Portrait of Mr. and Mrs. Charles Cutler*, c. 1940. Oil on canvas.

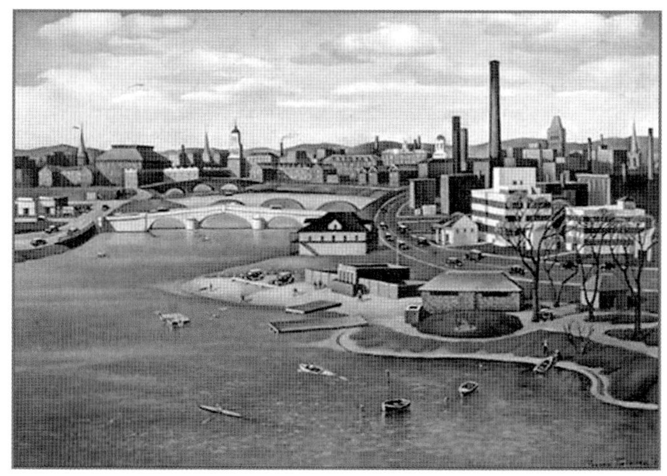

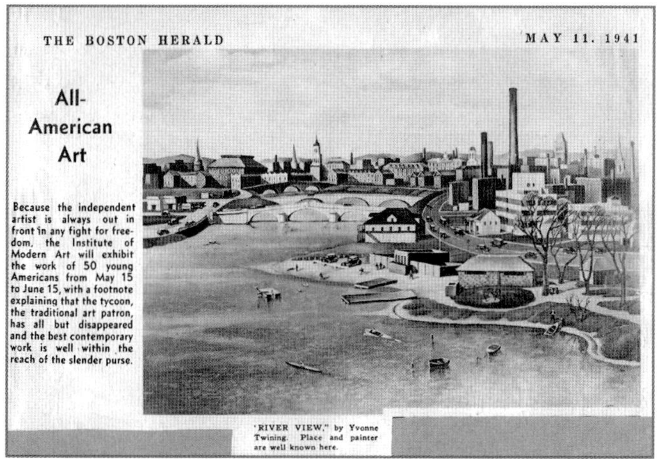

4.6 Yvonne Twining, *River View*, c. 1940. Oil on canvas, 20 × 28 inches.

4.7 "All-American Art," *Boston Herald*, May 11, 1941.

Charles River was tantamount to a "fight for freedom" the paper did not specify.[54]

The Cummings portrait, which Plaut ranked as "easily his most distinguished to date," offered a likeness of Charles Gordon Cutler, a New England stone sculptor, and his wife, Betty. Mr. Cutler, in coveralls, sits atop a wooden table at which Mrs. Cutler, in slightly nearer space, is seated. Mrs. Cutler rests her right arm upon the tabletop so that her hand nearly but not quite touches that of her husband. Also on the table, close to the couple's hands, lie what appear to be cursory sketches for the double portrait before us. It is as if the artist has incorporated his preliminary studies for the painting into its final composition. Or perhaps, within the narrative logic of the portrait, we are meant to understand that Cummings has just presented his sketches to the Cutlers, seeking their approval before proceeding to the full-fledged oil painting. In either case, the finished portrait includes a (painted) rendering of drawings that not only conjures up a third presence at the table—that of the artist who studies, sketches, and ultimately paints a portrait of Mr. and Mrs. Cutler—but also subtly underscores the importance of life drawing and direct observation to the making of art. When seen in tandem with Twining's *River View*, Cummings's portrait of the Cutlers conveys a sense of the realist and regionalist commitments that the Boston Institute shared with a community of local artists in the 1940s.

In 1946, Cummings and Cutler cofounded the Skowhegan School for Painting and Sculpture, a summer art colony in central Maine. While not adhering to any one academic method or tradition, the faculty offered courses in life drawing and painting and emphasized the importance of study from nature. Cummings would later recall that he and the other founder of Skowhegan "talked a lot about American art and American artists and the only

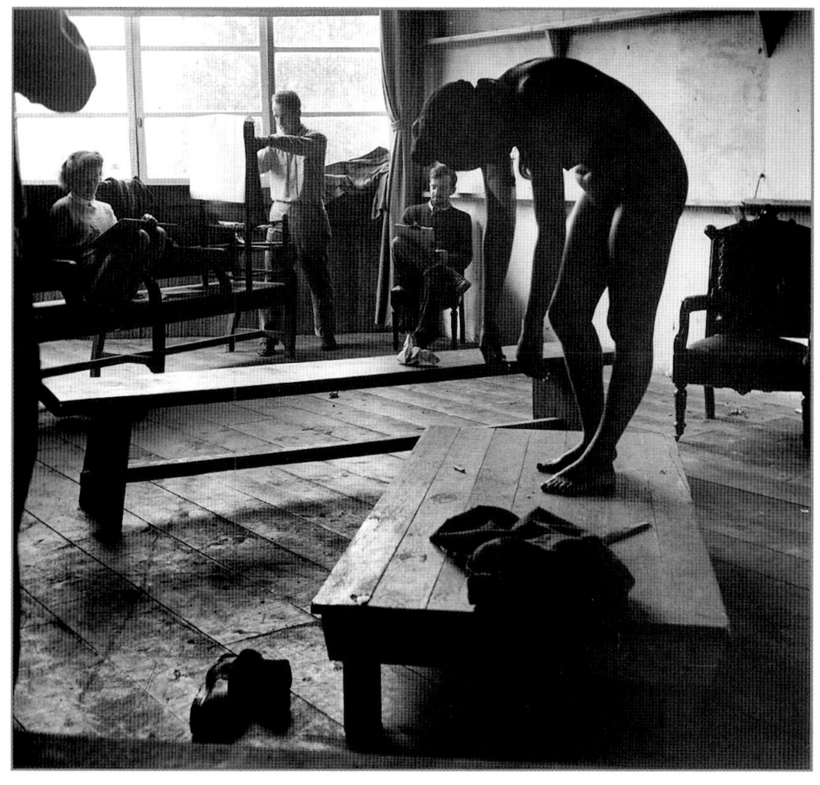

4.8 Gjon Mili, *Skowhegan School of Arts*, 1948. Photograph, 13.9 × 17.8 inches. © Gjon Mili/LIFE. (Collection Museum of Fine Arts, Boston.)

thing for an American art student to do before the war was to go to Europe … so we thought it would be good to have a school, using the summer which Americans just used for play, at least in those days where the very serious students could come and work."[55] Skowhegan challenged the need for American artists to seek Continental training and aesthetic inspiration from abroad. Like the Boston institute, the Maine art colony sought to demonstrate the independence of contemporary artists in the United States.

Throughout "50 Rising American Painters 50," Plaut is at pains to defend the "oncoming Americans" from the charge that their work is derivative of European sources. Thus, "John Koch's rich flower piece, *Gladioli*, betrays this painter's strong admiration for Renoir yet, in every sense, it is a highly individualized performance."[56] And while Jack Levine's "powerfully distorted *Neighborhood Physician*" recalls the pictures of Chaïm Soutine and Oskar Kokoschka, it remains "an utterly personal conception" of the Boston artist. Plaut ends the article by pointing to "conclusive evidence that a whole generation of American painters, on the threshold of emancipated maturity, are translating foreign doctrine into a persuasive native idiom."[57]

A figurative expressionist whose compositions tended toward the comic grotesque, Levine was among the most prominent young artists in the nation at the time of *Fifty Oncoming American Painters*, having already been shown three times at MoMA and twice in the Whitney Annual. Even as he developed a national reputation, the Boston-born and -based Levine frequently depicted New England themes and locales. The red and green gabled Victorian building in the background of *Neighborhood Physician* and the partially cropped advertisement for "[Narra]gansett Ale" would have been immediately recognizable to Boston viewers, not least because the latter was the best-selling beer in New England at the time.[58] For all its distortions of scale

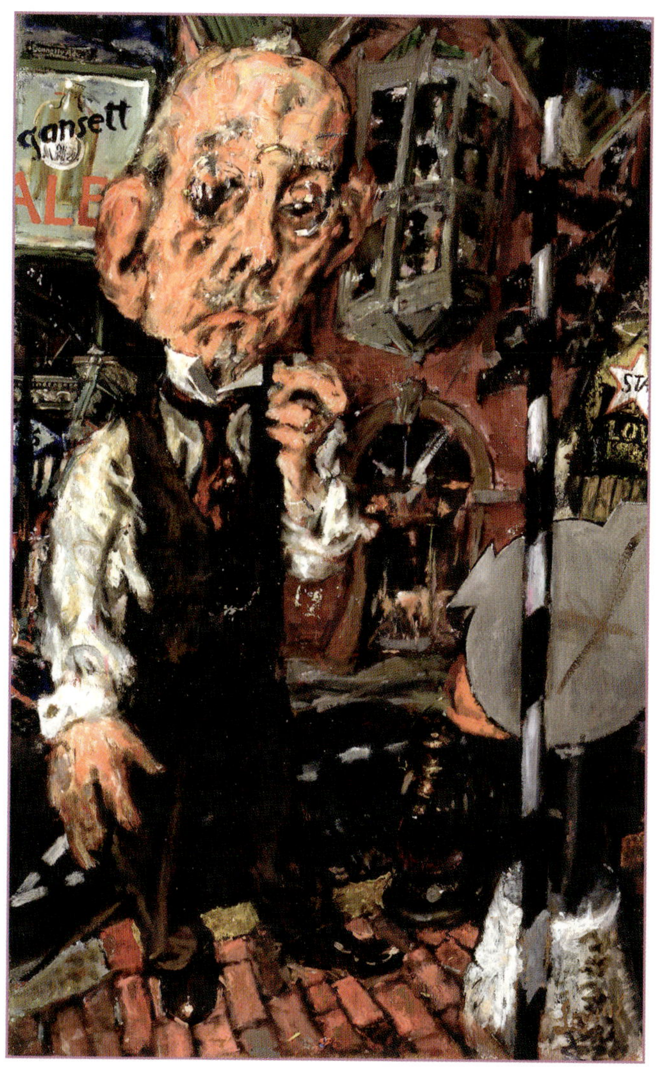

4.9 Jack Levine, *Neighborhood Physician*, 1939. Oil on pulp panel. (Collection Walker Art Center.) Art © Estate of Jack Levine/ Licensed by VAGA, New York, NY.

and perspective, *Neighborhood Physician* remains a portrait of a place as well as a character, a neighborhood as well as a physician.[59]

Of the fifty artists featured in the exhibition, nearly a quarter lived in New England. Plaut sought to cast the region's artists as representative of a "rising" American culture rather than as foot soldiers in a rearguard or otherwise provincial outpost. In place of abstraction, surrealism, and other forms of "foreign doctrine," the Boston institute advocated for a plurality of representational styles (from social realism and landscape painting to figurative expressionism and neoromanticism) as quintessentially American. Taken together, Cummings's *Portrait of Mr. and Mrs. Cutler*, Levine's *Neighborhood Physician*, and Twining's *River View* fairly suggest the range of local painters and realist idioms supported by the institute in 1941.

Plaut and the Boston institute came down on the wrong side of history, if by "wrong" we mean that the artists they supported either have disappeared from art-historical consciousness or are, at best, regarded as minor offshoots from the main road of modernist abstraction. Despite Plaut's prediction in the pages of *ARTnews*, the artists shown in *Fifty Oncoming American Painters* (including Levine, Twining, and Cummings) were not ones with which many critics or scholars felt they "had to reckon" in the postwar period.[60] Decades after the fact, Cummings would recall that he and Levine "weren't considered old-fashioned [in the mid 1940s], but a few years later we were so far out of date you couldn't see us in history even."[61] Though both men continued to exhibit after World War II, their careers were eclipsed by the rise of abstract expressionism.[62] As Levine would tell an interviewer in 2004, "I made quite a splash in the 1930s when I was still a kid and it seems to me that every year since, I have become less and less well known."[63]

When Cummings states, "we were so far out of date you couldn't see us in history even," he speaks to the ways in which established artists may disappear from art-historical consciousness even while they are still living and making art. This is not to say that the work of painters such as Cummings or Levine lies outside the history of American art at midcentury. But it is to acknowledge that these (and many other) realist artists were increasingly marginalized by the priority assigned to modernist abstraction. By returning to the work of "less and less well known" artists in the moment before they disappeared from art-historical view, we revive the range of possibilities that once constituted contemporary art. The aim of doing so is not to valorize obscurity for its own sake but to expand our retrospective view of art history. Our sense of 1940s American art changes, for example, when we place the paintings of Jack Levine and Willard Cummings in dialogue with contemporaneous works by (now-)canonical artists such as Jackson Pollock and Willem de Kooning. "Any given historical period," writes Serge Guilbaut in "The Frightening Freedom of the Brush," "generates one aesthetic that dominates as well as others that are dominated or repressed. It is the study of why such a split should exist that gives art history its great importance and worth."[64]

There is one additional aspect of *Fifty Oncoming American Painters* that needs to be taken into account: all the paintings in the exhibition were for sale. As Plaut wrote in *ARTnews*, "The exhibition has the secondary function of inculcating the museum-going public with the realization that a considerable quantity of first-rate painting is within the range of the small pocketbook. The prices in this exhibition, appearing, incidentally, both in the catalogue and on the labels in healthy contradiction to accepted museum practice, scale down from a $500 maximum (affixed to three pictures) to a $60 minimum."[65]

In defiance of "accepted museum practice," the Boston institute engaged directly in the marketing of contemporary American art. By placing the purchase price of paintings both on the wall labels and in the catalogue, the institute acknowledged its part in a network of commercial exchange.[66] The necessity of doing so, according to Plaut, followed in part from the inadequacies of local patronage for contemporary art. "Too many artists with great talent," he would lament in 1946, "have left a New England unappreciative of their gifts. We want to keep such people here, and keep them busy. We hope to supply increased patronage for them."[67] To do so, Plaut argued, it was necessary to "bring the artist in touch with industry, which, in using his output, will bring him into contact with the public."[68] By these lights, the joining of art and industry would furnish much-needed professional opportunities for the undervalued artists of New England. It would also, as we shall see, furnish much-needed proceeds to the Boston institute.

"A Certain Glass Company"

One of the last shows that the Boston Museum of Modern Art mounted before it "dropped affiliation with Manhattan" and became the Institute of Modern Art early in 1939 was an exhibition entitled *Contemporary American Glass*.[69] Opening in December 1938, the show followed *Contemporary American Watercolors* in 1936 and *Contemporary American Sculpture* in 1937. *Contemporary New England Oil Paintings* opened shortly after the glass exhibition closed in 1939. The link between the term "contemporary" and the display of American art and design in the museum's early years becomes even more striking when contrasted to its exhibitions of French art during the same period, which included *Gauguin* (1936), *Modern French Paintings from Boston Collections* (1937), and *Picasso-Matisse* (1938), none of which were designated as "contemporary." From its first years of operation, the Boston Museum of Modern Art emphasized American art and design as up-to-date and alive to the current moment.[70]

More than half of the nearly one hundred works on display in *Contemporary American Glass*, including the Gazelle Bowl that illustrated the catalogue's title page, were produced by the Steuben Glass Company. Another twenty-seven objects in the exhibition, including a Pyrex condenser coil and a double boiler, were manufactured by Corning Glass Works, the parent company of Steuben, and the maker of utilitarian objects and cookware.[71] Although presented as a national survey of recent glass production ("the first in a series of annual exhibitions conceived as demonstrations of the best design and craftsmanship prevalent in American industry today"),[72] the show was largely dedicated to the output of a single company. Taken together, products manufactured by Steuben and Corning represented more than three-quarters of the work on display.

In his foreword to the exhibition's catalogue, Plaut noted that *Contemporary American Glass* "arose from the Museum's belief that any institution concerned with modern art must focus public attention upon the newer and more vital manifestations of contemporary culture."[73] Notice the shift from "modern" to "contemporary" and from "art" to "culture" in the space of that one sentence. For Plaut, both Steuben's expensive crystal and Corning's utilitarian glass qualified as "newer and more vital manifestations of contemporary culture." But newer and more vital than what? Than older forms of American glass? Than current designs in European glass? Or than modern art conceived exclusively in terms of painting and sculpture?

In a positive review in the *Christian Science Monitor*, critic Dorothy Adlow linked the contemporary glass exhibition to a broader tendency within American curatorial practice at the time:

In recent years there has been an increasing practice among progressive art groups of including in their range of exhibition objects of utility, which for a century at least had been excluded from the category of fine art. . . . Interesting, is it not, that these objects are shown at a museum of modern art, where they are exhibited in a milieu which had seemed the property of sculpture and painting; where the rarefied designs of the

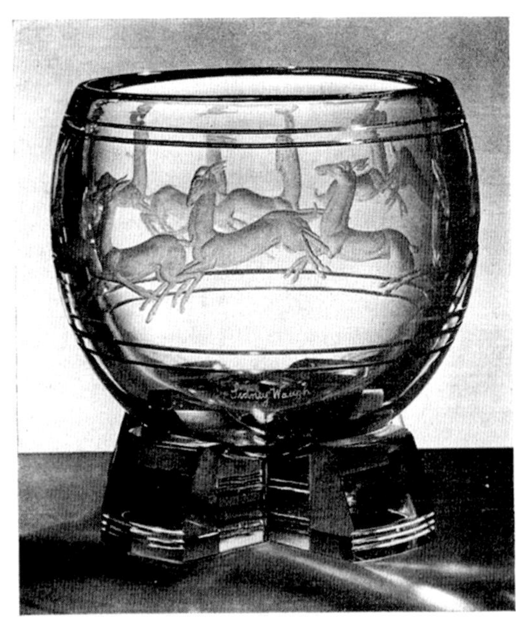

4.10 Exhibition catalogue for *Contemporary American Glass: Decorative, Utilitarian,
Structural* (Boston: Museum of Fine Arts,
1938), title page.

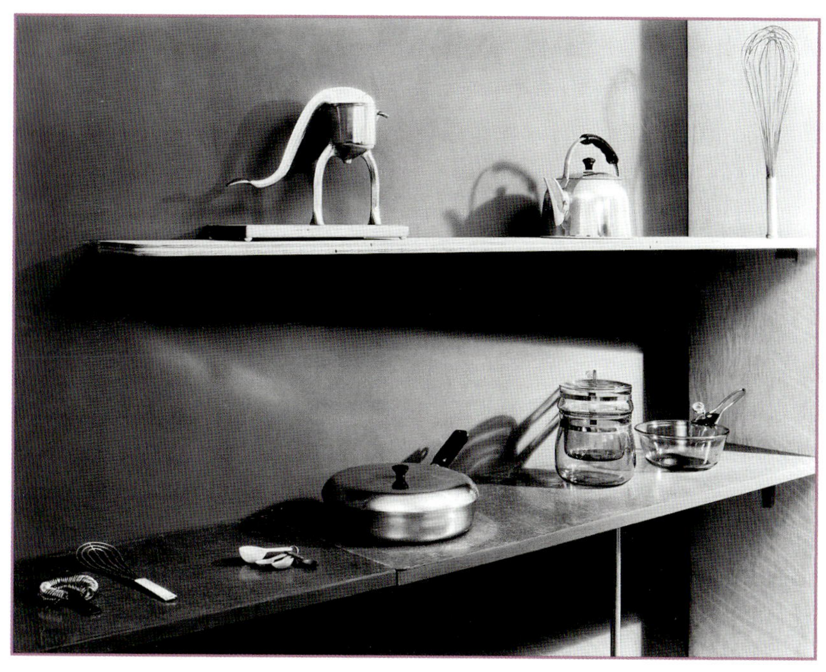

4.11 Installation view of the exhibition *Useful Household Objects under $5.00*, September 28–October 28, 1938. The Museum of Modern Art, New York. Photographic Archive. (Courtesy The Museum of Modern Art Archives, New York.) Photographer: Soichi Sunami. Digital image © The Museum of Modern Art/ Licensed by SCALA/Art Resource, NY.

abstract and incomprehensible artists of the Paris School are found akin to designs which occur in innumerable objects in everyday use![74]

Though she does not specify which recent shows of utilitarian objects she has in mind, Adlow was likely referring to MoMA's exhibitions of *Machine Art* (1934) and *Useful Household Objects under $5.00* (1938).[75]

A fundamental difference in curatorial philosophy separated MoMA's approach to industrial design from that of its Boston affiliate. Where the New York museum focused on mass-produced, inexpensive objects of household utility, the Boston museum showcased expensive, handblown glass vases and bowls alongside everyday wares such as saucepans and light bulbs. As employed by the Boston museum (soon to be institute), the term "contemporary" was expansive enough to include both art and design, both luxury and quotidian objects. At MoMA, functionalism and truth to materials were understood as the sine qua non of good design. In a press release for *Useful Household Objects under $5.00* (which closed six weeks before *Contemporary American Glass* opened in Boston), the museum noted that "machine production has recently shown the possibility of developing an esthetic peculiar to itself."[76] In adherence to the Bauhaus ideal of well-made objects of utility for the masses, MoMA sought to demonstrate that "it is possible to purchase everyday articles of excellent design at reasonable prices."[77] According to the museum's press release, "Some of the handsomest glassware and other articles are from the five-and-ten cent stores."[78] The inexpensive boiling flasks and laboratory beakers on exhibit at MoMA stood in vivid contrast to the crystal goblets and hand-engraved vessels featured in *Contemporary American Glass*. Priced at $650 upon its debut in 1935, the Gazelle Bowl was engraved with the signature of Sidney Waugh, Steuben's in-house sculptor/designer. Needless to say, the Steuben bowl was not available at the local five-and-ten. By exhibiting luxury wares that departed from modernist

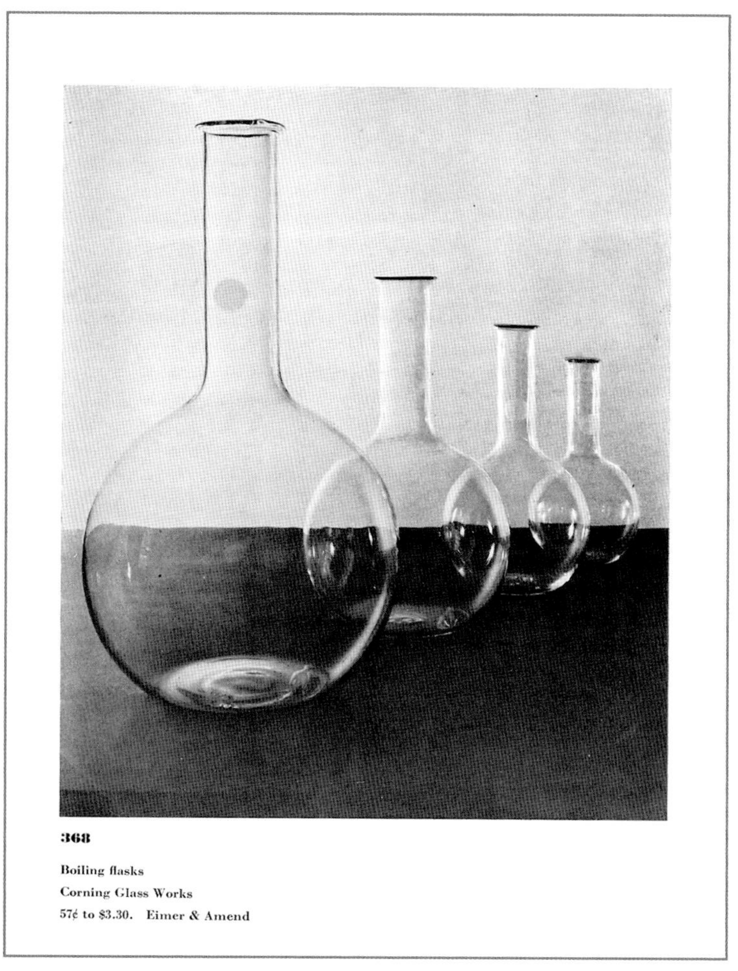

4.12 Corning Glass Works, "Boiling Flasks,"
exhibition catalogue for *Machine Art* (New
York: Museum of Modern Art, 1934), no. 368.
Digital image © The Museum of Modern Art/
Licensed by SCALA/Art Resource, NY.

ideals of functionalism, the Boston museum measured a pointed distance from its parent institution in New York City.

Throughout his career, Barr was dismissive of gratuitous streamlining and moderne designs, which he viewed as "modernistic" rather than genuinely modern insofar as they tended to conceal materiality, structure, and function beneath a sleekly decorative facade. Visitors to MoMA would, Barr hoped, learn to distinguish between "good modern design and modernistic cosmetics or bogus streamlining."[79] Among the objects he would likely have dismissed as "modernistic" were Steuben's copper-wheel engraved glass bowls, plates, and heavy-cut crystal vases.

In response to the Boston manifesto in 1948, Barr would recall *Contemporary American Glass* as an example of the Boston institute's substandard level of aesthetic taste and professional integrity. In a confidential memo to the president of the MoMA board of trustees, he tartly remarked, "I did not see the Boston Institute's show of modern, excuse me, contemporary glass in 1938, but I remember clearly hearing about its lack of discrimination and general adherence to commercial standards. It was subsidized, I believe, by the glass companies."[80] Barr expresses disdain for the Boston institute by purposely stumbling over the name of its ("modern, excuse me, contemporary") exhibition. He implies that *Contemporary American Glass* was co-opted by the glass companies whose products it displayed and, as we know, the show was in fact dominated by works from Steuben/Corning. Barr ascribes a measure of crassness to the institute for its "adherence to commercial standards" rather than to the rigors of legitimate curatorial practice.

Arthur Houghton, Steuben's president and chief executive officer since 1933, had sought to imbue every aspect of the company's product (design, retail display, packaging, print advertising) with the imprimatur of contemporary art. At Houghton's directive, Steuben abandoned the intricately frosted and colored glass with iridescent, art nouveau finishes it had promoted since

1903 and focused instead on colorless crystal heavy-cut into sleek geometries and engraved with moderne (or what would later be called art deco) designs. Steuben's transparent vases, bowls, and plates were meant to suggest both luxury and unparalleled technical achievement. "Our ideal," said Houghton, "was to see if we could make glass that a museum would buy. That would be the apotheosis of our existence."[81]

To promote its newly moderne glassware, the company opened a gleaming flagship store on Fifth Avenue across from the Plaza Hotel. According to Mary Jean Madigan's definitive study of Steuben, the store "evoked the atmosphere of a fine art gallery rather than a shop. The staff of seven, including three saleswomen, were selected for their knowledge of the fine arts."[82] An article in the March 1934 issue of *Architectural Forum* praised the store's "salon" for its combination of "good taste and good merchandising," by which it meant that the former cushioned and partially concealed the latter: "The company's merchandising plan is built upon elimination of salesmen as such. There are no counters. It is principally a room in which to create desire rather than to accomplish the definite sale."[83]

The commercial status of the objects on display was downplayed in favor of their aesthetic value and apparent rarity. At the far end of the main display room (or "exhibition space" as *Architectural Forum* put it), Waugh's cast crystal sculpture of a fawn crowned a glass cylindrical fountain which itself rested upon a mirrored base. An expanse of black rubber flooring "polished to the brilliance of jet"[84] provided a dramatic counterpoint to the play of light across an array of transparent glass vases, bowls, and *objets*, some of which were reflected in a mirrored wall or on mirrored circular tabletops. An illuminated chromium-and-glass balustrade led patrons up to the mezzanine. The sales floor was intended to "create desire" for Steuben's products through its luxe displays and deco glamour. The cash transaction to which that desire would

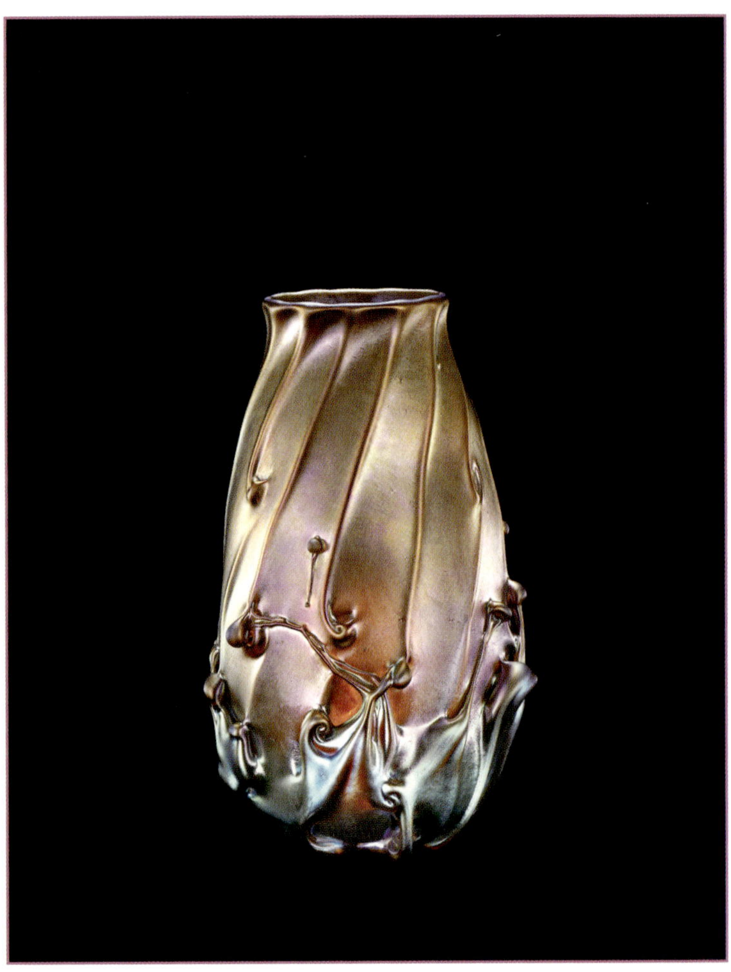

4.13 Frederick Carder, vase, about 1910.
Gold aurene glass with applied and tooled
decoration, height 17.1 cm. (Collection The
Corning Museum of Glass, Corning, New
York [75.4.113]. Gift of Corning Glass Works.)

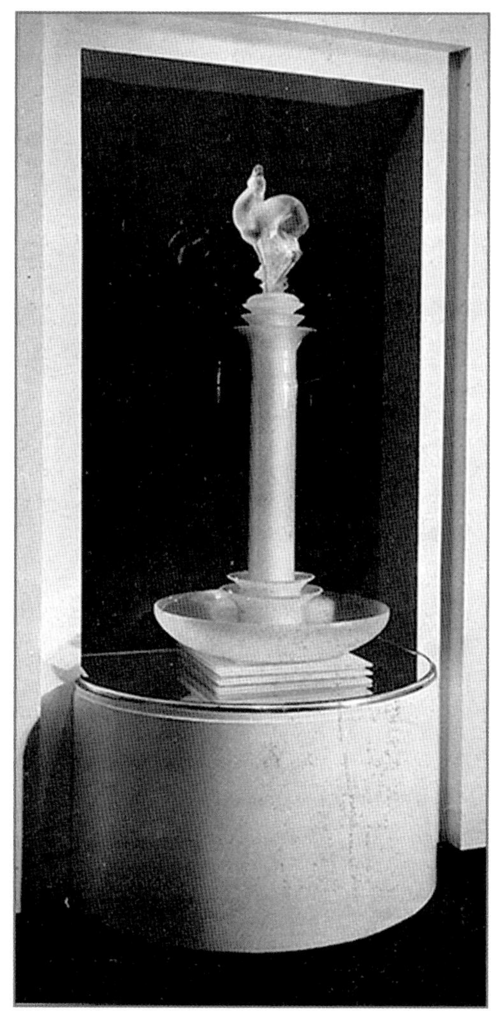

4.14 Photograph showing Sidney Waugh's cast crystal fawn sculpture atop a glass fountain in Steuben shop, *Architectural Forum*, March 1934.

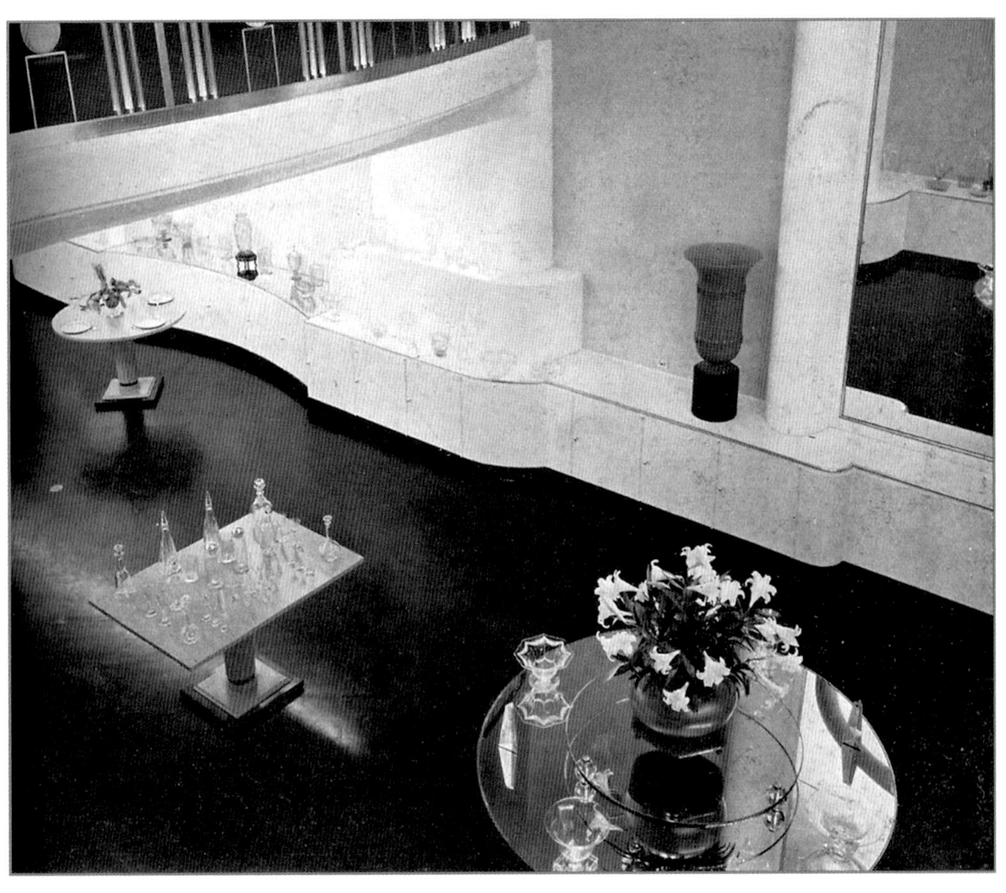

4.15 Steuben shop, *Architectural Forum*,
March 1934.

lead was confined to a small office space on the second floor, a space which was not shown in the *Architectural Forum* spread and to which, in general, Steuben drew little attention.

As in its shop, Steuben's advertising sought to present its glassware as museum-worthy art. A 1939 ad in *Fortune* magazine featured a black-and-white photograph of a starkly lit Zodiac Bowl under the headline, "Can the machine age create a Masterpiece?" The text in an accompanying cartouche implied that it could: "In the Permanent Collection of the Metropolitan Museum of Art." The ad copy proclaimed, in smaller type, "All the masterpieces aren't old! Here, for instance, is the Zodiac Bowl. It was designed by Sidney Waugh and handmade at Corning by Steuben craftsmen. Replicas are in the permanent collection of the Metropolitan Museum of Art in New York and the Victoria and Albert Museum in London." In something of a publicity coup for Steuben, the Zodiac Bowl was acquired by both the Metropolitan Museum and the Victoria and Albert Museum in 1935, the same year that it was designed by Waugh and debuted on the market.[85]

The Zodiac Bowl was included in *Contemporary American Glass* in 1938 (as was a version of the cast crystal fawn that adorned the fountain in the Steuben shop). That exhibition inaugurated a long and mutually beneficial relationship between Steuben and the Boston museum. Houghton joined the institute's board of trustees in 1946. The following year, he sent Plaut on a trip "to find out what was going on" with Steuben's competition in Europe.[86] According to Plaut's post-trip report, "The general debilitation of Europe has compromised greatly any opportunity which the glass industries of the liberated countries—and of Sweden—might have of evolving a successful and promising post-war pattern of recovery. The implications of this situation for American industry, and for Steuben-Corning in particular, are arresting."[87] Plaut contrasts the postwar health of U.S. industry—and of the glass industry

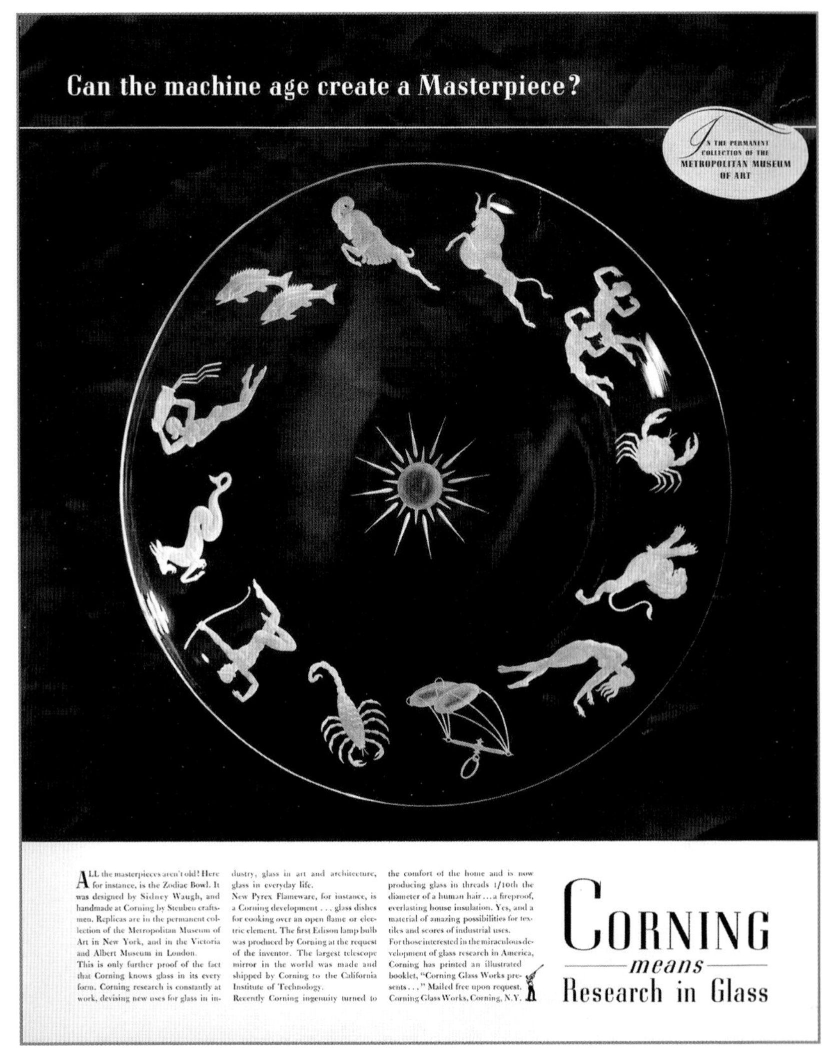

4.16 Ad, Steuben Zodiac Bowl, *Fortune*, 1939.

in particular—with the "general debilitation of Europe." Recall his similar argument in "50 Rising American Painters 50" several years earlier. Just as young American artists flourished to the extent that they cast off European influence and outmoded doctrine, so Steuben would benefit from the diminishment of its European counterparts.

In March 1948, the publishing house of H. Bittner and Company released a monograph on Steuben glass. Elegantly produced with sixty-one full-page plates in halftone, and eleven gravure reproductions, the book was priced at ten dollars (roughly ninety dollars in today's money).[88] An ad announcing the volume in the *New York Times* described Steuben glass as "America's greatest achievement in craftsmanship and art."[89] Previous monographs issued by the same publisher, the ad noted, focused on Raphael, Matthias Grünewald, Théodore Géricault, Auguste Renoir, and eighteenth-century Venetian drawings. The ad thus sought to align Steuben glass with a high art tradition reaching back to the Renaissance, even as it underscored the American independence and technical ingenuity of the company's designs. In a brief foreword, the book's author noted that Steuben's glassware was a "healthy American art form which its founders have compounded of their inventiveness, their ideals, and their tenacity."[90] All this might seem unremarkable save for the fact that the author of the monograph was James S. Plaut—and the fact that the month before Steuben had played an active role in distributing the Boston manifesto proclaiming modern art "a cult of bewilderment." The publication of a monograph on Steuben glass written by the director of the (newly christened) ICA extended the public ties between the two institutions.

Throughout *Steuben Glass*, Plaut's approach to his subject is at once celebratory and decidedly nationalistic: "This book has been devised to trace and illustrate the development of Steuben in terms of enlightened design and craftsmanship and their harmonious resolution. A straightforward American story, this is the romantic revelation of a pioneer industry's courageous investment in art and ideas."[91] As though to assert Steuben's quintessential Americanness, the work illustrated on the front cover of the monograph was the American Ballad Bowl, one of two engraved glass vessels from 1942—the other being the Paul Revere Vase—for which early American history served as pictorial inspiration.[92] Just as Plaut had previously celebrated U.S. painters who sought to "break free of European doctrine," so he now promoted Steuben as a producer of definitively American design. Indeed, as early as the *Contemporary American Glass* exhibition in 1938, Plaut was casting Steuben's achievement in strongly nationalistic terms: "No false patriotism provokes the categorical statement that … Steuben has come forward rapidly to challenge and often surpass the spectacular achievements of Orrefors in Sweden, Baccarat and Lalique in France, or Lobmeyr in Vienna. . . . The American glass industry has embarked on an ambitious course of production. The eventual realization of its momentary promise rests heavily upon the discernment of its patrons."[93] Ten years later, Plaut would draw contemporary art, commerce, and American design more closely together under the aegis of a new program at the Boston institute, and it is to that program that we now turn.

Design in Industry

In addition to renouncing "modern" in favor of "contemporary" art, the Boston institute initiated a new venture in 1948, the Department of Design in Industry. Rather than organizing exhibitions, this department's primary goal was to consult with corporate clients. According to the *Boston Daily Globe*, "What the Institute does depends upon the corporation employing it. It will set up an entire design department for a company. It will analyze a company's design problems. It will criticize, review, and make recommendations. It will recommend skilled design personnel, if desired."[94] The Department of Design

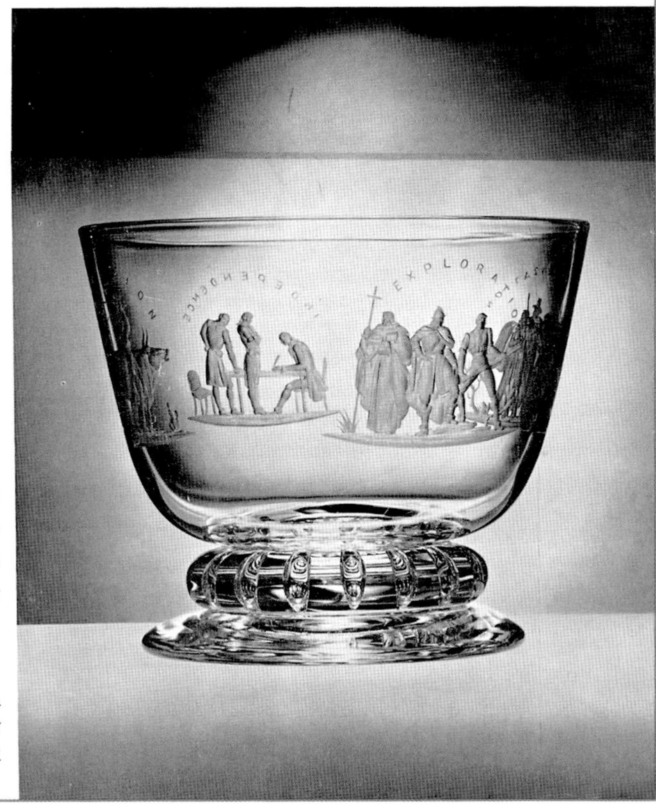

4.17 James S. Plaut, *Steuben Glass* (New York: H. Bittner & Company, 1948), cover.

in Industry fulfilled at least one additional function: it made money, much needed at the time, for the ICA.[95]

In a later interview, Plaut noted that he had "continued to preach as a gospel" the need for museums and other nonprofit institutions to devise money-making ventures such as the Department of Design in Industry:

> We charged fees to industry for consultation. It might be that under present tax laws this kind of activity would be more difficult for a non-profit institution, but I suspect that a formula can always be found if the work that is being done has legitimate educational ends, which this did. It certainly was a life-saver for the Institute. From the beginning to the present-day the Institute has always struggled financially in the absence of any significant endowment. The industrial design program, for a period of ten years, saved the Institute in that its income was able to offset the general operating deficit.[96]

The integration of cultural institutions and commercial industry would, according to Plaut's "gospel," enhance both.

The need for the ICA to raise funds—and to do so quickly—was apparent to both Plaut and his board of trustees (including Houghton) at the time the Department of Design in Industry was launched. In a report dated October 7, 1948, the acting treasurer of the ICA submitted a budgetary statement for the fiscal year ending the previous May. It was not reassuring:

> The operating deficit for the year was $80,633.96. This was partly alleviated by receiving temporary loans totaling a little over $15,000, but the cash position of the Institute is in a very precarious condition. It would be folly not to recognize this as a matter of immediate concern. In my opinion it is mandatory that sources of additional income be found or that operating and overhead expenses be reduced. It is recommended

that the latter course be put into effect immediately pending accomplishment of the former.[97]

The only optimistic note sounded by the report was that "Considerable progress was made in the Department of Art in Industry [soon to be renamed the Department of Design in Industry], which resulted in additional income, but this likewise entailed additional expenses."[98]

Though it eventually formed relationships with nearly fifty clients, including the Elgin Watch Company, Motorola, Gillette, and Cheney Fabrics, the Department of Design in Industry grew out of a year-long pilot program that the ICA developed with its first corporate patron, Corning-Steuben. The program involved training designers for potential employment by the glass company as well as periodic consultations about product design, retail display, marketing, and corporate policy. During this first year, Corning-Steuben covered a portion of Plaut's salary along with some of the other costs incurred while launching the new department.[99]

The close relationship between the ICA and Steuben did not sit well with a number of contemporary artists in Boston, including Jack Levine. At an artists' meeting called to protest the Boston manifesto in 1948, Levine noted

> the rather peculiar participation in the art world of a certain glass company. It is curious that when the Institute of Modern Art denounced modern art this glass company went to such trouble to circularize the statement and it is interesting that this glass company has further participated in the art field by means of recent book which demonstrates the intrinsic art values of their glass productions.... Modern art is driven from the field and this glass company picks up the marbles.[100]

By pointing out the "curious" collaboration of Steuben and the Boston institute, Levine suggests at least the appearance of a conflict of interest. Steuben promotes the "art values" of its glassware (in part through the publication of a book authored by Plaut) while supporting the Boston institute's critique of modern art as Continental and outmoded.

Like Levine, Barr believed that both the "art values" of Steuben Glass and the company's relationship with the Boston institute were questionable at best. In the context of the controversy over the Boston manifesto, Barr recalled:

> Back in 1940 I find that Mr. [John M.] Gates of Steuben proposed that we have an exhibition of glass designed by 27 artists. I doubt if we would have had the exhibition anyway since most of the pieces were not such as we would want to exhibit. Mr. Gates seemed to understand our reasons at that time. Indeed, one of our staff had a long conversation with Mr. Gates. In a memo of this conversation I find the following remarks:
>
> "The Steuben clientele consists of the peak of the economic triangle. As [their] taste is not in proportion to their income, it has been found that reminiscent design is what sells best. They [Steuben] have tried designs which approach the modern point of view and have not sold a piece, and they feel that the best they can do is edge taste along a little at a time. As their product is a handmade one and very expensive, their problem is rather a special one and does not fall in the category of mass production."[101]

Eight years after the fact, Barr retrieves a memo recording a conversation between a MoMA staffer and a senior executive at Steuben. The memo suggests that Steuben's customers have more money than taste and that nostalgic ("reminiscent") designs therefore sell better than those with a "modern point of view." In specifying that "their product is a handmade one and very expensive," the memo distinguishes Steuben glass from the machine-made, inexpensive objects of design that concerned MoMA.[102]

MoMA included industrial design within the curatorial purview of its Department of Architecture and Industrial Art. Describing the department's approach, Barr wrote in 1934 that MoMA "played up the anonymously designed industrial object rather more than the object which shows evidence of 'styling.'"[103] When glass objects were shown at MoMA, they were therefore simple Pyrex bowls and laboratory beakers rather than hand-etched crystal vases or signed, limited-edition plates.[104] It would be hard to think of objects more obviously stylized than Steuben's Zodiac Bowl or more self-consciously reminiscent than its American Ballad Bowl.

The 1940 exhibition to which Barr refers in his confidential memo was *The Collection of Designs in Glass by Twenty-Seven Contemporary Artists.* Following its rejection by MoMA, the show was mounted not at another museum but at the Steuben shop on Fifth Avenue. The exhibition presented the fruits of Steuben's first effort to collaborate with a group of living artists. Although the company claimed its selection criteria were inclusive, twenty-six of the twenty-seven designs chosen were figurative. The use of the term "contemporary" in the exhibition's title was important in this regard, since it could accommodate deeply traditional imagery that would not have qualified as "modern" in the sense of innovative, forward-looking, or self-critical: Grant Wood's stolid farmwoman feeding geese and chickens, for instance, or Jean Hugo's centaur hotfoot in pursuit of a unicorn, or Thomas Hart Benton's women gathering grapes encircled by leaf and vine. None of these designs would have passed muster as "modern" in Barr's MoMA, but they were all "contemporary" in the sense of having been produced by living artists of the time.

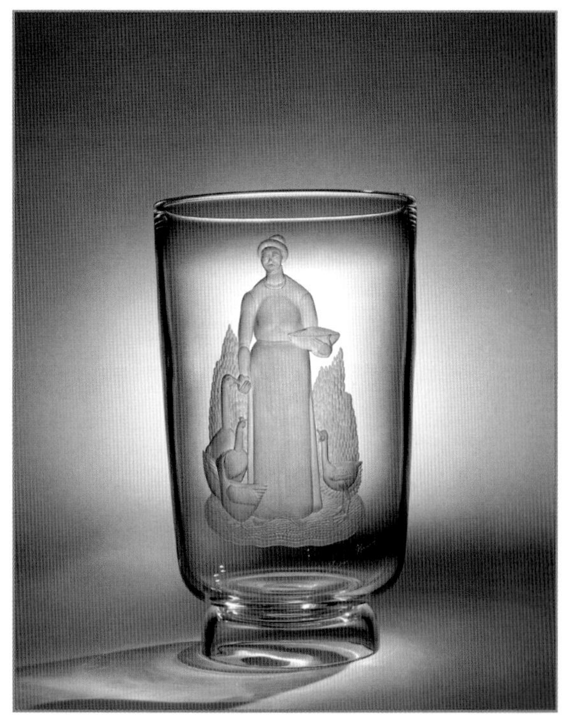

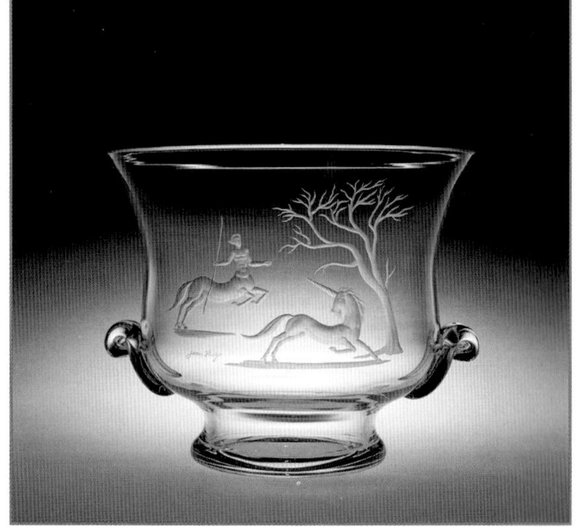

4.18 Engraved vase designed by Grant Wood and engraved by George Thompson for Steuben Glass, Inc., 1940. Colorless lead glass, blown and engraved, height 13¾ inches (35.5 cm). (Collection The Corning Museum of Glass, Corning, New York [89.4.33]. Gift of Harry W. and Mary M. Anderson in memory of Carl G. and Borghild M. Anderson and Paul E. and Louise Wheeler.)

4.19 Engraved bowl designed by Jean Hugo for Steuben Glass, Inc., 1940. Colorless lead glass, blown and engraved, height 8 inches (23.7 cm). (Collection The Corning Museum of Glass, Corning, New York [2003.4.56].)

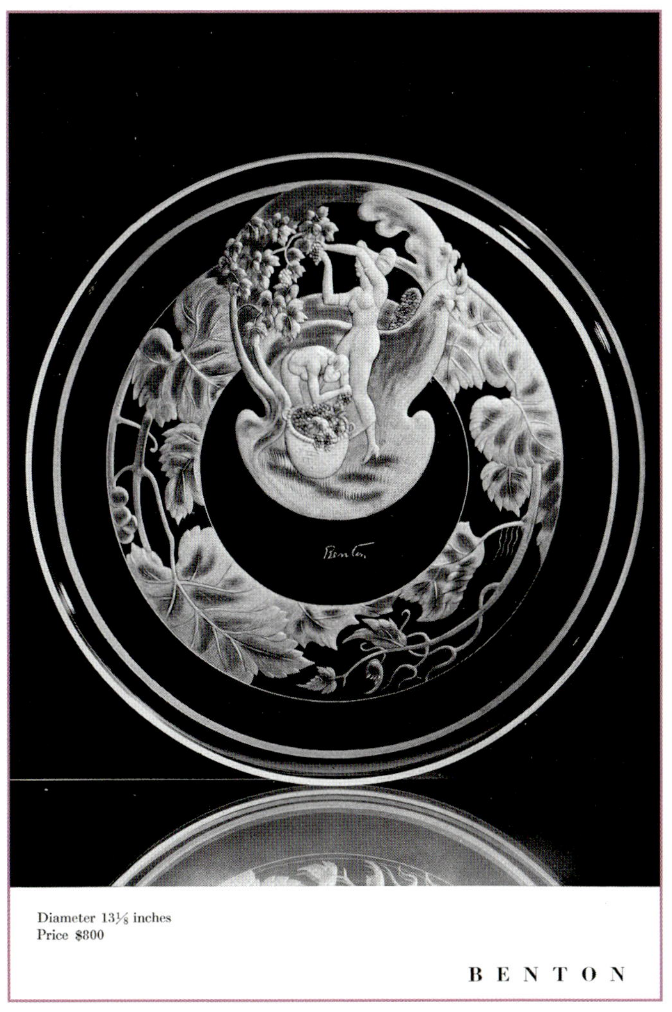

4.20 Engraved plate designed by Thomas
Hart Benton for Steuben Glass, Inc., 1940.
Colorless lead glass, blown and engraved,
diameter 13⅛ inches. (Collection Rakow
Research Library, The Corning Museum of
Glass, Steuben Archive.)

Each artist in the exhibition—Giorgio de Chirico, Jean Cocteau, John Steuart Curry, Marie Laurencin, Henri Matisse, and Georgia O'Keeffe, among others—submitted sketches which were then engraved onto handblown glass by Steuben craftsmen in Corning, New York. One unacknowledged irony of the project was that each vessel included a facsimile of the artist's signature engraved by an artisan whose own name appeared neither on the glass nor in the catalogue accompanying the exhibition.

In the Steuben shop, the twenty-seven "designs in glass" were displayed like museum artifacts, behind velvet ropes attached to polished stanchions. According to the *New York Times*, "The larger front showroom was decorated with daffodils and forsythia from which the guests passed in line to a small semi-circular room in the rear, where the twenty-seven pieces were shown on pedestals and lighted against a royal blue background."[105] Notwithstanding this rather grand presentation, Ruth Green Harris, the *New York Times*'s critic, expressed disappointment that many of "the designs bear little integral relation to the shape on which they are etched in intaglio; and some are etched in a way that destroys and grays the very nature of the material itself."[106] As Harris saw it, the form of the engraved image did not follow the function of the glass vessels on view. Or, rather, since these were objets d'art that were not intended for everyday use as bowls, vases, or plates, form did not follow the appearance of functionalism in an aesthetically appealing or convincingly modernist fashion.

Fernand Léger's vase, which bore the one abstract composition in the show, was deemed a particular failure in this regard. According to Harris, "The drawing here is just a lump on the surface of the glass, not an enrichment of the surface."[107] Léger's design was something like a tumor on the body of the bowl, a misshapen growth that had deformed rather than enhanced the glass. The unhappy marriage of the artist's machine-inspired abstraction and the hand-cut crystal onto which it had been engraved revealed the larger

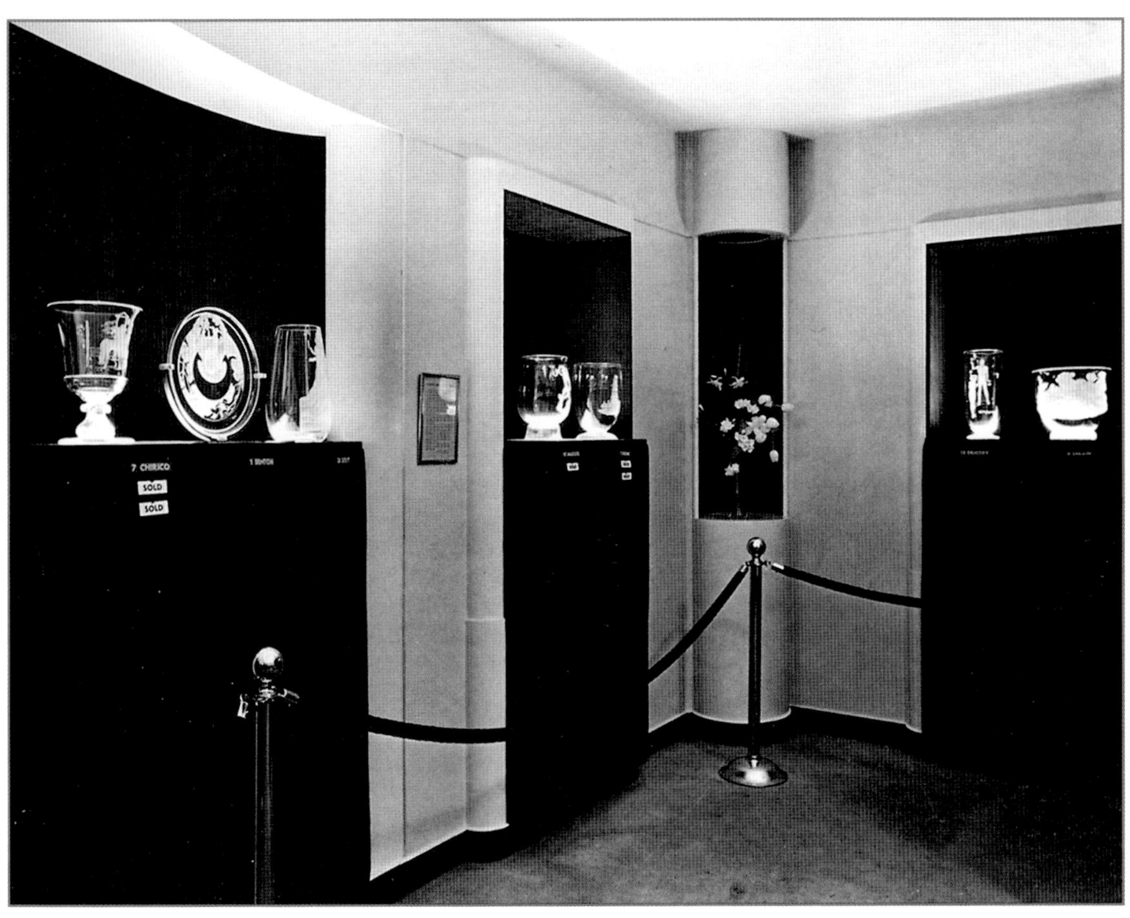

4.21 Installation view of the exhibition *The Collection of Designs in Glass by Twenty-Seven Contemporary Artists*, 1940, Steuben Glass shop, New York.

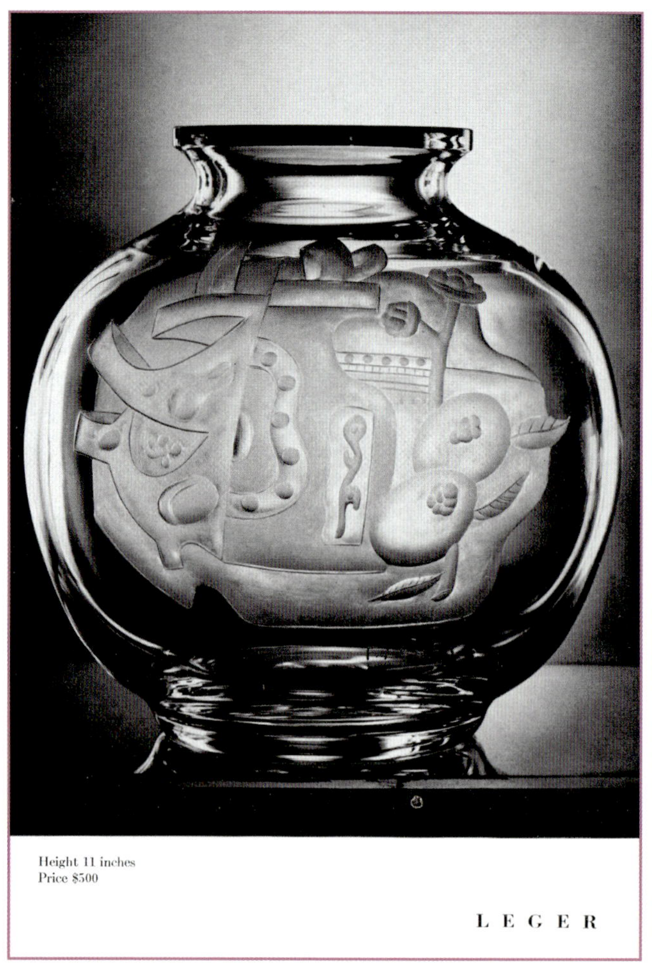

4.22 Engraved bowl designed by Fernand Léger for Steuben Glass, Inc., 1940. Color-less lead glass, blown and engraved, height 11 inches. (Collection Rakow Research Library, The Corning Museum of Glass, Steuben Archive.)

tensions between fine and applied art in the exhibition. Rather than being a genuine collaboration, the design of each vessel consisted of a two-part relay, in which the artist's drawing was passed on to and reinterpreted by the engraver. In Léger's case, the pairing of two-dimensional sketch and three-dimensional object—of artistic and artisanal labor—was especially ill-conceived.

It is easy to dismiss Léger's bowl, if not the entire exhibition, as what Clement Greenberg called "high-class kitsch for the luxury trade."[108] For Greenberg, kitsch not only was hostile to modernist values—to art for art's sake and medium specificity—it threatened actively to co-opt them: "Kitsch's enormous profits are a source of temptation to the avant-garde itself, and its members have not always resisted this temptation. Ambitious writers and artists will modify their work under the pressure of kitsch, if they do not succumb to it entirely."[109]

Once it had been translated onto the surface of Steuben crystal, Léger's cubism was no more or less "contemporary" than Wood's corn-belt regionalism, Hugo's neoclassicism, Salvador Dalí's surrealism, or Christian Bérard's neoromanticism (to name some of the artists and styles represented in the exhibition). The promise of the category of the contemporary in 1940 was that it would provide what Plaut called "the total picture of the art of our times dispassionately, without bias, and without undue emphasis on any particular aspect."[110] The danger was that it would devolve into kitsch.

Plastics

The Collection of Designs in Glass by Twenty-Seven Contemporary Artists opened at the Steuben shop in January 1940. In December of that year, the Boston institute mounted *Plastics* as a follow-up to its 1938 exhibition *Contemporary American Glass*. Like the earlier exhibition, *Plastics* was intended as a demonstration "of the best design and craftsmanship prevalent in

American industry today."[11] The show featured quotidian objects (umbrellas, door pulls, shower curtains) alongside decorative items such as "transparent angels molded of Lucite" and artworks such as a Plexiglas sculpture by Alexander Calder. Given the recentness of most types of plastic (Lucite, for example, was invented in 1931 by Dupont chemists) and the leading role of U.S. scientists and corporations in the development of these materials, the status of the exhibition as both contemporary and American would have been self-evident.

Photographs of the exhibition set up an amusing, slightly awkward standoff between individual female spectators (including the institute's receptionist) and the plastic items and pedagogical wall labels on display. In one view, a well-appointed woman ("Mrs. Hasket Derby of Boston," according to the photograph's caption) poses beside a poster-sized wall-text at the show's entrance, as though in the midst of reading it. The text announces: "In keeping with our policy of dispassionate presentation of significant contemporary trends, we submit this exhibition of current design in American plastics." "A policy of dispassionate presentation" suggests a range of styles and approaches to design extending well beyond the "machine art" aesthetic promoted by MoMA. Similarly, the institute's focus on "contemporary trends" and "current design" suggests a temporal distinction rather than a qualitative evaluation ("good design") of the sort typically made by the New York museum.

In contrast to MoMA's modernist emphasis on truth to materials, the institute pointed up the endless adaptability of plastic. As the supersized wall text for the exhibition put it, "A plastic is at once wood, rubber, metal, glass and yet none of them. Thus the designer cannot depend on the inherent nature of his material for inspiration but is obliged to draw from the heritage of the 'pure' materials which plastics resemble." Impure and synthetic, plastic must imitate other materials since it has no "inherent nature" to fall back

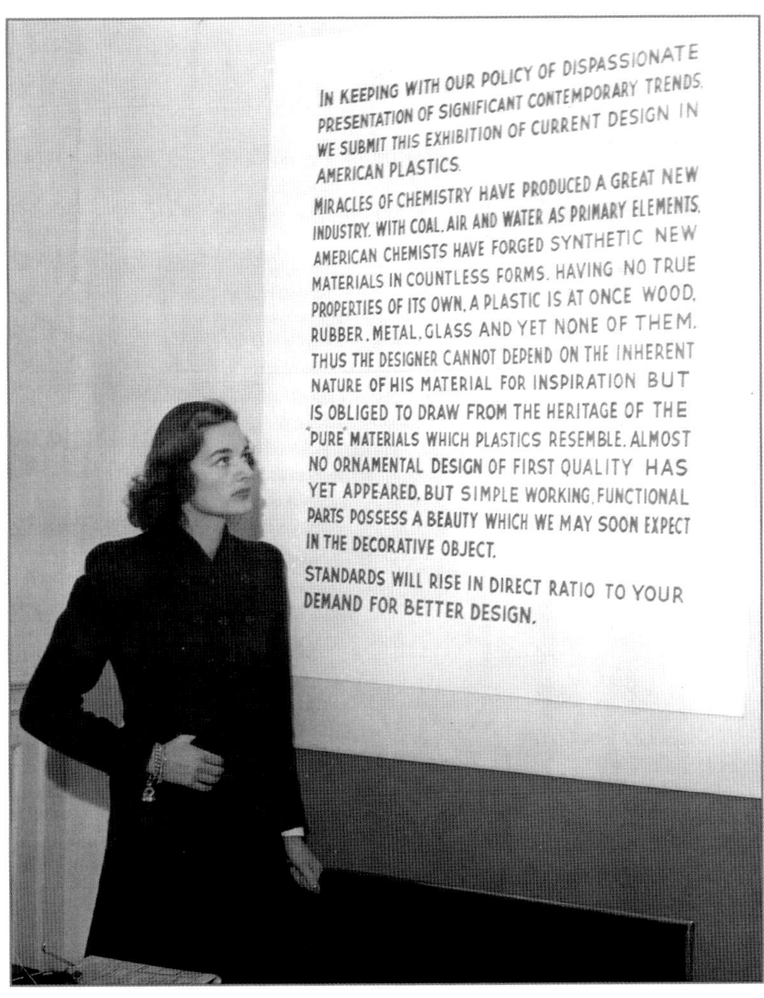

4.23 *Plastics*, The Institute of Modern Art,
Boston, December 20, 1940–January 12, 1941.
Mrs. Hasket Derby with the credo of the
Plastics exhibition. © Crosby of Boston.

upon. How, then, could the Institute of Modern Art display plastic objects to best advantage in its exhibition?

The installation views of *Plastics* seem unresolved, as though caught between emphasizing utilitarian value on the one hand and visual novelty on the other. In one photograph of the exhibition, institute staff member Anne Tredick sits on a bamboo chair while holding a plastic door handle in her left hand and an umbrella in her right. Behind her and to the left, a plastic shower curtain hugs the institute's wall. Of the several items on display in the photograph, only the (non-plastic) chair serves a functional purpose at the moment. The plastic objects—a shower curtain without a shower, a door handle unattached to any door, and an umbrella open in the absence of any water or rain—appear superfluous and vaguely absurd. The seemingly ornamental presence of Miss Tredick is thus revealed as necessary to the logic of the picture. By displaying the umbrella and door handle (and, not incidentally, herself) to the camera, Miss Tredick solicits visual interest in plastic objects that we might otherwise look past or, quite literally, through.

In another view of the exhibition, "Miss Polly Cotter of Boston" faces off against Alexander Calder's Plexiglas sculpture. The sculpture's concealed light source illuminates not only the test tube–like armature of the work but also, and slightly uncannily, the face of Miss Cotter. Whether she is transfixed or bemused by this particular experience of contemporary art is impossible to know.

Calder's work had recently won first prize among 250 entries in a Plexiglas competition sponsored by the chemical manufacturer Rohm and Haas. Created by the company as a shatterproof alternative to glass in 1933, Plexiglas was introduced to American markets within the context of military production (e.g., cockpit covers, windscreens, weapon mounts). The sculptural competition underscored the possibility of aesthetic—rather than strictly

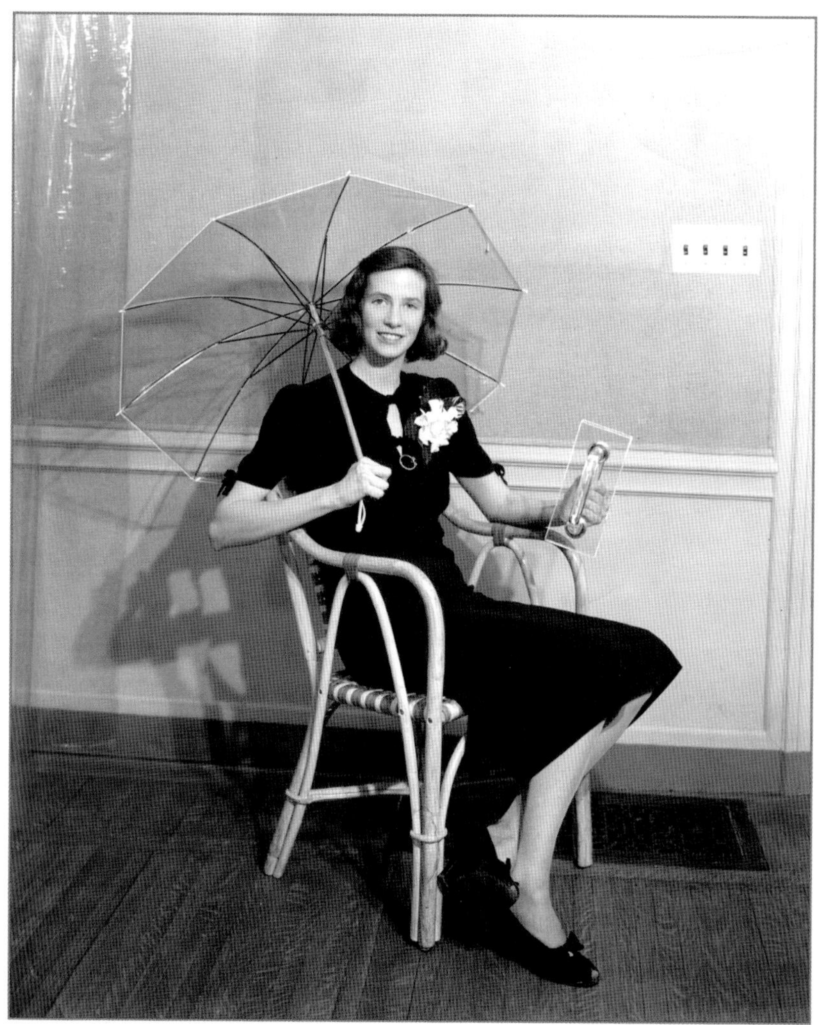

4.24 *Plastics*, The Institute of Modern Art,
Boston, December 20, 1940–January 12, 1941.
Miss Anne Tredick holds an umbrella of plastic material from Filene's, Boston, and Lucite
door pulls, W. C. Vaughan Co., Boston, Edward Pratt, designer. © Cloud Photographer.

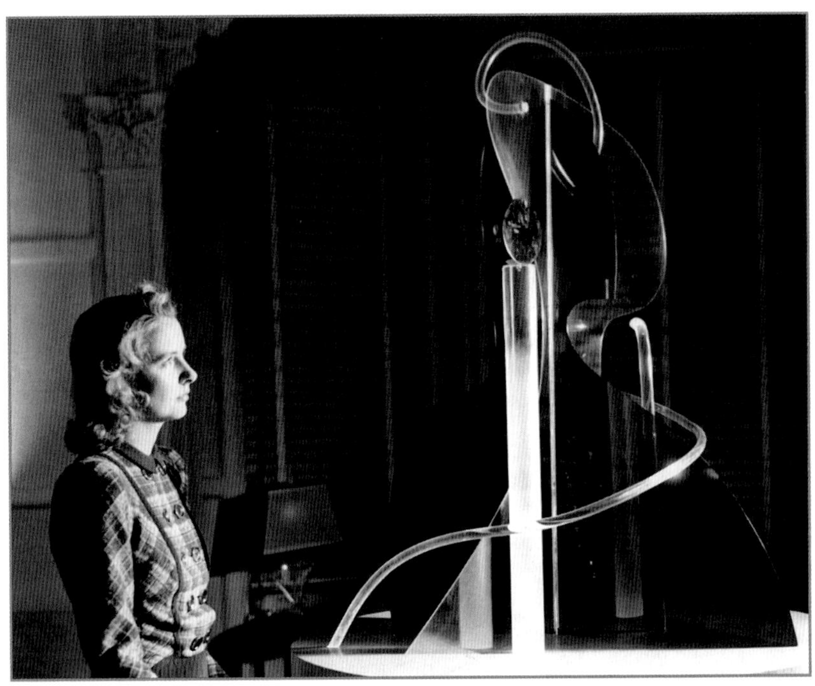

4.25 *Plastics*, The Institute of Modern Art, Boston, December 20, 1940–January 12, 1941. Miss Polly Cotter of Boston with Alexander Calder's prize-winning Plexiglas sculpture. © Crosby of Boston. © 2012 Calder Foundation, New York/Artists Rights Society (ARS), New York.

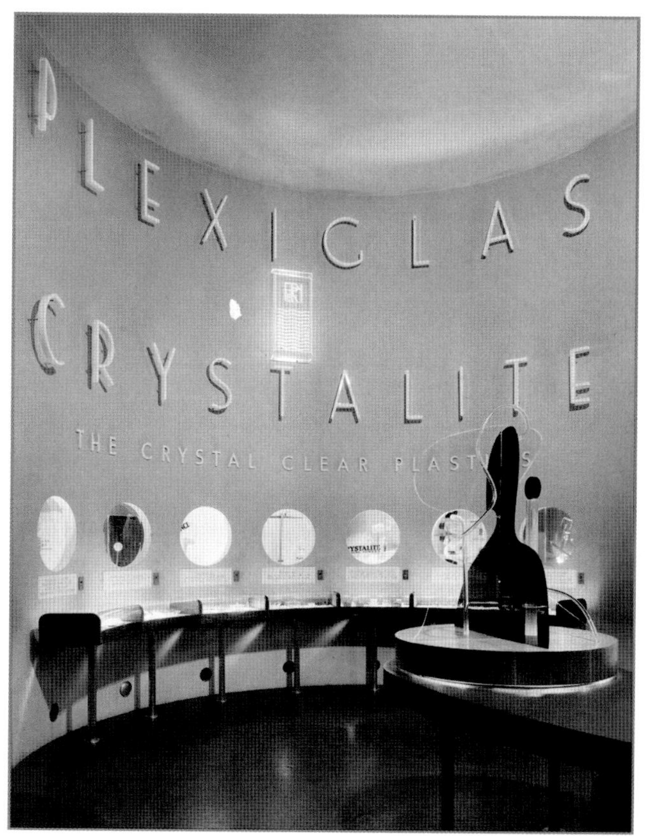

4.26 Alexander Calder sculpture, Rohm and Haas exhibit, 1939, New York World's Fair. (Collection Cooper-Hewitt National Design Museum, Smithsonian Institution, Gilbert Rohde Collection.) Photographer: Matt Flynn. © Smithsonian Institution. Photo credit: Cooper-Hewitt, National Design Museum, Smithsonian Institution/Art Resource, NY. © 2012 Calder Foundation, New York/ Artists Rights Society (ARS), New York.

utilitarian or militaristic—applications of the material. As the winning entry in the Plexiglas competition, Calder's sculpture was given pride of place in the Rohm and Haas pavilion at the 1939 New York World's Fair. Displayed on a circular table to allow viewers to approach from all sides, the sculpture was set against a series of seven backlit dioramas, each of which demonstrated a different property (flexibility, lightness, luminosity) of Plexiglas or its sister plastic, Crystalite.

Calder's sculpture took part in the corporate promotion of plastic at the World's Fair and, more broadly, in the affirmation of American industry and scientific ingenuity. It is worth noting, however, that the Plexiglas competition was cosponsored by MoMA and that James Johnson Sweeney, MoMA's director of Painting and Sculpture under Barr, served as one of its three jurors. Like its Boston offshoot, MoMA also forged alliances with private industry, if in a somewhat more discreet fashion. For example, while the museum agreed to cosponsor the Rohm and Haas competition, it did not (as was originally proposed) exhibit the winning entries in its galleries. And like the Boston Institute, MoMA occasionally engaged in the sale of art, as we saw in its 1932 exhibition of *Persian Fresco Painting*. As early as 1929, Barr would promote the new museum by telling the readers of *Vogue* magazine: "In the history of art as in more materialistic matters, money talks vividly. Let us not be ashamed to listen."[112]

Rohm and Haas was one of many corporate exhibitors at the 1939 World's Fair to present plastic as the very material of progress and prosperity. According to the *Chemical and Engineering News*, "The World of Tomorrow, to judge by the displays in the scientific exhibits of the New York World's Fair, 1939, will be plasticized, or at least dominated by plastics. As though by common consent, most companies have featured some variety of the many species of plastics."[113] As though consenting to the plasticized future of American culture and industry, the Boston Institute mounted its *Plastics* exhibition just a few weeks after the World's Fair closed. A last installation view of the exhibition suggests how tightly the institute linked the show to the promotion of plastic products.

In contrast to the photographs discussed above featuring individual women in the exhibition, this view presents a male mannequin seen through the slightly distorting scrim of a plastic curtain. "Equipped for anything," according to the photograph's caption, "this model at the current Plastics show at the Institute of Modern Art, Boston is ready for a morning of 'lab' work, an afternoon of football, and an evening of music. The Polyvinyl alcohol gloves were made by Dupont, the football helmet by John Riddell & Company; and the radio by Philco. Suspenders (and a belt to make sure) are made of Elastiglass, which, together with the Lumarith garters, were supplied by the Celluloid Corporation."[114]

The caption works overtime to name all the brands and products worn by the mannequin. In addition to sporting a gamut of plastic accessories, from garters to gloves to helmet, the mannequin is surrounded by additional tools and implements—flashlights, screwdrivers, a plastic key holder, a transparent cap—that have been affixed to the corner walls behind him. There is a slightly grotesque quality to the scene: the mannequin seems weighed down by his plastic props rather than efficiently outfitted or appropriately "equipped" by them. Why, after all, the need for both plastic suspenders and a plastic belt (just to be "sure"?) if both are reliably functional? Why obscure the mannequin behind a plastic curtain if not to further distance him from reality? It is almost as though the institute had summoned a dreamscape (or nightmare) of consumerism in which commodities take on a life of their own or threaten, like the objects strewn across the walls, to spin out of control.

In contrast to the highly ordered, Bauhaus-like rationalism of MoMA's exhibitions of industrial design, *Plastics* featured a dummy surrogate for an

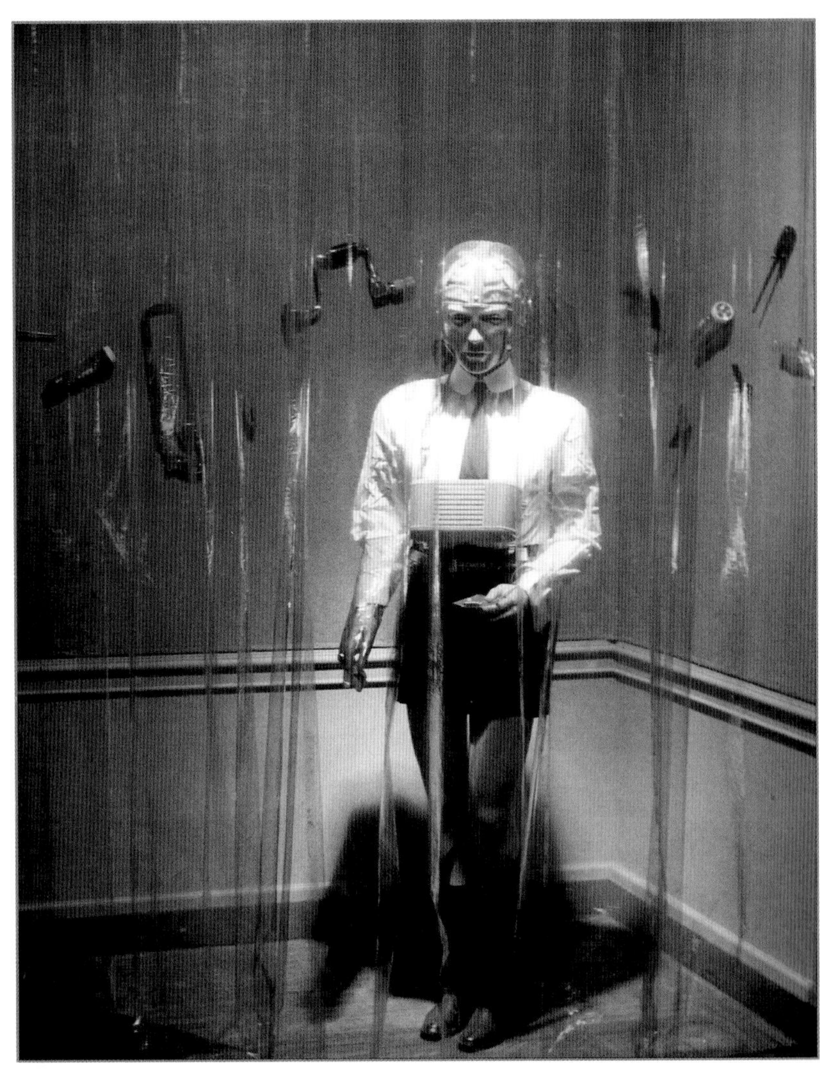

4.27 Installation view of *Plastics*, The Institute of Modern Art, Boston, December 20, 1940–January 12, 1941. © Cushing Gellatly, Boston.

American consumer all but overtaken by plastic products and accessories. Here it is useful to recall that MoMA's allegiance to the Bauhaus was itself criticized as out of step with contemporary American culture at the time. In a 1938 review of the museum's Bauhaus exhibition in the *Magazine of Art*, Mary Cooke argued that the school's methods of blending artistic and artisanal labor and its emphasis on workshop production were outmoded. Titling her review "Bauhaus Post Mortem," Cooke called upon MoMA to, as it were, drop the Bauhaus so as to keep up with the times: "Contemporary America with its highly developed capitalist system in which competition, overproduction, quick obsolescence, and the influence of consumers' choice play such an important role presents a new problem of design from the point of view of education and practical application."[115]

If, as Cooke suggested, MoMA was committed to a model of modernist design based on a nostalgic idea of collectivity, perhaps the *Plastics* show at the Boston institute could be seen as an effort to appeal to the "contemporary America" of "competition, overproduction, [and] quick obsolescence." At the institute, a range of American art and objects of design—from plastic door handles to glass Zodiac plates—could be claimed as contemporary quite apart from questions of modernity in terms of form or function. The institute's intermingling of curating and commerce would, for better or worse, increasingly come to mirror the logic of contemporary art in America.

Afterword: Stop and Shop (1959)

In this chapter I have argued that the category of contemporary art in the late 1930s and 1940s as taken up by the Institute of Modern Art accommodated a range of artistic practices and objects that were not modern in the sense of being modernist, self-reflexive, or medium-specific. Even before it changed its name to the Institute of Contemporary Art in 1948, the Boston institute tested the boundaries of museum practice by rejecting the premise of a permanent collection, emphasizing the relation of art to commerce, and by presenting American art and design—including the hand-blown and engraved glass created by Steuben—as exemplary of contemporary art.

In the late 1950s, the ICA found a different means to bring art and commerce together. In this instance, the institute intervened not in the process of design but at the point of purchase. An ad in the March 9, 1959, edition of the *Boston Globe* announced "A New Exhibition of Contemporary Art." Though "selected and arranged" by the ICA, the show was not held on its premises. Instead, it was presented at a nearby Stop & Shop supermarket. Titled *Young Talent in New England*, the show comprised paintings by regional artists. The works were displayed, to surprisingly strong effect, over the vegetable aisle of the grocery store. An installation view shows two young men, one with pipe in hand, looking at a large abstraction hanging over crates of avocados and rows of lettuce heads. A sign above the vegetables reads, "If you want smaller amounts, please ask clerk." Although the sign clearly refers to the large quantities of avocadoes on offer, one begins to think by analogy of the paintings as goods to be crated and shipped in larger or "smaller amounts."

Another installation view pulls back for a panoramic shot of the supermarket interior, recording multiple aisles of merchandise, various shoppers and their carts, and the same wall of paintings and vegetables that was captured close-up in the previous photograph. Seeing the packaged and canned goods in the other aisles of the market, we are reminded that the produce department offers the freshest—if also the most perishable—"selection" of items for sale in the store. The vegetables thus provide an appropriate companion for an exhibition of contemporary art, especially one promising that year's "selection" of *Young Talent in New England*.

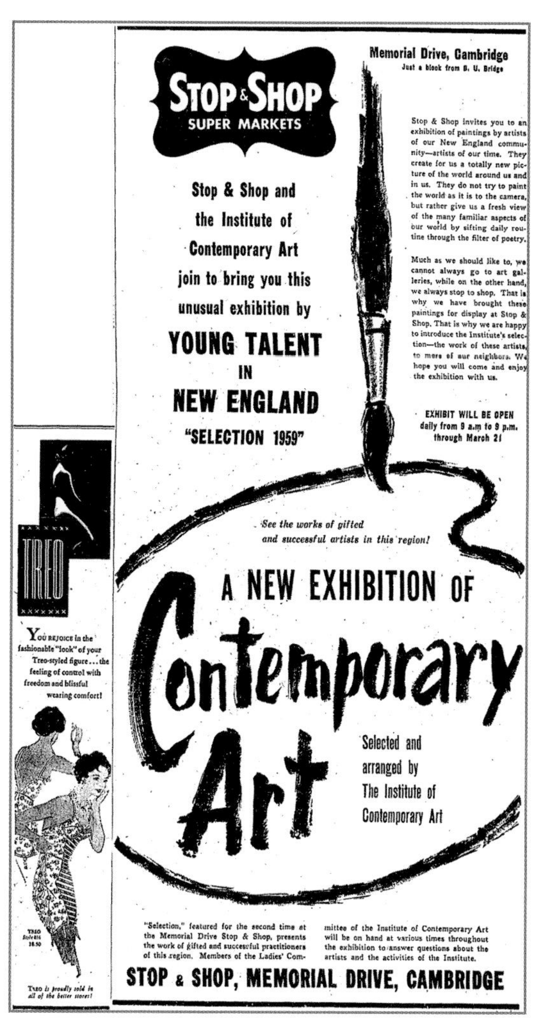

4.28 Display ad for *Young Talent in New England, Boston Globe,* March 9, 1959.

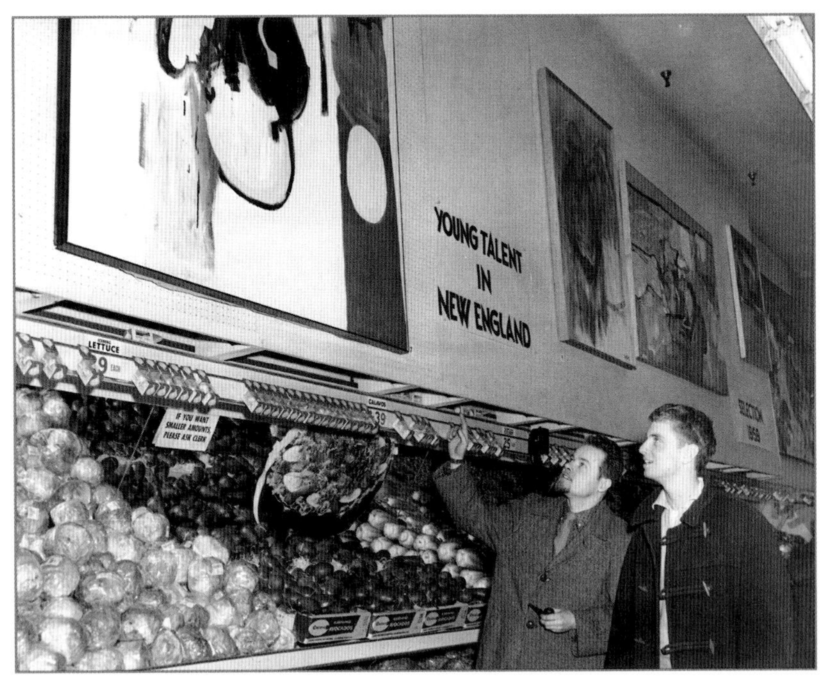

4.29 *Young Talent in New England: Selection 1959.* Installation view at Memorial Drive Stop & Shop supermarket, Cambridge, Massachusetts, March 9–March 21, 1959. Exhibition organized by the Institute of Contemporary Art, Boston.

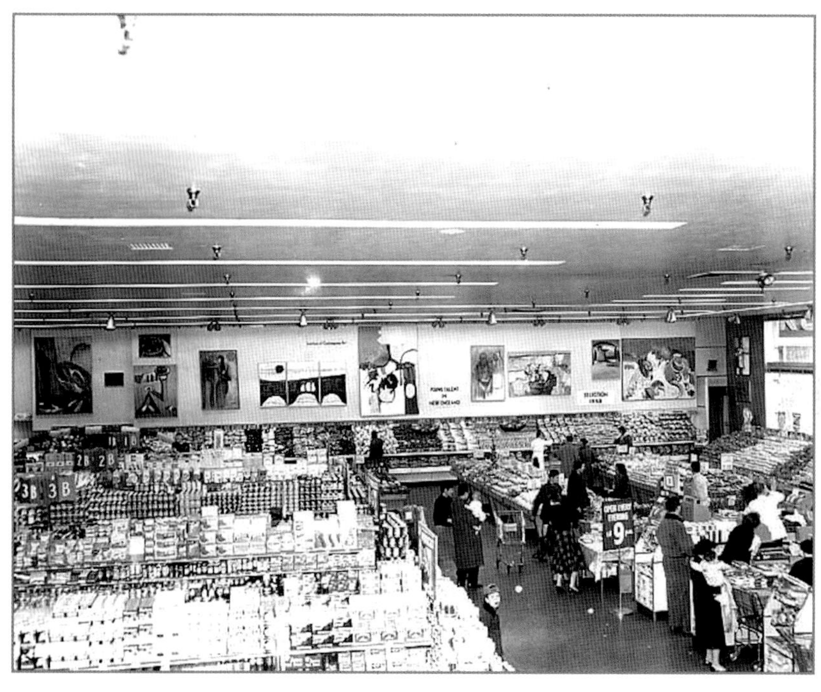

4.30 Young Talent in New England:
Selection 1959. Installation view at Memorial
Drive Stop & Shop supermarket, Cambridge,
Massachusetts, March 9–March 21, 1959.
Exhibition organized by the Institute of
Contemporary Art, Boston.

Throughout the 1940s and 1950s, the ICA was, according to Plaut, "very conscious of our obligation to American art, and particularly to the artists of our region. So that meticulously each year there were exhibitions of local artists and of American artists in general."[116] In showcasing New England artists, the ICA faced the risk of being dismissed as a provincial or strictly regionalist institution. One strategy it devised to address this challenge was to capitalize upon the looseness of the category of contemporary—rather than modern—art. The ICA applied that category broadly as a way to mix local and national surveys of art and to expand beyond painting and sculpture to objects of industrial design and décor. In addition, rather than downplaying the commercial status of contemporary art, the ICA embraced it.

Mounting *Young Talent in New England* at the local Stop & Shop was the logical extension of posting the prices for paintings on the walls of the Boston institute or partnering with Steuben on the design and promotion of its glassware. The exhibition at the supermarket anticipated the dovetailing of contemporary art and consumer culture that was to emerge a few years later under the name of pop art. To be sure, the works on display in the Cambridge Stop & Shop did not represent supermarket goods in the manner of Andy Warhol's *Green Coca-Cola Bottles* or Ed Ruscha's *Actual Size*, a painting of a can of Spam in flight (both from 1962). But the physical juxtaposition of contemporary paintings and perishable groceries in *Young Talent in New England* acknowledged a kindred commodification.

The ad in the *Boston Globe* noted that "Much as we should like to, we cannot always go to art galleries, while on the other hand, we always stop to shop. That is why we have brought these paintings for display at Stop & Shop."[117] Notice how the "we" in question shifts, all but imperceptibly, from the general public in the first sentence to the ICA in the second. The alignment of contemporary art and commerce could hardly be made more smoothly.

In 1963, the modernist critic Barbara Rose complained in print of a pop art exhibition at the Guggenheim Museum in the following terms: "I am annoyed to have to see in a gallery what I'm forced to look at in a supermarket. I go to the gallery to get away from the supermarket, not to repeat the experience."[118] The ICA understood what Rose and other modernist critics sought to disavow—namely, that the audience for contemporary American art would always find time to stop and shop.

Afterword: Not Now (1994/2005)

"Art history and art criticism are often distinguished on the grounds that one treats the art of the past, distanced in time from its subject, and the other deals with recent art or with older art from the vantage point of contemporary experience":[1] so, very sensibly, notes the art critic Irving Sandler. The peculiar hybrid that is contemporary art history, however, exists in the space between criticism and scholarship, between contemporary art and history. That space is necessarily unstable because the current moment keeps hurtling forward and the historical past likewise refuses to sit still for very long. This book has asked readers to consider contemporary art as a category that extends beyond—as well as before—the most recent biennial, issue of *Artforum*, international art fair, and emerging art star.

It takes about a year for a university press book to appear once the final manuscript has been submitted by the author. Given this, when writing *What Was Contemporary Art?* I knew that it would be at least twelve months out of date by the time it was published. Rather than regretting this delay, I have come to view it as a metaphor for the necessity of falling behind the times, for the importance of losing step with the ever-advancing march and marketing of contemporary art. By one recent accounting, there are now more than one hundred biennial exhibitions of contemporary art across the globe, from São Paolo to Seoul to Sharjah, with "almost one every ten days, on average."[2] The art market has never been more genuinely global, or more massively capitalized, than it is today. In researching this book, I attended versions of the Venice Biennale, the Whitney Biennial, the Athens Biennial, Documenta, and Art

Basel Miami, as well as various satellite events and expositions, including the 2007 "Art Now" Fair in Miami Beach. It soon became clear to me that trying to keep up with the pace of the contemporary art world was a practical impossibility, not least because I lacked the financial resources to do so. Archival research, critical thinking, the crafting of book-length chapters—these tasks do not lend themselves to the tempo or logic of "art now." In writing contemporary art history, it may therefore be necessary, paradoxically, to lag behind the time of the contemporary art world, behind the latest biennial opening, artist's project, or blog posting.

In approaching the contemporary as a historical phenomenon, I follow the example of my life partner, the performance scholar and theater historian David Román. In *Performance in America: Contemporary U.S. Culture and the Performing Arts*, Román observes that "critical efforts to theorize the contemporary are often accused of being 'presentist': a focus on the contemporary is presumed to come at the expense of history, as if the contemporary could only be understood as antagonistic to the past, or in a mutually exclusive relationship to it."[3] His 2005 book challenges this presumption by showing that "contemporary performance is itself already embedded in a historical archive of past performances that help contextualize the work in history. In this way, the contemporary participates in an ongoing dialogue with previously contemporary works now relegated to literary history, the theatrical past, or cultural memory."[4] *Performance in America* demonstrates how works of U.S. theater and performance from 1994 to 2004 revived a wide-ranging archive of British and American culture from the eighteenth through the mid twentieth centuries. Rather than trying to keep up with the ever-quickening pace of the contemporary, Román looked back through recent works to find a wealth of prior performances—from nineteenth-century saloon songs to golden-era Broadway musicals—embedded within them. In so doing, he revealed how a performance could be both contemporary and historical, both thoroughly up-to-date and deeply archival.

What Was Contemporary Art? has likewise sought to demonstrate the dialectical relationship of (once) current cultural production to the historical past. To do so, it has focused on visual art and its reproduction in the United States in the first half of the twentieth century. By way of conclusion, I want to step nearer to the present while still resisting the pressure of "art now."

I turn first to an artist's interview published in 1994, then to an art opening in 2005. In both cases, the event at issue triggers associations with other moments that unsettle the relation between contemporary art and history. In both instances, the past is reworked and challenged by what was then the current moment.

Warhol's Rhinestones (1994)

In 1994, the journal *October* published an interview with Andy Warhol conducted in 1985 by the art historian and critic Benjamin H. D. Buchloh. Throughout much of the interview, Buchloh is concerned with questions of artistic influence, with which art and artists mattered to Warhol when.[5] The following exchange is typical:

Buchloh: People have speculated about the origins of your early linear drawing style, whether it comes more out of Matisse, or had been influenced by Cocteau, or came right out of Ben Shahn. I was always surprised that they never really looked at Man Ray, for example, or Picabia. Were they a factor in your drawings of the late 1950s, or did you think of your work at that time as totally commercial?

Warhol: Yeah, it was just commercial art.

At several other points in the conversation, Warhol similarly rejects Buchloh's attempts to create a modernist pedigree for his art. When asked about the impact of meeting Marcel Duchamp in the 1960s, Warhol states,

"No, I didn't know him that well."[7] And, in a moment of terrifically unambiguous rejection, the artist responds to a question about the influence of Francis Picabia on his commercial drawings of the 1950s by saying, "I didn't even know who that person was" at the time.[8] Throughout the conversation, the famously impassive artist offers variations on his preferred response ("I don't know") to questions.[6]

The interview bespeaks the desire of the art historian to locate the artist within a genealogical schema of influence and innovation. The artist, however, will not play along. After Warhol has disclaimed Man Ray as an influence on his commercial art of the 1950s, Buchloh asks, "And you would not have been aware of Man Ray's drawings until the sixties?" Warhol responds, "Well, when I did know Man Ray he was just a photographer. I guess I still don't know the drawings really."[9] Not only does Warhol disclaim the knowledge about which Buchloh inquires but he also denies that knowledge in the present (1985) moment of the interview. By admitting that he (still) does not know Man Ray's drawings, Warhol precludes the possibility of identifying that body of work as a source for his own.

Warhol's criteria for judging art cannot be made to conform to Buchloh's, much to the latter's consternation. Throughout the interview, Buchloh invites Warhol to comment negatively on (then) current forms of neoexpressionist painting, which the critic feels have failed to heed the lessons of pop and minimalism:

Buchloh: So the shift that has occurred in the last five years has not at all bothered you? The return to figuration, the return to manual painting procedures—that's nothing that you see in conflict with your own work and its history?

Warhol: No, because I'm doing the same.[10]

Rather than seeing recent tendencies in contemporary art as contradicting his earlier work, Warhol blithely admits to practicing those same tendencies.[11] Far from judging the return to figuration or to painting by hand as regressive, the artist acknowledges that return within his own practice. By insisting that "I'm doing the same," he refuses the vanguardist logic proposed by Buchloh in favor of a model of repetition without conflict.

Toward the end of the interview, Warhol turns away from discussing art entirely to describe something he witnessed earlier that same day: "I don't know, this morning I went to the handbag district, and there were people that spend all day just putting in rhinestones with their hands, which is just amazing, that they do everything by hand. It would be different if some machine did it and . . . "[12] In a neat reversal of his oft-cited desire to be a machine, Warhol here finds himself fascinated by a labor of decoration that cannot be fully mechanized. Rather than rejecting "manual painting procedures" in the manner that Buchloh anticipates, Warhol directs the conversation to an unexpected time and place—this morning in the handbag district.

Earlier in the interview, the artist rejected an avant-garde lineage for his 1950s drawings and identified them instead as "just commercial art." Much of the appeal of Warhol's early commercial imagery lay, paradoxically, in its noncommercial, hand-wrought appearance and ornamental wit. Though he may not have attached rhinestones to actual handbags, Warhol did draw and trace rhinestones, beads, buckles, and gilt clasps in illustrations of ladies' handbags, shoes, belts, and other accessories for fashion advertisements and newspaper articles throughout the 1950s. In 1985, his mention of what he saw that morning not only marks a rejection of the model of avant-garde innovation and failure proposed by Buchloh; it also recalls the commercial imagery and materials with which the first decade of Warhol's career was largely concerned. The artist's mention of rhinestones on handbags reiterates his refusal to affiliate his 1950s drawings with Buchloh's pantheon of artists (Henri Matisse, Jean Cocteau, Man Ray, Ben Shahn, Duchamp, Picabia) and inscribes that work within a quite different order of manual labor and design. Warhol falls out of line—and out of time—with art history as a series of proper names and punctual movements.

Just after his mention of rhinestones, Warhol's voice trails off. As though recognizing the need to return to a discourse of the contemporary art world, he then asks Buchloh, "Have you been going to galleries and seeing all the new things?" Buchloh responds, "Yes, I go fairly consistently, and I never really quite understood why everything has been turned around in that way, why all of a sudden people start looking at painting again as if certain things never happened."[13] Here, Buchloh refers again to neo-expressionist painting, which he sees as outmoded and redundant in its insistence on painterly authenticity. But Warhol does not understand redundancy or outmodedness as a problem. In explaining this to Buchloh, Warhol again turns away from the art world and toward a quite different example:

> It's like in the sixties when we met our first drag queens, and they thought they were the first to do it. Now I go to a party and these little kids have become drag queens, the younger people now being drag queens. They think they are the only people who ever thought of being a drag queen, which is sort of weird. It's like they invented it, and it's all new again and stuff, so it makes it really interesting.[14]

Warhol sees the claims of "younger people now" to have "invented" drag as "really interesting." Instead of a model of heroic innovation in which each generation must create something radically different from the last, he proposes repetition as renewal in the sense of making newly relevant.

Warhol all but tells Buchloh to look beyond the paradigm of individual artistic achievement and influence if he wishes to understand his work. When

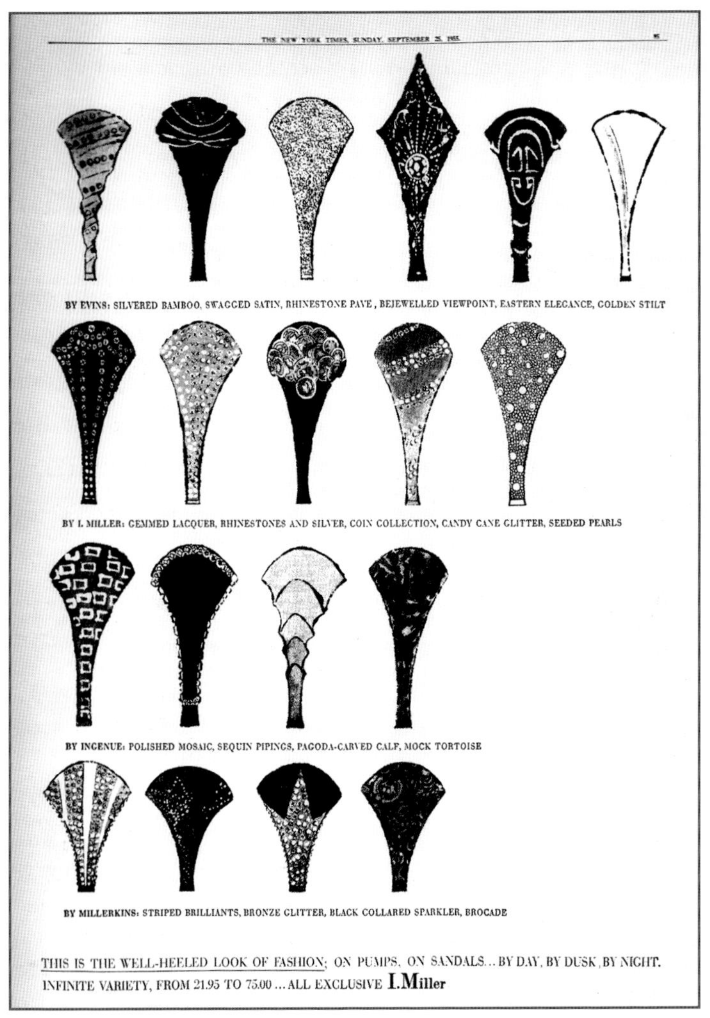

5.1 Andy Warhol's ad for I. Miller Shoes.
New York Times, September 25, 1955.
(Courtesy The Archives of the Andy Warhol
Museum, Pittsburgh. Founding Collection.)
© 2012 The Andy Warhol Foundation for the
Visual Arts, Inc./Artists Rights Society (ARS), NY.

the critic asks, for example, whether the accumulations of the French artist Arman inspired the serial nature of Warhol's pop silkscreens in the early
1960s, the artist's response is unequivocal: "No, well, I didn't think that way. I
didn't. I wasn't thinking of anything. I was looking for a thing."[15] Throughout the
interview, Warhol steps outside the canonical timeline proposed by Buchloh
and into the time "when we met our first drag queens" and the time "this
morning [when] I went to the handbag district." By situating art alongside
other things and people in the social and material world, Warhol eludes art-
historical periodization. Rather than fixing his art within a definitive sequence
of sources and influences, Warhol opts for multiple times and places. Like
the rhinestones he saw "this morning" that simultaneously recalled his commercial drawings from thirty years earlier, Warhol's present moment returns
to and reformulates the past rather than transcending it.

At the very start of the interview, Buchloh explains to Warhol that "I
am currently doing research on the reception of Dada and Duchamp's work
in the late 1950s and I would like to go a bit into that history if you don't
mind."[16] For Warhol, however, the reception of art, whether Duchamp's or his
own, could not be slotted into a stable time frame. It kept seeping out into
other times and places. In the final section of this book, I consider how we
might bring a similar sense of untimeliness to viewing—and writing about—
contemporary art.

Ligon's Light (2005)

I've just arrived in Toronto and am already running late. My taxi driver isn't
familiar with the Power Plant Contemporary Art Gallery, the art space I need
to get to. But he does know Harbourfront Centre, the cultural complex of
which the Power Plant is part. He drops me off beside an expanse of shops
and high-rise condominiums and I run into the building that looks the most
like a renovated factory. I am here for the opening of the survey exhibit *Glenn*

Ligon: Some Changes—but virtually no one else seems to be. The place is nearly deserted. I look over to the gallery assistant at the front desk, who says, "They're all out on the deck." After convincing her to stash my luggage behind the desk, I walk quickly through the galleries and out the back of the building. I enter a roped-off deck with a long bar, a table of hors d'oeuvres, and a sunny view of Lake Ontario. Two hundred or so people are listening to a speech by one of the two curators of the show. I don't see the artist or, for that matter, anyone I recognize among the crowd of attentive Canadians. As the curator acknowledges the various individuals and foundations that have supported the show, I decide to slip back inside the galleries. I figure I have at least ten minutes before the thank-yous end and the crowd disperses.

It takes a moment to adjust to the modified light of the galleries, and I turn to my right and enter a room that has only one work in it. It is a neon sculpture (the first, to my knowledge, of Ligon's career). In typewriter-like text, it spells out the words "negro sunshine." No caps, no quotes, just the two words illuminating the otherwise shadowy room with their slightly humming, off-white light. Outside, I think to myself, on that roped-off deck is the space of the contemporary art world, of collectors, curators, and gallerists socializing in the sun. Inside is Glenn Ligon's light—soft wattage, high impact, entirely unexpected yet exquisitely plugged in to both the historical past and the present. I spend the next fifteen minutes in this light, leaving only when some (other) white people begin streaming in from the reception outside.[17]

You have just read a portion of present-tense art criticism from the past. Occasioned by the June 2005 opening of a major exhibition by an artist I have long admired, the piece was published in the May 2006 issue of *Artforum*. Though already eleven months out of date by the time it was published, the piece began *in medias res* to give a sense of the ever-quickening pace of the contemporary art world and the challenge of keeping up with its accelerated tempo.[18]

Warm Broad Glow gave me permission to fall out of step with the social world of the opening in Toronto. Or rather, Ligon's artwork offered me entry into a different kind of opening—an imaginative and aesthetic opening onto the past rather than an opportunity for professional schmoozing and the exchange of hugs and business cards.[19]

Warm Broad Glow was the last work, chronologically speaking, included in *Some Changes*, and it was not reproduced or discussed in the exhibition catalogue. Almost nothing, in fact, had yet been written about the piece when I saw it in Toronto. I hesitated at the time to break the silence on it, even as, of course, I knew that the work would be widely written about and reproduced, given Ligon's stature as a contemporary artist. If wordlessness seemed an appropriate response to *Warm Broad Glow*, it was because the sculpture could not be made to mean something definitive about race or language, about the backlash against identity politics, or about the legacy of neon art in the wake of Mario Merz and Bruce Nauman. That the sculpture did not resolve into a stable meaning or message was not, however, to say that it lacked content. To the contrary, the oblique address of *Warm Broad Glow* was part of its content. The sculpture's material form—shaped glass tubes, black industrial paint, electrical cords and outlets, pulsating neon light—generated the "negro sunshine" that the work simultaneously named. *Warm Broad Glow* introduced a vernacular remnant from the segregationist past to a modern form of commercial signage and, in so doing, suspended the syntax of race in the light of anachronism.

Though often tethered by critics and curators to the concept of identity politics, Ligon's art has never been about the simple affirmation of identity (racial or otherwise) or about the positing of any "correct" form of racial politics. Take *Cocaine (Pimps)* (1993), one of the joke paintings the artist executed

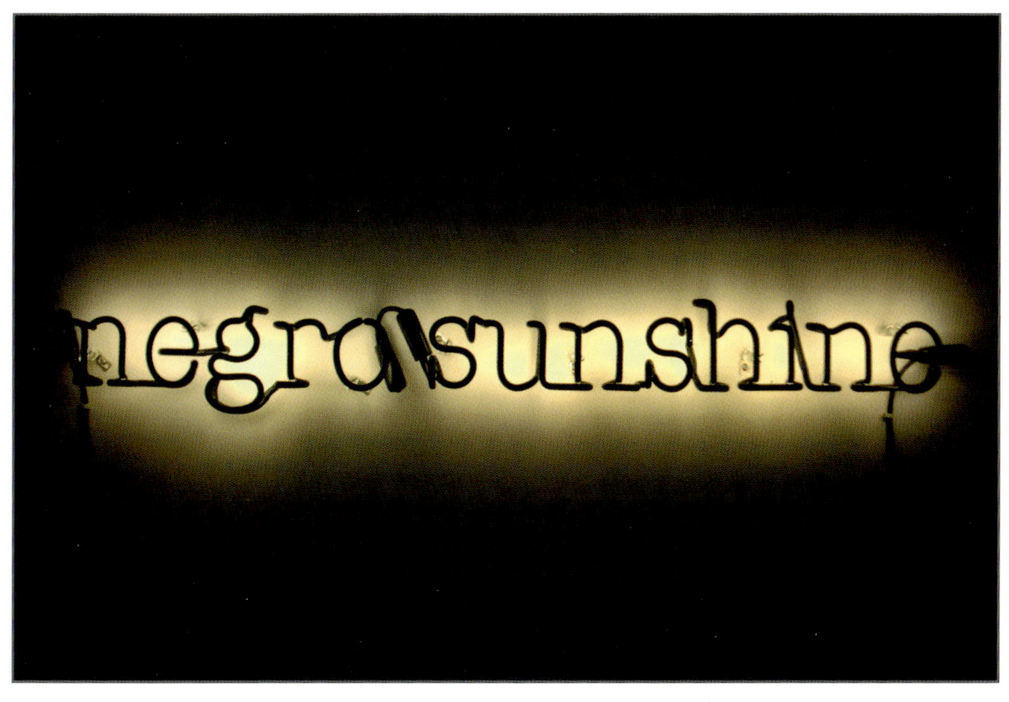

5.2 Glenn Ligon, *Warm Broad Glow*, 2005. Neon and paint, 36 × 192 inches (91.4 × 487.7 cm), edition of 7, AP 1/2. (Courtesy Regen Projects, Los Angeles.) © Glenn Ligon.

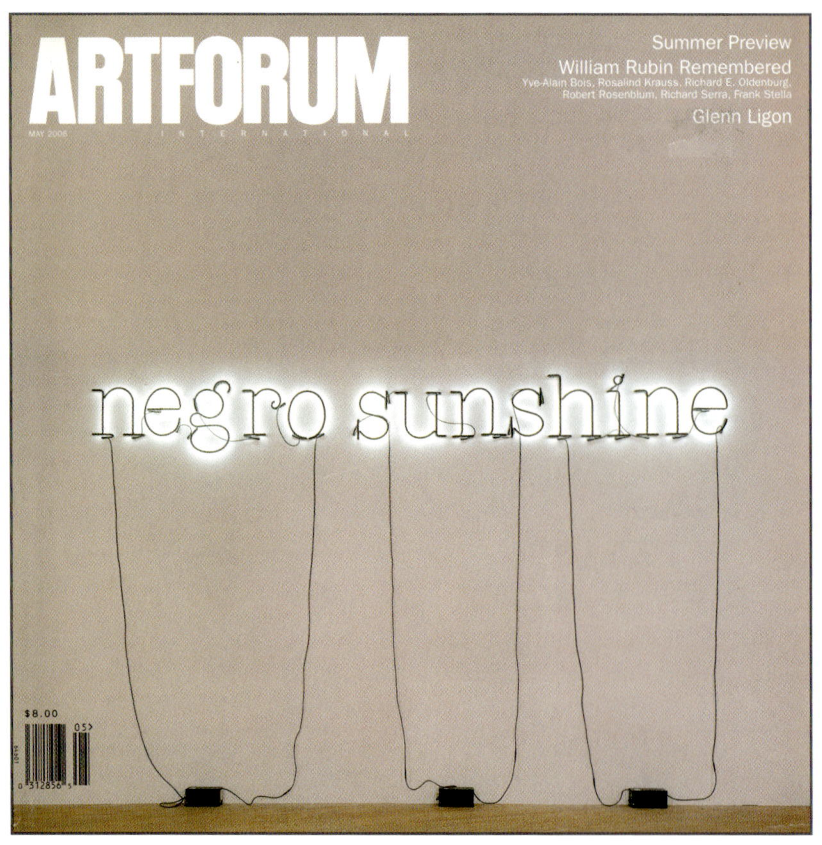

5.3 *Artforum* cover, May 2006. © Artforum.

in the early 1990s (the boom years of multiculturalism). The text of the painting, transcribed from a late 1970s LP of stand-up routine by Richard Pryor, reads:

Niggers be holding them dicks too . . .
White people go "Why you guys hold
your things?"
Say "You done took everything else
motherfucker."

As painted by Ligon, the raw language and syntax of the joke contribute to a broader sense of impropriety. For starters, the joke was meant to be heard rather than read, listened to rather than looked at. Its humor flows in part from the cadence and logic of Pryor's delivery. Reconstituted as a text painting, the joke is distanced, though not entirely dissociated, from Pryor's voice. It is now the viewer who mouths these words, whether silently or aloud, and thereby speaks the rage barely veiled beneath their humor. The visual form of *Cocaine (Pimps)*—the tiny flecks of paint jumping off the letters, the (off-) color combination of orange against red—changes and recharges its language. A raunchy joke from an old Richard Pryor album becomes, in Ligon's hands, an intricately painted surface of stencils, strokes, and smudges, a microworld of colored incident and inscription. The picture pays respect to the beauty of Pryor's obscenity.

Some Changes traced a recursive path, rather than a linear plot, through two decades of Ligon's career. Early projects and artistic concerns resurfaced through the lens of later experiences and creative commitments. The Pryor pictures provide a case in point. Having launched the series in 1993, Ligon abandoned it after just four canvases. According to the artist, the paintings "felt very raw to me. . . . Pryor's jokes are quite scatological and racially charged so in order to use those texts I had to inhabit them in a way that was frightening to me but also was the very power of those texts. . . . Basically, I got too scared to keep going with them."[20] In 2004, however, Ligon returned to Pryor's jokes and began to make additional text paintings. While similar in size to their predecessors and using the same square format, the later canvases feature a keyed-up, tartly Warholian palette and a multiplication of color contrasts. In *Especially If It's a Girl #1*, for example, the hot-pink text of a sex joke delivers an unexpectedly yellow punch line, while in *Mudbone (Liar) #3*, a purple passage on "the biggest dicks in the world" gives way to a long electric-blue conclusion.

In an essay written while he was working on this series, Ligon asks,

> So why have I returned to Pryor after all these years? Perhaps it is that Pryor is funny again. Not that he wasn't funny back in the seventies, it's just that all his militancy, his rage at social and economic injustice, his breaking down of sexual taboos seems amusing now, almost quaint. The jokes don't scare me anymore because the world they promised to bring seems even farther away than it did then. As Pryor says, "Remember the Revolution brother? It's over. Lasted six months." When I listen to Pryor records now, I laugh and am a little sad—nostalgic for my fear, I guess.[21]

Even as Ligon resumed work on his Pryor paintings, the jokes that were his source recalled a moment of black militancy and promised revolution receding ever further into the past. Pryor's death in 2005 can only have widened the distance between his jokes and Ligon's visual transcription of them.

Ligon's dialectical engagement with history is nowhere more intense than in his practice of self-portraiture. In the 1993 companion series of prints *Runaways* and *Narratives*, the artist speaks (or, rather, is spoken for) in the voice of the slave. In the latter series, Ligon mimics the rhetoric and typography of nineteenth-century slave narratives while replacing the details of the text with information drawn from his own biography:

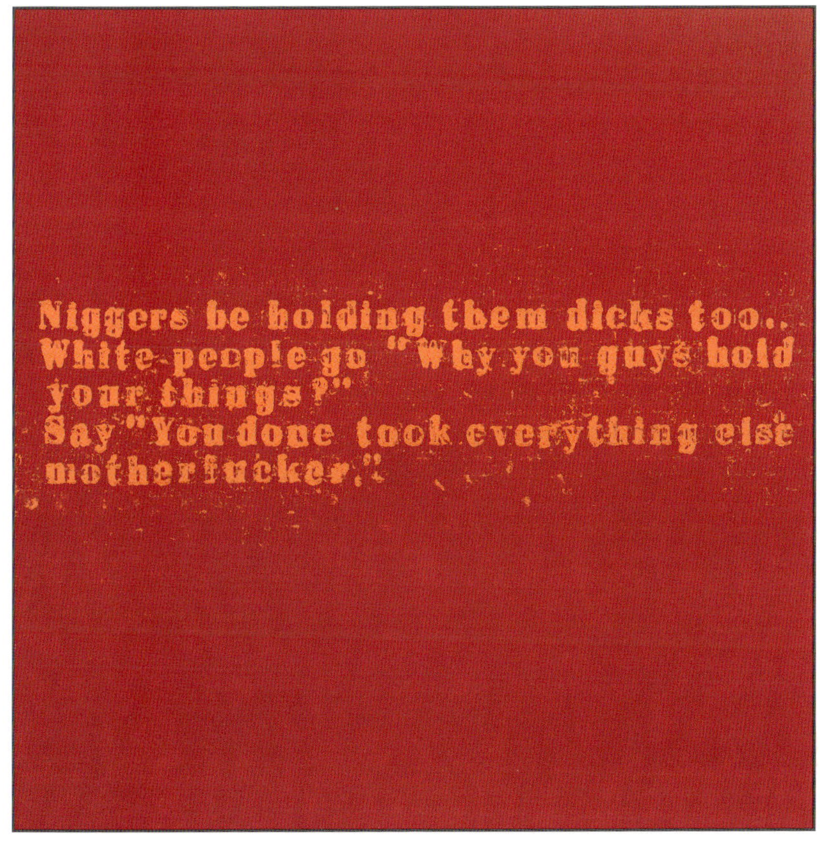

5.4 Glenn Ligon, *Cocaine (Pimps)*, 1993.
Oilstick, synthetic polymer, and graphite
on linen, 32 × 32 inches (81.3 × 81.3 cm).
(Courtesy Regen Projects, Los Angeles.)
© Glenn Ligon.

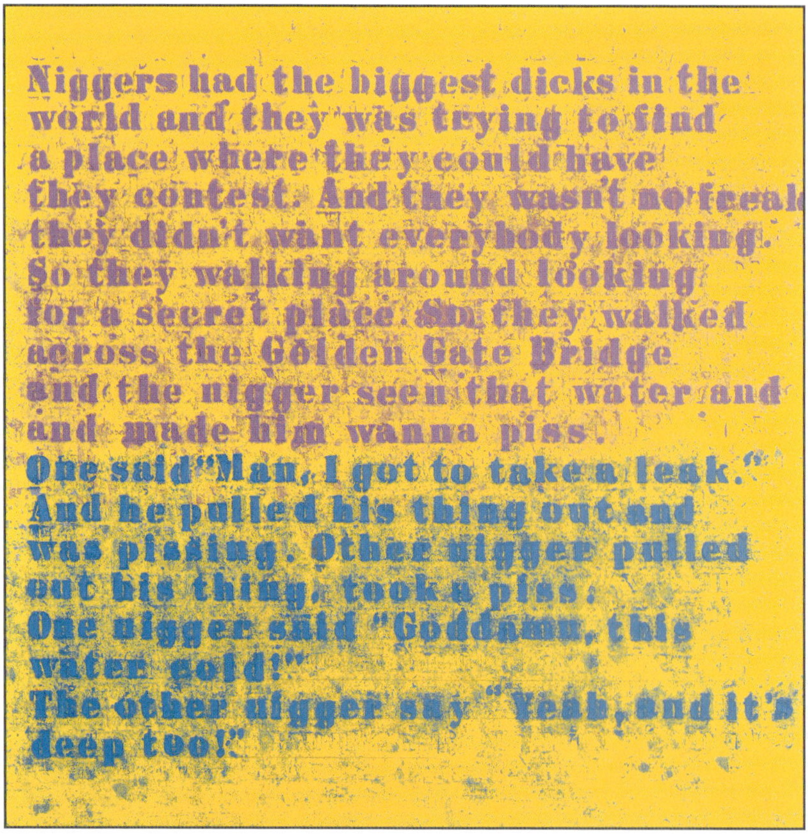

5.5 Glenn Ligon, *Mudbone Liar (#3)*, 2004.
Oilstick and acrylic on canvas, 32 × 32 inches
(81.3 × 81.3 cm). (Courtesy Regen Projects,
Los Angeles.) © Glenn Ligon.

The

Life and Adventures

of

Glenn Ligon

A Negro;

Who was sent to be educated amongst white people in the year 1966 when only about six years of age and has continued to fraternize with them to the present time.

By using the antiquated diction, style, and syntax of antebellum handbills and title pages to describe his own late-twentieth-century experience, the artist draws out the latent effects of history on the current moment, including (the current moment here being 1993) the art world's qualified embrace of multiculturalism:

Black Rage;

or,

How I Got Over

or

Sketches

of the

Life and Labors

of

Glenn Ligon

Containing a full and faithful account of his commodification of the horrors of black life into art objects for the public's enjoyment.

Or, to cite another print from the same series,

The

Narrative

of the
Life and Uncommon Sufferings
of
Glenn Ligon,
A Colored Man,
Who at a tender age discovered his affection for the bodies of other men,
and has endured scorn and tribulations ever since.
Written by himself.

Rather than situate the slave narrative securely in the past, Ligon insists on the continuing relevance of that narrative to contemporary black life, including, and especially, his own. The printed proliferation and stylistic back-dating of the character "Glenn Ligon" opens a space, at once critical and creative, for the artist to comment on various aspects of his personal and professional experience. Using the language of anachronism, Ligon remembers—but also sends up—his grade-school education among predominantly white students, his participation in the artistic commodification of black abjection, and the unsettling discovery ("at a tender age") of his contraband desires for other men. This last print deftly registers the queer force of sexuality as it brushes up against secrecy and stigma.

At the time of *Some Changes*, the current moment in contemporary African-American art was often referred to as "post-black," a term introduced by Thelma Golden in the context of *Freestyle*, an exhibit she curated in 2001 at the Studio Museum in Harlem.[22] As framed by Golden, the concept of post-black was intentionally double-edged, insofar as it referred to "artists who were adamant about not being labeled as 'black' artists, though their work was steeped, in fact deeply interested, in redefining complex notions of blackness."[23] For Golden, "post-black" named the push/pull effect of a

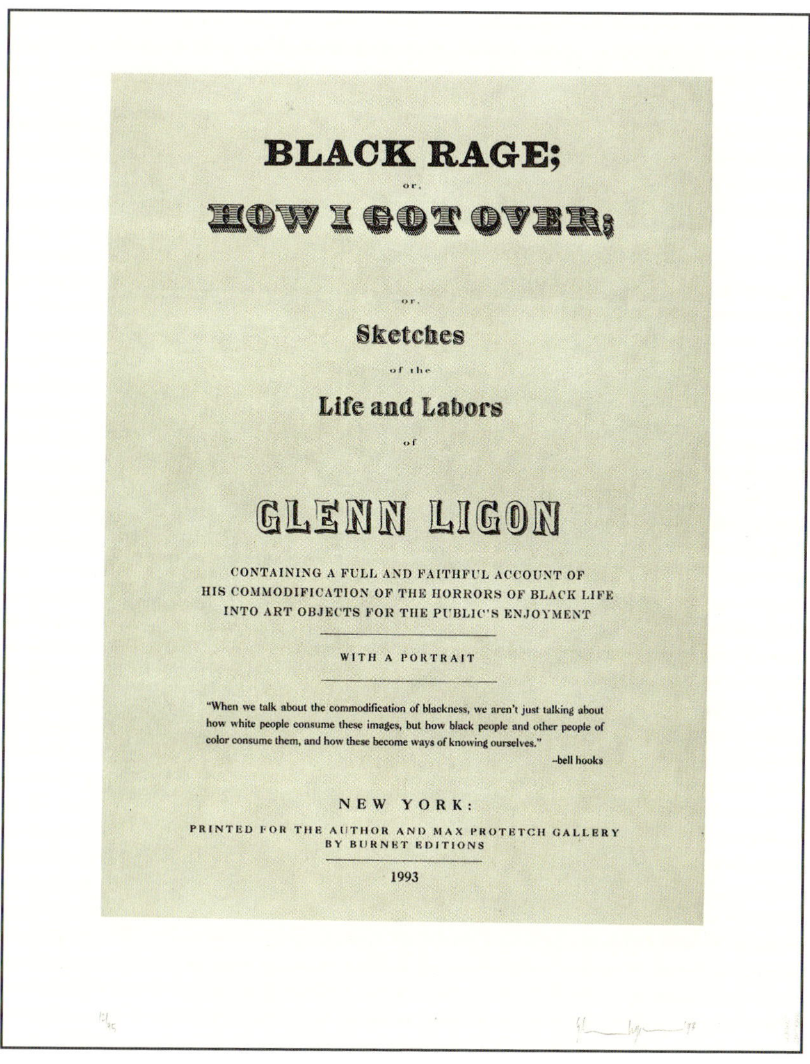

5.6 Glenn Ligon, *Narratives* (detail), 1993.
Suite of nine photo etchings on chine collé,
approx. 28 × 21 inches (71.1 × 53.3 cm) each.
(Courtesy Regen Projects, Los Angeles.)
© Glenn Ligon.

racial designation that could be neither comfortably claimed nor completely disowned.

In the immediate wake of *Freestyle*, the term created something of a minor media sensation. *Time* magazine, for example, (punningly) declared a "golden age for post-black art" with Golden as its "major cheerleader." *Time's* embrace of "post-black" was based in part on a blandly affirmative reading of the term as referencing "work by a generation whose approach to issues of racial identity has been liberated and informed by America's growing multicultural fabric."[24] Rather than situating post-black within a long and contested history of racial designation, *Time* presented it as a form of feel-good, multicultural liberation.

Warm Broad Glow registered a protest against such reductive formulations of post-black as expressed in *Time*. It did so by going back "before 'black'" to the lexical and historical moment of "negro" and back even further to the stereotype of shiny black servility and sunny obedience. Most specifically, *Warm Broad Glow* returned to Gertrude Stein's "Melanctha: Each One as She May," first published in 1909. On the opening page of the novella, Stein describes Rose Johnson, a friend of the mixed-race protagonist, in the following terms:

> Rose Johnson was a real black negress but she had been brought up quite like their own child by white folks.
>
> Rose laughed when she was happy but she had not the wide, abandoned laughter that makes the warm broad glow of negro sunshine. Rose was never joyous with the earth-born, boundless joy of negroes. Hers was just ordinary, any sort of woman laughter.[25]

Rose is contrasted against, rather than characterized by, the "warm broad glow of negro sunshine." Although genuinely black in parentage ("a real black negress"), Rose was raised "by white folks" and is, presumably for this reason, devoid of the "boundless joy of negroes." In such passages, Stein traffics in the most extreme of racial stereotypes. But she also scrambles the logic of those stereotypes by suggesting they are "earth-born" rather than "inborn," the product of social and domestic life rather than of blood or nature.

Many viewers of *Warm Broad Glow* (myself included) may not have recognized "negro sunshine" as a citation from Stein. This would not, I imagine, disturb Ligon very much. In declining to make the connection explicit, Ligon unbinds the sculpture from Stein and her place in the American literary canon. To view *Warm Broad Glow* is to confront instead the wider force of a past that has not passed away. Throughout his career, Ligon has traced the movement of language across multiple registers and contexts, from vernacular speech to printed texts, from common usage to obsolescence, from popular culture to literature to visual art and back again. *Warm Broad Glow* reaches back across a century of history, fiction, and stereotype to address a postmillennial audience that is supposedly beyond or "over" race.

According to Golden, "post-black" started as an irreverent comment, even a kind of joke, that she exchanged with Ligon. As she notes in the *Freestyle* catalogue:

> A few years ago, my friend, the artist Glenn Ligon, and I began using the term "post-black." Our relationship is grounded in a shared love of absurd uses of language, and our conversations, both serious and silly, are always full of made-up and misused words and phrases. "Post-black" was shorthand for post-black art, which was shorthand for a discourse that could fill volumes. . . . Glenn was better at identifying the traces and instances of it than I was, but the moment he said it, I knew exactly what he meant.[26]

Even as she introduces "post-black" into critical discourse, Golden locates it as private slang that cannot be fully calibrated or codified, a shorthand best apprehended in "traces and instances." It makes sense that Ligon should have shared that shorthand with Golden long before its presentation as a curatorial concept in *Freestyle* or its appearance in the pages of *Time* magazine. Ligon has always gravitated toward vernacular speech acts that trouble the protocols of proper usage ("you done took everything else / motherfucker") and to forms of language that have become antiquated to the point where they may now be renewed and recharged ("negro sunshine").

When I first saw *Warm Broad Glow*, I sensed but could not specify a slight indirection in the light cast by the sculpture. I later learned that Ligon had applied an industrial rubber-coating compound called Plasti Dip to the face of the sign. The Plasti Dip serves a double purpose: it traces the phrase "negro sunshine" in black and it blocks the emanation of neon from the front of the sign. These two functions were in fact one and the same. By partially obstructing the off-white light, the Plasti Dip created a halo effect that heightened—which is to say, softened—the visual drama of *Warm Broad Glow*. The viewing of a work such as *Warm Broad Glow* takes time. But it also makes time by clearing a space for other moments and associations to register in the living present.

The argument of this book has been that contemporary art is not simply a function of the current moment or the immediate past. Contemporary art is also a relation between an ever-shifting present and the volatile force of history. I have used the examples of Alfred Barr teaching contemporary art at Wellesley College in 1927, exhibitions of premodern art at MoMA in the 1930s and early 1940s, and the controversy over the naming of the Institute of Contemporary Art in 1948 to argue for a history of contemporary art. But many other examples could also be adduced to counter the present-ism of today's art world. Those examples would draw upon different institutional narratives, national contexts, and visual objects from those on which I have focused.

In 2012, as this book goes to print, the culture of contemporary art seems to be burning more intensely than ever. But the glare of now-ism—of the latest international art fair, *e-flux* posting, hot young artist, and auction-house record—can be fairly blinding. The spectacular immediacy of the contemporary art world threatens to overwhelm our ability to think critically about the relation of the current moment to the past.

By dimming the lights a bit, artworks such as *Warm Broad Glow* invite us to slow down, take a deep breath, and consider histories prior to our own. Should we accept the invitation, we will find ourselves envisioning a different place and time.

Not here. And not now.

Notes

1 Introduction: The Art-Historical Postmortem

1. Quoted in Judy K. Collischan Van Wagner, "Rosalind Krauss," in *Women Shaping Art: Profiles of Power* (New York: Praeger, 1984), 152.

2. The glossy, color image of *Cubi XXVIII* shown here is not from Krauss's dissertation, in which the illustrations are black-and-white photographs circa 1969, but from the catalogue to Sotheby's sale of contemporary art held in New York City on the evening of Wednesday, November 9, 2005. *Cubi XXVIII*, also known that evening as lot 23, sold for $23.8 million to dealer Larry Gagosian, who was bidding on behalf of the collector Eli Broad. The sale of *Cubi XXVIII* set a new record for the price of a single work of contemporary art sold at auction, a record that had, in fact, been broken just the night before when Christie's sold Mark Rothko's painting *Homage to Matisse* for $22.4 million. Though Rothko had been dead for thirty-five years and Smith for forty by the time these records were set, the prices paid for each man's work in 2005 raised the bar for the secondary market in postwar painting and sculpture (a bar that has been raised multiple times since). Here, then, we have a conception of contemporary art attuned to the logic and temporalities of the auction market rather than to those of the artist's life and death. See Carol Vogel, "Sale Sets Records for Eighteen Artists, and One for Christie's," *New York Times*, November 9, 2005, B6.

The rationale behind the intense bidding over the Smith sculpture, according to the *New York Times*, was "plain to lovers of contemporary art: this elegantly composed melding of boxes and columns may be the last example of the series to come on the market for some time. Most of the others are in museums or collections where they will stay for generations. So this last-chance opportunity was irresistible, which is why the sculpture's final price was nearly double its high estimate, $12 million." The last sculpture completed by Smith before his accidental death in 1965 thus becomes, 40 years later, the last of its highly prized series available for private purchase. See Carol Vogel, "$23.8 Million Steel Sculpture Sets Another Auction Record," *New York Times*, November 10, 2005, B4.

Krauss's dissertation complicates the narrative of *Cubi XXVIII*'s "irresistible" lastness in significant ways. As it turns out, Smith's physical death did not mark the endpoint of his artistic production. Krauss's catalogue raisonné includes eight sculptures that were begun by Smith but completed posthumously by Leon Pratt, the artist's "close associate and welder during the seven years before [Smith's] death." (Rosalind Krauss, "The Sculpture of David Smith" [Ph.D. diss., Harvard University, 1969], 381.) When the catalogue raisonné reaches these works, Krauss steps outside her own sequential system by designating them not with consecutive numbers but with letters, "Posthumous A–H." Just prior to the Posthumous group, another moment of sequential disturbance occurs in the catalogue raisonné. Ten undated tabletop figurines grouped under the heading "Miscellaneous" are assigned the last consecutive numbers in the sculptural count (nos. 686–696). Krauss characterizes the miscellaneous group by noting, in a tone bordering on contempt, that "the following works are undated and extremely difficult to place within Smith's oeuvre because even during the 1960s [he] made occasional, small-scale, exceedingly crude work that has no real stylistic reference point to anything important that was taking place in his sculpture" (381). Given the author's status as a doctoral candidate in art history at the time, the certainty with which she deems the table-top sculptures both "exceedingly crude" and irrelevant to anything "important" in Smith's sculptural production is striking.

3. Krauss, "The Sculpture of David Smith," 7. She also observes that such information may be found elsewhere in the scholarly literature on Smith.

4. Ibid., 7.

5. Ibid., 88.

6. Ibid., 73.

7. Ibid., 3

8. Ibid., 3.

9. The 1970s would see not only the flowering of Michael Fried's phenomenological art history and Krauss's theoretically informed criticism and scholarship but also the rise of a renewed social history of art led by T. J. Clark. Though their approaches were otherwise quite

distinct, one thing that Krauss, Clark, and Fried shared (along with Leo Steinberg, a historian/critic of a slightly older generation) was an orientation toward particular works of art rather than overarching movements or periods. As Svetlana Alpers put it in 1977, "While previously it was the history of art, conceived in terms of the development and achievement of period styles, which was studied in the historical context (resulting in books like *Der Barock als Kunst der Gegenreformation*), today it is individual works or groups of works, individual phenomena located at a particular time and place. Thus to amplify what I have just said: it is the work of art itself, not a history or sequence of works, which is seen as a piece of history." See Svetlana Alpers, "Is Art History?," *Daedalus* 106, no. 3 (Summer 1977): 1.

10. In "Is Art History?," Alpers described the self-critical turn in art history at the time: "The studies by Leo Steinberg, Michael Fried, and T. J. Clark that I particularly have in mind are perhaps more accurately called writings. For they are all acts of writing as much as they are reports of research accomplished. These three scholars differ greatly in subject, attitude, and manner of address. But they share a meditative stance which testifies in each case, I think, to work which is not only reflective in nature which might also properly be called reflexive. Each one clearly establishes where he stands" (10).

11. Krauss, "The Sculpture of David Smith," ii.

12. Referring to Smith, Krauss writes, "believing as I do that his is the greatest body of work produced by any American sculptor, I find myself wanting to explain this conviction" ("The Sculpture of David Smith," 3).

13. Recall that, according to Krauss, "certain objects" may "detach themselves from their historical background" as they "strike" the scholar with their "overwhelming importance" ("The Sculpture of David Smith," 3). It is as though the force of the artwork in the present moment—in the here and now of its viewing—all but supersedes any question of historical context.

Years later, writing from a perspective informed by poststructuralist and psychoanalytic theory, Krauss would come to question this ideal of modernist immediacy. Describing Fried's and Greenberg's formulations of modernism, she would write in 1993 that "Vision had, as it were, been pared away into a dazzle of pure instantaneity, into an abstract condition with no before and no after." See Rosalind Krauss, *The Optical Unconscious* (Cambridge: MIT Press, 1993), 7.

14. Clement Greenberg, as quoted in Peter G. Ziv, "Visit: Clement Greenberg," *Art and Antiques*, September 1987, 58. In its fuller context, the quotation reads as follows: "Do I exclude a lot of people? Yes. You don't choose your response to art. It's given to you. You have your nerve, your *chutzpah*, and then you work hard on seeing how to tell the difference between good and bad. The first obligation of an art critic is to deliver value judgments."

15. See Rosalind Krauss, "The Essential David Smith, Part One," *Artforum*, February 1969, 43–49; Rosalind Krauss, "The Essential David Smith, Part Two," *Artforum*, April 1969, 34–41. Neither article mentions Krauss's contemporaneous dissertation project at Harvard University. In "Part One," however, the author cites "an essay that is now in preparation for the Museum of Modern Art's forthcoming monograph on David Smith. Most of the material in this article, and another to be published in April, have been drawn from that manuscript." The manuscript would never be published by MoMA (in part because of a dispute over its content), appearing instead as *Terminal Iron Works: The Sculpture of David Smith* published by the MIT Press in 1971. Between 1969 and 1971, then, Krauss's work on Smith took multiple forms—a series of articles in *Artforum*, a doctoral dissertation, a manuscript in preparation for MoMA, and finally a university press book. On the circumstances of Krauss's work for MoMA and the dispute that led to the withdrawal of her Smith manuscript from the museum's Department of Publications, see Department of Publications Collection on Proposed David Smith Monograph, I.57, The Museum of Modern Art Archives, New York.

16. In the September 1969 issue of *Artforum*, the art historian Theodore Reff published a lengthy critique of Fried's dissertation. It concluded with a series of pointed remarks on how Fried's argument about the influence of art criticism on Manet neatly mirrored his own role as a contemporary art critic: "Is it not apparent that he [Fried] has claimed for Astruc, Chesneau, and Thoré the responsibilities and privileges he would claim for formal critics like himself? But then, is it not apparent throughout his essay that he claimed for Manet's art of the 1860s the ambitions and attitudes that he would claim for modernist art one hundred years later?" As Reff saw it, Fried's argument about Manet followed less from the historical record than from Fried's modernist agenda as an art critic and from the contemporary art he promoted at the time. See Theodore Reff, "'Manet's Sources': A Critical Evaluation," *Artforum*, September 1969, 47.

17. Michael Fried, "An Introduction to My Art Criticism," *Art and Objecthood: Essays and Reviews* (Chicago: University of Chicago Press, 1998), 8.

18. In a preceding passage, Fried outlines how his graduate coursework at Harvard University was punctuated by monthly trips to New York City to see contemporary art. The space of Cambridge, Massachusetts, correlates to the sphere of art-historical scholarship, the City of New York to that of art criticism.

19. Krauss, "The Sculpture of David Smith," 2.

20. See, for example, Krauss's remarks on the "vulgarization" that her fellow critics Barbara Rose and Lawrence Alloway "perform simultaneously on art history and on their own profession" of art criticism by setting "the two endeavors at variance with each another" ("The Sculpture of David Smith," 2).

21. In 2010, the Contemporary Art Think Tank was launched "to bring "together art historians, curators, and critics for discussions on pressing concerns in contemporary art. It breaks away from the traditional symposium model, and offers an intimate environment for spontaneous and collective thinking—one we hope will foster a growing collegiality in the field." See "About CATT," *Contemporary Art Think Tank*, 2008, www.cattdc.net/catt.html (accessed May 9, 2012).

22. Lobel presented his analysis of these statistics at a two-day workshop titled "The Short History of Contemporary Art" which he and I convened at the Sterling and Francine Clark Art Institute in Williamstown, Massachusetts, in summer 2006.

23. Holland Cotter, "Under Threat: The Shock of the Old," *New York Times*, April 14, 2011.

24. Patricia Mainardi, as quoted in Ibrahim El-Salahi, "Search Party," *Artforum*, February 14, 2011, http://artforum.com/diary/id=27540 (accessed May 9, 2012).

25. I do not recall discussing with any of my fellow students (or professors) why "Asianists" were designated by a continent rather than a historical period. Nor did I think at the time to question why "Americanists" referred only to those working on the art of North America, which, in turn, meant only the United States. I did come to understand one of the working (tacit) assumptions of "modernists": that the study of Asian art, like that of pre-1945 American art, was largely irrelevant to our pursuits. While aware of the cultural divides and Eurocentric traditions enforced by these field designations, I was less concerned with challenging

the discipline of art history than with finding a professional toehold within it. When I later realized that I was in fact an "Americanist" (though one trained by and alongside modernists), I began seriously to question these divisions. See Richard Meyer, "Mind the Gap: Americanists, Modernists, and the Boundaries of Twentieth-Century Art," *American Art* 8, no. 3 (Fall 2004): 2–7.

Miwon Kwon, in her response to *October*'s "Questionnaire on 'The Contemporary,'" lucidly described the tension between continental and chronological subfields within the context of contemporary art history:

> Contemporary art history sits at a crossroads in the uneven organization of the subfields that comprise the discipline of art history. Within most university art history departments, one group of subfields covering Western developments is organized chronologically, as periods (i.e., from Ancient to Modern, with Medieval and Renaissance in between). Another group of subfields that covers non-Western developments is identified geographically, as culturally discrete units even if they encompass an entire continent (i.e., African, Chinese, Latin American, etc.). The category of contemporary art history, while institutionally situated as coming after the Modern, following the temporal axis of Western art history as the most recent period (starting in 1945 or 1960, depending on how a department divides up faculty work load or intellectual territory), is also the space in which the contemporaneity of histories from around the world must be confronted simultaneously as a disjunctive yet continuous intellectual horizon, integral to the understanding of the present (as a whole). Contemporary art history, in other words, marks a temporal bracketing and a spatial encompassing, a site of a deep tension between very different formations of knowledge and traditions, thus a challenging pressure point for the field of art history in general. For instance, what is the status of contemporary Chinese art history? What is the time frame for such a history? How closely should it be linked to Chinese art, cultural, or political history? How coordinated should it be with Western art history or aesthetic discourse? Is contemporary Chinese art history a subfield of contemporary art history? Or are they comparable categories, with the presumption that the unnamed territory of contemporary art history is Western-American?

See Miwon Kwon, response to "Questionnaire on 'The Contemporary,'" *October* 130 (Fall 2009): 13.

26. Alexander Alberro, response to "Questionnaire on 'The Contemporary,'" *October* 130 (Fall 2009): 55.

27. Ibid.

28. Julieta Aranda, Brian Kuan Wood, and Anton Vidokle, "What Is Contemporary Art?" in *e-flux journal: What Is Contemporary Art?*, ed. Julieta Aranda, Brian Kuan Wood, and Anton Vidokle (Berlin: Sternberg Press, 2010), 6–7. A website and listserv as well as an online journal, *e-flux* describes itself as "an international network which reaches more than 50,000 visual art professionals on a daily basis through its website, e-mail list and special projects." See www.e-flux.com/about/. Originally published electronically, the *e-flux* double issue of *What Is Contemporary Art?* subsequently appeared as a book.

29. Cuauhtémoc Medina, "Contemp(t)orary: Eleven Theses," in *e-flux journal*, 11.

30. Terry Smith, *What Is Contemporary Art?* (Chicago: University of Chicago Press, 2009), 3–4.

31. Ibid., 6.

32. The art historians Alexander Dumbadze and Suzanne Hudson introduce their anthology, *Contemporary Art: 1989 to the Present* (Oxford: Wiley-Blackwell, forthcoming), by noting,

> One basic point of structural and historiographical organization is our periodization of the contemporary from 1989. We do this for a number of reasons. Among other geopolitical factors, the unprecedented growth of the contemporary art world coincided with the fall of the Berlin Wall and the tumultuous events surrounding the Tiananmen Square protests. The Velvet Revolution in Czechoslovakia, the Solidarity Movement in Poland, and the collapse of Communism in the Soviet Union and the rest of the Eastern Bloc irrevocably modified the landscape of contemporary European Art; it also provided the economic means for local collectors to become highly influential players in the international art world. (n.pag.)

As the editors themselves acknowledge, none of these "geopolitical factors" can be understood in isolation from the historical conditions and contexts that gave rise to them. Equally as important, there are other, no less relevant social, economic, and cultural phenomena (for example, the AIDS pandemic) and professional shifts (for example, the rise of MFA programs) that cannot be mapped cleanly onto a "1989 to present" timeline. More than any of this, however, the periodization of contemporary art tends to freeze the works created before 1989 (or, in other schemas, before 1960 or before 1945) into a pre-contemporary moment that is understood as more settled and sorted out than the present. My thanks to Dumbadze and Hudson for sharing the introduction to their manuscript with me prior to its publication.

33. In his response to "Questionnaire on 'The Contemporary,'" *October* 130 (Fall 2009): 122–123, Tom McDonough traced the semantic history of the term "contemporary" across several centuries:

> As a label for what belongs to or occurs in the present, this expression only materialized in the second half of the nineteenth century, its initial use appearing in the title of London's *Contemporary Review*, first published in 1866. . . . But this was not the first use of the term "contemporary," which developed from the Latin *contemporarius* in the seventeenth century as a fusion of spatial (*con-*, "together with") and temporal (*tempor-*, "time") indicators, describing, that is, something or someone dating from the same time as another. Which might naturally lead us to ask in the case of art: contemporary with what?

34. S.v. "contemporary, a.," *The Oxford English Dictionary*, 2nd ed. (1989), *OED Online*, Oxford University Press (accessed September 8, 2010).

35. By 1800, according to the entry in the *OED*, "contemporary [had] rapidly recovered its ground."

36. McDonough, response to "Questionnaire," 123.

37. In 1951, the art historian J. P. Hodin made a similar point in the *College Art* Journal: "Nobody could call the work of an academic artist modern though he might be called contemporary." This comment, as well as the title of Hodin's article—"Contemporary Art: Its Definition and Classification"—suggests that by the middle of the twentieth century, the conceptual limits of the category of contemporary art (and its relation to modern art) were of concern to the field. See J. P. Hodin, "Contemporary Art: Its Definition and Classification," *College Art Journal* 10, no. 4 (Summer 1951): 337–354.

38. Alexander Nagel and Christopher S. Wood, *Anachronic Renaissance* (New York: Zone, 2010), 9.

39. Thomas Crow, "The Practice of Art History in America," *Daedalus* 135, no. 2 (Spring 2006): 70–71.

40. Ibid., 71.

41. Randall Davies, *English Society of the Eighteenth Century in Contemporary Art* (London: Seeley, 1907), 69.

42. The rise of contemporary art as a field of scholarly study occurred in the wake of the theoretical turn in the humanities and the increasing emphasis laid on the critical act of interpretation, the deconstruction of language, and the overturning of the primacy of the individual author/artist. If the theoretical turn preceded and enabled the current fascination with the contemporary, so too did the prior convergence of art history and criticism (as in the work of Krauss and Fried in the late 1960s).

43. Alfred H. Barr Jr., "Modern Art Makes History, Too," *College Art Journal* 1, no. 1 (November 1941): 5.

44. When Barr mentions the MFA, he is referring to a master's degree in art history rather than studio art. On the rise of the MFA as the terminal degree in studio art after 1950, see Howard Singerman, *Art Subjects: Making Artists in the American University* (Berkeley: University of California Press, 1999). After noting that the first MFA degrees were awarded in the late 1920s, Singerman writes that "the Master of Fine Arts did not become widespread, nor did it become the terminal degree in studio art that it is now, until much later." Later in the book, Singerman discusses "the rapid expansion of university graduate-based education from the late 1940s through the mid-1960s" before turning to the explosion of interest in the MFA in the 1980s and 1990s (155).

45. Barr, "Modern Art Makes History," 5–6.

46. *Frank Lloyd Wright, American Architect*, The Museum of Modern Art, New York, November 12, 1940–January 5, 1941.

47. On the troubled history of the exhibition, see *The Show to End All Shows: Frank Lloyd Wright and the Museum of Modern Art, 1940*, ed. Peter Reed and William Kaizen with an essay by Kathryn Smith, Studies in Modern Art 8 (New York: Museum of Modern Art, 2004).

48. Milton Brown, "Frank Lloyd Wright's First Fifty Years," *Parnassus* 12, no. 8 (December 1940): 37.

49. Alfred H. Barr Jr., letter to editor, *Parnassus* 13, no. 1 (January 1941): 3.

50. See, for example, Linda Yablonsky, "Controversy over New Museum's Plans to Show Trustee's Collection," *The Art Newspaper*, November 2009, 207; Deborah Sontag and Robin Pogrebin, "Some Object as Museum Shows Its Trustee's Art," *New York Times*, November 10, 2009, A1. See also Christopher Knight, "Critic's Notebook: Private Collections Should Stay in the Living Room—With Their Owner's Ego," *Los Angeles Times*, October 10, 2010.

51. Barr thought that studying contemporary art would prepare college students for an ongoing engagement with and support of the arts in later life: "From these undergraduates will come the patrons of the living artists of the future. These future patrons, amateurs, museum curators, will thank the college teacher who sends them out in the world with a taste in art, recent and ancient, which is not twenty or thirty years behind the times." See Barr, "Modern Art Makes History," 4.

52. On this issue, see my "Artists Sometimes Have Feelings," *Art Journal* 67 (Winter 2008): 38–55.

53. Erwin Panofsky, "Introduction: The History of Art as a Humanistic Discipline," *Meaning in the Visual Arts: Papers in and on Art History* (Garden City, NY: Doubleday/Anchor, 1955), 24.

54. This gesture is inspired in part by the structure of *Art since 1900: Modernism, Antimodernism, Postmodernism* (London: Thames & Hudson, 2005). It consists of 107 essays, or "entries," each written by one of the textbook's four authors: the influential art historians/critics Yve-Alain Bois, Benjamin H. D. Buchloh, Hal Foster, and Rosalind Krauss. Every "entry" is keyed to an individual year from 1900 to 2003 or, more precisely, to an event from that year—the creation of an artwork, the publication of a particular text, the mounting

of an exhibition, the death of an artist. While some events are predictably canonical (Pablo Picasso's completion of *Les Demoiselles d'Avignon* marks 1907), many are relatively obscure: a lecture by the constructivist painter Varvara Stepanova (1921); the critical and commercial failure of Barnett Newman's second show at the Betty Parsons Gallery (1951); the opening of the alternative art space P.S. 1 in Queens (1976). The selected events provide the starting point rather than the focus of the entries that follow. In "1976," for example, Krauss contrasts the opening of P.S. 1 with the contemporaneous "King Tut" show at the Metropolitan Museum of Art and the rise of the exhibition blockbuster in the late 1970s and 1980s. In a sharp critique of art-world commercialism, she concludes with an account of the "globalized museum" of the 1990s (read: the Guggenheim) as a "nightmare" of "simulacral spectacle." Like Krauss, the other authors often slide forward or backward from their assigned start dates in order to develop a line of argument or trace a sphere of influence. They approach modern art less as a sequential record of events to be reported than as a series of interpretive problems to be pursued.

55. "'Modern Art' and the American Public," statement by the Institute of Contemporary Art (1948), reproduced in *Dissent: The Issue of Modern Art in Boston*, exh. cat. (Boston: Institute of Contemporary Art, 1985), 52.

56. For characterizations of Barr and MoMA in this spirit, see Alan Wallach, *Exhibiting Contradiction: Essays on the Art Museum in the United States* (Amherst: University of Massachusetts Press, 1998), 75; William B. Scott and Peter M. Rutkoff, *New York Modern: The Arts and the City* (Baltimore: Johns Hopkins University Press, 1999, 2001), 169; Terry Smith, *Making the Modern: Industry, Art, and Design in America* (Chicago: University of Chicago Press, 1993), 387; and Judith Zilcer, "Beyond Genealogy: American Modernism in Retrospect," *American Art* 15, no. 1 (Spring 2001): 4–9.

57. Sybil Gordon Kantor, *Alfred H. Barr, Jr., and the Intellectual Origins of the Museum of Modern Art* (Cambridge: MIT Press, 2001); Rona Roob, "Alfred H. Barr, Jr., a Chronicle of the Years 1902–1929," *New Criterion* 5, no. 11, special issue (1987): 1–19; Kirk Varnedoe, "The Evolving Torpedo: Changing Ideas of the Collection of Painting and Sculpture of the Museum of Modern Art," in *The Museum of Modern Art at Mid-Century: Continuity and Change* (New York: Harry N. Abrams, 1995), 12–73.

58. Nagel and Wood, *Anachronic Renaissance*, 9.

59. Thomas Crow, "The Graying of Art Criticism," *Artforum*, September 1993, 186.

2 Young Professor Barr (1927)

1. According to Sybil Kantor, "The outline of the course … would eventually be an analogue for the structure of the Museum of Modern Art and its contents." See Sybil Gordon Kantor, *Alfred H. Barr, Jr., and the Intellectual Origins of the Museum of Modern Art* (Cambridge: MIT Press, 2001), 91 n. 18, 396. Though it revisits Barr's early career with somewhat different questions in mind, this chapter is greatly indebted to Kantor's magisterial study.

2. Alfred H. Barr Jr. to Paul Sachs, October 5, 1929; as cited in Kantor, *Alfred H. Barr*, 366. In the context of the Wellesley course, Barr's neat separation of "Modern" from "contemporary" became blurred when "contemporary" arose from its "supine neutrality" to imbue particular forms of art and architecture with a sense of vitality and immediate relevance. If "contemporary" sometimes conveyed a sense of urgency (rather than neutrality), the term "Modern" could also suggest a more neutral (rather than progressive) sense of currency. Thus, Lloyd Goodrich writing about the new Museum of Modern Art in 1929: "As its name indicates, the new institution is to be devoted primarily to the work of living artists and their immediate predecessors"; see Lloyd Goodrich, "A Museum of Modern Art," *The Nation*, December 4, 1929, 664. By 1934, Barr was less confident about the use value and specificity of either "modern" or "Modern":

> The term *modern art* chronologically speaking is then so elastic that it can be scarcely be defined. But the colloquialism "Modern Art" in caps and quotes is no mere question of academic chronology. "Modern Art" is recurrently a matter for debate, to be attacked or defended, a banner for the progressive, a red flag for the conservative. In this sense the word modern can become a problem not of periods but of prejudices.

See Alfred H. Barr Jr., "Modern and 'Modern,'" *Bulletin of the Museum of Modern Art* 1, no. 9 (May 1934): 2, 4.

3. It was also the only job to which he could easily commute from Cambridge, where he was sharing an apartment with friend and fellow graduate student Jere Abbott. While teaching at Wellesley, Barr was thus able to continue his research at Harvard and sit in on the occasional graduate course.

4. Wellesley College, "Courses of Instruction: Art," *Wellesley College Bulletin Calendar 1926–1927*, ser. 15, no. 7 (1926): 41.

5. In his 1943 article "The Teaching of Art," Robert Goldwater tabulated the rise in undergraduate art history courses at fifty major American colleges and universities between 1900 and 1940. According to Goldwater's findings, there were 23 college classes designated "Modern" in the year 1920 as compared to 17 classes available in "Baroque," 63 in "Renaissance," 34 classes in "Medieval," and 88 classes in "Classical." See Robert J. Goldwater, "The Teaching of Art in the Colleges of the United States," *College Art Journal* 2, no. 4, part 2 (May 1943): 31.

6. Alfred H. Barr Jr., preface to *Bauhaus, 1919–1928*, ed. Herbert Bayer, Walter Gropius, and Ise Gropius (New York: Museum of Modern Art, 1938; reprint, 1979), 5.

7. Wellesley College, "Courses of Instruction: Art," 41.

8. Alfred H. Barr Jr. to his parents, February 1926, Alfred H. Barr Jr. Papers [AAA: 2166; 1109]. The Museum of Modern Art Archives, New York. (Hereafter cited as AHB Papers.)

9. List of Wellesley slides, AHB Papers [AAA: 2164; 450]. MoMA Archives, NY.

10. "Wellesley and Modernism," *Boston Evening Transcript*, April 27, 1927, 10. This article, written by a student in the class with Barr's input, will be discussed in detail below.

11. The Wellesley College Archives provided the author with a course roster for Art 305. The nine students enrolled in the class were Mary C. Bostwick, Ernestine Fantl, Alice Farny, Phyllis Holt, Natalie F. Jones, Rosamond Lane, Madeleine Schafter, Katharine Sterne, and Lois Whitaker. Letter from Wilma Slaight, Wellesley College Archivist, to the author, January 5, 2006. The author placed an announcement in the *Wellesley Alumnae Magazine* in 2007 as part of an effort to locate a surviving member of the class so as to interview her about the experience. The effort was not successful.

12. Helen Franc, interview, Oral History Project, 1991, p. 20. The Museum of Modern Art Archives, New York.

13. As Franc would later recall, "he was one of very few men on the faculty, and a very young one at that. Everybody was falling into swoons. I think one reason he liked me is that I did not have this great crush on him." See Helen Franc, Oral History Project, 1991, p. 24, MoMA Archives, NY.

14. A 1942 article on the history of laboratory work at Wellesley strongly distinguished the practice from studio art: "the principle aim should not be to train future artists, but rather to acquaint students as directly as possible with the purely formal aspects. The artistic quality of the student's own work is far less important in this case than his intelligent understanding of the problems involved and a person with no skill at all may derive as much benefit from the exercises as his more gifted companions." See Sirapie Der Nersessian, "The Direct Approach in the Study of Art History," *College Art Journal* 1, no. 3 (March 1942): 54–60.

15. The Motor-Mart seems to have been among the first garages in the United States to institute a policy of parking validation: "the principle is that if the claim check is stamped by the merchant, the owner may reclaim his car without cost. The garage, in turn, bills the merchant." See Harold S. Buttenheim, "The Problem of the Standing Vehicle," *Annals of the American Academy of Political and Social Science* 133 (November 1927): 153. Buttenheim refers to the Motor-Mart as "recently completed" (153), which suggests that the garage may have been under construction during the semester in which Barr's class was offered at Wellesley.

16. Paraphrasing Barr, the local newspaper article on the course identified industrial architecture as "America's distinctive contribution to art" ("Wellesley and Modernism," 10).

17. "Wellesley and Modernism," 10. The article continues, "The graphic arts include drawings, the etching and wood-cut and other prints, cartoons, and comic strips. Advertising is the happy hunting ground of this group, showing how modern pictorial style has followed into the ordinary environment of life."

For information on Bostwick, I am indebted to Kantor, *Alfred H. Barr Jr. and the Intellectual Origins of the Museum of Modern Art*, 397, note 51. "Wellesley and Modernism" has been attributed to Barr by Irving Sandler and Amy Newman. Given the existence in the Wellesley College Archives of a typescript for the article with Bostwick's name on it, however, I follow Kantor's attribution of the article to the student. The typescript includes hand-written corrections which were likely made by Barr when he reviewed the text prior to publication. See

Mary C. Bostwick, untitled typescript of article for *Boston Daily Record*, "Monday Evening, April 25, Tuesday A.M., April 26 [1927]," Wellesley College Archives.

18. "Annual Auto Show Opens in Splendor," *New York Times*, January 9, 1927, E1.

19. J. Brooks Atkinson, "*The Dybbuk* in Hebrew," *New York Times*, December 14, 1926, 24.

20. When the Habima production moved to Boston later in the semester, it was reviewed by the *Wellesley College News*. In an extraordinary passage, the anonymous reviewer linked the expressionist distortions of the production to the modernist distortions of the paintings on display in the controversial art exhibits organized by Barr on campus (and discussed later in this chapter):

> Such unconventionalities of treatment are particularity interesting in view of the furor raised by the current Modern Art Exhibit. It is pertinent in this connection to compare the abstract use of line, mass, and color, the accent of the rectilinear, the arbitrary foreshortening and manipulation of planes [on stage] with the similar use of plastic means in some of the more iconoclastic canvases; and to correlate the Hebrew legends with the cubist practice of introducing words into their pictures; to notice the similarity between the totally unnaturalistic make-up—the ochre faces, triangular eyebrows, and vermillion chins with the green faced rabbi of Chagall in the earlier exhibit or the "lead poisoned girl" of present horror.

See "Moscow Theatre Habima Wins Boston with Its Uniqueness," *Wellesley College News*, April 28, 1927, 3.

21. "Wellesley and Modernism," 10.

22. The ten-cent store competition foreshadows Barr's interest in industrial design at the Museum of Modern Art, including exhibitions such as *Useful Household Objects under $5*, mounted during the 1938 Christmas season, and its sequel, held in 1939 (and in several consecutive years), titled *Useful Objects under $10*. As Kantor astutely notes of Barr in the context of the Wellesley course, "One of the fundamental aspects of his taste was that he found utility objects, such as refrigerators and filing cases, more interesting than intentionally decorative forms." Kantor, *Alfred H. Barr, Jr. and the Intellectual Origins of the Museum of Modern Art*, 103.

23. Alfred H. Barr Jr., "A Modern Art Questionnaire," *Vanity Fair*, August 1927, 85.

24. On the monthly circulation of *Vanity Fair* in the late 1920s, see Kitty Hoffman, "A History of *Vanity Fair*: A Modernist Journal in America" (Ph.D. diss., University of Toronto, 1979).

25. Barr, "A Modern Art Questionnaire," 85.

26. "Wellesley and Modernism," 10.

27. Like Barr, *Vanity Fair* editor Frank Crowninshield valued advertisements as forms of creative expression in their own right. In a 1913 issue of the magazine [then known as *Dress and Vanity Fair*], Crowinshield wrote,

> The advertisements in a modern magazine furnish an independent and entirely different element of interest [from the articles]—an element that no editorial department can either duplicate or replace. . . . [E]ach advertisement in *Dress and Vanity Fair* is a special message definitely planned to interest the small and homogenous circle of which you, gentle reader, form a part . . . and frankly, we ask you to make this advertising a regular part of your reading—not on our account, not on our advertisers' account, but because these pages are worthy of it in their own right.

Quoted in Hoffman, "A History of *Vanity Fair*," 112.

28. Barr, "A Modern Art Questionnaire," 85. Later in his career, Barr would exhibit department-store window displays at MoMA, most notably in the 1949 exhibition *Modern Art in Your Life.*

29. In 1930, Frederick Kiesler would publish his influential book *Contemporary Art Applied to the Store and Its Display* (New York: Brentano's, 1930). Kiesler argued that the shop window is a purveyor not only of select commodities but of modernist style and sensibilities more broadly conceived.

30. Except for A. H. Fish, Covarrubias illustrated the greatest number of the magazines covers between 1925 and 1935.

31. "Wellesley and Modernism," 10.

32. As Irving Sandler has pointed out, "*Vanity Fair*, the chic and informed cultural monthly (which, by the way, was the source of much of Barr's earliest acquaintance with modern art) allowed its sophisticated readers to flatter (or embarrass) themselves with their scores [on the questionnaire]." See Alfred H. Barr Jr., *Defining Modern Art: Selected Writings of Alfred H. Barr, Jr.*, ed. Irving Sandler and Amy Newman (New York: Abrams, 1986), 56.

33. In smaller print, the ad proclaims: "Today is never new enough for *Vanity Fair*. . . . That's why intelligent moderns have accepted it, for ten years, as the forecast of what is new and the judge of what is significant in this gay and charming world. Don't look backward—think what happened to Lot's wife!"

34. "Don't Be a Yesterday," *New York Times*, October 2, 1925, 17. As Hoffman points out in "A History of *Vanity Fair*," *Vanity Fair* appealed to readers in part by refusing to specialize as an art, news, sports, or movie magazine.

35. The portrait is typically identified as *Portrait of Braque* although, according to Picasso, "It was painted in the studio without a model. Afterwards, with Braque we said that it was a portrait of him. He wore a hat a bit like that." Picasso quoted in Pierre Daix, *Picasso: The Cubist Years, 1907–1916: A Catalogue Raisonné of the Paintings and Related Works*, translated by Joan Rosselet (New York: Bulfinch, 1988), 252.

36. In that context, Barr employed the painting to demonstrate Picasso's gradual shift away from the faceted but still recognizable figuration of analytic cubism to the flattened, more fully abstract forms of synthetic cubism. See Alfred H. Barr Jr., *Cubism and Abstract Art: Painting, Sculpture, Constructions, Photography, Architecture, Industrial Art, Theater, Films, Posters, Typography* (New York: Museum of Modern Art, 1936), 31.

37. Barr and his staff were apparently less vigilant about the reproduction of Gino Severini's *Armored Train*, which was printed upside down in *Cubism and Abstract Art*. On this mistake, see Robert Rosenblum's foreword to the reprint of the catalogue that was published by Belknap Press of Harvard University Press in 1986.

38. Quoted in Rona Roob, "Alfred H. Barr, Jr.," *New Criterion* 5 (August 1987): 4, 6.

39. *The Studio*, a London-based art magazine with tipped-in illustrations under tissue guards, would likely have been seen by the "grey-beards" as a more legitimate source of knowledge about modern art.

40. Alfred H. Barr Jr., memo to A. Conger Goodyear about 1929 plan for MoMA, August 1941, as cited in Helaine Ruth Messer, "MoMA: Museum in Search of a Message" (Ph.D. diss., Columbia University, 1979), 27.

41. According to a 1953 profile of Barr in the *New Yorker*, "By his junior year [at Princeton], Barr was majoring in art history, and was developing an interest in modern art, partly because he liked what he saw of it in *Vanity Fair* and *The Dial* and partly because his teachers made fun of it." See Dwight MacDonald, "Profiles: Action on West Fifty-Third Street, Part 1," *New Yorker*, December 12, 1953, 70.

42. "An American Museum of Modern Art," *Vanity Fair*, November 1929, 76, 136. Barr published a similar piece in *Vogue*, *Vanity Fair*'s sister publication at Condé Nast: "A New Museum Which Will Devote Itself to the Masters of Modern Art," *Vogue*, October 26, 1929, 85, 108.

43. Cited in Messer, "MoMA," 24. *Vanity Fair*'s reproduction of modern painting was a point of contention between Crowninshield and the magazine's publisher, Condé Nast. According to Kitty Hoffman's cultural history of the magazine, the two men "disagreed about the merits of modern art, and the editor spent a good part of his time arguing with his publisher over the desirability of including full-page colour reproductions of modern masters in *Vanity Fair*. 'Crowny' finally won, and from 1921 to 1936 this became a famous feature of the magazine." See Hoffman, "A History of *Vanity Fair*," 62–63.

44. The British magazine *Vanity Fair* (1869–1914) was celebrated for its inclusion of a full-page caricature of a contemporary social or political figure in each issue. The caricatures were typically published as chromolithographic prints.

45. "A. H. Fish" was the professional name of the English illustrator Anne Harriet Fish Sefton, who created the August 1927 cover mentioned above.

46. Stein had, by this time, published with some regularity in *Vanity Fair*.

47. Millay had worked for *Vanity Fair* on assignment in Europe from 1921 to 1923, and Monroe had been profiled and photographed "in Chinese Dress" in the August 1920 issue.

48. The absence of women painters on the questionnaire is underscored by Barr's description of Alfred Stieglitz (#12) as "American photographer, pioneer, and prophet of modern art in America . . . [and] husband of Georgia O'Keeffe."

49. Agnes A. Abbott, "Department of Art at Wellesley College," *Art Journal* 21, no. 4 (Summer 1962): 264.

50. Wellesley's innovative course was introduced into the curriculum in 1911 by Alice Van Vechten Brown and her colleague Myrtilla Avery. When Paul Sachs started his now-famous course in museum training at Harvard University in 1921, he sought Avery's advice. Yet it is significant that while the Wellesley course initially aimed at "the training of museum assistants," the Harvard program envisaged the instruction of future museum directors and curators. On the Wellesley course, see Edith R. Abbott, "Training for Museum Workers," *Metropolitan Museum of Art Bulletin* 11, no. 5 (May 1916): 111–113.

51. Florence Converse, *The Story of Wellesley* (Boston: Little, Brown, 1915), 136–137.

52. "Art Museum Training Course," *Announcement for 1928-29, Farnsworth Art Museum,* Wellesley College Archives, file: President's Office; Academic Departments: Art. According to the announcement, "Because of the renewed call for trained museum officials, the Wellesley College Art Museum is reviving the Museum Training Course which was successfully conducted from 1911–1917. The aim is to give women graduates the opportunity to be among those who are developing museums, as museum instructors, assistants, museum librarians, curators, and directors."

53. On Wellesley's founding, see Jean Glasscock, gen. ed., *Wellesley College, 1875-1975: A Century of Women* (Wellesley: Wellesley College, 1975).

54. In 1936, Fantl married a British book dealer and moved to London, where she mounted exhibitions for the Ministry of Exhibitions as well as the American Office of War Information. See Barbara Burman, "Carter [née Fantl], Ernestine Marie (1906-1983)]," *Oxford Dictionary*

of National Biography (Oxford: Oxford University Press, 2004-2008), www.oxforddnb.com (accessed May 9, 2010).

55. Ernestine Carter, *With Tongue in Chic* (London: Michael Joseph, 1974), 16-17.

56. According to a biographical note from a book she coauthored, as of 1976 Helen M. Franc held "graduate degrees from the Institute of Art History of New York University and the Sorbonne. Before joining the staff of the Museum of Modern Art in 1954, she had been successively the assistant to the Director and Acting Curator of Drawings at The Pierpont Morgan Library, Assistant Editor of the *Art Bulletin*, Associate in Education at the Philadelphia Museum of Art, Managing Editor of the *Magazine of Art*, and Associate Editor at Harry. N. Abrams, Inc." See Jean Lipman and Helen M. Franc, *Bright Stars: American Painting and Sculpture since 1776* (New York: E. P. Dutton, 1976), 206.

It was Franc who oversaw Rosalind Krauss's work on (what was to have been) MoMA's monograph on David Smith in 1968 and 1969. The monograph was ultimately cancelled following a series of conflicts between Krauss and MoMA. Krauss, herself a Wellesley graduate, was thus in direct contact (if also, ultimately, in some dispute) with a Wellesley alumna who was both a student and a colleague of Barr's. On the troubled history of the Smith monograph, see Department of Publications Collection on Proposed David Smith Monograph, I.57. The Museum of Modern Art Archives, New York.

57. See "Katharine G. Sterne: Former Art Reviewer for the Times Dies Up-State," *New York Times*, September 1, 1944, 13.

58. "Wellesley and Modernism," 10.

59. "Wellesley Viewing Noted Paintings," *Christian Science Monitor*, January 19, 1927, 5B.

60. Walter Benjamin, "The Work of Art in the Age of Mechanical Reproduction" (1936), in *Illuminations: Essays and Reflections*, ed. Hannah Arendt, translated by Harry Zohn (New York: Schocken, 1969), 220.

61. Alfred H. Barr Jr., "Boston Is Modern Art Pauper," *Harvard Crimson*, October 30, 1926, 1.

62. Ibid.

63. Alfred H. Barr Jr., letter to the editor, *Art News*, December 18, 1926, 8.

64. Barr, "Boston Is Modern Art Pauper," 1.

65. Ibid.

66. Lewis Mumford, "Living Art," *New Republic*, February 6, 1924, 290. The facsimiles of watercolors were singled out for their visual excellence and technical accuracy. According to Thomas Craven's review of the portfolio, "The water-colours and temperas are facsimiles in the true sense of the word. By a process perfected in Germany it is now possible to duplicate in inks not only the colours of the original media, but the technical minutiae of the artist's handiworks: the delicate transparencies, the flat tones, the charcoal interpolations, and even the pencilings of the preliminary sketch are faithfully preserved." See Thomas Craven, "Living Art, Twenty Facsimile Reproductions after Paintings, Drawings, and Engravings, and Ten Photographs after Sculpture, by Contemporary Artists," *The Dial*, February 1924; as reprinted in *The Dial: Arts and Letters in the 1920s: An Anthology of Writings*, ed. Gayle L. Brown (Worcester, MA: Worcester Art Museum, 1981), 76.

67. See Barr, "Boston Is Modern Art Pauper," 1. For the public announcement of the gift, see "Fogg Museum Gets Art Gift," *Christian Science Monitor*, October 23, 1926, 5B: "A series of reproductions of 'Living Art' has been presented to Fogg Museum by Alfred H. Barr and Jere Abbott, graduate students at Harvard University. The collection will be on exhibition until Nov. 1."

68. Cited in Roob, "Alfred H. Barr, Jr.," 10–11.

69. D.A. [Dorothy Adlow], "Moderns at Wellesley," 8.

70. Ibid.

71. Ibid.

72. "Seniors Find Modern Art Queer and Incomprehensible," *Wellesley College News*, April 28, 1927, 1.

73. A brief notice in the *Christian Science Monitor* announced that "contemporary art and paintings of the nineteenth century are on exhibition at the Farnsworth Art Museum at Wellesley College in connection with the course on modern art here. Among painters represented the majority are French or foreigners residing in Paris." See "Wellesley Stages Exhibit of Paintings," *Christian Science Monitor*, April 12, 1927, 15.

74. Alfred H. Barr Jr., "The Exhibition of Modern Art," *Wellesley College News*, April 21, 1927, 5; clipping, Wellesley College Archives.

75. Ibid.

76. Ibid.

77. Alfred H. Barr Jr., "The Necco Factory," *The Arts* 13 (May 1928): 292–295. *The Arts* was a New York-based magazine focused largely on American art and architecture; see Lloyd Goodrich, "*The Arts* Magazine, 1920–31," *American Art Journal* 5, no. 1 (May 1973): 79–85. Goodrich cites the mission of Forbes Watson, editor in chief at the time: "Whenever it is possible, articles will be secured by artists. Those who are engaged in creating pictures, sculpture, and so forth, are not always, as everybody knows, the most impartial critics. But the most impartial critic is seldom the most stimulating critic, and a special interest and character are often found in the words of a craftsman about his own craft" (82).

78. Barr was especially impressed that there were "altogether over twenty kinds of windows in the Necco factory." See Barr, "The Necco Factory," 295.

79. Ibid., 294.

80. Ibid.

81. Indeed, the broader argument of Barr's essay on the Necco factory involved the superiority of American industrial architecture to other kinds of public building projects in United States, whether "ecclesiastical, academic, civic, or commercial." The question of beauty surfaces in Barr's article in a revealing way (ibid., 295):

The New England Confectionary Company, in addition to its industrial requirements, desired a building which would be beautiful. The demand for "beauty" in a factory usually implies the intervention of an architect, who courageously contributes a few Gothic arches or Renaissance cornices, sometimes both, thus reducing the factory to the mongrel level of the usual skyscraper. It was very fortunate therefore that Lockwood, Greene, and Company [the building firm] left the design of the Necco factory as well as the construction entirely in the hands of its engineering department. . . . It will exist for the new generation not merely as a document in the growth of a new style, but as one of the most living and beautiful buildings in New England.

82. Abbott's photographs of the Necco factory were first published in the inaugural issue of the Harvard University magazine *Hound and Horn* in September 1927.

83. Leah Dickerman, "The Radical Oblique: Aleksandr Rodchenko's Camera-Eye," *Documents* 12 (Spring 1988): 34.

84. Barr, "The Necco Factory," 294.

85. Kantor, *Alfred H. Barr Jr. and the Intellectual Origins of the Museum of Modern Art*, 104–105.

86. Sachs's Museum Course, first offered in 1921, became the curatorial and professional training ground for graduate students who ultimately "took up positions of authority in over 100 art institutions." In addition to Barr and Abbott, those students included James Plaut, who later became the Director of the Institute of Contemporary Art in Boston. Plaut and the Institute will be discussed at length in chapter 4. On Sachs's Museum Course, see Sally Anne Duncan, "Paul J. Sachs and the Institutionalization of Museum Culture between the World Wars" (Ph.D. diss., Interdisciplinary Doctorate Program, Tufts University, 2001).

87. Roob, "Alfred H. Barr, Jr.," 12. In a 1953 profile of Barr for the *New Yorker*, Dwight MacDonald cites Barr's "application for a Harvard fellowship 'to enable me to spend a year in Europe . . . I wish to study contemporary European culture . . . Contemporary art is puzzling and chaotic but is, to many of us, living and important in itself and as a manifestation of our amazing though none too lucid civilization. I confess I find the art of the present more interesting

and moving than the art of the Sung or even the Quatrocento" (quoted in MacDonald, "Profiles . . . Part 1," 71).

88. According to Elaine Hochman, "When Barr was unable to obtain a grant to study contemporary art abroad in 1927, Sachs personally arranged for funds to be made available to him. Two years later, as one of the Museum of Modern Art's founding board members, Sachs would offer twenty-seven-year-old Barr as a candidate for the museum's directorship." See Elaine Hochman, *Bauhaus: Crucible of Modernism* (New York: Fromm International, 1997), 173.

89. Alfred H. Barr Jr., to Alan McCullough, 1967, AHB Papers [AAA: 2196; 1198]. MoMA Archives, NY; as cited in Kantor, *Alfred H. Barr*, 159, 407.

90. Barr, as quoted in Margret Kentgens-Craig, *The Bauhaus and America: First Contacts, 1919–1936* (Cambridge: MIT Press, 1999), 83.

91. Barr, preface to *Bauhaus, 1919–1928*, 5.

92. Ibid.

93. Alfred H. Barr Jr., "Russian Diary 1927–28," *October* 7 (Winter 1978): 12.

94. Ibid., 15.

95. On Rivera's visit to Moscow and his interactions with Barr while there, see Leah Dickerman, "Leftist Circuits," in *Diego Rivera: Murals for the Museum of Modern Art* (New York: Museum of Modern Art, 2011), 14–21.

96. Barr, "Russian Diary," 24.

97. Ibid., 49.

98. Elizabeth Jones, "A Note on Barr's Contribution to the Scholarship on Soviet Art," *October* 7 (Winter 1978): 4.

99. Barr, "Russian Diary," 21.

100. Varvara Stepanova, diary entry for January 10, 1928, as cited and translated in Varvara Rodchenko, "Days in the Life . . . ," in *Aleksandr Rodchenko* (New York: Museum of Modern Art, 1999), 140. The entry continues, "Barr showed us a book on Russian art, in English, by [Louis] Lozowick. Everything was accurate—even the parts on the Constructivists—and there was a list of all their names. . . . There's an entire chapter on Rodchenko. Barr made us check it for accuracy. O'C (an Irishwoman) was there, and she interpreted. There turned out to be only one error. . . . In America this Barr lectures on art." As pointed out in the curator's preface to the diary entry, "Barr dates this visit a week before Stepanova does, on January 3, 1928" (143 n. 1).

101. The heir to a Maine textile fortune, Abbott later served as the treasurer of his family's successful business, the Amos Abbott Textile Company in Dexter, Maine. On Barr's recommendation, Abbott was appointed associate director of MoMA (1929–1932). He left MoMA to become director of the Smith College Museum of Art (1932–1947). See biographical note, Jere Abbott Papers, George J. Mitchell Department of Special Collections and Archives, Bowdoin College Library.

102. Alfred H. Barr Jr., "Sergei Michailovitch Eisenstein," *The Arts* 14, no. 6 (December 1928): 316–321.

103. According to Denise Youngblood, "After March 1928 . . . [r]eal [film] criticism, while still possible, was rare; it had been replaced by violent diatribes couched in the vituperative jargon which characterized the Cultural Revolution." See Denise J. Youngblood, "The Fate of Soviet Popular Cinema during the Stalin Revolution," *Russian Review* 50, no. 2 (April 1991): 155.

104. In his article on Lef, Barr noted that Stepanova "composes the adventurous typography of *Sovietskoi Kino*, the foremost of Russian cinema periodicals"; see Alfred H. Barr Jr., "The Lef and Soviet Art," *Transition* 13/14 (Fall 1928): 270.

105. There is a certain irony to this location, given the enmity between Barr and Arthur A. Houghton, who endowed the Harvard library and after whom it is named. The dispute between Houghton and Barr will be treated in chapter 4.

106. "Modern European Posters and Commercial Typography," *Wellesley College News*, May 9, 1929, 3.

107. Ibid.

108. Barr, "The Exhibition of Modern Art," 5.

109. "European Poster Exhibit," *Wellesley College News*, May 13, 1929, 3.

110. Ibid.

111. Ibid.

112. Cited in Dwight MacDonald, "Profiles: Action on West Fifty-Third Street, Part 2" (on Alfred H. Barr Jr.), *New Yorker*, December 19, 1953, 40.

113. "Wellesley and Modernism," 10.

114. Tim Studt, "Novartis Creates Research Magic in a Candy Factory," *R&D Magazine*, May 17, 2005, www.rdmag.com/Awards/Lab-Of-The-Year/2005/05/Novartis-Creates--Research-Magic-in--A-Candy-Factory (accessed May 8, 2012).

115. Ed Tsoi, cited in Naomi Aoki, "Candy Coated: Power-Cleaning Clears Way for Labs at Old Necco Factory," *Boston Globe*, July 9, 2003, C1.

3 Prehistoric Modern (1937)

1. According to Jewell's subsequent article, respondents to his questionnaire included Henri Matisse ("that veritable prince of modernism"), realist painter John Sloan, and Princeton art historian (and Barr's undergraduate professor) Frank Mather. See Edward Alden Jewell, "Again a Storm Rages over Modern Art," *New York Times*, February 22, 1931, 71.

2. Ibid.

3. Press release, "Definition of Modern Art for E. D. [*sic*] Jewell of Times—with Notes from A. H. Barr" (response to "What Is Modern Art?"), January 21, 1931. The Museum of Modern

Art, New York. Pdf available at www.moma.org/learn/resources/press_archives (accessed June 12, 2012).

4. Ibid.

5. Ibid. Jewell quoted extensively from Barr's response in his *New York Times* article "Again a Storm Rages over Modern Art."

6. In a December 1931 article on the museum, A. Conger Goodyear looked forward to a show resembling the one Barr described: "What may be the most interesting exhibition of the year [1932] might be called 'Modern Art, Past and Present.' As planned, it will place side by side the work of today and of the distant past—Egyptian, Persian, Greek, Aztec, Chinese, European—whatever may definitely illustrate relationships and throw light on the sources or contribute to the understanding of Modern Art." See A. Conger Goodyear, "Museum of Modern Art," *Creative Art* 9, no. 6 (December 1931): 456. In an official statement dated April 1931, the Museum noted that "Modern Art, Past and Present" "is not to be a pot-pourri but is planned to demonstrate definite relationships." Though the exhibition never came to pass, its proposed title suggested that "Modern Art" was not a new category but an ongoing dialogue between contemporary and historical forms of creative expression. See "An Effort to Secure 3,250,000 for the Museum of Modern Art, New York City" official statement, April 1931, 17; Alfred H. Barr, Jr. Papers, 9a.2. The Museum of Modern Art Archives, New York. (Hereafter cited as AHB Papers.)

7. Rather than confining these objects to the rarefied realm of connoisseurship or specialized scholarly discourse, Barr opened them to broader questions and contexts.

8. Alfred H. Barr Jr., "Russian Icons," *The Arts* 17, no. 5 (February 1931): 297.

9. In this sense, Barr follows the pro-Soviet tone of the Boston Museum of Fine Arts as expressed in its bulletin: "The Soviet revolution made all the icons of the Greek Church the property of the Russian government and the government undertook immediately to collect and care for them. They have been swept into the various museums but in most cases not before they have passed through the Central National Restoration Workshops which have been set up at Moscow within the walls of the Kremlin." See P. H., "The Exhibition of Russian Icons," *Bulletin of the Museum of Fine Arts* 18, no. 169 (October 1930): 90.

Where both Barr and the *Bulletin of the Museum of Fine Arts* present the Soviet government as benevolent in its treatment of religious art and architecture, alternative accounts offer a starkly different version of the same history. In the *Art Journal* in the midst of the cold war, the American scholar Leo Teholiz wrote, "The Bolsheviks ravaged the churches in Russia after the 1918 October Revolution. They burned, pillaged, destroyed, and confiscated church property, including hundreds of objects of religious art. Icons were defaced and defiled. The Bolsheviks originally set out to destroy and trample into the ground all 'religion' but only managed to scratch the surface during the period of the 1920's." See Leo Teholiz, "Religious Mysticism and Socialist Realism: The Soviet Union Pays Homage to the Icon Painter Andrey Rublev," *Art Journal* 21, no. 2 (Winter 1961–1962): 76.

10. Barr, "Russian Icons," 297.

11. Ibid., 303.

12. Barr credits the American Russian Institute with overcoming these challenges by "courageously assum[ing] legal responsibility" for the show; see Barr, "Russian Icons," 303.

13. J. J. Lissitzyn, general secretary of the National League of Americans of Russian Origin, to the president and trustees of the Metropolitan Museum of Art, as cited in "Russian Icon Show Stirs New Protest," *New York Times*, January 11, 1931, 36.

14. Ibid.

15. Barr, "Russian Icons," 303.

16. Ibid.

17. Sybil Gordon Kantor, *Alfred H. Barr, Jr., and the Intellectual Origins of the Museum of Modern Art* (Cambridge: MIT Press, 2001), 165.

18. Alfred H. Barr Jr., "Russian Diary 1927–28," *October* 7 (Winter 1978): 39 (entry for Tuesday, January 24, 1928).

19. During their visit to workshops, Barr and Abbott purchased multiple photographs of icons, several of which were used to illustrate Barr's 1931 essay "Russian Icons."

20. Alfred H. Barr Jr. to Paul Sachs, January 17, 1928, as cited in Kantor, *Alfred H. Barr*, 164.

21. Alfred H. Barr Jr. to Paul Sachs, January 17, 1928, as cited in Kantor, *Alfred H. Barr*, 164.

22. Barr, "Russian Icons," 305.

23. Igor Grabar, "Introduction: Ancient Russian Painting," in *A Catalogue of Russian Icons Received from the American Russian Institute for Exhibition* (New York: Metropolitan Museum of Art, 1931), xi–xii.

24. Teholiz, "Religious Mysticism," 77, describes the complex process whereby religious icons could be repurposed as Soviet cultural patrimony:

> From one point of view, the Soviet authorities seem to allay their fears and direct concern about the deceptive and fraudulent quality of religion, and from another viewpoint, religious art really was not "reactionary," or an "opiate," but instead it could be appreciated as a work of art. It could be discussed as an example of a national folk art and appreciated for its decorative beauty, elements of design and harmony of color; and the church buildings and other historical monuments acknowledged as fine examples of the building tradition of the Russian nation. It might even be possible to link together the past and the present: the development of past art forms, trends, styles in the different arts, the folk art, monumental art, religious art, applied art, architecture, sculpture and the fine arts, to show how all of these ultimately evolved through the centuries into what is today considered "the people's art"—the art of socialist-realism. In the final process of its development, those qualities which the Soviets consider decadent, formalistic and bourgeois would have been conveniently cast off.

25. Barr, "Russian Icons," 363.

26. The complete title of the exhibition, as listed in the catalogue, was *Persian Fresco Paintings, Reconstructed by Mr. Sarkis Katchadourian from the Seventeenth Century Originals in Isfahan*. It was most often referred to simply as *Persian Fresco Paintings* and appears as *Persian Fresco Painting* on the Museum of Modern Art's own inventory of exhibitions. See MoMA's exhibition history list (http://www.moma.org/learn/resources/archives_exhibition_history_list).

27. Press release, "Reconstruction of Persian Frescoes on Exhibit," September 24, 1932. MoMA, NY. Pdf available at www.moma.org/learn/resources/press_archives (accessed June 12, 2012).

28. Ibid.

29. Myron Bement Smith, "Notes," in *Persian Fresco Paintings, Reconstructed by Mr. Sarkis Katchadourian from the Seventeenth Century Originals in Isfahan* (New York: American Institute for Persian Art and Archaeology, [1932]), 14.

30. Ibid., 14–15.

31. Edward Alden Jewell, "Color of the East in 'Reconstructions,'" *New York Times*, October 16, 1932, 10.

32. Press release, "Reconstruction of Persian Frescoes on Exhibit."

33. *Reconstructions of Seventeenth-Century Persian Fresco Paintings in Isfahan by Mr. Sarkis Katchadourian* was on view at the Arts Club of Chicago from November 15 to December 27, 1932; see "Past Exhibitions," *Arts Club of Chicago*, www.artsclubchicago.org/exhibitions/past-exhibitions-1930.html (accessed June 12, 2012). Two years later, the show was displayed at the Leicester Galleries in June 1934; see gallery exhibition chronology at *Ernest Brown & Phillips Ltd.*, www.ernestbrownandphillips.ltd.uk (accessed January 14, 2012).

34. Smith, "Notes," 15.

35. Writing in 1974, the scholar Ernst Grube noted that centrality of painted decoration to the architectural logic of the Ali Qapu Palace. Painting, he writes, "is not employed only in specific areas or for specific subjects, but literally covers the entire interior surface . . . and most of the exterior recessed areas . . . in a tight continuous pattern. In this sense, painting becomes truly the interpretive agent of tectonic values, emphasizing the arches of vaults, the central circular elements of the cupolas, the division between wall and vault spaces. Painting defines and interprets architecture but it also envelops it." See Ernest Grube, "Wall Paintings in the Seventeenth Century Monuments of Isfahan," *Iranian Studies* 7, no. 3–4 (1974): 521.

36. On the influence of Persian art, textiles, and architecture on Matisse, see Fereshteh Daftari, *The Influence of Persian Art on Gauguin, Matisse, and Kandinsky* (New York: Routledge, 1991).

37. Malcolm Vaughn, "Modernism from Persia," *New York American*, October 15, 1932, clipping in A. Conger Goodyear scrapbooks [18.4]. The Museum of Modern Art Archives, New York.

38. *New York Sun*, October 15, 1932, clipping in "1932 Persian Fresco Paintings," A. Conger Goodyear scrapbooks [18.4]. MoMA Archives, NY.

39. Katchadourian was in a sense caught between two different moments in the cultural development of the copy—a premodern, artisanal culture of handmade reproductions and a modernist culture that privileged originality. In "Reproductions, Cultural Capital, and Museums: Aspects of the Culture of Copies," *Museum and Society* 2, no. 1 (March 2004): 47–67, Gordon Fyfe analyzes the work of nineteenth-century British artisan engravers as part of a "pre-modern culture of the copy . . . a world in which the boundary between originals and reproductions was more permeable than that of ours and where the relationship between them was more visible than it is today" (62). Fyfe's discussion of "handi-craft reproductions" is particular relevant to Katchadourian's later example.

40. See Douglas C. Fox, "Prehistoric Rock Pictures in Europe and Africa," *Bulletin of the Museum of Modern Art* 4, no. 5 (April 1937): 2. According to Goodyear, it was Barr's idea to bring *Prehistoric Rock Pictures* to the museum; see A. Conger Goodyear, *The Museum of Modern Art: The First Ten Years* (New York: n.p., 1943), 65.

41. Alfred H. Barr Jr., preface to Leo Frobenius and Douglas C. Fox, *Prehistoric Rock Pictures in Europe and Africa, from Material in the Archives of the Research Institute for the Morphology of Civilization, Frankfort-on-Main* (New York: Museum of Modern Art, 1937), 9–10. In this sense, the prehistoric rock art facsimiles contrast with Katchadourian's copies of Persian frescoes, which tended to reverse the historical process of decay.

42. Leo Frobenius, "The Story of Rock Picture Research," in Frobenius and Fox, *Prehistoric Rock Pictures in Europe and Africa*, 19.

43. Barr, preface to *Prehistoric Rock Pictures in Europe and Africa*, 10.

44. H. C. Woodhouse, "Rock Paintings of Southern Africa." *African Arts* 2, no. 3 (1969): 44.

45. A facsimile of a wall-sized rock painting from the Mtoko cave appeared in the MoMA exhibition, though its composition does not appear to match the (admittedly) indistinct imagery on the cave wall in the background of the photograph. Nor does the extreme width of the facsimile (9 x 25 feet) conform to the vertical orientation of the artist's canvas in the photograph. It may be, however, that the larger facsimiles were painted in vertical fragments and then pieced together.

46. Edward Alden Jewell, "Art Museum Opens Prehistoric Show," *New York Times*, April 28, 1937, 21.

47. Fox, "Prehistoric Rock Pictures in Europe and Africa," *Bulletin of the Museum of Modern Art*, 5.

48. Goodyear, *The Museum of Modern Art*, 65.

49. Robert Goldwater, "Prehistoric Rock Pictures," *Magazine of Art*, June 1937, 380. Barr sounded a similar note in his preface to the catalogue: "That an institution devoted to the most recent in art should concern itself with the most ancient may seem something of a paradox, but the art of the twentieth century has already come under the influence of the great tradition of prehistoric mural art which began around the 200th century B.C. . . . [and] which living artists and many others who are interested in living art have admired"; see Barr, preface to *Prehistoric Rock Pictures*, 9.

50. Robert Goldwater, *Primitivism in Modern Painting* (New York: Harper, 1938), xxii. In this passage, Goldwater is referring specifically to European modernist art of the early twentieth century, the "primitivizing" tendencies of which he contrasts to the "archaizing" effects of late nineteenth-century art nouveau. He writes, "How their [late nineteenth-century] idea of the primitive, imbued with the old conception of a return to a harmonious golden day—if not of culture at least of a controlled style in the arts—differs from the ferocious primitivizing of the last thirty years we will try to determine in our closing definition."

51. Barr, preface to *Prehistoric Rock Pictures*, 9.

52. This disparagement is particularly striking given MoMA's show *New Horizons in American Art*, which opened in September 1936 and featured work produced under the Federal Art Project of the Works Progress Administration; see Holger Cahill, *New Horizons in American Art* (New York: Museum of Modern Art, 1936).

53. "Art: Dawn Pictures," *Time*, May 10, 1937, 25. The *New York Times* similarly noted that "Mr. Barr has placed in galleries on the fourth floor of the museum a few shrewdly selected examples of work by such moderns as Miro, Arp, Klee, Masson and others. This supplement offers much that is suggestive and provides several interesting parallels"; see Jewell, "Art Museum Opens Prehistoric Show," 21. In a follow-up review, Jewell adds two more artists to the list of those included in the companion show: "The relationship between prehistoric and modern art (implicit and at times, perhaps, explicit too) is patent. Mr. Barr has performed a service by assembling on the fourth floor, for the purposes of comparison, some work by Miro, Arp, Klee, Masson, Lebedev, and Larionov, artists of the twentieth century." See Edward Alden Jewell, "In the Realm of Art: From the Stone Age to Modernism," *New York Times*, May 2, 1937, 9.

54. Alfred H. Barr Jr., "Cubism and Abstract Art," in *Cubism and Abstract Art: Painting, Sculpture, Constructions, Photography, Architecture, Industrial Art, Theater, Films, Posters, Typography* (New York: Museum of Modern Art, 1936), 11.

55. Douglas C. Fox, "Rock Pictures in Europe and Africa," in Frobenius and Fox, *Prehistoric Rock Pictures in Europe and Africa*, 48–49.

56. Siyakha Mguni, "Research into the Formlings in the Rock Art of Zimbabwe," *Antiquity* 75 (December 2001): 807–808. See also Siyakha Mguni, "Cultured Representation: Understanding 'Formlings,' an Enigmatic Motif in the Rock-Art of Zimbabwe," *Journal of Social Archaeology* 4, no. 2 (2004): 181–199. For his most recent interpretation, see Siyakha Mguni, "Iconography of Termites' Nests and Termites: Symbolic Nuances of Formlings in Southern African San Rock Art," *Cambridge Archaeological Journal* 16 (2006): 53–71.

57. Siyakha Mguni, "Continuity and Change in San Belief and Ritual: Some Aspects of the Enigmatic 'Formling' and Tree Motifs from Matopo Hills Rock Art, Zimbabwe" (M.A. thesis, University of Witwatersrand, South Africa, 2002), 8.

58. All of the other reproductions include figurative forms (whether of antelopes, elephants, humans, or other beasts).

59. The previous year, in the *Cubism and Abstract Art* catalogue, a futurist painting by Gino Severini titled *Armored Train* (1915) had been printed upside down; see Robert Rosenblum's foreword to the reprint of the catalogue published by Belknap Press of Harvard University Press in 1986.

60. Barr, "Cubism and Abstract Art," 13.

61. Alfred H. Barr Jr., "Understanding Modern Art," *Wellesley Alumnae Magazine*, June 1929, 304.

62. Ibid. In the pages of the *Park Avenue Social Review* a few years later, Barr would similarly point out: "It must be remembered that the whole history of art as well as much scientific and psychological knowledge is available to the contemporary painter. He picks and chooses whatever he wishes. Side by side today are artists who paint exactly what they see in nature, and artists who paint story-pictures, romantic landscapes, sociological and political problem pictures, sentimental portraits, dreams—and still a few who paint merely squares and circles." See Alfred H. Barr Jr., "Who's Crazy Now?" *Park Avenue Social Review*, November 1933, 10.

63. Alfred H. Barr Jr., *A Brief Survey of Modern Painting* (New York: Museum of Modern Art, 1932), n.pag.

64. Ibid.

65. Alfred H. Barr Jr., "Brief Analysis of the Installation of the 'Italian Masters' at the Museum of Modern Art," June 19, 1940, AHB Papers, 9.B.1. MoMA Archives, NY.

66. Press release, "Italian Masters Go Back April 13," *New York Times*, April 2, 1940, 26; as well as "All Attendance Records," February 5, 1940. MoMA Archives, NY. Pdf available at www.moma.org/learn/resources/press_archives (accessed June 12, 2012).

67. Barr, "Brief Analysis of the Installation of the 'Italian Masters' at the Museum of Modern Art," AHB Papers, 9.B.1. MoMA Archives, NY.

68. The two shows shared the same checklist, though each museum produced its own catalogue and the exhibition titles differed slightly. "Masterpieces of Italian Art Lent by the Royal Italian Government" was on display in Chicago from November 18, 1939, to January 9, 1940.

69. In a note to the church's pastor Father Shannon, the Art Institute's director expressed his gratitude for the "loan of your candlesticks [which] helped to suggest the Italian atmosphere which we were so anxious to achieve"; see Daniel Catton Rich to the Right Reverend Thomas Vincent Shannon, January 16, 1940, "Italian Masterpieces" exhibition file, Archives of the Art Institute of Chicago.

70. Eleanor Jewett, "World Famous Art Show Will Open Tonight," *Chicago Daily Tribune*, November 17, 1939, 25.

71. Edward Alden Jewell, "Of Old (and Contemporary) Masters," *New York Times*, February 4, 1940, 127.

72. Ibid.

73. Barr, "Brief Analysis of the Installation of the 'Italian Masters' at the Museum of Modern Art," AHB Papers, 9.B.1. MoMA Archives, NY.

74. Press release, "Italian Masterpieces to be Shown at the Museum of Modern Art," no. 1–2, December 28, 1939. MoMA, NY. Pdf available at www.moma.org/learn/resources/press_ archives (accessed June 12, 2012). Clark mentions both the museum's "emphasis on the contemporary arts" and its "interest in the field of modern art." At the time these words were written, it was still possible to use the two phrases interchangeably. As will be discussed in the next chapter, however, in the 1940s the category of "modern art" would increasingly be posed against a more expansive, less exclusive notion of "contemporary art" (or "arts").

75. Jewell, "Of Old (and Contemporary) Masters," 127.

76. Dorothy C. Miller, foreword to *Modern Masters from European and American Collections* (New York: Museum of Modern Art, 1940), 37.

77. See "All Attendance Records."

78. The rankings were reported in "Italian Masters Go Back," 26.

79. The lone German artist selected, Wilhelm Lehmbruck, was described in the catalogue as "One of the greatest of twentieth-century sculptors, [though] much of his art is now officially repudiated in his own country"; see Miller, foreword to *Modern Masters*, 37.

80. Alfred H. Barr Jr. to Commander Eugenio Ventura, February 15, 1940, AHB Papers, 6.B.15. MoMA Archives, NY.

81. Camille M. Cianfarra, "Italy Is Preparing for Spread of War," *New York Times*, January 8, 1940, 5. As Sergio Cortesini has demonstrated, "during the Thirties the Fascist Italian government promoted Italian culture in America as a form of 'parallel diplomacy.'" See Sergio Cortesini, "Unseen Canvases: Italian Canvases and Fascist Myths across the American Scene," *American Art* 25, no. 1 (Spring 2011): 53. In June 1940, less than three months after the works in *Italian Masters* were returned to Rome, Italy declared war on France and England. "The hand that held the dagger has struck it into the back of its neighbor," said President Roosevelt in reference to Mussolini in an address he gave at the University of Virginia on June 10, 1940; as cited in *Annals of America* (Chicago: Encyclopaedia Britannica, 1968–1977), 16:8.

82. Press release, "The Museum of Modern Art Broadcasts to Italy at Opening of Exhibition of Italian Masters," January 25, 1940. MoMA, NY. Pdf available at www.moma.org/learn/resources/press_archives (accessed June 12, 2012).

83. Emily Braun, "Leonardo's Smile," in *Donatello among the Blackshirts: History and Modernity in the Visual Culture of Fascist Italy*, ed. Claudia Lazzaro and Roger J. Crum (Ithaca: Cornell University Press, 2005), 174. According to Braun, "The Fascists co-opted the Italian Renaissance concept of 'humanism' to counter the impression of Fascism as a regime of thugs. The symbolic capital of Italy's past allowed Fascist propagandists to distance the

regime from the policies of Nazi Germany and the Soviet Union" (174–175). On the fascist uses of the Renaissance, see also Francis Haskell, "Botticelli in the Service of Fascism," in *The Ephemeral Museum: Old Master Paintings and the Rise of the Art Exhibition* (New Haven: Yale University Press, 2000), 107–127; and D. Medina Lasansky, *The Renaissance Perfected: Architecture, Spectacle, and Tourism in Fascist Italy* (University Park: Pennsylvania State University Press, 2004). According to Lasansky, "Mapping a continuum between modern and Renaissance culture was essential to the success of Fascist cultural programs" (96). This book was already in press when Raffaele Bedarida's important article on the display of Italian art at MoMA in the 1940s was published. See Bedarida, "Operation Renaissance: Italian Art at MoMA, 1940–1949," *Oxford Art Journal* 35, no. 2 (2012): 147–169.

84. Guido Clemente di San Luca, "Government and the Arts in Italy" (working paper, Institute for Policy Studies, Johns Hopkins University, 1988), 12, available online at *JScholarship* (accessed June 12, 2012). On the Bottai Law, see John Henry Merryman, Albert E. Elsen, and Stephen K. Urice, *Law, Ethics, and the Visual Arts*, 5th ed. (Alphen aan den Rijn, The Netherlands: Kluwer Law International, 2007), 171–172.

85. Giuseppe Bottai, Mussolini's minister of education, drafted some of these laws and was instrumental in their passage. See Eden Rebecca Knudsen, "Recasting the Italian: The Influence of Fascist Racism" (paper, International Security Studies Colloquium, Yale University, February 9, 2010), available at *Yale University International Security Studies*, iss.yale.edu/node/30/attachment (accessed June 12, 2012).

86. According to the scholar Kate Flint, "The notion that Italian art should be entirely Italian, that, like any ideal Fascist family circle, it should be racially pure, grew throughout the 1930s"; see Kate Flint, "Art and the Fascist Régime in Italy," *Oxford Art Journal* 3, no. 2 (October 1980): 51. One manifestation of this notion was the Italian government's establishment, in 1940, of an official "Department of Contemporary Art" which Flint describes as "partly a reflection of Mussolini's suspicion of the arts as tending to foster individuality. . . . The Department's statement of its function indicates the amount of control the regime wished to exert over artistic life. It saw itself as, 'simply, the means by which the State proposes to protect the artistic patrimony of contemporary art and to explain all its useful, educative content to the nation'" (51).

87. Behind closed doors, however, the museum carefully choreographed its negotiations with Italian officials. In a letter dated February 1, 1940, Barr expressed relief that Nelson Rockefeller, MoMA's president, had declined an official commendation from the Italian government in honor of the exhibition:

> I am glad to know that you have decided to refuse the decoration.
>
> I really feel, aside from my own personal convictions, that any attendant publicity would be unfortunate for the Museum. In view of the fact that the Museum stands for free development of cultural and spiritual matters in a liberal democracy and the Italian Government stands for exactly the opposite, I do not think the Museum or its officials can afford to accept decorations any more than they could afford to accept them from Stalin or Hitler—for accepted decorations imply a certain obligation toward, if not sympathy for, the Government awarding them, and that fact will be made the most of by the Italian authorities.

In a handwritten postscript to the typed letter, Barr adds, "Do you remember the row over Lindbergh's taking the decoration from the Nazis?" The episode to which Barr refers occurred in October 1938, when the aviator Charles Lindbergh accepted a Service Cross of the Order of the German Eagle with Star from the Nazi official (and Luftwaffe pilot) Hermann Göring. Even after the outbreak of World War II (and to the dismay of many Americans), Lindbergh declined to return the medal. Barr's postscript suggests both the heightened political stakes of the *Italian Masters* exhibition and his concern about the "unfortunate" publicity it might occasion. See Alfred H. Barr Jr. to Nelson Rockefeller, February 1, 1940, AHB Papers, 6.B.15. MoMA Archives, NY.

88. MoMA Advisory Committee to Alfred H. Barr Jr., AHB Papers, 6.B.15. MoMA Archives, NY.

89. Alfred H. Barr Jr. to MoMA Advisory Committee, December 6, 1939, AHB Papers, 6.B.15. MoMA Archives, NY.

90. Lincoln Kirstein to Monroe Wheeler, November 8, 1939, MoMA Exh. #98 "Italian Masters," MoMA Archives, NY. Kirstein continues, "I realize it would not be difficult for Alfred Barr or somebody he might select, to show the close connection between Botticelli and Modigliani. But this kind of rationalization would not, I think, convince the serious people whose good will the Museum wishes to hold." In lieu of the *Italian Masters* exhibition,

Kirstein proposed that "a very interesting exhibit cold be arranged on the effect of war on modern art. I realize that Alfred would be too busy to arrange it, but he could delegate somebody to do this."

91. Barr, "Understanding Modern Art," 305.

92. The fact that only two American artists, Alexander Calder and Man Ray, had been included in "Cubism and Abstract Art" was among the group's complaints.

93. See "The Artist as Reporter," *Bulletin of the Museum of Modern Art* 7, no. 1 (April 1940): 6.

94. Susan C. Larsen, "An Interview with George L. K. Morris," February 2, 1973; transcript published as an appendix to Larsen's dissertation, "The American Abstract Artists Group: A History and Evaluation of Its Impact Upon American Art" (Ph.D. diss., Northwestern University, 1975). The passage cited from the interview appears on page 484.

95. George L. K. Morris, "Art Chronicle: The Museum of Modern Art (as Surveyed from the Avant-Garde)," *Partisan Review* 7, no. 3 (1940): 202.

96. "The Work of Sharaku" was on display at MoMA from April 3 through May 1, 1940. According to the *New York Times* review of the exhibition, "Of the 136 prints by Sharaku known to exist, 108 were secured and the remaining twenty-eight are represented by photograph"—so once again, a mix of originals and reproductions were hung on the museum's walls. See "Prints of Sharaku at Museum Here," *New York Times*, April 3, 1940, 30.

97. "Artists Denounce Modern Museum," *New York Times*, April 17, 1940, 23.

98. AAA's contemptuous attitude toward the *Artist as Reporter* exhibition opened onto a series of challenges to the display of journalistic illustration within a museum of art: "Is the Artist a Reporter? Is the museum a business? . . . What is journalistic art? . . . Will the Museum sponsor the Police Gazette? What about Eastman, Leica, and the News?"

99. In explaining the need for the addition, MoMA Board chairman John Hay Whitney told the *New York Herald Tribune* that "the museum is literally bursting at the seams" because of a doubling of attendance figures over the previous five years. As a result, Whitney said, the

"present museum building, constructed in 1939, can no longer accommodate the crowds of New York City and out of town visitors. In the last year, more than a half-million people visited exhibitions and attended special events at the museum." See "Building Drive On for Museum of Modern Art," *New York Herald Tribune*, February 9, 1947, 42.

100. In 1934, Barr wrote, "The truth is that modern art cannot be defined with any degree of finality either in time or in character and any attempt to do so implies a blind faith, insufficient knowledge, or an academic lack of realism." See Alfred H. Barr Jr., "Modern and 'Modern,'" *Bulletin of the Museum of Modern Art* 1, no. 9 (May 1, 1934): 2.

101. Alfred H. Barr Jr., "Confidential Notes on the ICA Statement," 1948, AHB Papers. MoMA Archives, NY.

102. Terry Smith, *Making the Modern: Industry, Art, and Design in America* (Chicago: University of Chicago Press, 1993), 387.

103. William B. Scott and Peter M. Rutkoff, *New York Modern: The Arts and the City* (Baltimore: Johns Hopkins University Press, 1999), 16.

104. "Present Status and Future Direction of the Museum of Modern Art" (1933), drafted by Alan Blackburn Jr., AHB Papers, 9a.8. MoMA Archives, NY. The full sentence reads, "The Director believes the Museum should frankly state its right to appraise, by exhibition, any art of any age from a modern point of view" (9).

105. Miwon Kwon, "Response to Questionnaire on 'The Contemporary,'" *October* 130 (Fall 2009): 16.

4 Midcentury Contemporary (1948)

1. "'Modern Art' and the American Public," February 17, 1948, reprinted in Serge Guilbaut, "The Frightening Freedom of the Brush: The Boston Institute of Contemporary Art and Modern Art, 1948–1950," in *Dissent: The Issue of Modern Art in Boston*, exh. cat. (Boston: Institute of Contemporary Art, 1985), 52.

2. Ibid., 53.

3. Ibid., 52.

4. Ibid.

5. Ibid.

6. According to the art historian Serge Guilbaut, "10,000 copies were printed and distributed internationally by a professional firm from New York … not only to the worlds of art and journalism but also to the business world—5017 copies to industrial companies, 1150 to college presidents, and 435 to 'prominent women' mainly culled from *Who's Who*." See Guilbaut, "The Frightening Freedom of the Brush," 58.

7. Steuben's plan to distribute 30,000 copies of the statement to its client list is noted in the minutes to the Executive Committee Meeting of the Institute of Modern Art, January 23, 1948, ICA Archives, Boston, MA.

8. See Emily Genauer, "Boston Hits 'Cult of Bewilderment,'" *New York World Telegram*, undated clipping, Alfred H. Barr Jr. Papers [AAA: 2171; 235]. The Museum of Modern Art Archives, New York. (Hereafter cited as AHB Papers.) See also "Modern Art Loses Its Face in Boston," *New York Times*, February 17, 1948.

9. "The Boston Tea Party," *American Artist*, April 1948, 55.

10. "Modern into Contemporary," *Newsweek*, March 1, 1948, 73.

11. In the passage from which this quotation is drawn, Plaut continues in the same vein, "We were very conscious of the need to establish total independence in the public mind and not be considered a small sister of our larger friends in New York. But there was also a philosophical principle involved here, which is that we felt that the term 'Institute of Modern Art' was misleading to a great many people." See James Plaut, interview by Robert Brown, June 29, 1971, typescript, p. 24, ICA Archives.

12. Alfred H. Barr Jr. to Paul Sachs, October 5, 1929, as cited in Sybil Gordon Kantor, *Alfred H. Barr, Jr., and the Intellectual Origins of the Museum of Modern Art* (Cambridge: MIT Press, 2001), 366.

13. "'Modern Art' and the American Public," 52.

14. In its place, the Boston institute proposed "contemporary," the very term Barr conceived as a zone of "supine neutrality" that would admit all current forms of art and culture, including the "safe and academic."

15. In his "confidential notes" on the ICA manifesto, Barr railed against the contention that "modern" had ever defined a neutral or stable style, whether in art or in the broader culture:

> For three centuries modern has been a term which involved the most challenging, original, and not yet accepted movements in philosophy, theology, and the arts. Even in science, economics, and technology the word modern is not a neutral term. That is why we used the word when the Museum of Modern Art was named. The word modern, or its equivalent, has been used probably since the beginning of civilization to denote what innovators created and what conservatives and reactionaries disliked.

See Alfred J. Barr Jr. to William A. M. Burden, March 3, 1948, AHB Papers [AAA: 2170; 20]. MoMA Archives, NY.

16. During the years immediately following World War II, modern art, as Amy Newman puts it, "was being attacked as subversive by the popular press, by conservative intellectuals and academic artists, and by Members of Congress. Barr responded to these sloppily reasoned attacks (what he called 'a campaign of muddleheaded reaction') . . . with his characteristic zeal for the precise presentation of facts and brilliance at adapting his delivery to the subject and audience addressed." See Amy Newman in Alfred H. Barr Jr., *Defining Modern Art: Selected Writings of Alfred H. Barr, Jr.*, ed. Irving Sandler and Amy Newman (New York: Abrams, 1986), 203.

The politicization of modern art during the McCarthy era has been widely discussed by art and cultural historians, several of whom have linked it to the ICA controversy of 1948. For the purposes of this chapter, the most relevant contribution is Guilbaut's comprehensively researched "The Frightening Freedom of the Brush: The Boston Institute of Contemporary Art and Modern Art, 1948–1950" (see above, note 1). Guilbaut's essay pivots on the following issue:

> What could the substitution of the two small words, *modern* and *contemporary*—which had hitherto appeared to be interchangeable—contain that would prove so explosive?

Evidently these two words brought into play much more than the aesthetic choices they implied. The simple fact of the matter was that they had acquired political connotations that—in the context of a growing debate on American art and American foreign policy—became of vital import for the international image of the United States. (61)

This chapter considers the same episode through a slightly different optic by looking at the exhibition program of the Boston institute and its alliance with Steuben Glass in the context of its claims about "contemporary art" in the 1948 manifesto.

17. Guilbaut, "Frightening Freedom," 61.

18. Ibid., 61–69.

19. After being recalled from abroad, the works in *Advancing American Art* were promptly auctioned off as military surplus by the U.S. State Department. Although there were several abstract paintings among them, the paintings most often singled out for opprobrium by conservative politicians and commentators at the time were figurative, albeit in highly stylized and expressionist form. In their study of the exhibition, Taylor Littleton and Maltby Sikes note that the show was presented in the popular press as "a distorted and disfigured portrait of the American scene" that "contained no examples of art which depicted the nation's values and traditions in recognizable forms." See Taylor Littleton and Maltby Sikes, *Advancing American Art: Painting, Politics, and Cultural Confrontation at Mid-Century* (Tuscaloosa: University of Alabama Press, 1999), 27.

20. "Your Money Bought These Paintings," *Look*, February 18, 1947, 80.

21. "Art for Taxpayers," *The Republican News*, 1947, as reproduced in Lana A. Burgess, "'Advancing American Art' and Its Afterlife: From the State Department to the University Museum" (Ph.D. diss., Florida State University, 2010), 116.

22. In Guilbaut's estimation, Plaut and the ICA "obviously did not have a direct political purpose in mind. But the attempt to redefine the modern paradigm, and the need to decree in the manifesto that the end of Modern experiments dated from 1939" provoked the ideological firestorm that Guilbaut charts in his essay. See Guilbaut, "Frightening Freedom," 61.

23. James Plaut, interview by Robert Brown, 24.

24. In Greenberg's estimation, the large, abstract paintings of what would later be called the New York School furnished the most important and genuinely progressive form of American art at the time. For examples of this view, see Clement Greenberg, "The Situation at the Moment," *Partisan Review*, January 1948; and "Review of Exhibitions of Worden Day, Carl Holty, and Jackson Pollock," *The Nation*, January 24, 1948; both are reprinted in Clement Greenberg, *Arrogant Purpose, 1945–1949*, vol. 2 of *The Collected Essays and Criticism*, ed. John O'Brian (Chicago: University of Chicago Press, 1986), 192–196, 200–203.

25. Clement Greenberg, "Review of an Exhibition of Mordecai Ardon-Bronstein and a Discussion of the Reaction in America to Abstract Art," *The Nation*, March 6, 1948; reprinted in Greenberg, *Arrogant Purpose, 1945–1949*, 217–218.

26. Ibid.

27. Clement Greenberg, "Towards a Newer Laocoon" (1940); reprinted in Clement Greenberg, *Perceptions and Judgments, 1939–1944*, vol. 1 of *The Collected Essays and Criticism*, ed. John O'Brian (Chicago: University of Chicago Press, 1988), 29. The passage from which this quotation is excerpted reads:

> Nineteenth century painting made its first break with literature when in the person of the Communard, Courbet, it fled from spirit to matter. Courbet, the first real avant-garde painter, tried to reduce his art to immediate sense data by painting only what the eye could see as a machine unaided by the mind. He took for his subject matter prosaic contemporary life. As avant-gardists so often do, he tried to demolish official bourgeois art by turning it inside out.

In the immediately preceding paragraph, Greenberg expressed contempt for storytelling painting in which, as in the work of Norman Rockwell,

> everything depends on the anecdote or the message. The painted picture occurs in blank, indeterminate space, it just happens to be on a square of canvas and inside a frame. It might just as well have been breathed on air or formed out of plasma. . . . Everything contributes to the denial of the medium, as if the artist were ashamed to admit that he had actually painted his picture rather than dreaming it forth. (28–29)

28. Clement Greenberg, "Avant-Garde and Kitsch" (1939), reprinted in Greenberg, *Perceptions and Judgments, 1939–1944*, 13.

29. See "Your Money," 80.

30. As Guilbaut points out, the Boston manifesto promised "an expansion of the field of interest to include contemporary art forms that were usually seen as outside the scope of advanced Modernism, and at the expense of abstraction itself and of its most experimental forms, such as the work of Pollock, de Kooning, and Gorky." See Guilbaut, "Frightening Freedom," 62.

31. Reinhold Heller, "The Expressionist Challenge: James Plaut and the Institute of Contemporary Art," in *Dissent: The Issue of Modern Art in Boston*, 18.

32. Nathaniel Saltonstall, "The Boston Museum of Modern Art," *Bulletin of the Museum of Modern Art* 5, no. 3 (March 1938): 3.

33. Shortly after this name change, *Time* magazine ran an article that recounted the institute's brief run to date:

> [In 1936] a drifting spore from Manhattan's Museum of Modern Art took root in Boston as an "affiliate," was watered by about 50 members, made $1,500 on a Modern Arts Ball (now annual and famous as the only dance at which Boston Society stays up until dawn). By 1937 there were 300 members. Two months ago, with 800 paying members, Boston's offshoot became a lusty shoot, dropped affiliation with Manhattan, [and] changed its name to the Boston Institute of Modern Art.

See "Shoot in Boston," *Time*, March 13, 1939, 41.

34. According to Judith Bookbinder, the name change "signaled that the institute would forego a permanent collection, which might codify one trajectory of modern art, in favor of a continually evolving project which would study without prejudice all contemporary developments." See Judith Bookbinder, "Figurative Expressionism in Boston and Its Germanic Cultural Affinities: An Alternative Modernist Discourse on Art and Identity" (Ph.D. diss., Boston University, 1998), 354 n. 91.

35. As cited in Russell Lynes, *Good Old Modern: An Intimate Portrait of the Museum of Modern Art* (New York: Atheneum, 1973), 167.

36. On the founding of MIT and its curricular innovations, see Elizabeth Andrews, Nora Murphy, and Tom Rosko, *William Barton Rogers: MIT's Visionary Founder*, October 2004, a virtual exhibition posted online by the MIT Institute Archives and Special Collections at http://libraries.mit.edu/archives/exhibits/wbr-visionary/.

37. *Institute of Modern Art Bulletin* 1, no. 1 (March 1939), as cited in Laser Antonsen, "An Outline for a Comprehensive History of the ICA, Boston," summer/fall 1983, p. 2, ICA Archives.

38. Nathan Saltonstall, "Report of the President," in *Annual Report for the Year 1939–1940 (Incorporating the Reports of the President, Director, and Treasurer)* (Boston: Institute of Modern Art, 1940), 2. The relevant passage of Saltonstall's report reads as follows: "Two years ago we changed our name from The Boston Museum of Modern Art to the Institute of Modern Art as the Trustees considered that our importance to the community should be educational rather than as a museum of objects never long contemporary."

39. James Plaut, interview by Robert Brown, 15–16.

40. According to Plaut,

> From the very beginning there was an ideological conflict as to whether the Institute would acquire and collect works of art for permanent retention or whether it should eschew this course in the direction of simply being an experimental laboratory in which one would present a platform for things that were happening on the contemporary scene (where people would simply come and see and explore and learn and evaluate). Whether these two things should happen side-by-side or whether one should do only one and not the other, was debated long and hard. And the eventual decision, which in retrospect can still not be said to have been right or wrong, was not to acquire works of art to form a permanent collection. Even in those days one looked at the Museum of Modern Art, which was the only institution that was devoted wholly to the art of our time, and realized that many of the works that were in its permanent collection were not contemporary art all. They were works of the nineteenth century. Great paintings from the [Lizzie] Bliss collection and others represented a paradox for the Museum of Modern Art.

See James Plaut, interview by Robert Brown, 15–16.

The institute's policy of not collecting art remained in place until 2000, at which time it was decided to start building a permanent collection. According to the ICA's website,

The development of a permanent collection began a new era for the ICA.

To provide our visitors with broader and more lasting experiences, the ICA made the pivotal decision in 2000 to start collecting. The core of the museum's collection is work by contemporary artists featured in ICA exhibitions, many at seminal moments in their careers. A diverse overview of national and international artworks in a range of styles and media, the collection represents the very best art being made today and provides an important resource for contemporary culture in Boston.

See "Exhibitions: Permanent Collection," *ICABoston.org*, www.icaboston.org/exhibitions/permanent-collection (accessed February 18, 2012).

41. "Shoot in Boston," 41.

42. Alfred H. Barr Jr., "Boston Is Modern Art Pauper," *Harvard Crimson*, October 30, 1926.

43. When Barr wrote in his 1926 letter to the *Harvard Crimson* of the "foremost living painters," the artists he mentioned by name were Henri Matisse, Pablo Picasso, Pierre Bonnard, and André Derain.

44. James Plaut, "Emotionalism in Modern Painting" (1939), as cited in Isabel S. Wilcox, "The Evolution of Modernism in Boston: The Institute of Contemporary Art—The First Twenty Years" (M.A. thesis, Hunter College of the City University of New York, 2002), 93 n. 11.

45. Ibid.

46. Ibid.

47. James Plaut, "Sanity in Art," transcript of a radio address broadcast by WBZ (Boston, NBC), May 13, 1940, as cited in Guilbaut, "Frightening Freedom," 90 n. 11, and John O'Brian, *Ruthless Hedonism: The American Reception of Matisse* (Chicago: University of Chicago Press, 1999), 207. Unfortunately, this transcript could not be found in the ICA Archives despite repeated efforts in 2009 and 2010.

48. Cited in Antonsen, "An Outline for a Comprehensive History of the ICA, Boston," 3.

49. Plaut had not yet been hired by the museum in 1937. At the time, the Boston Museum of Modern Art operated primarily as a regional branch of MoMA and a venue for touring exhibitions. Though I have discovered no commentary by Plaut on the surrealism show, one gathers that he would have agreed with the local critic Dorothy Adlow who, in reviewing the exhibition, noted that "As much as one may object, even feel violently antipathetic to Surrealist methods, it is reasonable to try to understand the origins" of the movement. See Dorothy Adlow, "Surrealists in Boston," *Christian Science Monitor*, March 16, 1937, 8. See also "Baby Auto in Cage Surrealistic Art," *Christian Science Monitor*, March 10, 1937, 12.

50. James S. Plaut, "50 Rising American Painters 50," *ARTnews* 40, no. 8 (June 1941): 25.

51. Ibid.

52. On May 11, 1941, the *Boston Herald* reproduced a suite of four paintings from the show in its Rotogravure Section, under the headline "All-American Art." These were *The First Born* by Daniel Celetano, *River View* by Yvonne Twining, *The Gallants* by O. Louis Guglielmi, and *Little Girl* by John E. Heliker. Adlow's review in the *Christian Science Monitor* was also illustrated with Twining's *River View*. See Dorothy Adlow, "'Oncoming Americans' Show at Institute of Modern Art," *Christian Science Monitor*, May 19, 1941, 7.

53. "All-American Art," *Boston Herald*, May 11, 1941, Rotogravure Section (left page).

54. Underscoring the local appeal of *River View*, the *Herald*'s caption noted that both "place and painter are well known here" (ibid.).

55. Willard Cummings, oral history interview, March 20, 1973, available online at "Research Collections," Smithsonian Institution, Archives of American Art, www.aaa.si.edu/collections/interviews/oral-history-interview-willard-cummings-12296 (accessed June 12, 2012).

56. Plaut, "50 Rising American Painters 50," 25.

57. Ibid.

58. This according to the admittedly partisan history of Narragansett Beer and Ale posted on the company's website, www.narragansettbeer.com/home (accessed February 18, 2012).

59. In a 1943 letter, Levine specifies that the building portrayed in *Neighborhood Physician* is "on the corner of Gainsborough Street and Huntington Avenue in Boston." He notes as well that he "was intrigued by the idea of a portrait of a man together with a portrait of his home." See Jack Levine to "Dan," September 14, 1943, Archives of American Art, Downtown Gallery Collection, Series 2, Artists Files, Box 24, Reel 5549, frames 945-946.

60. By contrast, works by the American artists from the 1940s who are today most celebrated—Jackson Pollock, Willem de Kooning, Mark Rothko—were not included in *Fifty Oncoming American Painters*.

61. Willard Cummings, oral history interview, Archives of American Art.

62. In an exhibition catalogue on Boston expressionism, art critic Theodore F. Wolff notes:

> Abstract Expressionism's rapid growth and extraordinary success, coupled with our growing tendency to view creativity in stylistic, evolutionary, and categorically art historical terms, has helped fashion a somewhat distorted picture of that period. It throws the spotlight of significance on everything that in any way contributed to the emergence of The New York School, and casts into relative or deep shadow—or even into disrepute—the work of anyone not associated with it. . . . [Abstract Expressionism's] victory was so total and dramatic, in fact, that the critics, in a burst of euphoria, decreed that American art had never really quite existed before it came into being. Furthermore, they insisted that everything of genuine significance and originality in American painting was embodied in the work of Pollock, Still, Rothko, Kline, and de Kooning, and that anyone who didn't agree, or refused to paint in a similar manner, would be cast into outer darkness—or at least, never be taken seriously again.

See Theodore F. Wolff, *The Persistence of the Expressionist Mode in Boston and Environs, 1945-1985* (Lincoln, MA: DeCordova Museum, 1986), 6.

63. Cited in Dennis Raverty, "The Painting of Jack Levine and the Politics of Criticism," *Prospects* 29 (2005): 361.

64. Guilbaut, "Frightening Freedom," 86.

65. Plaut, "50 Rising American Painters 50," 25.

66. MoMA also engaged, on occasion, in the sale of artworks. It did so rather more discreetly, however, than the Boston institute. For example, prices were neither posted on gallery walls nor printed in catalogues but supplied on price lists that the interested buyer had to request.

67. Lawrence Dame, "Plaut Plans New Era for N. E. Modern Art," *Boston Herald*, June 14, 1946, clipping in James Plaut Papers, ICA Archives.

68. Ibid.

69. *Contemporary American Glass: Decorative, Utilitarian, Structural* was on view at the Boston Museum of Modern Art from December 17, 1938, through January 22, 1939.

70. While American art was represented by a range of media and objects (watercolors, oil paintings, sculpture, glass), French art was presented in terms of painting alone. When the Boston institute renounced "modern art" in 1948, School of Paris painting was the target it had in mind.

71. Highly resistant to heat, chemicals, and electricity, Pyrex was developed by Corning for use in scientific laboratories, then extended into kitchen cookware.

72. James S. Plaut, foreword to *Contemporary American Glass: Decorative, Utilitarian, Structural* (Boston: Institute of Contemporary Art, 1938), n.pag.

73. Ibid.

74. Dorothy Adlow, review of *Contemporary American Glass*, *Christian Science Monitor*, January 3, 1939, 10.

75. Adlow may also have been referring to an even earlier exhibition, the Newark Museum's *New Jersey Pottery and Porcelain* (1915), which famously included a room full of bathtubs, and its *Inexpensive Items of Good Design* (versions of which were seen in both 1928 and 1929). On the innovative display of everyday wares at the Newark Museum, see Carol Duncan, *A Matter of Class: John Cotton Dana, Progressive Reform, and the Newark Museum* (New York: Prestel, 2009).

On the rise of exhibitions of industrial design in the United States, see "Where to See Everyday Art," *Everyday Art Quarterly*, no. 13 (Winter 1949–1950): 1–11. The category of "everyday art" referred to industrially produced objects, usually for household use. It was rarely applied to handcrafted objects or to designs in the style of older historical periods. The "everyday" at issue, then, was almost always "today."

In reference to Barr and the curatorial staff at MoMA, the scholar A. Joan Saab writes,

> for the most part they followed traditional collecting practices and displayed the pieces as sacred masterpieces imbued with timeless auras that would ensure value in the future. In the industrial design shows, however, they challenged traditional standards for determining, collecting, and displaying art by focusing instead on the temporality of the pieces—their value was rooted in their contemporary usefulness. In a way, . . . their emphasis on function rather than exchange value presented a new type of aesthetic experience rooted in the quotidian and tied to everyday life.

See A. Joan Saab, *For the Millions: Art and Culture between the Wars* (Philadelphia: University of Pennsylvania Press, 2004), 103.

76. Press release, "The Exhibition of 'Useful Objects under Five Dollars' Now on View," October 13, 1938. MoMA, NY. Pdf available at www.moma.org/learn/resources/press_archives (accessed June 12, 2012).

77. Press release, "Three New Exhibits," August 31, 1938. MoMA, NY. Pdf available at www.moma.org/learn/resources/press_archives (accessed June 12, 2012).

78. "The 'Exhibition of Useful Objects,'" 2.

79. Alfred H. Barr Jr., "The 1929 Multidepartmental Plan for the Museum of Modern Art: Its Origins, Development, and Partial Realization," prepared for A. Conger Goodyear, August 1941, AHB Papers, 9a.15A, p. 9. MoMA Archives, NY. On the distinctions drawn by Barr and Philip Johnson between the genuinely "modern" and the superficially "modernistic" or "modernoid," see Saab, *For the Millions*, 100–104.

80. Alfred H. Barr Jr. to William A. M. Burden, March 3, 1948, AHB Papers [AAA: 2170; 20]. MoMA Archives, NY. Burden, who joined MoMA's board of trustees in 1943, was a prominent art collector, diplomat, and investor. He would be elected president of the Board in 1953.

81. Houghton, as cited in Mary Jean Madigan, *Steuben Glass: An American Tradition in Crystal*, rev. ed. (New York: Harry N. Abrams, 2003), 77. Upon taking over at Steuben, Houghton was said to have smashed much of the colored glassware in the company's stockroom. Whatever its truth value, the story might be taken as a metaphor of Houghton's desire to destroy Steuben's past so as to present its current products as both up-to-date and unprecedented. According to Houghton's obituary, "It is part of company folklore that about a month after assuming control of the new subsidiary, Mr. Houghton, dissatisfied with its products, spent a Sunday smashing every piece of glass in a company warehouse in Corning, N.Y." See George James, "Arthur Houghton Jr., 83, Dies; Led Steuben Glass," *New York Times*, April 4, 1990. See also Madigan, *Steuben Glass*, 72.

82. Madigan, *Steuben Glass*, 71.

83. "Steuben Shop, New York," *Architectural Forum*, March 1934, 195.

84. Ibid.

85. According to Donald Albrecht, it was Steuben's practice in the 1930s and 1940s to try to place its work in museum collections: "As part of its skillful marketing strategy, the company also donated signature designs ... to major museum collections, discreetly mentioning these associations in their advertisements." See Donald Albrecht, "Glass and Glamour: Steuben's Modern Moment, 1930–1950," *Antiques*, January 2004, 175.

86. Houghton, as cited in Madigan, *Steuben Glass*, 95.

87. Cited in Madigan, *Steuben Glass*, 96.

88. Ten dollars in 1948 has the relative value of about $90.60 in 2012. See the simple purchasing power calculator at Lawrence H. Officer and Samuel H. Williamson, "Purchasing Power of Money in the United States from 1774 to Present," *MeasuringWorth*, 2011, www.measuringworth.com/ppowerus (accessed February 18, 2012).

89. Display ad, *New York Times*, March 28, 1948.

90. James S. Plaut, *Steuben Glass: A Monograph* (New York: H. Bittner, 1948), 1.

91. Ibid.

92. The four scenes engraved around the bowl represent "Exploration," "Colonization," "Independence," and "Expansion."

93. Plaut, foreword to *Contemporary American Glass*, 1.

94. John Harriman, "New England Leadership in Industrial Design," *Boston Daily Globe*, undated clipping, Department of Design in Industry File, ICA Archives.

95. On the history and mission of the Department of Design in Industry, see David Joselit, "The Postwar Product: The ICA's Department of Design in Industry," in *Dissent: The Issue of Modern Art in Boston*, 94–105. Joselit's account of the department is more idealistic than the one I have presented here. He writes, for example, "The Institute hoped to show how the artist could benefit the businessman, not just by providing designs for products, but by offering industry an attitude of openness and exploration associated with creativity. The ICA asserted that the artist and businessman were not just separate but equal partners, but men and women who could work from a shared experience of culture" (104).

96. James Plaut, interview by Robert Brown, 23–24.

97. Samuel H. Wolcott Jr., "Institute of Contemporary Art: Acting Treasurer's Report," October 7, 1948, ICA Archives.

98. Ibid. Corporate clients were charged an annual fee of $2,000.

99. According to the scholar Isabel Wilcox,

> At this trial stage, Steuben underwrote most of the Institute's added costs (including a portion of Plaut's salary) relating to the establishment of a training program for designers. The success of the venture led to an expanded program involving the collaboration of educators, designers, manufacturers, and retailers eventually spilling beyond the limits of New England into the international arena. A productive and lucrative venture, this involvement with industry lasted for ten years and fizzled out only after Plaut's departure in 1956. During those ten years the department not only was self-sustaining,

but it also contributed significantly to the Institute's finances by off-setting its general operating deficit and allowing it to survive as an independent institution.

See Wilcox, "The Evolution of Modernism in Boston," 62. Wilcox's thesis provides the most comprehensive account of the ICA in the 1940s and 1950s, and this chapter is indebted to her research and insights.

100. Jack Levine, quoted in "Report of the Panel Discussion Sponsored by the Modern Artists Group of Boston, March 25, 1948, The Old South Meeting House, Boston, Massachusetts," AHB Papers [AAA: 3263; 801]. MoMA Archives, NY.

101. Alfred H. Barr Jr. to William A. M. Burden, March 3, 1948, AHB Papers [AAA: 2170; 20]. MoMA Archives, NY.

102. Ibid.

103. Alfred H. Barr Jr. to Norman Bel Geddes, December 4, 1934, as cited in Jeffrey L. Meikle, *Twentieth-Century Limited: Industrial Design in America, 1925–1939*, 2nd ed. (Philadelphia: Temple University Press, 2001), 181.

104. In a 2003 essay on the history of design at MoMA, curator Paola Antonelli notes that "Deploring style for the sake of style—or for the sake of commerce—has become a trademark of the collection and resulted in several exclusions, the first of them being Art Deco and the streamline manner." According to Antonelli, the "current curatorial choices" continue to "privilege objects whose form is generated from within." See Paola Antonelli, "Objects of Design," in *Objects of Design from the Museum of Modern Art* (New York: Museum of Modern Art, 2003), 15.

105. "New Glass Designs Seen," *New York Times*, January 10, 1940, 26.

106. Ruth Green Harris, "New Designs in Glass by Contemporary Artists," *New York Times*, February 11, 1940, 135.

107. Ibid.

108. Greenberg, "Avant-Garde and Kitsch," 13.

109. Ibid.

110. Plaut, "Sanity in Art" (1940), as cited in Guilbaut, "Frightening Freedom," 90 n. 11.

111. Plaut, foreword to *Contemporary American Glass*, n.pag.

112. Alfred H. Barr Jr., "A New Museum," *Vogue*, October 26, 1929, 85.

113. "New York World's Fair, 1939," *Chemical and Engineering News*, September 1, 1939, 574.

114. Typewritten caption taped on an installation view of the *Plastics* exhibition featuring male mannequin, ICA Archives.

115. Mary Cooke, "Bauhaus Post Mortem," *Magazine of Art* 32 (January 1939): 40.

116. James Plaut, interview by Branka Bogdanov, summer 1995, as cited in Judith Bookbinder, *Boston Modern: Figurative Expressionism as Alternative Modernism* (Durham: University of New Hampshire Press, 2005), 226–227.

117. Display ad, *Boston Globe*, March 9, 1959, 13. The phrase "Contemporary Art" is set in large type, dwarfing the other words in the ad and effectively promoting it as a brand no less than "Stop & Shop Super Markets" (in a cartouche at the top of the ad) or, for that matter, "Treo Undergarments" in the adjacent ad.

118. Barbara Rose, "Pop Art at the Guggenheim," *Art International*, May 1963, 20–22; as reprinted in *Pop Art: A Critical History*, ed. Henry Madoff (Berkeley: University of California Press, 1997), 84.

Afterword: Not Now (1994/2005)

1. Irving Sandler, "The History of Contemporary Art: A Contradiction in Terms?" *Art Criticism* 1 (Spring 1979): 42.

2. Gustavo Grandal Montero, "Biennalization? What Biennalization? The Documentation of Biennials and Other Recurrent Exhibitions," *Art Libraries Journal* 37, no. 1 (2012): 13.

3. David Román, *Performance in America: Contemporary U.S. Culture and the Performing Arts* (Durham: Duke University Press, 2005), 12.

4. Ibid., 12–13.

5. Benjamin H. D. Buchloh, "Three Conversations in 1985: Claes Oldenburg, Andy Warhol, Robert Morris," *October* 70 (Autumn 1994): 40.

6. On Warhol's penchant for answering "I don't know" (or variants thereof) to interview questions, see Reva Wolf, "Introduction: Through the Looking-Glass," in Kenneth Goldsmith, ed., *I'll Be Your Mirror: The Selected Andy Warhol Interviews* (New York: Carroll & Graf, 2004), xi–xxxi.

7. Buchloh, "Three Conversations in 1985," 37.

8. Ibid., 40.

9. Ibid.

10. Ibid., 42.

11. The artist is referring here, as the broader context of the interview makes clear, to his recent Rorschach and oxidation (or "piss") paintings and to other works in which he manipulated pigment by hand or brush.

12. Ibid., 45.

13. Ibid.

14. Ibid.

15. Ibid., 39.

16. Ibid., 37.

17. This passage was first published in Richard Meyer, "Light It Up, or How Glenn Ligon Got Over," *Artforum*, May 2006, 241.

18. *Glenn Ligon: Some Changes* was still on view in May 2006, though no longer at the Toronto venue at which I had seen it. The show traveled to the Contemporary Arts Museum, Houston.

19. Since 2005, there have been other major exhibitions of the artist's work, notably *Glenn Ligon: America*, a midcareer survey organized by the Whitney Museum of American Art in 2011.

20. Glenn Ligon, quoted in Stephen Andrews, "Glenn Ligon: In Conversation," *Glenn Ligon: Some Changes*, exh. cat. (Toronto: Power Plant Contemporary Art Gallery, 2005), 177.

21. Glenn Ligon, quoted in "The Ubiquitous Censor: Artists and Writers on Self-Censorship: Glenn Ligon," in *Censoring Culture: Contemporary Threats to Free Expression*, ed. Robert Atkins and Svetlana Mincheva (New York: New Press, 2006), 328–329.

22. Golden was also the co-curator, with Wayne Baerwaldt, of *Glenn Ligon: Some Changes*.

23. Thelma Golden, introduction to *Freestyle* (New York: Studio Museum in Harlem, 2001), 14.

24. Ron Stodghill II, "Curator: A Golden Age for Post-Black Art," *Time*, October 15, 2001, 89.

25. Gertrude Stein, "Melanctha: Each One as She May," in *Three Lives: Stories of the Good Anna, Melanctha, and the Gentle Lena* (Rockville, MD: Serenity Publishers, 2008), 57.

26. Golden, introduction to *Freestyle*, 14.

Index